2nd Edition

Web.Studies

Edited by
David Gauntlett and **Ross Horsley**

ARNOLD

First published in Great Britain in 2000
Second edition published in 2004 by
Arnold, a member of the Hodder Headline Group,
338 Euston Road, London NW1 3BH

http://www.arnoldpublishers.com

Distributed in the United States of America by
Oxford University Press Inc.
198 Madison Avenue, New York, NY10016

The advice and information in this book are believed to be true and
accurate at the date of going to press, but neither the editors nor the publisher
can accept any legal responsibility or liability for any errors or omissions.

British Library Cataloguing in Publication Data
A catalogue record for this book is available from the British Library

Library of Congress Cataloging-in-Publication Data
A catalog record for this book is available from the Library of Congress

ISBN 0 340 81472 1

2 3 4 5 6 7 8 9 10

Typeset in 9.5/13 Baskerville BT by Dorchester Typesetting Group Ltd
Printed and bound in Malta

What do you think about this book? Or any other Arnold title?
Please send your comments to feedback.arnold@hodder.co.uk

Contents

ACKNOWLEDGEMENTS

We would both like to thank the contributors, of course, without whom this book would be rather poor value. As well as being insightful internet critics, they have been thoughtful and helpful correspondents too.

At Arnold, the editor of the first edition, Lesley Riddle, was a very enthusiastic supporter of the book, and her successor Abigail Woodman has been a wonderful editor of this edition.

David's acknowledgements: Many thanks to Ross, for being incredibly efficient and for doing his half just how I would have done it, but better. Colleagues at Bournemouth Media School have been very supportive, especially Richard Berger, Chris Wensley, Jonathan Wardle, Sherryl Wilson, Jim Pope and Roger Laughton. Thank you also to Graham Roberts, Steve Lax, Jayne Rodgers, Kirsten Pullen, Susan Giblin, Kevin Robins, David Buckingham and Annette Hill. Finally, but most of all, to Ilse Devroe, for being lovely and everything.

Ross's acknowledgements: I'll always be grateful to David for giving me the opportunity to be part of this project, and for being such a helpful co-editor and good friend. Special thanks are also due to Mum and Dad for guiding me along a rather twisty academic path; to Mark Gundill who puts up with me as a housemate; Chris Furminger who paints and inspires; and Matthew Browne who's great.

PICTURE CREDITS

Flanagan's '[collection]' (Chapter 10) reproduced by kind permission of the artist. Copyright © Mary Flanagan 2003. Images of breast cancer blog and resources (Chapter 12) reproduced by kind permission of Jeff Siddens. Images from the Marilyn Manson Australian Webpage (Chapter 13) reproduced by kind permission. (The website shown is not affiliated in any way with Marilyn Manson. The information on this, and adjoining, pages is provided solely as an informative and entertaining resource. No copyright infringement is intended nor implied. Other borrowed materials and images are owned and copyrighted by their original owners. All rights reserved.) Image of the website of the Australian Copyright Council (Chapter 16) reproduced by kind permission. Image of the Kazaa Media Desktop (Chapter 17) copyright © Sharman Networks 2002–2003. Images of Indymedia sites (Chapter 18) reproduced by kind permission of Indymedia (www.indymedia.org). Images from *Women's Net* (womensnet.org.za) and the South Asian Women's NETwork (sawnet.org) (Chapter 20) reproduced by kind permission. Images from *The Cherokee Nation* (cherokee.org) and the official home page of the Eastern Band of Cherokee Indians (cherokee-nc.com) (Chapter 21) reproduced by kind permission.

CONTRIBUTORS

Mark Andrejevic is an Assistant Professor in the Department of Communication Studies at the University of Iowa, USA. He writes about new media, surveillance and television, and is the author of *Reality TV: The Work of Being Watched* (Rowman & Littlefield, 2003).

Jayne Armstrong is a Lecturer in Media and Cultural Studies at Falmouth College of Arts, UK. She is interested in cyberfeminisms, grrrl culture and alternative media.

Ellen L. Arnold is an Assistant Professor at East Carolina University, Greenville, North Carolina, USA, where she teaches multicultural literature, ethnic studies and women's studies. She has published essays on Native American studies and literature, and edited *Conversations with Leslie Marmon Silko* (University Press of Mississippi, 2000). Website: www.ecu.edu/english/profiles/arnold.htm.

Meredith Balderston splits her time among Los Angeles, Chicago, and her home town of Washington, DC, while finishing her Master's thesis for Georgetown University's Communication, Culture and Technology programme. Her academic work explores the overlap of sex, capitalism and activism, and her paid work explores design, technology, gaming, sex, capitalism and activism. She speaks five languages and makes her own furniture. Website: www.cavityshack.com.

Richard Berger is a Senior Lecturer in Film and Broadcast Media at Bournemouth Media School, University of Bournemouth, UK. He is an experienced journalist and broadcaster, currently writing a PhD on the changing relationship between different media, in particular, emerging new forms of adaptation and translation. He writes about film and television for BBCi's *Collective* website, and talks about the internet on BBC radio.

Charles Cheung is a PhD candidate at the University of Leeds, UK. His interest is in the social influences of popular culture. He has co-edited the book *Reading Hong Kong Popular Culture: 1970–2000*, the most comprehensive collection of articles on Hong Kong popular culture and identities (Hong Kong: Oxford

University Press, 2000). He has previously taught Hong Kong Cultural Studies at the Chinese University of Hong Kong.

Nick Couldry is Senior Lecturer in Media and Communications at the London School of Economics and Political Science, UK. He is the author of three books, *The Place of Media Power: Pilgrims and Witnesses of the Media Age* (Routledge, 2000), *Inside Culture* (Sage, 2000) and *Media Rituals: A Critical Approach* (Routledge, 2003), as well as many articles on media power and public space. Website via: www.lse.ac.uk/depts/media.

Ian Dobie is project manager for Freeflow UK, Salford University's music and media showcase website for student work. His PhD thesis chronicled and analysed the impact of new technologies and the internet on the music industry, 1997–2001. Website: www.quercus-circus.co.uk, www.freeflow.uk.com.

David Gauntlett is Professor of Media and Audiences at Bournemouth Media School, University of Bournemouth, UK. He is author of the books *Moving Experiences* (John Libbey, 1995), *Video Critical* (John Libbey, 1997), *TV Living* (with Annette Hill, Routledge, 1999), *Media, Gender and Identity: An Introduction* (Routledge, 2002), and edited the first edition of this book. He produces the website www.theory.org.uk. See www.theory.org.uk/david.

Laura J. Gurak is Professor and Department Head (Rhetoric) and Director of the Internet Studies Center, University of Minnesota, USA. Her specialisms include rhetoric of technology, intellectual property and internet studies. Among her many publications, she is author of *Cyberliteracy: Navigating the Internet with Awareness* (Yale, 2001) and *Persuasion and Privacy in Cyberspace: The Online Protests over Lotus MarketPlace and the Clipper Chip* (Yale, 1997). Website: www.rhetoric.umn.edu/faculty/lgurak.

Wendy Harcourt is Editor of the journal *Development* and Director of Programmes at the Society for International Development in Rome, Italy. She has written widely on gender, globalization and ICTs, including editing the book *Women@Internet: Creating Cultures in Cyberspace* (Zed Books, 1999). From 1997–2002 she coordinated a global training and research project on women and ICTs: 'women on the net'. Website: www.sidint.org.

Ross Horsley is a PhD candidate at the University of Leeds, UK, researching men's lifestyle magazines and the construction of male identity. He teaches Web design and HTML, and runs seminars in sociological theory for undergraduate students. Website: www.readinginto.com.

Stephen Lax is a Lecturer in Communications Technology at the Institute of Communications Studies, University of Leeds, UK. His research explores the social role of communications technologies and claims about the potential of technological developments. He is the author of *Beyond the Horizon: Communications Technologies Past, Present and Future* (John Libbey, 1997), and the editor of *Access Denied in the Information Age* (Palgrave, 2001). Website: www.leeds.ac.uk/ics/sl1.htm.

Vincent Miller is currently a Lecturer in Sociology at Lancaster University, UK. He has research interests in the information society, the political economy of new media and new media and 'intimacy'. He is also interested in urban social space in global cities, and has published on the topics of interextuality, intimacy, and mobility in the construction of urban space. Website: www.comp.lancs.ac.uk/sociology/vince.html.

Jodi O'Brien is Associate Professor of Sociology at Seattle University, USA. She teaches and writes in the areas of sexuality, religion, social psychology, social theory and social inequalities. Her recent published works include, 'Writing in the Body: Gender (Re)Production in Online Communication', in *Communities in Cyberspace* (Routledge, 1999), *Everyday Inequalities* (co-editor, Blackwell, 1998) and *The Production of Reality: Essays on Everyday Interaction* (co-editor, Sage, 2001).

Kathleen K. Olson is an Assistant Professor of Journalism and Mass Communication at Lehigh University in Bethlehem, Pennsylvania, USA. She is a licensed attorney and conducts research in the fields of media law and online journalism. Website: www.lehigh.edu/~kko2.

Shani Orgad is Lecturer in Media and Communications at the London School of Economics, UK. She completed her PhD on the online communication of women with breast cancer. Her research interests include media and everyday life, study of narrative, media and globalization, and methodological aspects of doing internet research. She has lectured on these issues at both Cambridge University and the London School of Economics.

Darcy C. Plymire is an Assistant Professor of Kinesiology at Towson University, USA. She is the author of 'Running, heart disease, and the ironic death of Jim Fixx' (Research Quarterly for Exercise and Sport, 2002) and co-author of 'Speaking of Cheryl Miller: Interrogating the lesbian taboo on a women's basketball newsgroup' (NWSA Journal, 2001). She is currently writing a critical cultural history of the wellness movement in the USA.

Kirsten Pullen is Assistant Professor of English at the University of Calgary, Canada, where she teaches Performance Studies and New Media Studies. Her book, *Actresses and Whores: Society and Stage*, will soon be published by Cambridge University Press.

Graham Roberts is Senior Lecturer in Communications at the Institute of Communications Studies, University of Leeds, UK, Director of the Louis Le Prince Institute and MD of Endgame Pictures. He is currently researching European cinema in the television age, and is the author of books including *Man with the Movie Camera* (IB Tauris, 2001) and *Nicolas Roeg* (MUP, forthcoming). Website: www.leeds.ac.uk/ics/gr1.htm.

Eve Shapiro is a PhD candidate in Sociology at the University of California Santa Barbara, USA. Her research areas include social movements, sexuality and (trans)gender. She is currently working on a dissertation examining the relationship between drag performance and political consciousness. Forthcoming work includes 'Virtual Activism: The Impact of the Internet on Transgender Organizing', in *Transgender Rights: History, Politics, and Law* (University of Minnesota Press).

Christopher R. Smit is an Assistant Professor of Communications at Calvin College, USA. His specialisms include disability and media, cultural theory and popular music. Smit's edited collection (with Anthony Enns) *Screening Disability: Essays on Cinema and Disability* was published by UPA in 2001. His essays on a wide variety of topics can be seen in *Studies in Popular Culture*, *Journal of Popular Culture*, and *Disability Studies Quarterly*.

Philip M. Taylor is Professor of International Communications at the University of Leeds, UK. He is the author of numerous books and articles, including *Munitions of the Mind: A History of Propaganda from the Ancient World to the Present Day* (3rd edition, 2003). Website: www.leeds.ac.uk/ics/pt1.htm.

Douglas Thomas is Associate Professor in the Annenberg School for Communication at the University of Southern Calfornia, USA. He is interested in the relationship between subculture and technology, and is the author of *Hacker Culture* (2002), and co-editor of *Technological Visions* (2004) and *Cybercrime: Law Enforcement, Security and Surveillance in the Information Age* (2000). Website: www-rcf.usc.edu/~douglast.

Nina Wakeford is Director of INCITE (Incubator for Critical Inquiry into Technology and Ethnography) in the Department of Sociology, University of Surrey. She has written about internet cafés as well as the sociology of mobile phones. She is currently working on projects funded by Intel on ubiquitous computing and Sapient on collaborative ethnography with technology designers. Website: www.soc.surrey.ac.uk/incite.

Part 1:
Web Studies

Chapter 1

WEB STUDIES: WHAT'S NEW

DAVID GAUNTLETT

The first edition of *Web.Studies* began with a story about how I didn't get into the internet at first, in the mid-1990s, because it seemed too nerdy. Bloody internet, I said: full of computer geeks swapping episode guides for *Babylon 5*. This was, of course, intended to reassure 'cool' readers that they weren't reading a book aimed at an audience of computer scientists and boys who go to sci-fi conventions.

Today, such apologies are not necessary: the Web is so much a part of everyday life – and, in particular, so often at the heart of popular culture, or used to *communicate* pop culture – that there is no need to justify it, or be embarrassed. During the final years of the last century, the Web had only really managed to be 'cool' as defined by *Wired* magazine, the stylish but technology-obsessed fanzine of new media culture. Now, the Web is cool as defined by the worlds of fashion, music and art. In 1999, the Web was full of idiotic capitalists who thought they could become millionaires just by having a website. But in 2000 it all went wrong (of which, more later). That 'dot-com crash' was a blessing. Nowadays, the capitalists, like everybody else, have to be cool: thoughtful, streamlined, intelligent.

The idea behind *Web.Studies* was to have a book that treated internet media like any other popular media that appeals to people (without, of course, forgetting about the things that made it unique). In a world where people are still burbling about 'cyberculture' – a term whose useful potential has been killed off by the staggering number of tedious things that have been written about it – I believe we can still be confident that this is refreshing and appropriate. New media would be nothing if it wasn't *meaningful* to people, if it wasn't a site of sociability, politics, art, emotion, music and dancing. (Of course, that's what 'cyberculture' refers to – maybe without the dancing – but I'm not sure we need new nerdwords.) *Web.Studies* was designed to address a cross-section of interesting cultural and social things happening on the net.

This second edition, like the first, came together entirely on the internet. We have never spoken to most of the contributors, but we've exchanged a lot of e-mails. The new edition is not just an 'update' of the previous one: half of the chapters are newly written versions of the most popular chapters from last time, and are often substantially different, since three and a half years is a long time on the net. The other half are brand new contributions, from invited experts, on important areas that have become more striking recently, or were requested by users of the first edition, or are dealt with here in a more contemporary way. These include the chapters on digital film-making; copyright issues; self-help online; new media art; online zines; pornography for lesbians; masculinities; the 'digital divide'; and the debate about one of the internet's biggest and most controversial applications in the twenty-first century, the free exchange of music online via peer-to-peer sharing programs like Kazaa.

This introduction contains revised versions of some old parts, but a greater amount of new material. Those of you who read the first edition will get a sense of *déjà vu* when you get to the obligatory 'origins of the Web' section, soon, but hang in there for all-new stuff about the collapse of the dot-com bubble, illegal file-sharing, and an interesting theme about how the Web has (partly) returned to its authentic, non-corporate, community roots with the help of things like wikipedia, Google and blogs.

NEW HORIZONS

In the previous edition, I argued that the arrival of new media offered a much-needed kick to the world of media and communications studies. (You can read this material from the first edition at www.newmediastudies.com.) In general, media studies had entered a 'middle-aged, stodgy period', characterized by pointlessly contrived 'readings' of media texts, an inability to identify the real impact of the media, and a black hole left by the total failure of vacuous US-style 'communications science' quantitative research, which remained unfilled due to a corresponding absence of much imaginative qualitative research. In particular, I said, media studies was looking weak and rather pointless in the face of media producers and stars, including media-savvy politicians, who were already so *knowing* about media and communications that academic critics were looking increasingly redundant: chasing humbly after the media's top artists and manipulators, saying, 'Ah, I see what you've done there' – and publishing wilfully unreadable articles about it three years later – and these didn't really seem to add up to much, especially when the phenomena had already been dissected perfectly well by newspapers or magazines as they were happening.

Most of these things are still true: you wouldn't expect old-school media studies to reinvent itself within three years. But the arrival of new media within the mainstream *has* had an impact, bringing vitality and creativity to the whole area, as well as whole new areas for exploration (especially around the idea of 'interactivity'). In particular, the fact that it is quite easy for media students to be reasonably slick media *producers* in the online environment means that we are all more actively engaged with questions of creation, distribution and audience. But before we consider the exciting implications of new media for today and the future, we'd better lay down some basic internet history.

ORIGINS OF THE WEB

This is the internet

The internet is a global network of interconnected computers. Rumours that it started life as a sinister US military experiment may be somewhat exaggerated, although a computer network called ARPANET run by the US Defense Department from 1969 was a primary component of the super-network which would eventually become the internet, and the US government was definitely interested in a network which could withstand nuclear attack. In fact, the first talk about an internet can be traced back to 1962, when J.C.R. Licklider of MIT wrote a number of memos about his idea of a 'Galactic Network' linking computers worldwide (see www.isoc.org/internet/history).

The first event in the life of the internet as we know it today came in 1974, when Vint Cerf and Bob Khan defined the Transmission Control Protocol (TCP) and internet Protocol (IP) by which information could be put into a 'packet' and addressed so that computers on the network would pass it along, in the right direction, until it arrived at its destination. Various tests and demonstrations were successfully conducted, and internet-style networks started to take off, but it was ten years before the TCP/IP-based internet rolled out across the USA in 1983. And then it would primarily remain the domain of academics and scientists for another ten years.

So what is the World Wide Web?

The World Wide Web is a user-friendly interface onto the internet. It was developed by Tim Berners-Lee (www.w3.org/People/Berners-Lee) in 1990–91, and caught on in 1993, when a freely available Web browser called Mosaic, written by Marc Andreessen and Eric Bina, started the 'Web revolution'. (Mosaic went on to become Netscape Navigator, the hugely popular early Web browser which managed to keep Microsoft at bay for most of the 1990s.) Berners-Lee is sometimes mistakenly credited with inventing the internet. But his actual achievement was perhaps more socially significant: he recognized that the internet was 'too much of a hassle for a noncomputer expert' (Berners-Lee, 1999: 20), and created an elegant solution.

1.1 Tim Berners-Lee, the eminently nice inventor of the World Wide Web

Berners-Lee's idea was to create a set of agreed protocols and standards so that documents could be stored on Web servers anywhere in the world, but could be brought up on a computer screen by anyone who wanted them, using a simple address. Central to Berners-Lee's dream was the use of hyperlinks, so that web-pages would be full of highlighted words or phrases, which would take the user to other relevant pages elsewhere. (Today, websites often only link to their own internal pages, to prevent users from wandering off to other sites too easily. 'External' links might be offered on a separate 'links page', or not at all. Berners-Lee had really want-ed everyone to be much more liberal in their interlinking across these boundaries.)

More surprisingly, Berners-Lee hoped that the World Wide Web would be built through *collaboration* – he wanted Web users to be involved in a two-way process, not only reading webpages, but also adding to and amending them, creating links and, of course, creating new pages. The Web's creator did not expect Web brows-ing to be a one-way experience, but the browser software which became popular, from Mosaic onwards, would only read and present webpages, not alter them. The World Wide Web Consortium, the advisory body which Berners-Lee estab-lished and still directs, has developed its own browser/editor, Amaya, which will both read and edit webpages. (See the Consortium's website, www.w3.org, for the latest, and Berners-Lee's book, *Weaving the Web*, 1999, for the story of the Web's development.) But this idea never caught on: almost all sites refuse to allow users to rewrite their main content.

Indeed, it is difficult to picture how this could work: who on earth is going to create a nice website, only to pass control over to visitors who can change, delete, amend, scribble, add their own links and 'contributions', and generally mess the whole thing up? An optimistic answer to this pessimistic question can be found at www.wikipedia.org, the online enyclopedia launched in 2001 and built entirely through the contributions of its users. Anybody can add the beginnings of an article, but – most importantly – that article, like every Wikipedia article, can be edited, changed and added to by any other visitor. All previous versions of an article can be viewed, or reinstated, making it easy to put things right if any user does indeed spoil an entry – although this happens rarely. The site, which reached the milestone of 100,000 articles in January 2003, contains interesting discussions about how this apparently free-for-all system works (see 'About Wikipedia' and 'Our replies to our critics').

The success of Wikipedia suggests, heart-warmingly, that Tim Berners-Lee was not being entirely naïve when he dreamed of a Web built on the love and free labour of nice people all around the world, summarized in this 'vision' of what the Web should be about:

> The dream behind the Web is of a common information space in which we communicate by sharing information. Its universality is essential: the fact that a hypertext link can point to anything, be it personal, local or global, be it draft or highly polished. There was a second part of the dream, too, dependent on the Web being so generally used that it became a realistic mirror (or in fact the primary embodiment) of the ways in which we work and play and socialize. That was that once the state of our interactions was on line, we could then use computers to help us analyse it, make sense of what we are doing, where we individually fit in, and how we can better work together.
>
> ('The World Wide Web: a very short personal history' at www.w3.org/People/Berners-Lee)

A FEW WEB ESSENTIALS

It is worth emphasizing that the Web is something that runs *on* the internet. It is not, however, the *same* as the internet. The internet is the network of networked computers. Since it is basically all cables, wires and microprocessors, the internet can carry any kind of data, such as e-mail, computer programs or illegally copied music files. The Web, however, is made up of a particular type of (easy to use, universally readable) data. At its heart is Hypertext Markup Language, HTML, a simple computer language which can be used to create webpages which include links, graphics and multimedia components. The simplicity of HTML is also its weakness: it is difficult (but not impossible) to create graphically stunning, or amazingly interactive websites using just HTML. For this reason, other languages and formats have appeared, such as ASP (for sites which are driven by an underlying database, such as online shopping sites where the site is like a 'window' on the catalogue database, or indeed news websites where the site is used to view the news database), XML (an advanced sibling of HTML, which can also deal with databases), and Macromedia's well-established Flash (for fancy, interactive, scalable graphics in quite small file sizes).

For the first few years of the Web, there was a range of different search engines, often with fancy logos and complex layouts, and a substantial advertising budget. Everyone had their own favourite: Excite, Lycos, Altavista, and numerous others, all used different search methods, and were all a bit disappointing in different ways – especially in their desire to style themselves as 'portals', full of adverts and paid-for information and links. These sites were crippled under the wheels of the word-of-mouth juggernaut surrounding Google, which was launched in autumn 1998 with the no-frills layout and simple logo which the majority of Web users know and love today. As well as being impressively free of marketing gimmicks, Google had the cleverest way of ranking websites, developed by Larry Page and Sergey Brin at Stanford University. Google's system, as the site itself explains, 'relies on the uniquely democratic nature of the Web by using its vast link structure as an indicator of an individual page's value'. Every link to a page is taken as a vote in favour of that page; and links from pages which themselves rank highly in this system carry more weight than links from pages that nobody links to. In other words, links equal popularity, and Google will always give you the most popular pages on anything. Even Yahoo!, which previously was an excellent *directory* put together by humans (rather than a search *engine* put together by software algorithms), seems poor now, simply because Google is so damn good.

THE WEB TODAY

In 2000, I complained that while the Web had become a colourful, complex, multimedia environment where people connected in new ways, many internet scholars were still writing about text-based applications (such as newsgroups, MUDs and MOOs) which ran on the internet (not the Web) and which were generally unknown to the mainstream Web users who had come online in the late 1990s. There was also an emphasis on the most basic, text-based uses of webpages. Thankfully, since then, academia seems to have caught up a bit. And the Web has helped out a little, too, by becoming a bit more simple and old-fashioned: less obsessed with ill-conceived 'get rich quick' schemes, and with more opportunities for Web-based sociability via easy-to-use outlets of self-expression, such as blogs. Let's explore both sides of this change.

The money thing, and where it all went wrong

At the time when the first edition of *Web.Studies* was being prepared – but not, ahem, for much longer – the internet was seen as a source of great wealth.

Internet companies were valued very highly on the stock market, even though most of them had not made any money and showed little sign of doing so. In the first *Web.Studies* I felt obliged to explain this phenomenon. Indeed, the capitalist obsession with the Web was so great that some internet scholars felt that the creative potential of the global network had already been killed off by big business. I had to argue that this was not quite right, because the business and non-business spheres of the internet could exist quite happily side by side:

> For example, let's say your town has an excellent public library which you enjoy using. One day a company opens a large supermarket next to the library. The library continues to be good and well-stocked, and indeed picks up more users from the influx of supermarket customers. Now, if your friend said, 'I see the supermarket has destroyed the library', you would think they were a bit of an idiot.
>
> In the same way, the commercial and non-commercial parts of the internet ought to be able to exist side by side. The problem, alas, is that in this town, we would probably see marketing people from the supermarket sneaking into the library, taking down the community notices in the foyer, and replacing them with adverts. They would also interfere with the library catalogue, so that it told library users that the answers to their questions would be found in the supermarket. Such forces obviously need to be kept in check.

1.2 Concerns remain that business sharks may try to gobble up the Web

This all remains true, and indeed the behaviour of obnoxious marketers online has only got worse: witness the huge amounts of spam (junk e-mail) which jam up the average inbox. But clearly there was a huge shakedown in the much-hyped world of e-business – this event has now become a recognized phrase: 'the day the dot-com bubble burst'. It's not clear exactly which day this was, but during the spring and summer of 2000 – when *Web.Studies* first hit the streets, though we claim no responsibility – it became clear that things had gone very wrong.

A classic example is the case of online fashion store Boo.com, which went online in November 1999 in a flurry of expensive publicity, only to collapse spectacularly, six months later, in May 2000. Enterprising to the last, its co-founder turned this story into a book, *Boo Hoo* (2002), written in the style of a John Grisham page-turner: 'The story of how an international model and former poetry critic from Sweden dreamed up an ambitious and glamorous internet start-up; how they

---

HOW CAN BUSINESSES MAKE MONEY OUT OF PEOPLE VIEWING WEBPAGES?

A longer explanation of this appeared in the first edition's introduction, which you can read at www.newmediastudies.com. Simply put:

- popular websites can generate profits by carrying advertising; it's the same as commercial TV stations, which make their money by showing you adverts during the programmes that you actually switched on the TV to watch; search sites are in a particularly good position to show users targeted adverts, related to the topic that they are searching for

- some sites can charge money for access, but only if the service is special or unique, and something you can't easily get elsewhere; pornography is the most obvious, and successful, example.

---

convinced the world's biggest fashion houses and Wall Street to invest $135 million in their plan; and how they burned through it all in just over a year', as the blurb has it. Boo.com seemed to have a staggering mismatch between the amount of money that people were willing to pour into it and what the company could actually offer. But its case was not untypical. For five years (1995–2000), venture capitalists and other investors threw money at all kinds of e-business ideas, based on the confident hope that these enterprises would become the hugely profitable corporations of tomorrow. They knew that some would fail, of course, but they didn't count on it being almost *all* of them. In the real world, it turned out, there just isn't room for *everybody* to run a super-successful internet business. Furthermore, many of these new businesses were neither as innovative nor as in-demand as their creators had liked to imagine. Investors lost faith, realizing that their internet stocks weren't worth as much as they'd hoped, and so the values plummeted.

Some have survived, of course, by performing a useful service in a well-organized way. Amazon, the online bookstore that actually makes a profit, is your classic case: it's a simple and usually cheap way to buy books (or music, films, toys, and an ever-growing range of other goods). It makes basic but effective use of the Web's unique interactivity, allowing users to post reviews of products (even if they hate the item in question), make annotated lists for others, receive recommendations based on their past purchases, view what other people that bought a product also bought, and so on. Importantly, Amazon has built a reputation for delivering actual goods efficiently in the real world – something you don't get just by having a fancy website.

Nowadays, then, everything's much more sensible: there's a smaller number of internet businesses, which are having to work extra hard to dispel the now-standard assumption that internet businesses are money losers, and which have to demonstrate that they can provide effective and robust services in the real world.

The prevailing spirit of the first years of the twenty-first century has been a sense that we should stop being silly, or gimmicky and fancy, and get back to basics with what we know we can do best. And this hasn't just affected the business sector.

Back to basics, and the rise of blogs

In the late 1990s, the websites that got people excited, even away from the commercial sector, were glitzy, hyper-designed temples to individualism and glossy graphic design. But as the new century has rolled in, we have seen a revival of the kinds of social communication which the internet always stood for, but which were more suppressed – and perhaps seen as embarrassingly 'old-fashioned' – during the Web's business boom years.

In particular, blogging has unexpectedly taken off like never before. A blog, short for weblog, is a regularly updated diary of a person's fascinations, thoughts, and/or experiences. Sites such as blogger.com make it simple to set up a blog, and – just as importantly – easy to update the thing regularly with no need for special technical skills. In February 2003, *Wired* magazine noted that 'the meteoric rise of weblogging is one of the most unexpected technology stories of the past year', and estimated that at least half a million people actively maintain blogs. (The site www.diarist.net has a good set of resources about this phenomenon.) The 2003 war in Iraq brought particular attention to blogs. As William Gibson, himself a blogger, noted (in interview with Hamish Mackintosh, May 2003):

> I think during the first week of the war in Iraq, I feel as if I saw blogging go mainstream. On a Monday, I'd mentioned to a friend in Vancouver that there was a guy in Baghdad who was blogging and my friend asked me 'What the fuck is blogging?' By the Friday, blogging was being discussed on the evening news.

Articles about blogging seem to have appeared in all major newspapers, and all current affairs magazines, during 2002–3. Half of them say that blogging is the perfect democratic internet application, giving everyone a platform to express their views, and giving non-mainstream voices an opportunity to contribute to media culture. (See, for example, Steven Levy's *Newsweek* article, 2002.) The other half are by journalists furious that unqualified amateurs are being treated as legitimate commentators on current affairs – this, they feel, should be left to professional hacks (Naughton, 2003). Journalism professor Elizabeth Osder told *Wired* magazine, 'Bloggers are navel-gazers. And they're about as interesting as friends who make you look at their scrap books. There's an overfascination here with self-expression, with opinion. This is opinion without expertise, without resources, without reporting' (Shachtman, 2002). On the other hand, Steve Outing of the Poynter Institute argued that the diversity of bloggers is one of their strengths: 'What we're seeing more and more are webloggers breaking niche stories, and thus serving as an early warning system for traditional journalists' (ibid.).

The most striking thing about these recent debates is that it's all so … 1996! Blogging is a good old-style use of the internet, and thus we see just the same debates as when the first personal homepages were put on the Web in the early to mid-1990s. Those in favour see these things as 'democratic' and a chance for everyone to 'have their say'. The critics, usually professional print journalists who do not want to be usurped by the new technology, condemn the phenomenon as a sandpit for the rambling amateur.

There is a straightforward technical explanation for the newfound popularity of blogs: today they are much easier to create, on the Web, using simple tools which had not previously been readily available. But blogs also seem part of a new philosophy on the Web, that the best things are not necessarily noisy animated explosions of multimedia innovation, but are the simple and effective phenomena which use the medium in a measured, accessible way, and connect people around the world. It's what the World Wide Web was always meant to be about.

Whatever happened to the 'attention economy'?

Back in 1997, Michael Goldhaber argued that on the internet there is an 'attention economy'. I outlined this in the first *Web.Studies*, and it seems worth reviewing the idea to see if it still makes sense, several years on. Goldhaber's point was that the scarce resource, which everybody on the Web is struggling for, is *attention*. On the internet, money is not the most important scarce resource, for reasons which we will turn to in a moment. And information certainly isn't a scarce resource – the Web contains oceans of it. The Web's scarce resource is attention, because there is so much information out there, and everyone has so little time to look at it. To triumph on the Web is to have lots of people giving attention to your site, instead of giving it to someone else's. Attention is what everyone wants. So it's an *attention economy*.

Big companies don't get attention on the Web *just* because they have a lot of money. Having money can enable a company to make a stylish multimedia web-site, and generate awareness of it through conventional media and promotions, but if the website has no engaging content, it won't win much attention. Meanwhile, individuals and small groups are relatively empowered in this medium, because if they produce a website deserving of attention then, hopefully and ideally, word will spread around the internet and lots of people's attention will be drawn to that site. (The fact that Google has become the most popular search tool adds considerable weight to Goldhaber's argument: as we have seen, Google favours those sites which are talked about on *other* sites – so a buzz of attention has a significant impact on a site's visibility.)

A commercial website, set up to promote a chocolate bar or a book publishing company, say, has the great advantage that its website address can be promoted on all of its adverts and all of its products. A non-commercial website does not usually have such an opportunity, and so is at a disadvantage. (The publishing company is also in a good position because it can give away bits of its product directly, on its website, as a 'taster' for the full product, whereas the chocolate manufacturer usually has to settle for offering news, games and quizzes associated with the product.)

However, if the commercial website does not have any interesting content, other websites won't link to it, it will be ignored in Google's theme/topic listings (only appearing when users ask for it by name), people won't mention it in e-mail discussions or chatrooms, and the poor site will only ever be visited by curious individuals (and the company's employees, partners or competitors) who have seen the address advertised and who visit the site – once.

Meanwhile, any website which is full of appealing and regularly updated content has a better chance of getting attention. Today, one of the best ways of getting attention is to be mentioned in one or more of the most popular blogs (see above), which also, due to the power of the top blogs, leads to a better Google ranking. Popularity can also be cultivated by some online networking – by sending personal e-mails (not spam) to potentially interested, and ideally influential, people. The whole thing takes effort, but not a lot of money. By getting links from other websites, and listed in directories, search engines and magazines, a website can come to command a lot of attention. Of course, though, it needs to be a good site in the first place.

So, have the passage of time, and the dot-com collapse, shown Goldhaber to have been right about the 'attention economy'? Basically, yes. Goldhaber illustrated his point by saying: 'Money flows to attention, and much less well does attention flow to money.' The second part is definitely true: you can't buy attention. You can't *make* someone interested in what you have to say, unless they actually find the content of what you have to say engaging. This is what the now-extinct dot-coms found – there were so many sites, insufficiently unique or different from each other, and they were unable to capture enough attention to be successful, no matter how much money they had behind them. Meanwhile, 'Money flows to attention'? Well, this has turned out to be *mostly* true, but maybe the demands of attention were even greater than Goldhaber realized: only a relatively small number of people got enough attention via the Web that they were able to convert this into a successful business or writing/TV career.

OUTLINE OF THIS BOOK

Web.Studies 2nd Edition is not a mere updating of the first edition. The chapters are all either brand new or substantially rewritten, to address today's wired world, for as we know, these things change fast. The first, introductory part of the book consists of three chapters: this introduction, which can be read in conjunction with Laura Gurak's overview of recent developments and themes in internet studies, and Nina Wakeford's outline of methodologies for studying the Web. This is followed by the first themed section, Part II, 'Web Life, Identities, Arts and Culture'. This part is (even) bigger than in the first edition, because it seems especially important to look at the range of creative ways in which everyday people are using the Web, creating new cultures and interacting with existing ones. The contributors consider personal homepages, and the Web presences and interactions of fans, and women's zines, and online phenomena from virtual sex, and pornography for lesbians, to movie-making in the digital era, as well as a discussion of masculinities online. We also see how Web artists have reflected on the nature of the internet in their works which explore interactivity and online sociality; and the ways in which online connections have brought real benefit to people in the form of self-help sites (in particular for sufferers of breast cancer). Last, we consider how the idea of *fascination* can be used to understand how websites entice audiences.

Part III, 'Web Business, Economics and Capitalism', looks at the ways in which commercial interests are affecting today's internet and the way that people use it. We consider the Web's relationship to capitalism, and deconstruct the idea of the 'digital divide'. Then we look at internet copyright issues in general, and as fought out in the ongoing battles between the music industry and file-sharing music fans. The final themed section, 'Global Web Communities, Politics and Protest', is about people coming together, for political or social reasons, on the net, and the ways in which the Web might change those political relationships and processes. The contributors consider whether the Web is really a tool for democracy, and its use in contemporary warfare. We also look at internet use by women activists, and two quite different communities: the Cherokee Indians, and the subculture of virus writers. The last chapter takes a look at some possible futures of the internet and new media culture.

SOME OF THE MAIN ISSUES

This section outlines some of the main issues in Web studies. These are key themes which will recur in other chapters throughout the book. Being broad themes, they are reasonably timeless, and I set them out in the first edition. But since you may not have read that, and these are important points, here they are again, revised and updated where appropriate.

The Web allows people to express themselves

The Web offers people an opportunity to produce creative, expressive media products (or texts, or art works, if you prefer) and display them to a global audience. Without question, compared to the pre-Web era, this is a significant new development. We may be able to produce a painting, or a poem, or an amateur 'magazine', but without the Web, most of us would not have the opportunity or resources to find an audience for our work. We could force our family and friends to admire our masterpiece, but that would be about it.

When I was at school, I made a 'magazine' for a useless musical 'group' that I was in. My materials were biro and paper. I was aged 12 and photocopiers weren't very accessible, so the single edition of each issue had to be passed around between members of its audience – approximately four people.

1.3 *Powercut* magazine. Paper and ink. Hard to distribute

When I was a student, I published a fanzine (or 'small press magazine') with an anti-sexist theme, *Powercut*, which was reproduced by a professional printing company (in exchange for a significant chunk of my humble student finances). Producing and printing the thing was the (relatively) easy part: it was the *distribution* which would eat up my life. I spent hundreds of hours visiting and writing to bookshops, and getting magazines and newspapers to write about it – with ordering details – so that I could spend yet more hours responding to mail-order requests. I published two issues, and for each one, it took me a year to shift 800 copies. This was regarded as a considerable success in small press circles.

Today, like many people, I can write a review or article, stick it on the Web, then sit back and relax; 800 or so people can have read it – well, *seen* it – within a week. I largely enjoyed the *Powercut* experience, back in 1991–3, but think how much simpler my life would have been – and how much more of a life I would have had! – if Tim Berners-Lee had bothered to invent the World Wide Web just a few years earlier than he did.

A website can be your own magazine, or gallery. Anything that can be put into words or pictures – or animation, video or music – can be put there. This is what made the internet fantastic, and it still is.

Cynics and miserablists here pipe up with 'What if nobody visits your site?' Frankly, this isn't a very powerful argument. If you put some effort into the site content, and then put a bit more effort into establishing links with other sites, and getting it covered by search engines and directories, then there are sufficient millions of Web users out there that some of them will come and visit. The Web, then, offers an extraordinary explosion of opportunity for creativity and expression. A decade ago, almost all readily accessible media was made by a small bunch of companies (and the lucky people who had got jobs with them). Now look at it.

The Web brings people together, building communities

Since Howard Rheingold published *The Virtual Community* in 1993, much has been written about 'communities' on the internet. The basic point is simple enough: before the internet, communities were people who lived or worked close to each other. If you were lucky, you might have a community of *like-minded people*, although it was unlikely that you would get a very compatible bunch all in the same place. The global internet transforms this – for those, as always, who have access to it – because it enables like-minded people to form virtual communities regardless of where they are located in the physical world. Before the internet, scientists working in a particular field might have little contact with each other, and needed to organize expensive conferences in order to have a meeting of minds. Meanwhile, fans of obscure bands would have little to do with their counterparts elsewhere, and people interested in certain hobbies, or artists, or skills, could only feed their interest through one-way communications, such as reading a magazine or newsletter about it.

Again, the internet changed all that. Now, regardless of where they are in the world, people with similar interests, or with similar backgrounds, or with similar attitudes, can join communities of like-minded people, and share views, exchange information, and build relationships. Indeed, the Web has even been successful in virtually patching up previously existing real-world communities, in the case of sites like Friends Reunited (www.friendsreunited.co.uk), which puts old school friends back in touch with each other.

Virtual communities are inevitably different to real-world ones, of course. They are much more flexible, with people coming and going, making new connections, or choosing to ignore parts of the community they don't like. They don't rely on the physical impressions made when people see each other in the flesh. In practice, what these communities look like are people sending electronic text to each other. Most of the studies of virtual communities are about groups exchanging messages on newsgroups and e-mail discussion lists, or groups who often meet in the same chat rooms. Internet scholars are also waking up to the phenomenon of the communities which develop in and around similarly themed websites and their creators. I noted this in the first *Web.Studies*, saying: 'Participants in chattering groups may come and go, whereas the bonds of friendship and interdependence which the Web, by its interconnected nature, breeds amongst website-creators – expressed in public links and personal e-mails – may be more compelling.' This remains true, but maybe I was a little optimistic: website creators, and their interpersonal connections, come and go with some regularity too.

Nevertheless, it remains a good argument, that if more people had a website, and communicated with like-minded others, the more complex and deeply entrenched these community webs would be. Some of us are quite moralistic about use of the Web, and feel that you must *contribute*, and not merely 'surf'. Everyone who uses the Web should, ideally, have a website, where they endeavour to put some stuff that may be of interest to someone else. It is difficult to take seriously, for example, internet scholars who don't even have their own website. You might say that we don't expect film critics to have their own movie studio, but this is rather different – making a website requires some effort, but little in the way of many material resources.

While the net's global friendship-building is valuable, there is, as usual, a downside. As with any open-access communications medium, the Web can be used in ways which we may find distasteful. If the internet can foster communities of like-minded artists and poets, it can also give a home to groups of like-minded Nazis and child molesters. Many countries already have laws to deal with the real-world actions of such people, but we can't stop them talking to each other. It is important not to confuse the medium with the message: newspaper stories still appear which seek to show how evil the internet is because unsavoury characters communicate using it. But when unpleasant people appear on TV, or make use of the telephone, we don't normally blame the box of electronics. We can hope that the opportunities for education and creativity which the Web offers will lead to a kind of human society which can find ways to get along without causing harm to others. That's the optimistic view, obviously.

Anonymity and identity play in cyberspace

Since the early days of the internet there have been bulletin boards and 'chat' spaces where users can interact online and, today, many websites include chat or discussion rooms where visitors can interact in real time. Since participants cannot see each other, and are not obliged to reveal their real name or physical location, there is considerable scope for people to reveal secrets, discuss problems, or even enact whole 'identities' which they would never do in the real world, not even with their closest friends – in some cases, *especially* not with their closest friends or spouses. These secrets or identities may, of course, be 'real', or might be completely made up. In cyberspace, where the 'people' we 'meet' are usually only seen as text or icons on a screen, it's clearly more difficult to tell which voices are 'true'.

Some aspects of this 'identity play' can be annoying, such as the sad middle-aged man who pretends to be younger, more handsome and successful in the hope of attracting the online attention of a young woman (who, in the real world, may be another sad middle-aged man). Other aspects can be criminal – paedophiles have been known to present themselves as friendly children online, so that they can arrange meetings with (what they hope are) other children. Sometimes, they might find that they have unintentionally arranged a meeting with another paedophile; sometimes it can turn out to be a police officer. (Some police services employ staff to wander around chat rooms pretending to be children to see if anyone asks to meet them.)

Some internet chat stories are more heart-warming: men and women who have thought that they may be gay, but have been afraid to come out in the 'real world', have 'tested' this identity online. They have been so happy to be able to express their 'true' selves – and to receive such a supportive (and perhaps erotic) response – that this has given them the courage to come out in their everyday real-world lives as well.

And, of course, people of all sexual orientations have used the internet for 'cybersex', which involves people telling each other what they are doing to each other (within their shared cyber-imagination) as they fumble their way towards sexual satisfaction. Today, inexpensive webcams allow participants to see each other – although some may choose not to, preferring the pleasure of text.

The internet's scope for anonymous interaction, and therefore identity play, is significant for the way in which it fits in with contemporary queer theory. Queer theory suggests that people do not have a fixed 'essence', and that identity is a per-

1.4 Queer theory, and other media/identity resources, at www.theory.org.uk

formance (Butler, 1990; Gauntlett, 2002; www.theory.org.uk/queer). We may be so used to inhabiting one 'identity' that it seems to be 'natural' to us, but it's a kind of performance nonetheless. Because the internet breaks the connection between outward expressions of identity and the physical body which (in the real world) makes those expressions, it can be seen as a space where queer theory's approach to identity can really come to life.

However, the arguments made about this tend to be based on playful chat spaces which, in terms of most people's internet use, are not popular or mainstream today. As I argued in the first edition of *Web.Studies*, it has become more interesting, these days, to be studying expressions of identity, and community developments, within and between people's websites.

The Web and big business

In the previous edition, the main concerns regarding business and the Web were based on the idea that big corporations might ruin the Web, by filling it with corporate nonsense and advertising, and by buying up all the best bits. There was also the associated fear that Microsoft might become so powerful that it would be able to influence the open standards of the Web so that all users would become reliant on proprietary Microsoft products – a threat which seems to have subsided, not least because of the huge court battle which took up so much of its time in recent years (United States vs Microsoft – see www.usdoj.gov/atr/cases/ms_index.htm).

Nowadays, the bigger panics run in the opposite direction – big businesses are scared that the internet will ruin *them*. Peer-to-peer file sharing (via systems like Napster and its successors such as Kazaa) has famously upset the music industry, which is understandably distressed that pop songs (and videos) are being acquired free of charge, instead of via the traditional method of paying for them. Some file sharers argue that the music industry has lots of money already and that rock stars are rich, so it doesn't matter. However, since we don't live in a post-capitalist utopia, this view is short-sighted and means that promising new bands would have no chance of getting a record deal (and indeed, the record industry has already become very reluctant to foster new talent unless it has 'instant pop hit' written all over it). File-sharing fans also point out that people who download songs are also more likely to buy CDs of the music they like most, which is a better argument, although the evidence for this happening is mixed.

In its response, the record industry gets over-excited and asserts that people who steal music are straightforward thieves, who should be treated the same as someone who steals your car. The analogy is faulty, because if you steal my car, I have lost the car; but if you take a copy of a digital file, nobody is left *without* a digital file. Nevertheless, you could say that its creator has lost, or been denied, the money that they would normally have been paid for it.

The music industry is slowly realizing that online distribution is not going to go away, and so is working out ways to offer this facility itself. The debate goes on, and is covered by Ian Dobie's chapter in this book. Meanwhile, related cultural industries, such as the movie and publishing businesses, continue to fear digital threats to their well-established empires – although certain traditions, such as going to the cinema with friends, or curling up on the sofa with a book, are well loved and seem unlikely to be wiped out by a computer-based alternative in the next few years.

The Web is changing politics and international relations

This theme remains strong: the internet has the potential to create links between people and groups with shared political interests – and for them to promote their ideas to others. By increasing access to information – or propaganda – it is thought that the internet may bring about a greater engagement and interaction between the individual and larger political processes.

The public sphere

In an argument related to the idea of virtual communities, discussed above, internet scholars often relate the net to the idea of the 'public sphere', as developed by Jürgen Habermas (see, for example, Habermas, 1989). In an ideal public sphere, citizens would discuss issues of concern and arrive at a consensus for the common good. Back in the 1980s, Habermas did not feel that we had an effective public sphere in Western societies, partly because commercial mass media had turned people into *consumers* of information and entertainment, rather than *participants* in an interactive democratic process. Now you can see where this is heading. From the 1990s onwards, internet enthusiasts noted the kinds of discussions taking place in newsgroups (text discussion forums), and argued that, when even more people had access, the net would bring about a healthy public sphere.

The shortcomings of this view are equally obvious. Increasing numbers of people *do* have internet access, but most of them don't spend any time in online political debates. Intense discussion spaces, like newsgroups, will remain the province of the minorities of individuals who are so interested in a particular area that that want to spend their time debating specific issues. Most people won't bother.

Life in the webs

This conclusion led to the feeling that, alas, the internet will not help to foster a healthy public sphere after all. But that may not be true either. If we look carefully at the interactions between and around the thousands of websites which can be called 'political' in the broadest of senses, we do find cultures of engagement and discussion. The fact that people who are concerned about an issue can create a website about it, and then find themselves in e-mail conversations (or in different forms of electronic conference) with people who are interested, curious or opposed to their views, or who run related sites, *does* create a climate of greater public discussion. Compare it to the days when all you could do was read about an issue in a mass-produced newspaper, and then discuss it with a handful of friends in a pub. This Web-based political culture is not, of course, the same as a democratic online meeting where every member of society has their say, but that was never going to happen anyway. (How do several million people chat about an issue at once? The only workable method would be . . . voting.) There is also the problem that only interested people participate, which will always be the case. We can hope that the greater engagement with political issues which the Web can bring will mean that more people become interested in politics generally; but this is far from guaranteed.

HOW TO SUCCEED IN WEB STUDIES

Make your own

Unless you want to be a very detached critic who argues that all new media developments are really bad and that we're all doomed, in which case you won't really need to understand the Web very well anyway, then you'll need to experience the agony and ecstasy of building and promoting your own website.

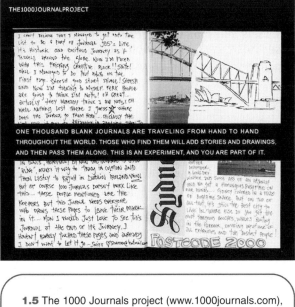

1.5 The 1000 Journals project (www.1000journals.com), an example of an incredibly creative project crossing the offline and online worlds

You'll find instructions on how to do this in numerous books and magazines, and of course on websites. To make a website really quickly, visit Tripod (www.tripod.lycos.com) – or type 'free homepage' into Google for similar alternatives – where they not only give you webspace for free, but have clever page-building facilities where you construct and publish your webpage(s) on the spot, within the website, with no extra software required. To make a blog, visit the wonderful Blogger (www.blogger.com) which does all the hard work for you. To make a really good website, though, you'll need Web design software (Macromedia Dreamweaver is the best, but costs money, although you may be able to get a perfectly good early version free of charge on a magazine CD) and graphics software (such as Paint Shop Pro, if you're paying, or use free demo versions or shareware of that or other packages).

Keep up to date

As well as making your own site, and then getting it noticed on the Web, you will also need to keep abreast of what's going on in the ever-changing new media world. One way of doing this is to subscribe (free) to the excellent *Wired Newsdrop* e-mail service, which will send you a daily message listing headlines and short summaries, with links to the full stories on its website (click 'Personalise this' at www.wired.com/news). Another method is to buy the more intelligent internet magazines, such as *.Net* and *Internet Magazine* in the UK, or *Internet World* and *Wired* in the USA. These magazines often come with free CDs containing copies of the latest Web browsers and plug-ins, other free software, and demo versions of new professional packages. Soon your home will be full of these shiny discs – especially promotional ones from AOL. Last time I suggested that these could be used as Christmas decorations, now I have so many that you could build an igloo out of them.

Here we go

We hope that you find this book useful. Please send comments to david@ theory.org.uk.

USEFUL WEBSITES

Blogger: www.blogger.com

Read other people's blogs, or make your own with the excellent blog-publishing facility.

Google: www.google.com

The invincible tool for finding anything on the Web.

The Internet Society: www.isoc.org/internet/history/

You want the history of the internet? It's here.

New Media Studies: www.newmediastudies.com

Where you can read the first edition's introduction (2000), and see how things have changed. You can also tut that, like many fickle Web producers, I have failed to keep this site very exciting, because my attention is more focused on Theory.org.uk (www.theory.org.uk), my regularly updated site about media and identity issues. Tsk.

Resource Centre for Cyberculture Studies: www.com.washington.edu/rccs/

Produced by David Silver, RCCS is 'an online, not-for-profit organization whose purpose is to research, teach, support, and create diverse and dynamic elements of cyberculture'. It's been growing for years, and so by now is an absolute goldmine of information.

Wired News: www.wired.com/news

Daily articles about internet developments, regulations and innovations, with an excellent searchable archive where you can find an article on anything Web-related.

The World Wide Web Consortium: www.w3.org

Lots of useful basic (and advanced) information about the World Wide Web, with Tim Berners-Lee's interesting Frequently Asked Questions page at www.w3.org/People/Berners-Lee/FAQ.html.

Chapter 2

INTERNET STUDIES IN THE TWENTY-FIRST CENTURY

LAURA J. GURAK

When the first edition of this book was published in 2000, David Silver kicked off the collection with a chapter entitled 'Looking Backwards, Looking Forward: Cyberculture Studies 1990–2000'. When it comes to the internet, a great deal has changed since 2000 – most notably the growth and burst of the inflated e-commerce bubble and the subsequent impact of this time period, forever and indelibly, on the internet and world cultures. Prior to 2000, it made sense in the context of this type of book to talk about 'cyberculture' as a reference for research about the internet. Today, we might say that most of the Western world is a cyber-culture, and that what we know about this culture from a research perspective is summed up in the phrase 'internet studies'. In the Fall of 2000, just as the first edition of this book came to press, the then-new Association of Internet Researchers (AoIR) held its first annual conference at the University of Kansas. The following Fall, we hosted the conference at Minnesota, and, in the Fall of 2002, the conference was held in Maastricht, in the Netherlands. This association, with its interdisciplinary membership and international reach, represents the state of the art in internet studies. In a moment, I will return to the Association and review some of the trends in research therein. But as always, it is useful to look back, just for a moment, to note how we began, who helped pave the way, and why it is that we study the internet and cyberspace as separate and unique technolo-gies and social spaces. Then, after looking back and looking at today's landscape, I will suggest four key terms – speed, reach, anonymity and interactivity – that articulate today's cyberculture, and help us understand how we need not only to rewire but completely reconceptualize media studies in our age. What is the role of major media companies when regular people can share music, news and infor-mation over the internet? What is the role of publishers in an age of heightened speed and broad reach across boundaries? How does peer-to-peer file sharing change our relationship to traditional forms of media? The chapters in this collection, and the ever-expanding world of information on the internet, will help answer these questions.

IN THE BEGINNING

Silver's chapter in the first edition of this book documents the rise of internet studies (then known as studies of computer-mediated communication) along roughly chronological lines, grouping this research by early studies of 'popular cyberculture', followed by what he calls a 'second generation' of cyberculture studies, and ending, at that time, with the 'critical cyberculture studies' of the late 1990s. Another way of looking at the history of how the internet has been studied is to look at the research perspectives and points of view brought to bear as the internet moved out of its roots in research and into popular culture. Today, internet usage in the USA is about as common as popping a piece of bread in your toaster but, in the early 1990s, the technology was still in its infancy and was used mainly by college professors and students, other researchers, and the military. Soon, however, internet technologies – mainly e-mail, gopher file sharing, and Usenet news – became of interest to private companies, who saw great opportunity for the technology in the workplace.

The first book to document the social and workplace aspects of the internet was Hiltz and Turoff's first edition of *Network Nation* in 1978 (reissued by MIT Press in 1993). If you look at the cover of that first edition, you notice that the image, a map of the USA with telephone lines, reflects the state of technology at that time – the telephone system as the basis of the 'highway' that would connect computers across place and time. (This system became the basis on which early metaphors, such as 'information superhighway', were based.) Even back then, the topics that Hiltz and Turoff noticed among users of networked computers were a foreshadowing of what was to come. Their work highlighted features such as impersonality and the freedom to be oneself (ibid.: 27), the social and psychological differences noted in online versus face-to-face communication (ibid.: 76), the difference in social cues (ibid.: 81), pen names and anonymity (ibid.: 95), and impacts on workplace hierarchies (ibid.: 133). These features are still much talked about in today's overly hyped internet news stories – for example, the notion of online anonymity, the crux of many news stories about children apparently 'stalked' over the internet, bogus online stock trading, and so on.

Hiltz and Turoff's work was the basis of a series of other studies, which continued looking into the ways in which the lack of social cues and novel features of online communication changed the workplace and interpersonal relationships. The 1984 paper by Kiesler, Siegel and McGuire in the journal *American Psychologist*, is interesting in several ways. First, it articulates the social features noted earlier by Hiltz and Turoff, and coins the phrase 'computer-mediated communication' in its title.

Also, this paper brought the social and language-based features of online communication to the attention of many other scholars and, soon, a field of study in computer-mediated communication (usually abbreviated to CMC) came to be. As internet technology became more and more accessible via e-mail in the workplace (see Sproull and Kiesler, 1986), a wider range of researchers from linguistics, rhetoric, composition, psychology, cultural studies, computer science and human–computer interaction, management studies and communication studies (especially interpersonal communication), came to see that this world of digital communication was incredibly rich for study. How was it, for example, that so much emotion could be carried in what seemed to be at first glance such a sterile kind of communication? (In these early days, all communication consisted of simple, typed text, without font or style changes or attachments, in a plain e-mail message.) But so much emotion could often accompany this seemingly simple message that huge 'flame wars' ensued, much to the concern of managers – and the interest of researchers.

Flaming, and the relationship of this behaviour to the lack of social cues, the setting, and even possibly to gender, was a serious line of research for many years. Rice and Love's 1987 paper on 'electronic emotion' was a foreshadowing of many papers to come, summarized quite nicely by one group of communication researchers (Lea *et al.*, 1992), who note that 'the notion that "uninhibited behaviour" is associated with communicating via computer has gained a great deal of attention. One manifestation, "flaming" (the hostile expression of strong emotions and feelings), has been widely reported.' But they note that most studies tried too hard to generalize and did not take into account the specific context of the behaviour. Yet some work did try hypothesizing about flaming and other behaviour with more specificity, the work of Susan Herring being the most notable here. Herring began the search for the relationship of gender to computer-mediated communication. She speculated that gender differences may account for some of this behaviour; that while the lack of face-to-face encounters may start the problem, masculine communication styles aggravate the situation, especially in certain online forums (1993).

Sherry Turkle's work raised the important question of how we consider the concept of *identity* in a digital age. Identity, of course, is a central concept for so many parts of human life: our psychological sense of self; how we portray ourselves in speech and writing; our financial and credit card identities; our workplace selves. Her book *Life on the Screen* (1995) asks us to consider our postmodern world, where one person can have many screen identities. One of the students interviewed in her book provides a very telling quote, that for him, real life (RL) is 'just another window' (page onscreen). Another central concept raised as the internet went from speciality product to everyday appliance during the mid to late 1990s was the concept of *community*. Online technologies appeared to have tremendous

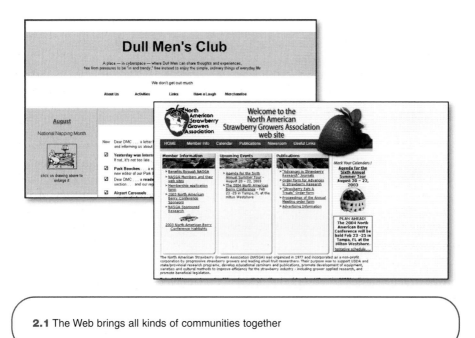

2.1 The Web brings all kinds of communities together

advantages and disadvantages in terms of community. On the one hand, groups of like-minded people from across states, countries, time zones and demographic groups could come together easily and for little cost. Howard Rheingold's (1993) book *The Virtual Community* paints this picture anecdotally, and *Persuasion and Privacy in Cyberspace* (1997) uses rhetorical analysis and case study methods to document the first two social actions of communities in cyberspace. Nancy Baym's work on Usenet news and soap opera fan clubs provides additional research-based evidence for the power of online community. But, as Steven Doheny-Farina argued in *The Wired Neighborhood* (1996), the downside of virtual community may come at the expense of knowing one's physical neighbours. Another downside is that, if the only people you communicate with are people just like you, you don't have as much reason to learn to communicate with people who are different. The power of the internet to create highly specific communities (such as people who own border collies and live in the Midwest and feed their dogs a natural diet and drive Harley-Davidson motorcycles) means that those folks are less likely to be exposed to the possibly alternative points of view of people less similar to themselves.

Thus arose the question of the relationship of the internet to democracy and politics. Many began to wonder if the internet could somehow 'reinvigorate' democracy by building coalitions, providing discussion sites, and perhaps even allowing for online voting. Several studies (Stromer-Galley, 2000; Haas, 2001) investigated the use of the Web for political campaigns, noting that the full potential of online communication was not being tapped. Soon, important legal issues began coming to the fore, most notably intellectual property (particularly copyright) and privacy. The work of Dan Burk (2000) is illustrative of questions raised by a technology that appears built to challenge copyright but is increasingly being subject to laws (such as the Digital Millennium Copyright Act, or DMCA) that restrict the possibilities of sharing and fair use of music, video and text from online sources. (All of Burk's writing is relevant here; see his website at www.law.umn.edu/FacultyProfiles/BurkD.htm for more.)

Other issues that have been important to the development of internet studies include questions about the digital divide; cross-cultural issues and online communication (although far more work is needed here); and, with the advent of the Pew Internet & American Life surveys, the use of the internet for increasingly mainstream issues such as medicine, education and governmental information.

That was then. Where are we today?

FROM GENERAL TO SPECIFIC

Probably one of the most fundamental shifts in internet studies at the dawn of the twenty-first century came in a move away from trying to generalize about all online behaviour to recognizing that, as the internet became the domain of many, and as websites covered everything from the news to college courses to home recipes, it was not possible to say that online communication is *one thing* and one thing only. In other words, context is key. On a student discussion site, folks may tend to behave one way. On a workplace website, behaviour may be more professional. On a self-help site, there may be more emotion; on a technical site, less. A news site may be less interactive than a site maintained by a high school student for discussing the most recent movies, or a site designed to allow real-time chats. And so on. Early work attempting to define what computer-mediated communication might and might not be seemed fine in a time when access was limited and the use of online technologies was simple. But today, saying 'the internet' is like saying 'the world'. Uses are many, technologies are complex, and levels of privacy and security are different from site to site. Research about the internet as a social, psychological and linguistic communication site is most fruitful when it is based on the specific case at hand.

A second major shift has been the coming together of many in internet research under the rubric of internet studies. During the heyday of the e-commerce boom, many universities even implemented entire majors or minors in internet studies. It became clear that just one discipline – rhetoric, communication, psychology, law, human-computer interaction – was not enough to address the interesting questions raised by the ubiquitous use of the internet. The rise of internet usage across income brackets, gender, social class and nation meant that there was a wealth of issues to be studied if we were to understand how best to use this new and powerful technology. Consequently, many researchers began going outside their own area to work with others who could lend a different perspective. The formation of the Association of Internet Researchers in 1999 along with the publication of some new interdisciplinary journals (for example, *The Information Society*) created the intellectual space for study that was focused on internet communication first and foremost.

Third, even with the demise of many dot-com companies, the world was left with some very sophisticated technologies relative to those that existed before 1999. New encryption technologies to protect credit card and banking transactions, new looks and functionalities for webpages, sophisticated programming in Flash and Java, and the move away from purely text-based online communication to a blend of text, sound, visuals and movement changed forever the expectations of those who use the internet. And, for internet studies, the new look of the place – interactive, sort of like TV, sort of like a picture of people talking, sort of like a movie – forced researchers to rethink what we need to be studying on the internet. Online community? Still seems relevant. Flaming? Is it even an issue any more? What about the way we now write, which looks more and more like speech? Does it matter? Studying the Web means knowing how to study not only text but also colour, design and interface functionality. Many of the 'original' internet researchers were trained to study text and conversation, but few have expertise in computer science, interface design, usability and visual analysis. A new group of researchers, raised in the dot-com age and emerging from their graduate studies, will lead the way for this new era of internet studies.

Finally, as the internet blurs and convergences with television, music, movies, and other forms of entertainment, legal issues become key. Major media and publishing companies wish to lock down the copyrights to intellectual property, lobbying governments to extend terms of copyright, and enforce rules that protect not only property but also technical systems that make access to DVDs or other media almost impossible. These legal issues are, ultimately, philosophical ones, in that they invite us to consider the cultural conditions that dictate the social uses of the technology. Studying these issues typically requires collaboration with a legal scholar and, increasingly, an understanding of international, rather than simply domestic, law.

KEY TERMS FOR INTERNET STUDIES CIRCA 2003

Yet let me backtrack for a second. Is it possible to identify several key terms that help describe, at a general level, issues that make internet studies important, that warrant a book such as this one to be published? In other words, even when you take context and situation into account, are there factors about the internet and how we use it that are somewhat universal? I believe it is quite possible, now that time has passed, to survey the research and observations about the internet and note that some features just seem to go along with online communication. The way in which the original internet was designed – the 'hardwiring' of internet technologies, if you will – seems to encourage and invite certain features of communication and certain behaviours from the end users. There are four 'key terms' that we can draw from internet studies to explain much of what makes online communication novel, powerful and significant. These are: speed, reach, anonymity and interactivity. Elsewhere, I provide case examples to illustrate these features and their implications (Gurak, 2000). Here, I will provide an overview.

Speed and reach

Two of the most obvious yet significant features of online communication are speed and reach. The combination of these two factors makes digital communication powerful indeed. In the split second you press the enter key, you can send your message across the globe, bypassing social and organizational structures and even bypassing government structures to reach millions. The internet was designed to be a flat structure, not a top-down structure with gatekeeping mechanisms along the way. You can jump around from server to server and get your message where it needs to go. Regular people can set up file servers to share files (peer-to-peer networking). We write quickly and move information with great speed. This speed and wide reach are generally true for all online communication, regardless of the situation, context or person using the system. Speed and reach inspire us to think about the following issues.

- *Oralness*: many people now write in a style more similar to the way they speak. In other words, online text often ignores conventions of spelling, punctuation, and so on. Online text uses symbols and 'emoticons' to inject oralness. We see these features creep back into everyday writing. Even Microsoft Word turns a colon followed by a dash and a closing bracket into a smiley face.

- *Redundancy and repetitiveness*: online information is often repeated because of speed. It's faster to cut and paste than it is to retype the same idea.

- *Casualness*: the oral quality of typed speech starts to lend itself to a casual communication style. Speedy communication seems to make people less serious. For example, students who used to address me as 'Professor Gurak' now just send a quick e-mail with no salutation whatsoever, or simply my first name.

- *Multiplicity*: as Kaufer and Carley note, 'mass communication technologies all have high multiplicity' (1994: 103). The broader the reach, the more people see the message – the popular website updated several times every day, or the 'chain' e-mail that travels around the world in seconds, for instance.

- *Visual reach*: online communication has a wide reach because it incorporates visuals to a high extent.

- *Community*: such broad reach, at such high speeds, combined with interactivity (see the next section) allows communities to come together across wider geographic distances.

Interactivity and anonymity

You might say that, to some extent, television has relative speed and reach. But when you add in interactivity and anonymity, you change the picture entirely. Interacting with the screen is not something we know about from television. It's at the heart and soul of what makes online communication so powerful. And, when you can have hundreds of e-mail addresses, IRC identities, and screen names, you have the ability to play hide and seek as you interact. You can be anonymous if you like (although only to some extent, since many e-commerce sites track you like never before). As with speed and reach, certain concepts are inspired by these features.

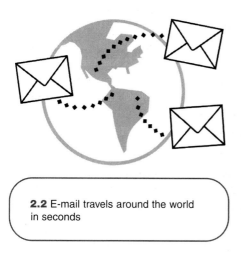

2.2 E-mail travels around the world in seconds

- *Gender and identity switching*: when you can be interactive and have multiple identities, you have the chance to experiment, to some extent, with what it feels like to be of a different gender or a completely different person altogether.

- *Ownership*: it's hard to know who owns what, or who said what, when the author of an e-mail message or website may be completely anonymous.

- *Flaming*: it's easier to say something nasty when you can hide behind the mask of an untraceable e-mail address.

- *Talking back*: suddenly, everyday people can talk back to the company or the media network. And if no one replies, that same person can set up a website instead.

- *Privacy*: you may feel anonymous on the screen, but internet technology (particularly web and e-commerce) makes it easy for website owners to track what you do, when you do it, how much you spend, and so on.

WHAT IS MEDIA STUDIES, AND WHERE DO WE GO FROM HERE?

Early research on online communication attempted to generalize about technology. More recent research recognizes that online communication happens in specific contexts; however, we can turn back to some of the earlier studies and synthesize all research to notice that four key features – the aforementioned speed, reach, interactivity and anonymity – run across almost all online communication situations and inspire certain forms of behaviour, challenges to legal and corporate ideas, and new ways of reading and writing. As we see the world of internet communication becoming more entrenched, and these features becoming more a part of our lives, we need to reconceptualize media studies for a digital age. At the outset of this chapter, I asked the following questions. Is there a place any more for major media companies when regular people can share music, news and information over the internet? What is the role of publishers in an age of heightened speed and broad reach across boundaries? How does peer-to-peer file sharing change our relationship to traditional forms of media? In the USA, and increasingly around the world, major media companies own almost everything. When a technology such as Napster (the controversial music file-sharing service) offers new ways of doing business, new ways of communicating and being creative, it is challenged in court for threatening the old models. To make any difference in communication and media in the coming century, we must think about media in terms of the implications of speed, reach, anonymity and interactivity.

Digital technologies are not going away; they are just becoming more pervasive. Wireless networks and satellite systems will allow internet connectivity even in parts of the world that do not have any telephone lines. Copyright and intellectual property will continue to be challenged, even as laws become more restrictive. The desire of news organizations, political campaign managers, companies and others to control information will not be easy to satisfy in an age of file sharing, networked personal computers and digital television. Traditional media studies concerns about free speech, freedom of the press, plagiarism, visual communication and good writing all become more complex in the digital age. If we look to past research, see what we know today, and envision a new and interesting future, we will learn that embracing the new technology may bring more interesting uses than if we stay beholden to models of the past.

USEFUL WEBSITES

Association of Internet Researchers: www.aoir.org

The Association of Internet Researchers' website has lots of useful links to internet research-related articles, journals and other information including the most upcoming international conference.

EFF's Digital Millennium Copyright Act Page: www.eff.org/IP/DMCA

This page, maintained by the Electronic Freedom Foundation, contains archival material related to the Digital Millennium Copyright Act.

Independent Media Center: www.indymedia.org

This group describes itself as 'a collective of independent media organizations and hundreds of journalists offering grassroots, non-corporate coverage. Indymedia is a democratic media outlet for the creation of radical, accurate, and passionate tellings of truth.'

Out There News: www.outtherenews.com

Out There News claims to be 'reinventing the way world news was reported for digital media'.

Pew Internet & American Life Project: www.pewinternet.org

The Pew Internet and American Life Project conducts surveys to determine 'the impact of the internet on children, families, communities, the work place, schools, health care and civic/political life'.

Chapter 3

DEVELOPING METHODOLOGICAL FRAMEWORKS FOR STUDYING THE WORLD WIDE WEB

NINA WAKEFORD

There is no standard technique for studying the Web. Rather, it is case of plundering existing research for emerging methodological ideas developed in the course of diverse research projects, and weighing up whether they can be used or adapted for our own purposes. Depending on the focus of the study, researchers may draw on a wide range of methodologies, which may originate in a variety of disciplines including communication studies, sociology, anthropology, visual studies, cultural geography and literary studies. This chapter offers four approaches for Web research. Readers are also encouraged to consult journals in the rapidly expanding discipline of internet studies, such as *New Media and Society*, *Information, Communication and Society* and the *Journal of Computer Mediated Communication*, which are a useful source of emerging thinking about methods for data collection and analysis.

The short history of social science research in this area has tended to prioritize interactive communication spaces over study of the Web. Much of the early communication research about the social aspects of the internet focused on 'computer mediated communication' (see, for example, Baym, 1995). Several authors examined the types of social world that existed online by studying the textual interactions that constituted so-called 'virtual communities' or 'cybersocieties' (Jones, 1995). At this stage, the Web did not appear to overlap with newsgroups, bulletin board services or e-mail discussion lists, which were the sites considered in this first generation of research.

Developments in communication technologies are constantly changing the way in which the Web is produced, represented and consumed. Chat or e-mail exchanges remain a key topic of research in communication studies, but as the Web develops, increasingly e-mail accounts and chat spaces are integrated into websites. As this happens, the boundaries between the Web and other internet spaces will become blurred. Projects which are currently developing ways to visualize the social networks of newsgroups and group chat will be increasingly relevant to the multiple social worlds of the Web. Also the overlaps of television, the internet and personal computing have led to a rhetoric of technological 'convergence' as well as corporate mergers such as the purchase of Time Warner by America Online (AOL) in January 2000. (Vincent Miller's chapter in this volume provides more information on this subject.) In the view of many technologists, the Web is poised to generate the convergence of previously segregated media technologies. Meanwhile, delivery devices are also in a state of radical upheaval. Wireless technologies, such as mobile phones, uncouple Web access from the desktop and the personal computer, particularly with the development of wireless Local Area Networks (LANs). Such technological transformation is likely to have methodological consequences. However, none of these changes *necessarily* alters the way in which users experience the Web. The relationship between technological developments and the rest of the social world cannot be *presumed*, but must be *investigated*.

IS THERE ANYTHING DISTINCTIVE ABOUT RESEARCHING THE WEB?

The Web is a technology and media form that can be understood at many levels, and this can lead to confusion when defining the parameters of a research project. Webpages are simultaneously computer code, cultural representations and the outcome of skilled labour, such as writing HTML. Webpages are complex artefacts that can be written, read, used or consumed, and therefore despite their apparently virtual nature, they are sometimes compared to other designed products that have a more traditional material form, such as a book or DVD. Although it is possible to do a fine-grained reading of an individual webpage as cultural text, as if it were a written paper document, it is equally feasible to take a broad view of the way in which the Web is becoming part of global culture and commerce. In methodological terms, the former project could be conducted entirely through online observation without ever gathering the opinions of those who created the webpages. In contrast, for a study of global contexts, it is likely that reference to secondary sources would be necessary, perhaps accompanied by interviews with those in relevant international organizations. Yet even though the Web is often portrayed as a global medium, it may involve experiences that take on a distinctive local flavour, such as Web browsing at an internet café in one particular town or neighbourhood. For this type of project, a researcher might use a place-based ethnography including extensive participant observation.

Some of the methodological challenges of researching the Web resemble those involved in studying other systems of mass communication, but there *are* distinctive technical features of the Web that allow the collection of particular kinds of data. For example, certain kinds of relationship between individuals or groups can be tracked by following hypertext links from one website to the next, as will be described in the section on mapping social networks. Ananda Mitra and Elisia Cohen (1999) have suggested that there are six special characteristics of Web text. First, it is overtly intertextual through the presence of 'links'. Second, it rarely has the linearity of more conventional texts. Third, the reader becomes the author, in a sense, as she or he actively selects which links to follow. Fourth, the Web is a multi-media text. Fifth, it has a global reach, albeit constrained by access and language. Sixth, the Web is characterized by the ephemeral and impermanent nature of many of its texts, files and filenames. All of these should be considered when making methodological decisions.

There are other new methodological problems. For example, webpages appear to allow us the possibility of conducting fast and cheap global surveys by administering an electronic rather than paper questionnaire. Yet we cannot rely on the same respondent behaviour online as we would on 'pencil and paper' questionnaires (Witmer *et al.*, 1999). The quantity of information that may be generated, and the speed at which answers can be collected, can result in satisfying piles of data, but we should be wary of being persuaded by sheer quantity of responses; data is only useful if it is representative of the larger population (Jones, 1999). Another issue is the model of webpages as public documents, which has been challenged by some research (Chandler, 1998). Furthermore, Web search engine databases themselves are rarely neutral; rather, they are constructed in such a way that advertising and other commercial values play a significant role in what is retrieved after a word search (Goguen, 1999). Such issues are a reminder of the inseparability of methodology with *ethics* and *politics* (Star, 1994; Goguen, 1999). Ethical guidelines are emerging for internet studies such as those produced by the Association of Internet Researchers (www.aoir.org), and individual disciplines often have professional codes of conduct (addressing issues such as anonymity) that should be consulted at an early stage of research planning.

Studying the Web is a matter of moving back and forth between long-standing debates in methodology and the distinctive challenges posed by new electronically mediated research. In thinking about which methodological frameworks we have at our disposal to study the Web, it is advisable to bear in mind that what is considered to be legitimate methodology is itself always in flux. Alongside the rise in new information and communication technologies over the past ten years, a substantial body of work has emerged which questions orthodox methodological practices (see Denzin and Lincoln, 1994; Denzin, 1997). In qualitative sociology, in particular, there have been extensive debates about the possibility and desirability of feminist methodology (Oelson, 1994) and alternative measures of validity (Lather, 1993). Another recent development has been the rise of writing as a method of enquiry (Richardson, 1994), which often draws on the notion of reflexivity (Woolgar, 1988). Several branches of social science are advancing the use of visual material, which holds much promise for the investigation of the graphics-laden new media. Their branches range from a long-standing tradition of using photography and film in anthropology (Banks and Morphy, 1997) to developments in visual sociology (Harper, 1994), multimedia anthropology (Pink, 2001) and computer-assisted analysis of qualitative material (Fielding and Lee, 1998). All of these developments can be used as a resource for studies of new media such as the Web. For example, Annette Markham has written a highly personal account of her online experiences, showing the impact of recent debates on autoethnography and reflexivity (Markham, 1999). Even though methods of data collection and analysis may change, questions of research design, selection of participants, choice of fieldsite, ethical practice and the influence of theoretical frameworks continue to be crucial, and cannot be sidestepped, however virtual the data collection.

MEASURING 'HITS'

Initially, the most common way of measuring the Web was through usage statistics. Webpage use was estimated through the analysis of 'access statistics' derived from information about the user when they connected to a site. Counting access 'hits' to one URL is a relatively simple way to analyse the Web, and one still frequently reported in the media and on the 'counters' of webpages. Yet these *hits* do not actually measure the number of individual *users*. A single user may access the same webpage more than once during one session, access the site on several occasions and log on from different machines. Any of these occurrences will artificially inflate the number of apparent users. Furthermore, the typical method of counting hits merely describes the number of files – including graphics, logos and bits of frames – served by the host, so the actual number of visitors may only be 10 per cent of the number of hits.

As well as individual page counters, examples of this kind of work on server log file data can be found by looking at research undertaken by market research companies. Web trend forecasting is provided by services such as Comscore's Media Metrix (www.comscore.com), which provides 'Internet Audience Measurement'. Rather than reporting 'hits', reports are now more likely to give 'unique visitor' numbers. For example, in December 1999, Nielsen's NetRatings reported that the two 'top shopping sites' were Amazon.com (4.4 million unique visitors) and eBay.com (3.9 million unique visitors) (*Los Angeles Times*, C4, 12 December 1999). Yet the same report also offered the information that if sites were ranked on the basis of minutes spent on the site, the order would have been reversed. The average time spent (or 'stay') on eBay.com was 52 minutes, compared to 11 minutes on Amazon.com. (Of course, this may simply show that Amazon is, by design, a faster site to use.)

The kind of measure reported – for example, number of visitors or average time of stay – depends on what we want to investigate. The range of variables that can be collected is shown in a study in which researchers sought to measure the internet audience of a Web-based online art museum (McLaughlin *et al.*, 1999). In this study, researchers used the server log files of webpages to assess the characteristics of the users. Using the software WebTrends, they identified the total number of hits, the total number of user sessions, the proportion of US and international user sessions, and average session length per user. The investigators then created profiles of the kinds of users who had accessed the museum. In such studies, these kinds of measures are useful to provide a broad overview of the behaviour and location of those accessing a site. They are of less help when studying the social importance of the Web, at least when used as a stand-alone technique. Just as we would not want to judge the social impact of television viewing by looking only at audience figures, we cannot rely on hits to tell us about the social significance of the webpage. Therefore, in the study of the online art museum, the researchers combined log file data with an analysis of the interactive 'chat' features of the site.

The rest of this chapter suggests ways in which we might go beyond counting hits, and begin to develop sociological and cultural approaches for the study of Web-based new media. These range from techniques that have been developed to visualize large segments of the Web, and how they are connected, to methodologies for studying those who produce and use the Web on a day-to-day basis.

Categorizing and mapping

It takes a relatively short amount of time looking at webpages to realize that the variety of purposes and formats cannot easily be summarized. Some are clearly advertisements, others are for public information. Some are transparent as to their authorship and location, while others appear to float free of any identifiable geographical base, and/or the authorship is unclear. In the face of such diversity, researchers have tried to work out ways to categorize webpages, and develop typologies for the Web. One way to do this is to use a list of generic features that can operate as a template against which to analyse a specific page.

Some researchers have been particularly interested in the ways in which individuals portray themselves on personal homepages, and have devised categorization schemes based on features found in this kind of webpage (Chandler, 1997, 1998; Chandler and Roberts-Young, 1998). These homepages generally have a single author, and he or she is often the subject of the page. Daniel Chandler has suggested that we can think about the cultural significance of these representations in terms of the system of signs they display. His approach is closely associated with the semiotic readings that one could make of texts such as films or literature, and it highlights the idea that webpages are linked to our sense of self or identity. His 'Generic Features' list is divided into five primary sections: themes, formulaic structures, technical features, iconography, and modes of address, which can be applied to a wide range of personal homepages (see Charles Cheung's chapter in this book for more).

Another type of project is to look at webpages that address one theme, such as a cultural event or a public issue. This might be a popular TV programme or a recent piece of government legislation. The content of the webpages could then be inspected and compared to other media coverage, including representations not usually heard in the traditional press. One of the challenges of doing this kind of categorization is that the sample of pages used to devise the scheme can be crucial. How do we know if we have all the examples of webpages on 'topic x', given the lack of neutrality of search engines and the fact that some webpages are not indexed by or linked to these services?

Another approach is to think about categorizing webpages according to what they are linked to, by creating maps based on the links between pages. Several mapping techniques are currently being developed which enable visualization of parts of the network. A database of attempts to provide a bird's eye view of the Web has been developed by Martin Dodge at www.cybergeography.com, and some of the projects listed offer free access to their software for researchers. One example is Touchgraph, which is an open source tool for visualizing relationships between websites. One of the applications created by Touchgraph is the GoogleBrowser, which uses the 'what's related' data from Google to construct the graph (www.touchgraph.com). Figure 3.1 shows a section of the map produced when the

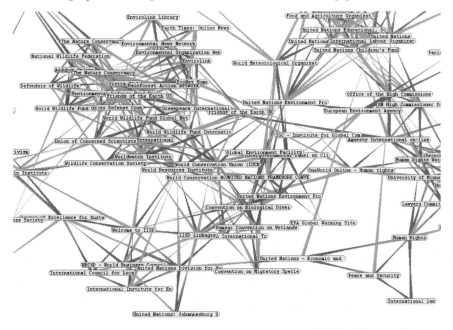

3.1 Touchgraph maps the relationships between Greenpeace and connected sites

webpage of the campaigning group Greenpeace is put into the GoogleBrowser.

Similarly, the Issue Crawler (http://govcomorg.oneworld.net) also provides a visualization of 'issue network' maps. One of the first visualizations produced using this technique was of the HIV/AIDS sites in Russia, Belarus and the Ukraine, undertaken by a researcher who was interested in the interplay between national and international groups, and their potentially different definition of the issues involved. Like the Touchgraph map, it shows a complex arrangement of interlinked points and related subject areas: you can see this at www.osi.hu/infoprogram/raidsnet.html.

Touchgraph and the Issue Crawler aim to give us maps of networks we would not be able to see using other methods, and plotting these can provide unexpected results. Such facilities have the advantage of being developed in an open dialogue with their users through their websites. Commercial software is also available, and an interesting map of the internet industry is provided at orgnet.com to promote one such product, InFlow. Yet still the greatest risk in their use is 'seduction' by the data itself, as reasonably unimportant patterns identified by the software may lead the researcher to draw premature conclusions. This, of course, is not an inherent problem with online research, but is an issue for all researchers dealing with this kind of data. The risk is that such visualization shows the result of tracking technological links, rather than ones that show a human-centred social network. Another way of thinking about this is that these programs offer a mapping geared to the technological parameters of association, rather than ones of collaboration, friendship, funding, and so on. The website blog-tribe.ryze.com shows a map of a network of friends within a Web-based writing community. In this case, each member submitted links to their friends, which were then used to construct the map of friendship. Hence, the result was based around what these users thought of as their social network.

The idea of virtual community has been explored by other visualization projects. The 'Sociable Web' research team has pioneered a way of seeing who else is simultaneously accessing a webpage while a user is browsing that page (Donath and Robertson, 1994). A custom browser allows each user to see the e-mail identifier or graphical icon of other users who are viewing the same page. The researchers hope that this is a way in which users can 'sense the presence of each other'. It could also be used for research purposes both to look at the dynamics of usage and group activity on the Web, as it allows people to browse the Web as a group. The user is required to create and present some information about him/herself either in terms of an identifying address or a pictorial representation. The researcher can monitor not only the behaviour of moving between sites, but also the relationship between the kinds of identities that are created by the user and their browsing behaviour.

Developing a critical visual methodology

We do not always need to rely on the networked features of Web documents in order to study them. Webpages are part of contemporary visual culture, alongside advertisements, photographs and television or film images. Another way to study the Web is to draw on the range of techniques that have been developed to study other forms of visual culture. Although many other professions deal in visual images, researchers need to develop a critical visual methodology in order to understand how webpages as images have a range of modalities: technological, compositional and social.

In his essay on how a visual sociologist would approach a photograph, as distinct from a photojournalist or a documentary photographer, Howard Becker (1998) points out that, when sociologists look at a picture, they search for contextual information such as explicit statements about cultural patterns and social structure. When researchers look at webpages, they also need to develop a set of questions related to the context in which the page was produced, but also to how it might be viewed by an audience. Gillian Rose has set out what she calls a 'critical visual methodology', by which she means

> an approach that thinks about the visual in terms of the cultural significance, social practices and power relations in which it is embedded; and that means thinking about power relations that produce, are articulated through and can be challenged by, ways of seeing and imaging.
>
> (2001: 3)

Thinking about webpages as part of visual culture entails thinking about the social effects of images, and Rose's book summarizes some central assumptions of this approach. First, there is a claim that images themselves do something. In other words, they have their own visual effects, and may be a site of power, seduction, pleasure or resistance. Second, images can either make visible or invisible social difference, by offering portrayals of social categories such as race, gender, and so on. Third, the visual culture approach also addresses how images are looked at, and in particular how the viewer (yourself or others) is positioned in relation to it. Fourth, images are treated as having a wider cultural context (which was Becker's point about looking at a photograph). Finally, the spectators of an image bring to their viewing their own sense of visuality, or ways of seeing and responding to what they see. Rose wants us to remember that images are not simply reflections of their social contexts, but have effects as images. She also encourages us to consider our own way of looking at images, and to be reflexive in our accounts of visual culture.

What does this mean for webpages? Rose suggests a checklist of questions that can be used to think about any item of visual culture (ibid.: 188–90). Her scheme was not intended to be directly applied to Web studies, so the ways in which the questions are asked might seem to apply more directly to traditional visual culture such as paintings. Nevertheless all of the themes are central to developing a critical visual methodology of the Web. Some questions about the production of an image are as follows:

- When was it made?

- Where was it made?

- Who made it?

- Was it made for someone else?

- What technologies does its production depend on?

- What were the social identities of the maker, the owner and the subject of the image?

- Does the genre of the image address these identities and relations of its production?

Applying these questions to a webpage sometimes proves difficult, and indicates the different ways a webpage is produced compared to an artwork in a gallery or photograph in a newspaper. These forms of image are often signed or attributed to an artist. What happens on the Web? It is often useful to look through a set of webpages to see how far this information is available on linked sites. Sometimes this may show surprising results in terms of who is hosting a site. At other times it is difficult to work out anything about the individual or individuals who have created the site. In this way, despite their supposed transparency and accessibility, webpages may in fact be more challenging to research than traditional images in terms of questions about their production.

When we study the image itself, a different but overlapping set of questions can be raised.

- What is being shown? What are the components of the image? How are they arranged?

- Where is the viewer's eye drawn to in an image, and why?

- What relationships are established between the components of the image visually?

- What use is made of colour?

- To what extent does this image draw on the characteristics of its genre?

- Does this image comment critically on the characteristics of its genre?

- What do the different components of an image signify?

Webpages have developed with a huge variety of components, both technological and aesthetic. They may combine moving images as well as banner advertisements, text as well as links to video downloads. However, they also operate as visual objects in themselves, and there are recognizable genres – for example, the personal homepage, the Web portal, the online store (such as Amazon.com), the search engine, and so on. Some of the questions above need to be adapted for the particular kind of webpage under investigation. For example, you might want to concentrate on the way in which links are visualized, through text or images, and how this fits into the components of the webpage.

Also important are the kinds of knowledge and skills which the user (or in visual studies 'audience') is expected to possess. Some questions about this 'audiencing' would include the following:

- Who are the original audience(s) for this image?
- How is it circulated?
- How is it stored?
- Is the image represented elsewhere in a way which invites a particular relation to it, in publicity materials, for example, or in reviews?
- Is more than one interpretation of the image possible?
- Is there any evidence that a particular audience produced a meaning for an image that differed from the meanings made at the site of its production or by the image itself?
- How do different audiences interpret this image?

By adapting this set of questions, a researcher can begin to develop a methodology that not only looks at a webpage as a set of technological links, but also as part of contemporary visual media. In the last set of questions, the emphasis is largely on the audience of the pages, and more conventional sociological methodology of interviews and ethnography can be used. The development of online focus groups is another way in which data about user experiences may be collected online. Ted Gaiser has discussed the mechanics of organizing and interpreting online focus group methodology (Gaiser, 1998).

Understanding webpage production

Webpages are produced as a basis of skilled work, often undertaken by professionals. Another way of researching the Web is to look at the kinds of work involved in producing it, and how the technical, social and political infrastructure of webpages translates into what Web designers or programmers actually do. This kind of approach becomes a way of studying the infrastructure of the Web. Although infrastructure sounds quite boring, by *not* studying infrastructure we risk overlooking other discourses. As Star notes: 'Study an information system and neglect its standards, wires and settings, and you miss equally essential aspects of aesthetics, justice and change' (1999: 379). As an information system, the Web has its own distinctive 'standards, wires and settings', most familiar to those who build and administer it.

Christine Hine has suggested that studying webpages using this framework can be a useful alternative to a framework that concentrates on webpages as identity performances on the part of the author or institution which produces them. Using methodological premises from media and technology studies, Hine interviews developers of webpages for the service departments of a UK university. She finds that the process of webpage design is largely a case of producing a working idea of who the audience might be. The responses suggest a range of such ideas, from a pre-existing imagined audience of university users and other developers to the use of technological features of the Web as a stand-in audience. For example, a design decision might be justified in the following terms: 'I refuse to have a logo here, because every different logo is an extra 3K of download' (see Hine, 2001: 194).

The use of an imagined audience as a guide to development of Web content can lead to particular depictions of the user being built into the imagery. Interviews with the creators of Web-based and non-Web-based virtual worlds suggested that programmers had clear visions of how to represent the user in graphical environments, and these visions were associated with the programmer's identities as predominantly white and male (McDonough, 1999). Images of women and non-white bodies were limited to a series of stereotyped choices.

Methods from historical sociology have also been employed to look at the development of Web design skill. A study by Kotamraju (1999) attempted to document the changes in the skills required by Web designers over a short period of rapid development (1994–8) in the San Francisco Bay Area. Nalini Kotamraju traced newspaper advertisements as well as recruitment sites on the Web. She also interviewed Web designers about their own changing skill sets and those of their colleagues in the Web development industry. The most interesting finding, methodologically, is that the history of Web design seemed to have largely disappeared. Most job openings had been filled by word of mouth or personal recommendation, and neither appeared in print nor electronically archived records. Nor were the practitioners themselves able to reconstruct the recent skill change. Web designers were not able to describe the changes in skills which producing the Web required. This research suggests that one of the puzzles of doing research on the Web may be trying to work out the appropriate place to study when online data yield no results. Kotamraju concludes that the problem is related to the topic of research itself: 'Data, the traces of technology-related phenomena, reflect Web technologies, and in doing so, increasingly mimic the high turnover, rapid obsolescence, and momentary existence of digital technologies' (1999: 468). Researchers need to be wary of the speed with which information about recent Web history may vanish into the haze of obsolete technology.

Web designers are at the higher end of the scale of status and income in terms of Web production. Research on the Web as an outcome of skilled work might also focus on computer chip assembly lines as an alternative and essential site of production. An interview study has shown that workers on the chip assembly lines in Silicon Valley are preferred if they are 'small, foreign and female' (Hossfeld, 1994). Karen Hossfeld's study was conducted using over 200 interviews with workers, and their family members, employers, managers, union organizations and community leaders. Such research shows how the computer industry is embedded within the wider system of social stratification in the United States. The author comments, 'The racial division of labor in the Silicon Valley high-tech manufacturing work force originates in the racially structured labor market of the larger economy, and in the "racial logic" that employers use in hiring' (ibid.: 89). Clearly the production of the Web cannot be separated from the wider questions of justice and equality for all of those who create it.

Studying 'real'-places

The previous section described studies that had used interviews to collect data on how the Web was produced. There are also an increasing number of qualitative studies on how the Web is being used by its consumers, including ethnographic studies of sites where the Web is accessed in public, and in contrasting cultural contexts. Qualitative studies of media usage in a domestic context are well established, including, for television (Morley, 1980; Gauntlett and Hill, 1999), radio (Tacchi, 1998) and personal computers (Silverstone and Hirsch, 1992). More recent studies are beginning to examine how the internet is used in households (see, for example, virtualsociety.sbs.ox.ac.uk). Ethnographers have shown that media devices are part of a world of material culture, which may operate in the background of other activities. Jo Tacchi explains that when it enters the home the sound of the radio is both material and social (1998: 43). She comments: 'The use of the radio adds to the sound texture of the domestic environment' (ibid.: 27). We can apply this kind of finding to other forms of media and communication to compare and contrast the entry of the internet into the household. How does the Web enter the different (sound, visual) textures of the household? Silverstone, Hirsch and Morley also claim that the computer becomes part of the 'moral economy of the household' in which households appropriate commodities into the domestic culture in accordance with the household's own values and interests (Silverstone and Hirsch, 1992: 16). If you wanted to repeat this kind of household study you might ask: how does the Web enter into this moral economy?

Ethnographies of previous technologies in a whole variety of settings can be used to provide the techniques for future qualitative studies (Suchman et al., 1999). Projects that have looked at office work practices, for example, can enable useful comparisons when the Web is under investigation in households. Researchers have increasingly looked for places where the Web is being used outside the household, for example, through internet cafés and kiosk services. British Telecom in the UK is one of the companies trying to encourage the use of broadband internet access through kiosks built into old telephone boxes. What impact does being outside the home have on our understanding of what the Web can do, or how it becomes culturally meaningful? Internet cafés are fascinating fieldsites, in part because they vary so widely in format and purpose. Wakeford's (1999) study of a London internet café involved the researcher working alongside the staff who served the coffee and showed customers how to use the machines. From participating in these activities, it was found that the kinds of interaction that happened around the machines were influenced by much more than the technical capacity of the machine or the level of user skill. Rather, the way in which the café functioned wove together its place in the London internet 'scene', its own spatial ordering, and the ideologies of age, race and gender that were perpetuated by both staff and customers. Use of the Web was not merely an experience of the human interaction with a terminal, but was filtered through a much broader experience of being one of the most well-established internet cafés in London. This information could not have been gathered by looking at the internet café's webpage, or even by interviewing customers. It relied on periods of extended observation and interviews with the staff.

Ethnographic researchers may also work across different fieldsites by combining methodological approaches. A team of anthropologists working on the meanings of genetic knowledge (such as that produced via the Human Genome Project) have been working with a methodology centred around '"multi-site" ethnography' (Marcus, 1995) in which participant observation at laboratories, clinics and support groups was combined with data collected from websites and other internet spaces (Heath *et al.*, 1999). This kind of approach contrasts with traditional anthropological practice in which a practitioner claimed a geographically defined place of research on the basis of long-term residency or contact. It also has methodological consequences. Individuals with genetic conditions who were initially contacted through their websites were later met face to face. Overall, the researchers described this process as advantageous. For example, they discovered that since leaving university (and losing her computer access), Karen, who has a blistering skin disorder, had been using the computers at the research laboratory where she was being treated to create her own independent informational webpages about the disorder. They state: 'Without these face to face interactions with Karen, we would not have recognized the extent to which her online work was entwined with the work of the university dermatology department where we were conducting fieldwork' (ibid.: 453). It was nowhere evident on her webpage.

However, this approach also generated research dilemmas. The team members realized that they could not isolate what they had learned (or assumed) from information on a participant's webpage from subsequent encounters. Reflecting on the

subsequent meetings with Karen, the researchers write about these methodological tensions:

> When we first met her, we wanted to interact with the woman that she
> presented to us in person and not with the woman that she presented to the
> public online. No matter how hard we tried, however, it seemed as if we could
> not disentangle the conversation from our earlier knowledge of Karen's online
> work. We found ourselves (often unintentionally) asking questions that reflected
> these earlier understandings, forming opinions about her statements based on
> them, and even interjecting details to what she was telling us about her life.
>
> (ibid.: 454)

The practical resolution was to *account for* this kind of overlap rather than try to
avoid it. Heath and her colleagues outline a model of 'network ethics' to cope with
these tensions. Writing about such methodological difficulties is a good sociological 'trick of the trade' (Becker, 1998). Another trick this team developed is to view
research as a 'modest intervention' of collaboration between the participant and
researcher in which both sides 'reveal and transform the boundaries which separate online and face to face lifeworlds' (Heath *et al.*, 1999: 462).

As these researchers began to investigate in more depth how the boundaries
between online and offline are continually crossed, any initial definition of what
the Web might be became unstable. Here the Web is not merely a network of
hyperlinks, but also represents an opportunity for Karen to claim access to computer resources, and negotiate her relationship with her condition through the
construction of her own webpages. Researchers need to recognize this broader set
of meanings connected to Web content.

CONCLUSION: CARRYING OUT MEANINGFUL RESEARCH

George Marcus has pointed out that the very subject of our research is
determined by the connections we make between objects, people and stories during our fieldwork (Marcus, 1995). Taking this view, we constantly construct the
Web as we conduct our research, rather than researching something that is
already 'out there'. Although this perspective might seem confusing, it is merely
another way of restating an earlier point. Limiting Web studies at the outset to the
collection and analysis of online data is restrictive, and in so doing we may miss
the central features of the behaviour or group we are studying. How we *define the
subject* of research will always be strongly related to the choice of methodology.
This is true both for what we represent as 'the Web', and the level at which we
study it. In this chapter, there has been the space to point out only briefly a range
of techniques and frameworks for studying the ever-changing phenomenon

that is the Web. Throughout, I have emphasized that even though the Web appears to be about electronic communication, every component is also set within the *social and economic context* within which this communication/information network has emerged. This context, in turn, influences our methodological options. The technical functions and infrastructure of the Web can drive the data collection and visualization. For some projects, this will be useful. However, many studies which seek to represent the perspectives of consumers or producers will find interviews, observation and participation in social contexts much more productive. Susan Leigh Star has written that methodology is 'a way of surviving experience' (1994: 13). In the world of rapidly changing technological products, platforms and visions, we need as many ways of surviving experiences as possible.

 USEFUL WEBSITES

Computer Assisted Qualitative Data Analysis Software Networking Project: www.soc.surrey.ac.uk/caqdas

This project aims to disseminate an understanding of the practical skills needed to use software designed to assist qualitative data analysis (e.g. field research, ethnography, text analysis). The website has links to software sites where free demo downloads of the products can be acquired, as well as its own useful bibliography.

Cyber-Geography Research: www.cybergeography.org

A gateway into research concerned with the spatial mapping of the internet, including the Web. It provides access to a directory of 'Atlases of Cyberspaces' (including links to many commercial and academic projects) and a regular research bulletin.

International Network for Social Network Analysis: www.sfu.ca/~insna

INSNA is a professional organization for those interested in social network analysis, and provides details of publications and conferences, as well as a newsgroup. A good place to start if you're interested in going beyond visualizing the networks shown in Touchgraph.

Visualising Ethnography: www.lboro.ac.uk/departments/ss/visualising_ethnography

A gateway site for researchers using visual methods of research and representation in ethnographic projects, this site has a range of links to existing online work, as well as its own interviews with visual researchers, and articles describing visual research projects.

Part 2:

Web Life,
Identities,
Arts and Culture

IDENTITY CONSTRUCTION AND SELF-PRESENTATION ON PERSONAL HOMEPAGES: EMANCIPATORY POTENTIALS AND REALITY CONSTRAINTS

CHARLES CHEUNG

HOW MANY PERSONAL HOMEPAGES ARE THERE ON THE WEB?

Although it is difficult to count the dispersed and ever-changing number of homepages on the Web, a look at the press relations sections of a handful of the sites offering free Web space shows that the numbers must add up quickly: large community sites like Yahoo! GeoCities and Angelfire claim over 4.5 million active homepage builders each, for example, and FortuneCity claims a further 2 million (July 2003). Millions more homepages reside in the numerous other free webspace services, and within commercial and educational sites. Personal homepage websites are also a popular Web destination. Nielsen/NetRatings' MarketView report shows that Yahoo! GeoCities had more than 27 million unique visitors within one month (October 2002). ComScore Media Metrix surveys also show that Tripod and Angelfire had around 16 and 12 million monthly unique visitors respectively (September 2002).

INTRODUCTION

If you are curious enough to browse through some personal homepages posted on the Web, you may quickly observe the following phenomena.

- Generally, personal homepages are websites produced by individuals, or sometimes a couple or family. On a personal homepage, people can put up any information about themselves, including autobiography or diary material, personal photos and videos, creative works, political opinions, information about hobbies and interests, links to other websites, and so on.

- People from all walks of life have started to use the personal homepage to tell personal stories about themselves: cancer patients, retired scientists, kids with disabilities, vinyl collectors, kung fu movie fans, transsexuals, DIY enthusiasts, pornographic movie lovers, to name but a few.

- Certain personal homepages seem to be made to display the strong personality and identity of the homepage authors, as if declaring: 'It is me! I'm cool!' These pages usually have stylish design, and contain details of specific aspects of the author's life.

- Some personal homepages seem to be made more for self-exploration than for making a strong identity statement. These pages usually contain an online diary or journal, in which the homepage authors put down how they feel about what happens to them every day.

- Having said all this, many personal homepages tell you little information about the author. These pages are unbelievably dull – they only include things like vital statistics, one or two photos, some links to other websites, and nothing else.

- Even worse, many homepages are listed in Web directories but actually not available.

Personal homepages have their critics, of course. Some internet commentators, for example, suggest that the contents of personal homepages reflect nothing but the narcissism and exhibitionism of many net users and the 'content trivialization' of the internet superhighway (DiGiovanna, 1995; Rothstein, 1996). Some web designers are appalled by the amateur appearance of many personal homepages. But these responses are inappropriate. This chapter argues that, to make sense of the above phenomena, we need to take the personal homepage seriously as a significant social phenomenon. This chapter has two arguments.

4.1 Personal homepages are traditionally where people put big pictures of their friends – and their cats

1 The personal homepage is an emancipatory media genre. The distinctive medium characteristics of the personal homepage allow net users to become active cultural producers, expressing their suppressed identities or exploring the significant question of 'who I am', often in ways which may not otherwise be possible in 'real' life.

2 Nevertheless, the fact that many personal homepages are poor in content, or have even been abandoned by their creators, suggests that the emancipatory potentials of the personal homepage are limited and often not fully exploited. In daily life, there can be a range of factors which preclude some people from producing 'content-rich' personal homepages.

People tell stories about themselves by making personal homepages, but not – to paraphrase Marx – in conditions of their own choosing, as this chapter will show.

'THIS IS ME!': THE PERSONAL HOMEPAGE AS A STAGE FOR STRATEGIC SELF-PRESENTATION

The first emancipatory use of the personal homepage is strategic and elaborate self-presentation. In everyday life, we usually try in vain to tell our partners, family, friends, employers, or at times even strangers who we 'really' are. Although we can one-sidedly complain that other people misunderstand us, sociologists suggest that self-presentational failure in everyday life actually involves other factors, such as social interactional contexts and our presentation skills.

According to Goffman (1990), in everyday encounters, the social settings and audiences we face always define the kinds of 'acceptable' selves we should present – a teenager performs as a hard-working student in front of teachers in class, an office worker as a responsible employee in front of his or her boss and colleagues, a CEO as a responsible company leader who cares for shareholders in front of financial journalists at press conferences, and so on. Nevertheless, sometimes we may wish to present certain identities but may not find the 'right' social settings and audiences, and if we present these identities in inappropriate social settings, we experience embarrassment, rejection or harassment. For example, a boy may entertain his friends with rap songs about his sexual conquests, but his grandparents might be a less receptive audience.

In face-to-face interaction, we present ourselves through the use of 'sign vehicles' such as clothing, posture, intonation, speech pattern, facial expression and bodily gesture. But Goffman also emphasizes that total control over these sign vehicles is difficult, since most face-to-face interactions proceed in a spontaneous manner and do not include an assigned block of time in which we can present ourselves in an orderly and systematic fashion. More often than not, our presentation of self in everyday life is a delicate enterprise, subject to moment-to-moment mishaps and unintentional misrepresentations. These mishaps typically lead us (again) to experience embarrassment, rejection or harassment and, consequently, the failure of self-presentation.

To put it simply, the core problems of our self-presentation in everyday life are that we lack enough control over (1) what 'selves' we should display in a particular social setting and (2) how well we can present them. The personal homepage, however, can 'emancipate' us from these two problems.

First, the personal homepage allows much more strategic self-presentation than everyday interaction. The personal homepage is a self-defined 'stage', upon which we can decide what aspects of our selves we would like to present. As previously mentioned, in everyday life we may wish to present certain identities but may not be able to find the 'right' audiences. On the personal homepage, however, this is not the case: once we put up our personal homepage on the Web, its global accessibility of the personal homepage means that we instantly have a potential audience of millions (with the emphasis on *potential*). In addition, even if some people dislike our 'homepage selves' and send us negative responses by e-mail, these responses are not instantaneous, so we feel less pressure to respond to them – in fact, we can even ignore these comments. For example, if a kung fu movie lover really wants to tell others that he is an expert in kung fu movies, his simplest solution is not to force strangers in pubs to listen to him but to construct a personal homepage. By creating a website featuring his essays on kung fu movies, photo collection of kung fu stars, or even digital videos of him doing karate, he would have millions of net browsers who also love kung fu movies as his *potential* audience. Of course, not everyone stumbling across his homepage will admire his identity as a 'kung fu movie fan', and sometimes people may even send him e-mails ridiculing his enthusiasm for these movies. But since these 'attackers' are not his targeted audience, he can always ignore their criticisms.

Second, the personal homepage is emancipatory for self-presentation since it allows the individual to give a much more polished and elaborate presentation, with more control over 'impression management', compared with face-to-face interaction. Indeed, the 'sign vehicles' used in the homepage self-presentation are more subject to manipulation. As discussed in the preceding paragraph, since we are less likely to experience immediate rejection from those who read our homepages, before releasing our personal homepage to the net public, we can always manipulate all the elements until we are satisfied: we can experiment with the colour scheme, choose the most presentable head shot, censor the foul language accidentally written in the draft biography, and ponder as long as we like before deciding whether to tell the readers that our partner just dumped us. Mishaps that may affect one's self-presentation in everyday life can be avoided on the personal homepage. Of course, not all responses can be controlled – I cannot prevent a homepage visitor from thinking that I am a self-indulgent fool.

Research evidence shows that people from all walks of life have started to use the personal homepage for strategic and elaborate self-presentation.

One prominent use of the personal homepage is to promote one's professional achievement in ways which may not otherwise be possible in everyday life. People seeking jobs, for instance, use the personal homepage to highlight and embellish aspects of their professional achievements, so as to reach potential employers or to create more lasting impressions than brief phone or face-to-face job interviews (Rosenstein, 2000). Likewise, artists use their websites to promote their artistic persona (Pariser, 2000), and young academics use faculty homepages to gain wider exposure (Miller and Arnold, 2001). As one young academic confessed: 'For the person visiting the webpage of my department, I am more visible than the professors [who don't have pages]' (ibid.: 105).

Some homepages are more relationship-oriented. On these homepages, the authors often highlight particular personal qualities (personalities, hobbies or political opinions) so as to share opinions and experiences with like-minded individuals (Walker, 2000), or to attract potential romantic partners who admire those qualities (Rosenstein, 2000).

The personal homepage is also particularly valuable for those with difficulty presenting themselves in face-to-face interaction, such as introverts with weak self-presentational skills, and people with any kind of visible or invisible disability such as amputees, the visually impaired, or the hearing impaired. As one homepage author with traumatic brain injury said concisely: 'Our disability is *invisible* so people can't respond (original emphasis; Hevern, 2000: 16). These homepage authors may feel better able to express themselves through the use of biographies, online writing or their photos (Chandler, 1998). People with Down's syndrome, for example, have used the personal homepage to assert that in many ways they are no different from other people, because, like anyone else, they have distinctive cultural tastes and are knowledgeable about certain things – such as making webpages (Seale, 2001).

The personal homepage may be most emancipatory for those whose identities are misunderstood or stigmatized in society – teenagers, gays and lesbians, fat people, the mentally ill, and so on – since they can reveal their identities without risking the rejection or harassment that may be experienced in everyday life. One gay respondent, for instance, explained how the personal homepage helped him to come out 'steadily':

> I was looking for some way of having a gay presence in the world and still feel protected from the adverse effects. [Making my personal homepage] was great because I didn't have to just 'come out' to somebody and risk rejection. I could do things a little at a time and build levels of trust along the way.
>
> (Hevern, 2000: 15)

Another gay author reports a similar experience. He would say to friends, 'Check out my website', and let them see his positive expressions of gay identity, and 'think about it before reacting' (Chandler, 1998).

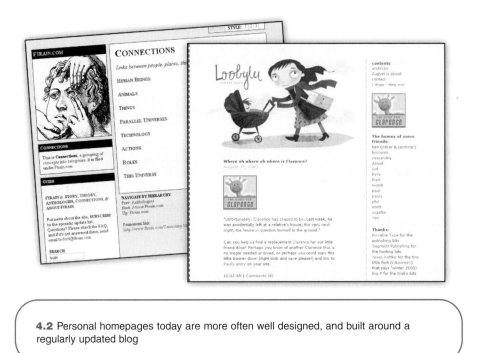

4.2 Personal homepages today are more often well designed, and built around a regularly updated blog

In fact, the emancipatory value of the personal homepage for self-presentation is even more evident if we look at how traditional mass media represent ordinary people. Generally, the mass media do not allow ordinary people to represent themselves on their own terms. Rather, ordinary people are represented by the creative personnel of the mass media, perhaps in stereotypical ways: the stupid teenager, the helpless disabled person, or the sexually available woman, for example. There may be radio phone-ins and TV audience talk-back programmes for the 'users' of these media to express their points of view, but the limited access to these shows, as well as the commercial nature of their topics, means that these media never allow people the degree of creative freedom offered by the personal homepage. Media scholars have longed for a medium which can help people who are often misrepresented in the mass media to move 'from silence to speech' (hooks, 1989: 9). The personal homepage can serve this very purpose.

'WHO AM I?': THE PERSONAL HOMEPAGE AS A SPACE FOR REFLEXIVE CONSTRUCTION OF IDENTITY

For some people, however, the personal homepage is emancipatory not because it is a stage for self-presentation, but because it can be a space for identity construction. My previous discussion on self-presentation more or less assumes that homepage authors have a stable sense of self-identity, and the only problem for these authors is to find some ways to present aspects of their identities. Some confident academics may use their webpage to advertise their academic persona, for example, and some lesbians who are very sure of their sexual identity may use their homepage to celebrate their lifestyle. However, for many people, their sense of 'who I am' is not that obvious, and may be highly uncertain. Their problem is not so much about presenting their identity, but concerns their exploration of 'who I am' and re-establishing a stable sense of self-identity. Much has been written on the sources of uncertain identity; here I have selected three examples for our discussion.

- *Multiple and contradictory identities*: unlike traditional society in which people only have a narrow range of ascribed identities, in late-modern society we are usually offered a bewildering range of choices over social and cultural identities, including those based on gender identity, nationality, religion, family relationships, sexuality, occupation, leisure interests, political concerns, and more. As Giddens (1991) suggests, these identity 'choices' are not marginal but substantial ones, since they allow us to define who we want to be. But Giddens (ibid.: 73) emphasizes that '[t]aking charge of one's life involves risk, because it means confronting a diversity of open possibility'. One 'unfortunate' consequence of this condition is identity confusion. Take for example a Chinese-American lecturing in the USA, who feels passionate about gay fiction but also about heterosexual pornographic movies, who loves both academic books and PlayStation games, and who supports feminism yet likes Sylvester Stallone's movies a lot. Who is 'he' actually? Gay, straight or bisexual? Is he really an American? Is he an intellectual or just a lowbrow who loves video games but pretends to be an intellectual? Can someone who loves macho movie stars like Sylvester Stallone still be a feminist?

- *Disrupted lives*: late-modern society is always undergoing rapid and extensive change, and accordingly, our lives and sense of stable self-identity are prone to disruption more than ever: a CEO who loses his job and cannot find another post for years may have serious doubts about his identity as a member of the middle-class elite; an American girl who moves to Paris to be with her French fiancé may feel totally disoriented in a new country; a man who has been divorced five times may seriously question whether he can really be a 'good' husband in the future. Furthermore, victims of serious illness or injury may also feel uncertain about their identities and their ability to function as 'normal' people (see Shani Orgad's chapter in this volume).

- *Stigmatized identities*: we may be doubtful about certain identities of ours if these identity categories are controversial, stigmatized or unacceptable in society at large. For instance, a young woman who is attracted only to females may still feel uncertain about her sexuality, because she has been told for years in her traditional Catholic school that homosexuality is sinful.

So how do people with uncertain identities re-establish their stable sense of self-identity? Giddens (1991) argues that, in late-modern society, we construct our sense of self-identity by creating a 'coherent' self-narrative. In such a coherent self-narrative, we successfully make ourselves the protagonist of the story, and we know clearly who we are, how we became the way we are now, and what we would like to do in the future – all these elements help to give us a stable sense of self-identity. However, if our identities are being challenged by new events or experiences, the coherence of our self-narrative can be disrupted, and we may experience an unstable and confused sense of self. In order to re-establish a stable sense of identity, we have to reflexively reappraise and revise our 'disrupted' self-narrative until its sense of coherence is restored. Take, for example, how the aforementioned CEO may rework his self-narrative when his identity as a member of the middle-class elite becomes uncertain as a result of his long-term unemployment. He may insist on finding work as another CEO, and interpret his long-term unemployment as just one of the roadblocks that all successful people might face at some point. In this case, he makes minor modifications to his middle-class elite self-narrative, but the overall meaning of the narrative remains unchanged. Alternatively, he may choose to abandon his middle-class elite identity and adopt a new 'simple-life-is-good' identity, and interpret his previous middle-class life as a worthwhile experience, without which he would not have been able to discover the true value of his new 'simple life' philosophy. In this case, he almost completely rewrites the overall meaning of his self-narrative. Anyhow, our concern here is not which concrete self-narrative this CEO finally adopts. Our point is rather that, if our sense of self-identity becomes uncertain, it is only through reflexive reappraisal and revision of our self-narrative that we can re-establish a stable sense of self-identity. Giddens describes this process as 'the reflexive project of the self'.

The personal homepage is a form of media which facilitates the reflexive project of the self. I mentioned in the last section that people who use their homepages for self-presentation can lay out, arrange, retouch and manipulate their 'homepage selves' until the outcome reflects the self-identities they intend to present. But for people with uncertain identities, or with a more free and fluid sense of self, this flexible creative process has a totally different meaning – experimentation and exploration of different identities. As Rosenstein (2000: 153) suggests, the 'hypermedia qualities of the home page can support linear, chronological narratives, but … they also lend themselves to a more episodic, situated and associational organization of materials that may be quite diffuse thematically and even spatially'. In other words, the hypertextuality of the personal homepage enables those authors who are in search of their self-identities – or who are happy to 'play' with their identities – to construct different self-narratives on their homepage and mull over which narrative (or narratives) makes most sense to them. This self-exploration process is akin to conducting internal dialogues within one's mind: 'I can be this or that, but who do I want to be?' However, the internal dialogue as a method of self-exploration has one major limitation. Since this dialogue is an internal mental process, it does not have any physical record. It is impossible to retrieve our internal dialogues conducted in the past without any loss and distortion of thoughts. In contrast, self-narratives on the personal homepage have a physical existence (at least as stored in webpage format) which can be completely retrieved for further self-contemplation whenever the author wants to. Undoubtedly, the self-narratives we compose in traditional written media such as a diary or biography also have a physical existence, but these forms often lack the revisability of the personal homepage, which allows or even invites the author to continually amend his or her homepage self-narratives. As Chandler (1998) suggests, completion of any personal homepages 'may be endlessly deferred' since every homepage is always 'under construction'.

In fact, recent research shows that people with uncertain identities have started to use the personal homepage to reflexively explore and reconstruct their identities. Personal homepages 'permit some authors to explore aspects of themselves in ways that they have never previously done,' claims Hevern (2000: 14). As one homepage author admitted: 'It helps to define who I am. Before I start to look at/write about something then I'm often not sure what my feelings are, but after having done so, I can at least have more of an idea' (Chandler, 1998). Another author commented: 'as a process for doing, for seeing yourself reflected on a screen, being able to draw connections where there weren't connections is really rich' (Rosenstein, 2000: 154).

By continually exploring and clarifying their thoughts and feelings, some people use the personal homepage to reclaim a sense of identity which is continuous with their previous one. As one homepage author who relocated from New York to California said: 'Moving to a place where I had to make so many changes, I needed a way to convince myself I was still okay and the things that were important to me are still important' (Rosenstein, 2000: 159). Some authors, however, may fashion new identities. For example, by building websites which provide health information, people whose lives have been disrupted by serious accidents or chronic illness may successfully re-establish a positive identity, as a health information producer (Hevern, 2000; Hardey, 2002).

The personal homepage surpasses the internal dialogue and other traditional media in one more respect. The internal dialogue and traditional diary writing are 'private' identity construction activities, the audience of which is generally the author him/herself. But the global reachability of the personal homepage enables the homepage author to get validatory feedback from net browsers who empathize or share with the author's identity or narrative. I am not arguing that we cannot consider our self-identities in the absence of others, but getting recognition from other people is still important for establishing affirmative identities (Cooley, 1902; Blumer, 1969). After all, if no one ever tells you that you are smart, for how long can you convince yourself that you really are?

This identity validation function of the personal homepage is also identified in recent research. Undeniably, some homepage authors do not actively *seek* readers at all (Rosenstein, 2000: 96–9). As one author said: 'I was the intended audience, as strange as it sounds' (Chandler, 1998). Yet, many homepage authors use the personal homepage to re-establish their self-identities by getting positive comments from other net browsers. One disabled homepage author said: 'Do you have any idea how many people wallow in self-pity, spend the rest of their lives crying about what happened to them? Through the internet I have been challenged to grow, to blossom, to meet others who understand me' (Hevern, 2000: 15). A gay author said: 'I think we all sometimes need to know that, no matter how alone we feel, there are witnesses' (ibid.: 14). A Spanish-speaking homepage author explained his motive for homepage publishing this way: 'I was looking for other people that were my color or listened to my kind of music or spoke my family's language … I was really looking for a part of me out there that I could make contact with' (Rosenstein, 2000: 168).

REALITY CONSTRAINTS ON THE MAKING OF PERSONAL HOMEPAGES

So far, our story of the personal homepage appears quite heartening. But some critics tell a more gloomy story, cautiously warning us not to uncritically celebrate the emancipatory potentials of the personal homepage and the creative autonomy of the homepage author. This more pessimistic story can be divided into two parts: (1) concern that social background may preclude certain people from making personal homepages; and (2) the view that commercial and ideological factors may work against the expressive creativity of homepage authors.

Who can build personal homepages?

One key factor that influences people's chances of reaping the emancipatory benefits of the personal homepage is their internet access. The reason is simple: if a social group has less internet access than others, members of this social group will have less opportunities to build personal homepages and, accordingly, they are less likely to benefit from the emancipatory potential of this media genre. One factor which influences one's opportunities to access the internet is country of residence. Take some countries as examples: the internet access rate of people living in China is 3.5 per cent; France, 28.4 per cent; Germany, 38.6 per cent; Greece, 13.2 per cent; Iceland, 79.9 per cent; Malaysia, 25.2 per cent; Russia, 12.4 per cent; Singapore, 51.9 per cent; Sweden, 67.6 per cent; Spain, 19.7 per cent; Thailand, 7.4 per cent; United Arab Emirates, 36.8 per cent; United Kingdom, 57.4 per cent; United States, 59.1 per cent (these are 2002 figures; see Nua.com, 2003). Indeed, internet statistics show that, in many countries, additional factors such as ethnicity, gender, age, educational attainment and income level may also affect internet access, although the significance of individual factors varies greatly from country to country.

Statistics show that demographic factors like gender, age, occupational status and educational level have noticeable effects on levels of internet access. For example, a survey shows that, in 15 Western European countries, females, manual workers, the elderly and the less educated have less internet access than males, professionals, the young and the well educated (European Commission, 2002). The USA shows similar internet access patterns (except that females and males have virtually identical internet access rate in the USA; see below) (Victory and Cooper 2002). Nevertheless, the specific extent to which each demographic factor affects the internet access rate of individual social groups varies from country to country. Take gender as an example. According to a recent survey of internet users in 25 developed countries, the internet access rate of females varies from country to country: in France, females make up 40.8 per cent of total internet users; Germany, 38 per cent; Sweden, 46 per cent; the UK, 44.5 per cent; the USA, 51.9 per cent. (Nielsen//NetRatings, 2002). In some countries like Romania and Ukraine, females occupy less than one-third of the total population of internet users (Taylor Nelson Sofres Interactive, 2002).

But will equal internet access bring about equal opportunities in making personal homepages? Not necessarily. In a study of the homepages produced by students at four US universities and four German universities, Döring (2002) finds that females only make up 27 per cent and 13 per cent of the student homepage authors in the US and German universities respectively, despite the fact that at all of these universities there was an equal balance of male and female students. One possible explanation is that females tend to feel alienated from the male-dominated computer culture (as certain studies have suggested: Morbey, 2000; Turkle, 1988), making them less motivated to learn website-building skills. In other words, even if females and males have similar opportunities to 'log on' to the internet (as is already the case in certain countries), females may not have the same degree of motivation and learned skills to create and maintain personal websites. In short, equal internet access does not necessarily mean equal opportunities in making personal homepages.

Dominick's (1999) study illustrates how factors such as gender, age and occupation may influence people's chances of making homepages. From 317 English-language personal homepages randomly sampled from the Yahoo! homepage directory, Dominick found that 87 per cent of homepage authors were men, 79 per cent were under the age of 30; more than half of those who mentioned an 'occupation' were students, and around 90 per cent of the rest were white-collar workers. This data suggests that females, the unemployed and blue-collar workers may have less chances of building homepages than other people. (Note, however, that the gender balance, at least, is likely to have changed since the mid-to-late 1990s when this study was conducted; and note that the sample is based only on those homepage owners who submitted their site to the Yahoo! directory, and had that submission accepted by Yahoo! staff.)

The poverty of self-expression and creative constraints

Undeniably, those who have no opportunity to make personal homepages are unable to enjoy the emancipatory benefits of the personal homepage. However, it is not necessarily the case that people who have already made personal homepages for themselves are able to fully realize the emancipatory potential of this media genre. From his sample of 500 English-language personal homepages, Dominick (1999) found that 30 per cent of the pages were either abandoned or no longer available, and most of the remaining 'analysable' homepages had been produced with little creative effort, offering predictable elements such as a brief biography, an e-mail address, some authors' photos, or links to other sites. Only 12 per cent of those analysable homepages included in-depth biographies, and only 23 per cent contained 'creative expressions' like original poems or stories. Dominick argues that most personal homepages show nothing but superficial self-expression. It is perhaps no wonder that some critics will say that many personal homepages lack creativity and thoughtfulness, since many homepage authors build their websites not for self-presentation or identity construction, but for instrumental reasons like passing time, learning HTML, distributing information to peers, and so on (Buten, 1996: Papacharissi, 2000: Walker, 2000). This argument, however, cannot really explain why some personal homepages which are built for the purpose of self-presentation or identity construction still lack thoughtful and in-depth self-expression (Killoran, 2002). To answer this question, we need to examine how commercial homepage providers and ideological forces suppress the expressiveness of homepage authors.

Commercial homepage providers

Using Yahoo! GeoCities as an example, Harrison (2001) offers a number of compelling critiques of how major commercial homepage providers may undermine users' freedom of self-expression on the personal homepage. Two of these criticisms are as follows.

- *Standardizing homepages*: Yahoo! GeoCities provides novice homepage authors with sets of pre-created homepage 'templates'. These 'templates' offer homepage authors standardized suggestions of where to place text, images and links, and encourage them to add Yahoo! services to their homepages. (Other major commercial homepage providers like Tripod, Angelfire and AOL Hometown also offer similar 'simple' homepage building tools.) Although these 'templates' enable novices to build homepages without the need to learn more advanced website-building tools like HTML, they indirectly lead homepage authors to produce 'cookie-cutter' personal homepages (ibid.: 55–62).

- *Homepage content control*: all Yahoo! GeoCities homepage authors have to abide by the Yahoo! Terms of Service, which allow Yahoo! GeoCities to delete without prior warning those homepages with content the company and its advertisers deem inappropriate (ibid.: 62–4). Indeed, most commercial homepage providers such as Tripod, Angelfire and AOL Hometown, also have content regulation policies, which grant them the right to remove any homepages at any time, for any reason, with or without notice. According to some journalists and homepage makers, personal homepages deleted by commercial homepage providers often contain 'sensitive' content, including anti-abortion, death penalty and anti-Malaysian government opinion, nude photos of the author, and information that directly criticizes certain commercial homepage providers (Standen, 2001; Scheeres, 2002; Zeman, 2002). Recently Yahoo! has signed a voluntary pledge with the Chinese government, promising that Yahoo! China will avoid 'producing, posting or disseminating pernicious information that may jeopardize state security and disrupt social stability'; it also pledged to monitor personal websites and will 'remove the harmful information promptly' (*Washington Post*, 2002).

Ideological forces

Killoran's (1998, 2002) study shows that the poverty of self-expression on personal homepages is also caused by the ideologies of commercial and bureaucratic organizations as well as commercial homepage providers. He argues that since the personal homepage is a new media genre, it has no established generic conventions which homepage authors can follow when representing themselves in this medium. Under these conditions, the well-established, powerful and prevalent ideologies of commercial and bureaucratic organizations tend to 'colonize' the speaking spaces of the authors. Consequently, homepage authors abandon the opportunity to explore their distinctive self-identities, and represent themselves as 'domesticated, innocuous subjects and objects of a capitalist and bureaucratic order' (Killoran, 2002: 27). Killoran describes this process in which personal homepage authors adopt commercial and institutional ideologies to express themselves as 'synthetic institutionalization'. He argues that when individuals present themselves using visual styles borrowed from brands, organizations or corporations, or with devices designed to attract returning viewers (such as the promise of regular updates), they suppress their own creative identities in favour of institutionalized conformity. (Of course, it could be argued that the homepage authors are often wittily parodying corporate language, and that the promise of a regularly updated site does not necessarily represent some kind of tribute to capitalist 'customer loyalty' schemes, as Killoran seems to think.)

Gender ideologies may also affect personal homepage design. In two studies of faculty homepages hosted in university departments, Miller and Arnold (2001) and Hess (2002) found that, generally, female academics were more hesitant and cautious than males about putting their personal photos on their faculty homepage. Many female academics explicitly admitted that they feared their photos may 'give off' sexist impressions and encourage people who read their homepage to focus on their appearance rather than their academic work. As one female lecturer said:

> Putting my own picture on my webpage … seems like something that would allow people to see me as vain (like, 'Oh, she thinks she's so good looking she put her picture on the Web') or at least read outside a professional context.
>
> (Hess, 2002: 181)

Instead of resisting these ideological pressures, some female academics opt for self-censorship – they choose not to put their pictures on their homepage and become 'faceless' authors (see also Cheung, 2000, for a discussion of self-censorship).

CONCLUSION

My analysis clearly demonstrates that, although the personal homepage is an emancipatory media genre for some people, its emancipatory potentials have not yet benefited everyone. Many people may still lack the resources and technological knowhow to build their own personal homepage. Even for those who are capable of making personal homepages, their individual expressiveness might still be suppressed by content censorship of commercial homepage providers or ideological pressures. Some statistics show that the internet access gap between countries is narrowing (UNCTAD, 2002), and that in many countries the internet access gap by gender is closing rapidly (Nielsen//NetRatings, 2002). These trends certainly imply that more people will be able to build personal homepages. But it remains the case that many constraints upon making personal homepages will not disappear in the near future: low-income groups in many countries still have great difficulty accessing the internet; ideologies of various types will continue to exist and suppress individual expression; and control over homepage content may also be further heightened by some homepage providers. If more people are to enjoy the emancipatory benefits of a personal homepage, we must endeavour to remove these constraints. Homepage authors need to protest against any censorship of homepage content practised by commercial homepage providers (Zeman, 2002); non-profit organizations may seek ways to provide free internet access, censorship-free website hosting services, and even free training courses on website-building skills; academics and critics should also find ways to raise awareness among homepage authors about the commercial and ideological constraints which may suppress self-expression on the personal homepage. Only through such efforts can we hope that more people will be able to use the personal homepage to work through their identities, or present their suppressed selves to audiences around the world. Indeed, in a world where many people are plagued by identity problems, enabling more people to fully realize the emancipatory potential of the personal homepage is a timely and important task.

USEFUL WEBSITES

Homepage providers

Millions of people use the free and easy homepage building tools offered by commercial homepage providers to build their personal homepages. These personal homepages are usually listed in the sites of these providers, unless their creators opt to stay 'hidden'. Major commercial homepage providers include:

Angelfire: www.angelfire.lycos.com
AOL Hometown: www.hometown.aol.com
Tripod: www.tripod.lycos.com
Yahoo! GeoCities: http://geocities.yahoo.com

Homepage directories

Sometimes personal homepage authors also list their websites in Web directories. Some of the major directories are:

Google:
http://directory.google.com/Top/Society/People/Personal_Homepages
Lycos:
http://homepages.whowhere.lycos.com/Personal_Profiles/About_Me
Yahoo!:
http://dir.yahoo.com/Society_and_Culture/People/Personal_Home_Pages

Webrings

Webrings connect every type of homepage you could imagine – and some you would never dream of. Homepages with similar concerns are linked together in a 'ring' so that browsers can navigate through similar kinds of homepage. Two major webring sites are:

Ringsurf: www.ringsurf.com
WebRing: www.webring.org

Online diaries

Online diaries are a special type of personal homepage, in which the authors put down their intimate thoughts and feelings about what happens to them in everyday life.

Diarist: www.diarist.net
Diaryland: www.diaryland.com

Personal websites

About.com – Personal Web Pages: http://personalweb.about.com

A diverse range of articles about personal homepages: statistics, technical know-how, recommended books and selected sites.

Reflections on the making of personal websites

www.nathan.com/thoughts/personalsites/index.html
Designer Nathan Shedroff offers a thoughtful discussion on designing personal homepages.

www.writing.ucsb.edu/faculty/sorapure/wa
Scholar Madeleine Sorapure offers some general observations on various types of Web genre such as homepages, online diaries and blogs, and hypertext stories and anthologies.

Chapter 5

MASCULINITIES ON THE WEB

ROSS HORSLEY

It seems that issues of gender attract as much interest and analysis in relation to cyberspace as they do to every other form of media in existence. Elsewhere in this book, you will find chapters about women's online magazines, lesbian pornography, and campaign work carried out by Web-savvy women's groups around the world. While all different kinds of people use the internet for all different kinds of purposes, the women discussed in these chapters have found that it provides them with new ways to express themselves as women, and address some specifically female-oriented concerns. Conversely, this chapter will look at the ways in which certain men (and groups of men) have made use of the Web, and ask if these indicate any changes or new developments in the social and cultural constructions of masculinity we are familiar with.

A BRIEF WORD ABOUT 'MASCULINITY' AND 'MASCULINITIES'

The notion of masculinity is notoriously difficult to define. In fact, Robert Connell (1995) – who went as far as to actually write a book called *Masculinities* – argues that '"masculinity" does not exist except in contrast with "femininity"' (ibid.: 68). His point is that the concept of masculinity does not have any meaning in itself; it is only when men and women are assumed to possess particular and *different* character traits associated with their genders that notions of *what it means to be a man* arise.

For our purposes, Steve Craig's assertion that 'masculinity is what a culture expects of its men' (1992: 3) is a useful one because it suggests that masculinity essentially exists only in a cultural context, as something rooted in the traditions, codes and – in particular – *expectations* commonly held by society. Similarly, George Mosse's definition of masculinity as 'the way men assert what they believe to be their manhood' (1996: 3) implies that it is widely understood as a way of behaving in accordance with one's sex-defined characteristics, either as a manifestation of one's underlying sexual identity, or by way of a perceived responsibility towards the 'general order' provided by understandings of gender.

At any given time, then, a certain version of masculinity is likely to become dominant in a society, and possibly idealized by some people as the most 'natural' or wholesome form of manhood. Connell refers to this as 'hegemonic masculinity' (1995: 77) and argues that it exists because it 'embodies the currently accepted answer to the problem of the legitimacy of patriarchy' (ibid.) – that is, it validates (and is, in turn, validated by) traditional gender roles that see men as powerful and women as more submissive. Whether or not we think these roles continue to pervade our society, we will recognize that ideas of 'traditional masculinity' tend to incorporate such character traits as strength, aggression, assertiveness and the value of reason over emotion.

Finally, you will note that this chapter is entitled '*Masculinities* on the Web'. It is clear that masculinity, as just one aspect of identity, can take on an entire *range* of potential meanings. Frank Mort suggests that 'we are not dealing with masculinity, but with a series of *masculinities*' (1988: 195). As well as recognizing that class, race, sexual orientation, and many other factors all enter the equation at the level of identity, the term 'masculinities' refers to the fact that no two people's performance of any so-called masculine traits will ever be exactly the same. Therefore, whenever the term is used here, it is in recognition of the fact that, as Roger Horrocks puts it, 'there is clearly not a homogenous monolithic identity possessed by all men in all contexts' (1995: 3). With these points in mind, we can now turn to look at a number of ways in which the Web has allowed some of its male users, whether overtly or not, to both express and re-evaluate their masculinities.

E-MALES: MEN'S VIRTUAL DISCUSSION GROUPS

Some of the most obvious online discussion of aspects of masculinity takes place in men's forums set up specifically for that purpose. These range from the rather academically minded Yahoo! Men's Studies Discussion Group (http://groups.yahoo.com/group/ms-discussion), to the more light-hearted Dull Men's Club (www.dullmen.com). The former is an active bulletin board where members typically report and discuss current news stories pertaining particularly to men – such as, at the time of writing, an article from the BBC news website about male longevity, and a report from the *USA Today* newspaper concerning domestic abuse targeted at men. The group's stated aim is 'to promote intelligent (and civil) discussion of these issues from academics and non-academics alike'. Masculinity on the forum is viewed as something in a state of flux; it is constantly being reshaped by social trends, and challenged by the attitudes of the media and, in some cases, feminists. Perhaps for this reason, there is an air of defensiveness on the board, as posters seek to protect their rights as men to equality and respect in a chaotic world.

In contrast, the tongue-in-cheek Dull Men's Club defines itself as 'a place where dull men can share their (dull) experiences and (modest) goals'. Here, such topics as park bench styles and whether it's *duck* or *duct* tape dominate the discussion, while beer-loving accountant Norm from the sitcom *Cheers* is hailed as a role model. 'Many Dull Men are shy,' explains the site. 'But with the anonymity of the web, now they are free.' This freedom gives voice to a common man who is 'polite … helpful around the house … predictable, reliable, and safe' – everything, the site slyly remarks, a woman could want. In its celebration of the trivial, with only a mildly bitter tone, the Dull Men's Club hints at the plight of a modern masculinity downtrodden by domestic commitments and the 'daily grind'.

One of the most interesting men's discussion sites is the Australian-based *Manhood Online* (www.manhood.com.au), dedicated to the promotion of 'a masculinity that is protective and gentle, energetic and positive, open and self aware'. This constructive face of manhood, the site's editorial suggests, is a recent development linked to society's increased awareness of women's rights, and the gradual erosion of traditional and more restrictive gender roles: 'A more exuberant and loving kind of man is emerging from old, uptight and distant models of the past.' Despite a tone that some may find slightly off-putting in its New Age earnestness, the refreshing feature of this forum is its encouragement of readers to share stories and experiences, rather than simply opinions.

On the front page, we find a section entitled 'Snapshots', which poses 'the 16 big questions about what it means being a man today' by way of an online form that visitors can fill in and submit for publication on the site. While most of its questions could apply as much to females as males, this survey manages to provide an interesting insight into the thoughts, dreams and anxieties of men from around the world. The prompt 'Your defining moment(s) as a man?' provokes a wide range of responses, including:

> Leaving home and joining the Navy at 16. (Chris, UK)
> To give a shoulder to my better half. (Digvijay, India)
> Rescuing a 14-year-old in turbulent, shark-infested waters in a storm, and dragging us both to safety at the top of a limestone cliff. I discovered my capacity for endurance, strength, care in the face of terror … and my smallness before the vagaries of nature. (Bart, Australia)
> Realizing my manhood and becoming okay with it and myself as a gay man. (Jase, US)

Such examples only hint at the enormous variety of feelings and beliefs that different men associate with their male identity. For some men, it is demonstrations of independence or heroism that define their masculinity; for others, the foundations lie in a quiet moment spent with their partner, or a personal journey of their own.

Similar elements of contradiction are apparent in visitors' reflections on the 'key issues facing men in the 21st century' – from 'recognizing that traditional roles do change', to 'being a "man" … not some lame, scared pussy'. It would appear that many men are well aware of the responsibilities assigned to them by certain established notions of their 'role' in society, and judge themselves accordingly. These expectations also feed into respondents' 'greatest fears', where such 'inadequacies' as being unable to fix a car or suppress emotions appear to reflect male worries of not living up to qualities associated with being a man. By compiling the thoughts of those living through such experiences, *Manhood Online* offers a valuable, interactive space for men of all ages and nationalities to discuss and come to terms with many aspects of their identity. It is difficult to imagine such a service being made possible by any medium other than the Web.

DESIGNS FOR LIFE: MEN'S GUIDES ONLINE

'Being a bloke doesn't have a set of clear-cut instructions anymore,' advises the *UK Men's Guide* (www.ukmensguide.co.uk), with its aim 'to help you get the most out of your masculinity'. This, it seems, can be achieved with the help of several links (many off-site) to pages about health, dating and fashion, as well as a Web directory for all men's DIY, car, motorcycle, sports, betting and gambling needs. And there are also 'extensive listings of recipes to help you impress on that first date, or maybe to earn some extra brownie points with your current partner!'

The *UK Men's Guide* is one of a number of portal-type sites that aspire to provide a starting-point or 'online home' for men using the Web. Assuming that these services are doing something right in order to remain in business, they are interesting because, in their efforts to offer 'everything a man could need', they help us to identify the likely interests and concerns of a theoretical 'satisfied customer'. The directory categories of the *UK Men's Guide* listed above, then, would seem to paint a familiar picture of the somewhat macho leisure pursuits commonly associated with men, although some other popular men's portals take an even more aggressively masculine stance. The American *Bullz-Eye.com* wastes no time in introducing us to the month's featured female model, while *Nutz.co.uk* mixes its soccer and computer games headlines with prominently positioned 'Top Babe Site Links'. *Hunney Club Magazine* (www.hunneyclub.com) – which gathers 'all of the things that men love into one forum so that they will NEVER have to leave home again to mix business with pleasure' – is unusual in that its selection of links, girls, articles, girls, dating tips and girls is apparently served up by two *female* webmasters, ex-models Jazmine and Venice.

5.1 The popular online men's magazine FHM.com

From the 'blokey' titles of these portals to their apparent preoccupations with sex, sports and tools, they appear to offer, at first glance, nothing out of step with some of the most entrenched notions of rugged masculinity. This may be less true, however, of the obvious value they also place on the traditionally more feminine matters of fashion, dating and health. Men's seemingly growing interest in these areas is something that has only relatively recently come to be exploited by the media, in the form of men's lifestyle magazines like *FHM*, *Maxim* and *GQ* (all of which also have their own companion websites). One of the most popular purely Web-based equivalents of these is *AskMen.com*, boasting five million readers a month, daily updates, and sections that include 'Dating & Love', 'Fashion & Lifestyle', 'Sexuality', and even 'Men's Horoscopes'. (By the way, Sagittarius, 'you may find your woman somewhat perturbed this week'.) Several scholars have suggested that the current popularity of such subjects in men's media is evidence of a new form of masculinity characterized by a greater level of self-awareness and uncertainty.

According to David Gauntlett, in his book *Media, Gender and Identity*, 'today's magazines for men are *all about* the social construction of masculinity. That is, if you like, their subject-matter' (2002: 170, his emphasis). It is only fairly recently, he argues, that feminist-driven critiques of traditional masculinity have combined with a wider recognition of changing gender roles to create a modern environment in which we are all aware of the many choices we can make regarding our identities. In such a climate, men's magazines provide men not with any concrete 'answers', but a framework of ideas, ideologies and role models from which they can rework and redefine their individual identities.

Similarly, in their study *Making Sense of Men's Magazines*, Peter Jackson, Nick Stevenson and Kate Brooks (2001) argue that the contradictory assortment of problem pages, relationships advice, scantily clad women, and well-dressed male models found in the pages of most men's lifestyle magazines in fact represents the very mixture of insecurity and instability that typifies the life of the modern man who, as the *UK Men's Guide* puts it, 'doesn't have a set of clear-cut instructions anymore' (see ibid.: 145–6). Ultimately, it is clear that many different kinds of men are catered for by sites like *AskMen.com* and *Hunney Club Magazine*, and that these men may pick and choose from the range of information and representations available in much the same way that they work to construct their own different masculinities.

One issue that affects all men, however, is that of health. Some recent academic studies have suggested that current increases in men's health problems can be linked to men's apparent reluctance to visit their doctors, possibly based on notions that seeking help is a sign of weakness or 'not being a man' (see White, 2002; Williams, 2003). With such concerns in mind, Peter Baker set up *Malehealth* (www.malehealth.co.uk), a UK-based website dedicated to providing health information specifically to male readers. He notes:

> Seeing a doctor is not part of the traditional male role but this doesn't mean that they are not interested about their health. The site takes men as they are. It's not about telling them to give up beer, go to the gym and eat 33 types of seaweed.
>
> (Quoted in Martin, 2000)

Malehealth is one of many similar, often localized resources on the Web, including *BBCi Health* (www.bbc.co.uk/health/mens), the Toronto Men's Health Network (www.menshealthnetwork.ca), *Gay Men's Health* (www.gmhp.demon.co.uk), and the website of *Men's Health* magazine (www.menshealth.com). Together with self-diagnosis sites like the UK's *NHS Direct* (www.nhsdirect.nhs.uk), these make access to medical information a simple matter of typing a few search terms into a computer. Whether or not the Web will have a genuine impact on the state of men's health in this way has yet to be seen. In terms of male identity issues, however, it poses an interesting question: will improved access to medical advice help to normalize health awareness in men, making it a more acceptable characteristic of masculinity – or does it simply make it easier for men to avoid their doctors and deflect potential accusations of weakness instead of facing them head on? Whatever the case, it seems certain that the Web will have some role to play in this particular aspect of developing masculinities.

VISUAL MASCULINITIES: ART IN CYBERSPACE

A naked man stares out from your computer screen. As you slide a row of switches with your mouse, his waistline swells, his shoulders broaden to cartoon-like proportions before pinching in again, and his calves shrink from sturdy muscles to spindly sticks. This is John Tonkin's *Elastic Masculinities* (www.johnt.org/meniscus/body/body.html), an online artwork based on an installation displayed in Sydney's Performance Space gallery in 1997.

The aspect of this piece that makes it so relevant to our discussion of masculinities on the Web is the challenge it poses to the visitor: 'Construct a brave body,' urges an instruction at the top of the page. Once you have fiddled and clicked until you're certain the physique on your screen is indeed a *brave* one, you may submit your creation to the site's database, where it will be used, along with the hundreds of other stored responses, to form the average user's perception of what a courageous man looks like. You can repeat the process to design a man who is arrogant, or graceful, or vulnerable, or sensual. 'In a culture obsessed with self-observation

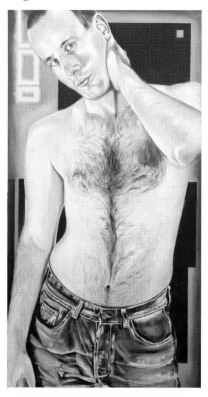

and the observation of self by others, it seems that most of us have a distorted body image,' observes the artist. 'Our bodies change shape according to their state of mind and the cultural messages they have been digesting'. In *Elastic Masculinities*, the psychological is made physical, and men's bodies *literally* transform before our eyes to match our expectations of their masculinity.

The work of Christopher Lucas Furminger, at the straightforward URL www.gayartist.co.uk, uses more traditional artist's tools to explore aspects of masculinity from a gay man's perspective. His six oil on canvas paintings based on the colours of the gay rainbow flag (www.gayartist.co.uk/rainbow.htm), however, have a uniquely digital-age twist. He explains:

[The flag's] creator Gilbert Baker gave each colour a separate meaning, which I have interpreted to portray various aspects of gay culture in a positive way. The models are all gay men who I found on an internet chat service.

5.2 *Art*, the fifth work in Christopher Lucas Furminger's rainbow series

Thus, *Life* (the first colour of the flag) depicts a young man in T-shirt and shorts against a vivid red background reminiscent of a pouch of blood. Furminger writes: 'As a gay man I haven't been able to give blood since I first had sex, so this piece is basically offering the blood of a gay man to the national blood service. I must admit I'm quite annoyed at their prejudice shrouded in safety guidelines.'

The blue-themed *Art* portrays a bare-chested man in jeans against a background suggestive of microchips or computer motherboards. Furminger reveals that he commissioned the model to create this design himself, which the artist then reproduced in paint. In a gesture that takes the piece around a further self-reflexive loop, this particular model also designed and built the website on which Furminger's paintings are displayed.

Works like those of John Tonkin and Christopher Lucas Furminger are blurring the boundaries between art, communication and computer programming, while the Web itself gives us access to their creations as easily as it does to an online DVD retailer or the publicity shots of a popular celebrity. Both artists' meditations on manhood ask us to question our own perceptions of masculinity before, with a click of a mouse, we wander off on another journey into cyberspace.

ADVENTURES IN GENDER

Perhaps the most extreme negotiation of masculinity possible is the adoption of a female persona. On the Web, assuming an identity of the opposite sex is commonly referred to as 'gender-swapping' or 'gender-switching' (see, for example, Turkle, 1995; Roberts and Parks, 2001), and tends to inspire a large number of chapters in a great many books on cyberculture studies. Unfortunately, the majority of these, even in recent volumes, continue to concern themselves with old-fashioned, text-based MUD and MOO environments. Still, the authors of such pieces often make interesting points about the relationship between online and real-life masculinities, and many of their observations can also be applied to less esoteric Web spaces, such as contemporary chat rooms and bulletin boards.

Sherry Turkle's *Life on the Screen* (1995) offers some enlightening insights into the motivations for users' gender-switching behaviour on various internet role-playing sites. When participating in one herself for the first time, for instance, Turkle found it easier and less intimidating to appear as a male character: 'I finally experienced that permission to move freely I had always imagined to be the birthright of men. Not only was I approached less frequently, but I found it easier to respond to an unwanted overture with aplomb' (ibid.: 211). Here, Turkle's online experience bears out the expectations of masculinity she brings in from real life – specifically, those she associates with being branded a prudish 'wallflower' as a non-participating girl at the school dance, while boys who similarly declined to take a partner were instead considered 'shy in a manly way – aloof, above it all' (ibid.: 210).

Turkle also relates the story of a male role-player called Garret, who plays a female character online (albeit a female frog) for the reason that he enjoys helping other, less experienced players to learn the ropes (ibid.: 216). He finds this role to be in such conflict with the aggressive, competitive nature he feels he has been encouraged to adopt as a man in real life, that he actually feels uncomfortable performing it as a male in the fantasy environment. As Turkle notes, however, 'all he had to do was to replace male with female in a character's description to change how people saw him and what he felt comfortable expressing' (ibid.: 218).

These accounts are interesting because they demonstrate the ways in which notions of masculinity shape people's actions and behaviour, even in non-face-to-face situations. To date, the most talked-about strategy that the Web offers for dealing with such notions is the practice of gender-switching. This appears to occur mainly because it is easier to accomplish online than in a physical location, where elements of *actual* disguise and performance would be required in order to pull off a successful switch. In itself, the practice is not much of a step towards the reassessment of gender roles. In fact, it could be argued that simple binary gender-switching actually further entrenches traditionally held ideas, by suggesting that conventional roles are so firmly established that a person must simply pick one or the other, based on the package of qualities it comes with, and how appropriate these are for the situation at hand.

Evaluating a statistical analysis of online gender play, Roberts and Parks conclude that 'gender-switching for most people is best understood as an experimental behaviour rather than as an enduring expression of their sexuality or personality' (ibid.: 282). Their findings suggest that it is more common in fantasy-based Web environments than more socially oriented ones, implying that people are less comfortable with the idea the closer it comes to their 'actual' life and self (ibid.: 281).

Nevertheless, any regular user of the Web is likely to encounter situations where the genders of others are not immediately apparent – or, indeed, find themselves at some point having to explicitly state their own gender. In my own experience of a bulletin board called *Dark Dreams* (www.darkdreams.org), on which fans of Italian horror film director Dario Argento converge, it is not long before active members with gender-ambiguous usernames – such as acidstars, Perfume V, absorbinglife and Inferno – are gently encouraged to reveal their sex. It would seem that we regard this information as one of the most important aspects of another person's identity, as if it reveals fundamental facts about their attitudes and character, when, of course, it really only allows us to impose some expectations of our own. Whether or not an online friend is 'telling their truth' about their gender may even by a moot point; ultimately, gender-switching matters most on a personal level. As Turkle puts it, 'by enabling people to experience what it "feels" like to be the opposite gender or to have no gender at all, the practice encourages reflection on the way ideas about gender shape our expectations'

(1995: 213). In this respect, the Web brings contemplation about gender and identity into the everyday lives of all its users, and may prove to have a significant influence on the shaping of masculinities in the future.

CONCLUSION

In our brief exploration of men's activities on the Web, we have looked at the shaping of male identities in discussion forums, online magazines, internet artworks and virtual environments where aspects of gender identity can be 'transformed' at the press of a key. It has been suggested that, in the multifaceted media environment of the present, many men are more aware of their masculinity as a social and psychological construction than ever before. This can lead, naturally, to uncertainty and even anxiety, but eventually to a greater level of self-awareness and personal freedom. The Web is a place that appears to have fired the public imagination in recent years, and led to a lot of predictions about how human lifestyles will change in the coming decades. How it might ultimately affect our identities, and shape our perceptions of masculinity – and, indeed, gender in general – will, of course, remain to be seen. But, for now, what the Web most definitely offers is a new space for increased thinking about gender and identity on the parts of both men and women.

USEFUL WEBSITES

Manhood Online: www.manhood.com.au

An Australian site on which men share their experiences of life from a male perspective, including discussion forums and profiles of readers' masculinities.

Media, Gender and Identity: www.theoryhead.com/gender

David Gauntlett's website for the book of the same name, but offering DVD-style bonus materials, including discussions and interviews about men's media consumption which do not appear in the book.

Men's magazines on the Web:

www.fhm.com (international *FHM*)

www.maxim.com (American *Maxim*)

www.gq-magazine.co.uk (British *GQ*)

www.loaded.co.uk (British *Loaded*)

http://askmen.com (online-only *AskMen.com* magazine)

MensNewsDaily: www.mensnewsdaily.com

'The leading website for daily news, information and commentary geared exclusively toward men and the women who love them.'

Menstuff: www.menstuff.org

A huge collection of resources and editorial comment relating to men's lives, including sections on men's issues, fatherhood, health, men's book reviews, and links.

Chapter 6

EVERYBODY'S GOTTA LOVE SOMEBODY, SOMETIME: ONLINE FAN COMMUNITY

KIRSTEN PULLEN

The relationship between the media text and the audience has been described within contemporary media studies as a dialogue: texts are presumed to be open to various interpretations, and audience members are presumed to interpret those texts in various ways and for various uses. Some audience members dialogue more aggressively and sustainedly than others: they are fans. In the last dozen years, several academic studies of fan communities have been undertaken; though early fan studies focused primarily on science fiction fans taking part in conventions, or the hysteria surrounding certain musical groups, or the activities of sports fans, the net has recently been cast more widely. The World Wide Web has opened up the boundaries of fandom, allowing more people to participate in fan culture, and designating more television programmes, celebrities and films as worthy of fan activity.

Significantly, the publishing and networking capabilities of the internet have enabled more viewers to participate in activities usually associated with long-term, committed fandom, such as writing fan fiction, collecting images and information, and following the activities of those associated with their text. Literally anyone with access to a computer and modem can create a fan webpage, as many internet access providers offer free cyberspace and instructions for new members, as well as space for individual webpages. Counting the number of fan websites nestled within the vast World Wide Web is nearly impossible. However, approximate data is available, and suggests that there are thousands of fan websites, and that the number continues to grow. For example, when I wrote the first version of this chapter in 1999, the Yahoo! search engine listed more than 33,000 websites about individual actors and actresses, television programmes, and films. Then, I suggested that the number would continue to grow; by July 2003, Yahoo! listed over 58,000 such websites, and we can assume that there are thousands of further sites not listed on Yahoo!. On the internet, it can seem as though nearly everyone is a fan, and nearly everything is worthy of fan adulation. This chapter continues my earlier inquiry, suggesting that online fan activity has retained some traditional fan behaviours while encouraging both greater community action and greater commercialism.

WHAT MAKES A FAN?

So what do fans do? How do you know a fan when you see one, on the World Wide Web or in the world? Media scholar Henry Jenkins (1992: 277–80) has identified five characteristics that fan communities share. First, fans watch and re-watch favourite programmes, looking for meaningful details, internal contradictions and ambiguity in order to find the gaps that suggest a space for intervention. Second, fans learn to understand and analyse texts in terms of the fan community. Watching this way, fans create what Jenkins calls a 'meta-text', one that has more information about characters, lifestyles, values and relationships than the original. Third, because fans have a particular investment in a programme, they often write letters about plot lines and characters, and have in some cases successfully lobbied to keep favoured series on the air; fans are active consumers. This kind of activity is especially evident (though not necessarily successful) on the Web. For example, message boards for soaps may urge reconciliation for the popular *General Hospital* couple Luke and Laura, demand that Susan Lucci's notorious Erica Kane finally receive her just reward, or plead with writers to bring *Passion*'s popular Timmy back from the dead (even though the actor himself recently died). Fourth, fans create unique forms of cultural production such as: zines publishing stories about major characters; information about actors' appearances and production schedules; episode guides; gossip about the show; videos of moments from the series set to popular music and resembling music videos; fan artwork; and 'filk songs' about particular shows or characters and fan activity. On the Web, this cultural production includes websites dedicated to the programme or the programme's stars, online zines, and posts to official and unofficial fan bulletin boards. Finally, fans create an alternative social community. In conversation and correspondence with other fans, viewers of a particular television text create a space that is more 'humane and democratic' than the everyday world (Fiske, 1992; Grossberg, 1992; Jenkins, 1992; Penley, 1991). Brought together by their love of a particular programme, these fans form alliances with others who may have different political, social and economic backgrounds but are committed to the ideals expressed by their favoured text. Within the community, fans also frequently express pleasure and relief to find others who are like them. Posts to official bulletin boards and individual websites often praise the support that online fandom provides, such as this example from *The Buffy Cross and Stake* (2002), a webpage for *Buffy the Vampire Slayer*: 'Thanks for making me part of the Scooby Gang.'

6.1 Fan art inspired by *Buffy the Vampire Slayer*, and posted on the net by the artist at www.geocities.com/roseveare

Although fans are often stereotyped as obsessive losers, lacking ties to the real world and living in a fantasy universe populated with characters from *Star Trek*, media scholars have reframed discussions of the fan, generally arguing that fan culture is unfairly maligned for a variety of reasons, often explicitly tied to class and gender. For example, John Fiske (1992) suggests that fandom is linked with aesthetic and cultural choices made by subordinate groups. In addition, Fiske points out that fan activity can include empowered social behaviour that merely substitutes for political and social action (ibid.: 30). For Fiske, then, fandom is a way for disenfranchised groups to engage with mass media products like television shows in a way that makes the content meaningful for them but does not necessarily offer models for political action. Similarly, media scholar Lawrence Grossberg (1992) suggests that fans of rock music and rock musicians choose to identify with certain behaviours and personalities in order to confirm their own sense of self. Identifying with 'rock and roll', rock fans borrow some of the anti-authoritarianism associated with rock culture in order to mark their own politics, behaviours and identities (ibid.: 58–63). Thus, according to these analyses, fans are not fringe extremists with an unhealthy and unrealistic interest in a particular media text, but savvy consumers who are able to use popular culture to fulfil their desires and needs, often explicitly rearticulating that culture in unique and empowering ways. On the Web, this is particularly evident in fansites that include fan fiction, links to similar sites that form an online fan community, and support for charitable activities.

Traditional fan studies tend to insist on the marginality of fan-worthy texts, paying particular attention to science fiction programming. Media scholars suggest that the choice of these particular programmes is not coincidental, as they specifically lend themselves to fan intervention. According to John Fiske (1992), all television texts are polysemic – that is, open to interpretation and requiring viewers to make their own meanings – but some texts are more polysemic than others, and are thus more likely to be appropriated and used by fans. Fiske defines these texts as 'producerly'. Producerly texts contain internal contradictions and ambiguities, providing opportunities for fans to fill in the gaps and make their own meaning (ibid.: 42). According to Constance Penley's (1991) study of female *Star Trek* fans, science fiction and fantasy offer more freedom than other genres, because these texts allow for discussion of real-life issues unconstrained by real-life circumstances (ibid.: 138). Shows set in the future or in alternate universes, such as science fiction programmes, and shows with a strong element of fantasy, such as *Xena: Warrior Princess*, lend themselves to being worked on and activated by fans: the fantasy included in the original text legitimizes the flights of fancy engaged in by the fans as they revise, continue and rework plot lines. Producerly texts invite fans to incorporate their own ideals and practices into the narratives provided.

Further, traditional fan studies posit an ideal and particular fan. According to traditional accounts, fans choose programmes that are presumably more open to interpretation and intervention than critically acclaimed and popular programmes. They are drawn to polysemic texts because they see something in them that critics and the mainstream audience have missed. Further, fans form an alternative community which rebels against mainstream norms and creates a space for open communication of liberal, democratic ideals. Members of disenfranchised groups, such as women and the working class, find in favoured programmes a more equitable society and seek to replicate that society within the fan community. In fact, some media scholars (most notably Jenkins and Penley) express a certain romantic attachment for fan activity, appearing to uncritically assume that fans who rework television's meanings are somehow better than the average viewer.

Internet fans, however, overturn both these assumptions. The Web has mainstreamed fandom, making visible a wider variety of texts and allowing more viewers to participate in activities usually reserved for alternate communities, as evidenced by shifts in fansite content. The traditional objects of fan culture are still well represented, but the number of *Star Trek* websites (still over a thousand) seems to be falling, while other programmes have an increased online presence – for example, the number of fansites for the soap opera *Guiding Light* have more than tripled in the past three years. With only 31 sites, *Guiding Light* is hardly a major presence; however, this increase suggests that as the Web becomes more accessible, fans of different kinds of programming increasingly use it. Ultimately, fans' pervasive presence on the internet may mean that stereotypes of the fan as a fringe obsessive will give way to views of the fan as a typical internet user.

BUILDING FAN COMMUNITIES ONLINE

With the World Wide Web now readily available on college campuses, in public libraries, and in most middle-class homes, fan communities have staked out online territory to celebrate their favourite programmes. Most important for Web-based fan communities are the distribution and production of fan-created texts, and the sense of community that talking about a favoured television programme can impart, even to viewers separated by thousands of miles. Further, the immediacy of the internet enables fans to get an immediate response to their interpretations of a particular text or fan production. Rather than waiting weeks or months for a new zine or newsletter, within hours a fan can expect an internet reply. For example, fans of *Buffy the Vampire Slayer* can choose from and interact with nearly 150 websites devoted to the programme. Most of the sites are hyperlinked to each other, often including plugs for other sites and the people who have created them. In addition, many of the sites offer tips for creating webpages and offer the use of graphics to those designing new sites. By checking out a search engine and surfing the Web, even a fan new to either *Buffy* or the internet can quickly find other fans and information about joining the online fan community.

Joining an online fan community also frequently entails interacting with an official (and market-driven) website. Most television programmes and films now have accompanying internet addresses and official websites advertising the production, providing information, and serving as a clearing house for fan activity. Most of these websites provide the kind of information previously available only through fan clubs and fan activities such as newsletters and conventions. For example, CBS, NBC and ABC all have extensive websites for their daytime soap operas, which provide plot summaries, actor biographies, behind-the-scenes footage and information, and chat rooms; in the UK, the BBC and Channel 4 have provided similar websites for their top soaps. In addition, celebrities from all forms of media engage in live, interactive, online discussions with their fans, especially when promoting a new film, special television programme, new season, or music release. For example, the website for the US entertainment channel E! features weekly chats with stars ranging from Anna Nicole Smith (the former model and *Playboy* centrefold) to Academy Award-winning actor Benecio Del Toro. These chats are conducted by E!'s online columnists, who also participate in weekly chats with their fans. As this example demonstrates, not only has access to celebrities increased, but the number of 'celebrities' whom one can access has increased as well.

In addition to offering correctives to the assumptions about fan-worthy texts made in traditional fan studies, internet fan activity also suggests different models for understanding online identity and community formation. In *Tune In, Log On: Soaps, Fandom, and Online Community*, researcher Nancy K. Baym (2000) suggests that earlier assumptions about identity play online need to be modified in light of fan activity. Rather than supporting the idea that the internet offers a space for trying on new identities (especially *vis-à-vis* gender), Baym's study suggests that soap opera fans, specifically those on the rec.arts.tv.soaps usenet group, 'build identities [online] congruent with those they present face-to-face' (ibid.: 155). Further, Baym suggests that people who post to the group 'self-disclose ... to let more of themselves seep into their messages and to promote [community]' (ibid.: 152). Since 'community' is an important characteristic of both on- and offline fan activity, Baym's comments are particularly relevant. As Baym's study makes clear, fan communities often interpret texts through reference to their own lives which in turn encourages 'a group norm of (relatively) honest self-representation' (ibid.: 157). In general, those who frequent chat rooms for, say, *Buffy the Vampire Slayer*, tend to post comments that relate the programme to their daily lives, comments that are treated as factual by the other participants.

WRITING BACK: THE RISE OF 'FAN FICTION'

Of course, fan activity also includes fantasy and free play, as evidenced by the tremendous amount of fan fiction available on the Web. Within traditional accounts, fan fiction is often suggested as the basis for creative, interventionist fan activity. Fans write and circulate stories about particular television programmes, continuing narratives, creating alternate endings, and most frequently suggesting romantic relationships not explicitly designated by the original text. This fiction, nearly always containing homoerotic themes, is called slash fiction, named for the '/' that separates the character names, as in fiction about a homosexual relationship between Captain Kirk and Mr Spock. Penley asserts that the original, polysemic *Star Trek* text explicitly invites this kind of rearticulation, and further that only texts like *Star Trek* offer the ambiguity necessary for such textual intervention (1997: 138). However, internet fan fiction suggests otherwise. Yahoo! lists nearly 1000 fan fiction sites (up from 700 three years ago), many with multiple stories and multiple authors. While marginal, presumably polysemic texts like *Highlander*, *Babylon 5* and *Stargate SG-1* (all syndicated US programmes) constitute the subject of most fan writing, mainstream and critical successes are also reworked. Further, the multitude of programming choices now available to the average North American television viewer makes it difficult to differentiate between marginal and mainstream texts. For example, *The X-Files* was an ambiguous, conspiracy-driven science fiction programme that invited an active, more traditional fan community. On the other hand, *The X-Files* was an Emmy Award-winning programme that regularly showed in the top 20 US television shows according to Nielsen ratings. With dozens of fansites and hundreds of fan fiction stories, *The X-Files* suggests that internet fandom may bridge the marginality usually associated with fan texts and the mainstream success most traditional fans eschew.

Even solidly mainstream programmes have active internet fan communities, however. For example, *The West Wing*, an Emmy-winning programme for best television drama for the past three years, has at least 14 fan fiction sites, with plots ranging from the imagined homosexual relationship between presidential aides Sam Seaborn and Josh Lyman, to crossovers with other television programmes, to the imagined love story between Josh and his assistant Donna. *Sports Night*, a critical favourite but ratings-loser airing on US television in the late 1990s, still maintains an active fan fiction archive. The case of *Sports Night* is particularly interesting; as a sitcom with a traditional narrative structure it would seem impervious to the kinds of interventions fan fiction usually makes. At the same time, its sudden cancellation meant that many fans were left hanging at the end of the second season. One site, *(I Can't Believe It's Not) Sports Night*, offers a 22-episode 'virtual third season' written by three fans. Soap operas, such as *Guiding Light* and *All My Children* also engender fan fiction about popular romantic couples. Though mainstream texts have generally been considered (by fandom scholars) closed to the plurality of readings necessary to fan activity, on the World Wide Web fan fiction has been created for nearly every genre of programming.

Though not all fan fiction is (homo)erotic, the ubiquity of slash fiction does suggest that rewriting and reimagining open texts to alternate readings. *Xena: Warrior Princess* demonstrates how fan fiction offers an intervention within official constructions of narrative meanings. *Xena: Warrior Princess*, a syndicated US programme produced from 1995 to 2001, had a loyal following among three distinct fan groups: lesbians, straight men and straight women. When *Xena* first became a cult hit, these groups were often openly hostile toward one another, with lesbians and straight women in particular battling over the 'meaning' of the show and its depiction of the relationship between Xena and her sidekick, Gabrielle. Lesbian websites generally focused on the relationship between Xena and Gabrielle, which most of the fans refer to as the 'subtext' of the show. Subtext fans watch the show for what one fan calls 'the electricity that runs just beneath the surface of *XWP*' (Dax), and some catalogue each instance of homoerotic contact on their individual websites. *Dax's Museum of Xena Subtext* (1997) is such an archive, begun because the fan is 'tired of hearing the mental gymnastics created and executed by the [homo-]'phobes on other Xena lists'. In addition to recognizing the subtext in the original programme, lesbian viewers actively rearticulated the relationship between Xena and Gabrielle through fan fiction. *Xena: Warrior Princess* has dozens of fan fiction sites, and many develop a lesbian relationship between Xena, Gabrielle and other female characters. Recognition, discussion and expansion of the subtext are important activities for many *Xena* fans. By acknowledging and celebrating the subtext, lesbian viewers create a critical framework for understanding the programme, one that distinguishes between fans and suggests at least a contingent political position. Fan fiction, particularly slash fiction, is an important and visible way for a specific fan community to articulate its values and identity.

Not surprisingly, the explosion of fan fiction has resulted in negative consequences for many fan writers. First, as fan fiction becomes more accessible, the stereotype of the fan as a socially backward obsessive spinning tales of imaginary friends seems to be proven correct. In the last year, nearly a dozen mainstream US, British and Australian newspapers have reported on the 'new phenomenon' of fan fiction. While some, like Robbie Hudson (2002) of *The Times*, note that adaptations and continuations of classic novels have been produced at least since the mid-nineteenth century, most mainstream commentators have focused on the absurd plotlines and sensationalism of slash fiction. Barber (2001) quotes a slash *Harry Potter* ('Draco eyed a sweat droplet as it ran down Harry's cheek and neck, to disappear into the collar of his robes. Every instinct suddenly cried out to follow the damp trail with his tongue...') to warn his readers that 'the internet is weirder than you thought'. Though the internet has made fan fiction publishing much easier, cheaper, and quicker for fan writers, the increased visibility may also have renewed and expanded negative stereotypes.

Even more important, the ubiquity of fan fiction on the internet has led to increased regulation from the copyright owners who view these stories as infringing on their property. Battles between Twentieth Century Fox, the company that produces the *Buffy the Vampire Slayer* television series, and *Buffy* fans have been particularly intense. In August 1999, Fox ordered webmistress Anya McLerie of *Slayer Fan Fiction* to 'cease and desist' publishing episode transcripts and the 'derivative infringement' of her fan fiction. Fox further demanded that McLerie's site acknowledge Fox's ownership of the characters, images and plotlines through official disclaimers whenever they were used. Fox's actions were roundly criticized; obviously, fans support the programme, and McLerie and others argued that fan websites, rather than detracting from favourite programmes, actually offered valuable publicity. Fox, however, persisted, and McLerie's site was modified. In March 2001, US-based internet service provider Lycos shut down hundreds of websites without warning. Many of the sites were personal webpages celebrating *Buffy* (many others were sites critical of the Malaysian government – internet copyright makes for strange bedfellows); Lycos feared the sites were infringing on Fox's copyright, and worried that it would be held liable. Again, fans were outraged. In an article on *Salon.com* (2001), webmistress Bridget O'Donoghue complained that 'the Web is where a lot of us get together to display and share our love for particular fandoms. When the sites are unceremoniously destroyed, well, it leads to large amounts of resentment and makes it difficult to share our mutual admiration for a fandom.' *Buffy* has an active fan following, many of whom see the programme as an alternate universe where friendship, freedom of choice and redemption are celebrated and affirmed. For these fans, then, the actions of Fox seemed to negate their positive experiences as a community. Fans of *Star Wars*, *Star Trek*, *Scooby Doo* and the novels of Anne McCaffrey have also been subject to legal action because of Web-based fan activities. Though the ease of publication and circulation offered by the internet has increased the amount of fan fiction and

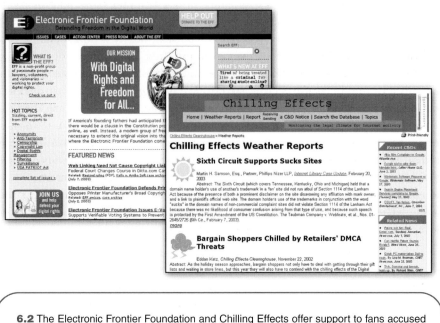

6.2 The Electronic Frontier Foundation and Chilling Effects offer support to fans accused of copyright infringement

arguably enhanced a sense of community, this increased visibility has also curtailed some fan activity that had previously existed under the radar of the copyright owners.

Most fans agree that the threat of lawsuit used by copyright owners is an over-reaction to legitimate fan activity; so do many lawyers and free speech activists. *Chilling Effects* (www.chillingeffects.org), a website operated by the US Electronic Frontier Foundation and students at the Harvard, Stanford, Berkeley, University of San Francisco, and University of Maine law schools offers free, concise advice about how to avoid copyright infringement, much of it targeted directly to fans who use the internet to celebrate a particular text. *Chilling Effects* is also a free speech watchdog group; it operates a clearing house for copyright cases on the internet in order to 'encourage respect for intellectual property law, while frowning on its mis-use to "chill" legitimate activity'. As other chapters in this volume demonstrate, copyright law is an important component in current debates about the limits and use of the internet; fan activity plays a major role in shaping those debates.

CONCLUSION: THE FUTURE FACE OF FANDOM

Debates about the ceaseless commercialism of the internet are also informed by fan activity. Because movie studios increasingly target the internet audience, websites advertising films are becoming more visually complex and interactive in order to create fans before a film's release. In 1999, the marketing for the independent Artisan Entertainment release *The Blair Witch Project* launched a new synergistic relationship between film and the internet. By establishing an enormous internet presence, with a detailed and interactive website, Artisan created fans of the movie before the movie even existed. In fact, many American reviewers noted that the pre-movie internet buzz and film website were more interesting than the movie itself. The pre-release activity guaranteed a huge opening weekend and steady growth in the USA. In the three years since I first wrote this chapter, the line between fan websites and official websites, especially for films, has increasingly blurred. *The Blair Witch Project*'s techniques have been copied and revised, most notably by the website for Steven Spielberg's *A.I.* (2001). The success of these marketing techniques represents one of the most radical ways the Web has expanded definitions of fandom, as advertising campaigns engender fans of their own.

Further, many official sites borrow the conventions of fansites. The website for the *Lord of the Rings* film trilogy (based, of course, on the novels by J.R.R. Tolkien, whose estate has been notoriously sticky about copyright) is a remarkable blend of fan and official content. Even before film production was announced, *Lord of the Rings* had a significant fan community with clubs both on- and offline dedicated to the cultures, languages, legends and ideals of Middle Earth. *Lord of the Rings* director Peter Jackson famously courted this fan base while developing the trilogy's Web presence, and the result is one of the most detailed film marketing sites on the Web. The official site includes message boards, interviews, information about appearances, downloads, and an invitation to 'join the fellowship' to receive free promotional material, updates and inside information. The kind of information circulated (as well as the community created by its circulation) mimics traditional fan activities. Of course, *Lord of the Rings*, like all other official sites pitched to fans and potential fans, offers merchandise for purchase: T-shirts resurrecting the counter-cultural slogan 'Frodo Lives', student planners embossed with Gandalf's visage, and a sculpted Orc head whose forehead hinges to reveal a thermal coffee mug are all available through one-click shopping. The multi-tiered commercial potential of linked fans is never ignored by producers and webmasters.

Though the Web has certainly commercialized fandom, the community offered to internet fans is equally real. In fact, the Web has encouraged not only friendship between fans otherwise separated by race, class, sexual orientation and geography, but also real-world action. Fan communities use the internet to facilitate charity giving and volunteerism. *Sword and Staff* (1997) is an online clearing house for charitable activity by *Xena: Warrior Princess* fans. Though the programme was cancelled in 2001, the charity is still active. Fans are invited to donate to different charities and take part in auctions to raise money. Generally, fans donate *Xena* merchandise and other celebrity memorabilia to auctions devoted to a particular cause. Between May 1997 and October 2002, nearly US$400,000 was donated by *Xena* fans to children's hospitals, women's shelters, rainforest preservationists and AIDS organizations. This charitable activity, though rare in fan communities, is facilitated by the Web. Since I wrote the first version of this chapter, fans have continued to use the internet to facilitate charitable activity. In particular, fans of the popular US boy bands Backstreet Boys and *NSync used the internet to donate to children's charities suggested by those bands. Wired, philanthropic fans can use the internet to deposit direct donations, participate in auctions modelled on the popular eBay site, and find information about local volunteer opportunities. This charitable activity seems to demonstrate the opportunities for social action the Web might offer, and suggests that fans are harnessing Web technology to move beyond merely talking about a favoured television programme and the ideals it espouses to putting those ideals into practice.

Despite the enthusiastic, sustained fan activity visible on the World Wide Web, the internet should not be assumed to have created utopian fan communities. Though more fans are able to take part in fan activity, and fan cultural production is more readily available to a larger number of fans, increased visibility has brought fans new challenges, especially in terms of copyright and commercialism. Further, despite a small increase in charity fundraising by fans online, few internet fans have moved from imagination to action. As the examples in this chapter suggest, fandom on the Web is a complex phenomenon. Though the internet may have led fandom towards the mainstream, it has not necessarily created a single, unified fan position or practice.

 **USEFUL WEBSITES**

The Buffy Cross and Stake: www.angelicslayer.com/tbcs/main.html

Links, images, fan fiction, episode guides and downloads pertaining to the world of *Buffy*.

Chilling Effects: www.chillingeffects.org

Non-profit site run by the Electronic Freedom Frontier and several US law schools to monitor online freedom of speech and offer advice on avoiding copyright infringement.

Dax's Museum of Xena Subtext: http://members.aol.com/Xenastry/subtext/subtext.htm

Scene-by-scene analysis of homoerotic content in the first three seasons. Still a fan favourite.

E! Online: www.eonline.com

Television, music, and film information, including live chats, gossip columns, special entertainment event coverage, and film information, including reviews. Online presence for the US E! cable television channel.

I'm Your Fan: www.walrus.com/~gibralto/acorn/fan.html

Clearing house for fan fiction based on *Star Trek, Highlander, The X-Files, The Sentinel* and more.

Slayer Fan Fiction: www.slayer.fanfic.com

A large collection of *Buffy the Vampire Slayer* fiction; subject to Fox's cease and desist order in 1999.

Chapter

7

WEB GRRRLS, GUERRILLA TACTICS: YOUNG FEMINISMS ON THE WEB

JAYNE ARMSTRONG

> We've entered an era of DIY feminism . . . Your feminism is what you want it to
> be and what you make of it. Define your agenda. Claim and reclaim your F-word.
>
> (thefword.org.uk)

In the mid-1990s a new generation of young feminist voices emerged on the Web through the medium of the grrrl e-zine. E-zines such as *Saucy Chicks* (saucychicks.com), *Fluffy Mules* (btinternet.com/~virtuous/fluffymules), *The F-Word* (thefword.org.uk), *Disgruntled Housewife* (disgruntledhousewife.com), *Planetgrrl* (planetgrrl.com), *Wench* (wench.com), *Bitch* (bitchmagazine.com) and *Cuntzilla* (cuntzilla.org) exemplify the ways in which young women and grrrls are appropriating the new technologies of the World Wide Web to build women and grrrl networks, create communities and alternative 'image spaces' (Castells, 2001).

Marginalized by academic feminist discourse, 'grrrls' are young feminists who use the Web to build networks and create space to articulate their interests and experiences. These spaces on the Web become a means through which grrrls can debate, negotiate and contest the meanings of femininity and create alternative feminist discourses and practices. Thus women's and grrrls' e-zines might be conceptualized as 'subaltern counterpublics', that is, discursive spaces 'where members of subordinated social groups invent and circulate counter-discourses to formulate oppositional interpretations of their identities interests and needs' (Fraser, 1993: 528).

WHAT IS A GRRRL E-ZINE?

E-zines are independently produced, self-published electronic zines or magazines that are produced as hypertexts and exist in cyberspace. Grrrl e-zines have been developed entirely with the medium in mind and will typically include a number

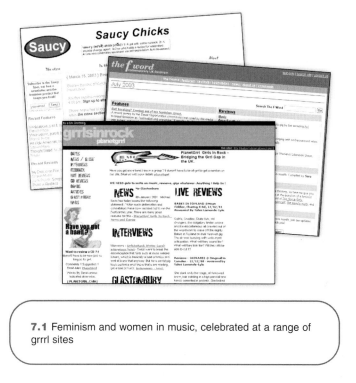

7.1 Feminism and women in music, celebrated at a range of grrrl sites

of themed sites or channels, comprising personal and autobiographical writing, feminist critique, features, humour, forums and fun.

Often opening with a declaration of their feminist identity, grrrl e-zines are by no means a homogenous genre, and producers will utilize a variety of practices to suit their feminist intentions: from autobiography, to critique, to the appropriation and transformation of the conventions of women's and girl's magazines. In this way, grrrls' lives and experiences, and the products and text of mass culture become resources for the articulation of new feminine and feminist identities.

Frequently cited as primary examples of third wave feminism (Garrison, 2000), women's and grrrls' e-zines share many characteristics, especially the use of numerous hypertext links to connect with other grrrl sites and to 'useful' resources on the Web. They also share an implicit, and sometimes explicit, urge to participate and contribute and an emphasis on DIY, not in the sense of domestic carpentry but as a form of Do-It-Yourself feminist practice, which describes both the ways in which young women and grrrls appropriate technologies and a form of feminist practice that is rooted in a reclamation of feminism for young women.

This chapter intends to offer an analysis of a range of popular grrrl e-zines, and will consider the tactics and practices adopted by young women and grrrls to construct a feminist identity on the Web. These practices and tactics include speaking in one's own voice, weaving grrrl networks and a range of textual tactics including mimesis, parody and irony.

SPEAKING IN ONE'S OWN VOICE

A significant feature of many grrrl e-zines is the autobiographical journals, articles and features that give voice to the experiences and concerns that face young women today. In a culture where the voices and experiences of young women are marginalized, journals and diaries enable women and grrrls to document their lives, publish their experiences and share their concerns with others. Emphasizing the 'personal' is by no means a new strategy for feminists. Truth telling, self-expression and sincerity underpinned the development of the consciousness-raising groups that were a feature of the radical feminist movement in the 1970s, whose aim (in part) was the identification of common concerns and issues. Telling the truth and speaking from experience thus become a tactic for the voices of the young feminist generation in the West.

Features and articles may focus on violence against women, the ways in which women and girls are represented in the media, body politics, identity politics and consumer culture as well as a diverse range of broader concerns about the environment, politics and education. These new feminist voices cannot easily be defined in terms of a singular agenda, and while clearly not uninformed by feminist debates and theorizing, they reject the forms and language of academic feminism for a form of 'vernacular feminism'. Thomas McLaughlin developed the notion of vernacular theory in relation to the writers and producers of zines (self-published, small-circulation, amateur magazines), who develop forms of practical criticism that give rise to theoretical questions. Here, vernacular

> refers to the practices of those who lack cultural power and who speak a critical language grounded in local concerns, not the language spoken by academic knowledge-elites ... They do not make use of the language or analytical strategies of academic theory; they devise a language and a strategy appropriate to their own concerns. And they arise out of intensely local issues that lead to fundamental theoretical questions.
>
> (1996: 6)

The 'vernacular', or 'vernacular feminism', thus refers to the language and critical practices that are used by women and grrrls to question the structures and discourses that construct them as women.

WEAVING THE GRRRL WIDE WEB

Commercial e-zines are characterized by their limited use of hyperlinks and a need to retain authorial control over the content of the site. Here, readers are limited to intra-site surfing and are afforded few opportunities to contribute – with the exception of the forums. However, independently produced e-zines, and particularly grrrl e-zines use the hypertext link to create networks and webs of grrrl spaces, to connect women and grrrls with 'useful' resources, and encourage women and grrrls to contribute to the site.

The primary purpose of hypertext links on grrrl sites is to construct relationships with other grrrl and feminist sites, webrings and resources. Drawing on the work of Sadie Plant and Donna Haraway, Nina Wakeford employs metaphors of networking and weaving to describe grrrl practices in cyberspace.

> Weaving could be a productive metaphor to describe the process of creating
> pages, and interlinking others. webpages could be construed as the woven
> products of electronic and social networks. Unlike the notion of the frontier,
> weaving could be used to emphasize the relationships within electronic networks,
> and between pages themselves, as well as the individuals who create them.
>
> (Wakeford, 1997: 62)

Weaving is a useful metaphor for describing the ways in which young women and grrrls are using the Web, but also describes grrrls' tactical use of hypertext links to connect and create relationships with other grrrl e-zines.

WEB GRRRL TACTICS

In his book *The Practice of Everyday Life* (1984), Michel de Certeau describes the 'tactics' or 'ways of operating' of powerless and marginalized people to create identities, maintain communities and achieve practical kinds of power. Tactics are forms of resistance, which may take the form of compromise, negotiation or subversion and can be understood as victories of the weak over the strong. For de Certeau, tactics are a form of poaching, the characteristics of which are trickery and guile.

De Certeau's theory rests on the idea that ordinary people find ways of resisting the structures of power through the practices of consumption. He argues that people utilize the goods and products of the consumer society for their own ends, and while they cannot escape the dominant cultural economy, they can appropriate its products for their own purposes.

Drawing on de Certeau, Constance Penley (1997) has discussed the ways in which female fans of *Star Trek* make tactical uses of *Star Trek* texts, and of technology to create their own texts. The producers and writers of women's and grrrls' e-zines use similar tactics to build communities and networks, challenge 'official' discourses of femininity and create grrrl spaces and identities. These tactics are purposeful and often politically motivated, combining techno-tactics, or the appropriation of computer, internet and Web technologies with semiotic tactics, including mimesis, parody, irony, exaggeration and critique. Such tactics are thus far more significant than the opportunist trickery that de Certeau describes; they are guerrilla actions, and, when combined, become powerful strategies for the construction of alternative feminine and feminist identities.

MIMESIS

> 'Grrrl', a word coined by Bikini Kill singer and activist Kathleen Hanna, is a spontaneous young-feminist reclamation of the word 'girl' ... 'Grrrl' puts the growl back in our pussycat throats.
>
> (Gilbert and Kile, 1996)

Many e-zines are characterized by their use of terms such as grrrl, wench, bitch and chick. Grrrl, in particular, has become synonymous with young feminist women on the Web, and has its roots in the Riot Grrrl movement that began in the underground music communities in USA in the 1990s and the underground zine movement. Riot Grrrls challenged the sexism of the underground music scene, and encouraged girls and women to assert themselves. The Riot Grrrl movement soon spread across the USA and Europe through print and electronic zines.

As Kearney suggests,

> These female youth have appropriated the word 'girl' from its dominant connotations and reformulated that social category by creating a new identity that better represents their revolutionary spirit. 'Riot grrrl,' therefore, symbolizes the enraged girl who empowers herself and others to speak out and fight against oppression. In turn, it is a call to action ('Riot, grrrl!').
>
> (1998: 156)

Exposing the contradictions and values within the many terms used to label women and girls is the first step towards transforming their meanings. Vološinov argues that, 'each living ideological sign has two faces, like Janus. Any current curse word can become a word of praise, any current truth must inevitably sound to many people as the greatest lie' (1973: 23). In exposing the contradictions and values that inhere in the many words used for 'woman', grrrls expose the multi-accentuality of the sign, and 'wench' and 'bitch' become sites for the struggle over meaning that is evident in every utterance and every speech event.

Drawing on the work of Luce Irigaray, philosopher Rosi Braidotti advocates a strategy of mimesis to interrogate the meanings culture ascribes to 'woman'. Mimesis involves returning to the images, words and definitions of 'the woman' and *dealing* with those images. She notes, 'One does not reinvent the subject "woman" by sheer willpower; rather, the process requires the deconstruction of the many, often contradictory, meanings and representations of "woman"' (Braidotti, 1996).

Many women's and grrrls' e-zines demonstrate the use of mimesis to deconstruct the meanings and representations of 'woman' in political and self-conscious ways. In the process of analysing their meanings, exposing their contradictions and the values that inhere in them, young women can begin to carve out new grrrl identities. The 'about' section in e-zines is often used as a means of explaining the choice of name for the site. *Wench*, for example, begins by questioning the meaning of the term.

> What exactly is a 'wench'? Kind of seems like an easy question until you try to answer it, doesn't it? The word has several definitions, and they cross at a dangerous intersection. According to Webster's, a wench can be:
> 'a young woman' or 'girl';
> 'a female servant';
> 'a lewd woman' or 'prostitute'
> 'Wench' is often thrown at women as a generic, vague epithet implying some sort of disapproval. But the word crystallizes the situation most women find themselves in today. This single, ambiguous word means three very different things at the same time; similarly, women today are often seen primarily as those same three things. A woman today is expected to be young (or look like she is), often a servant (especially if she has a family) and a sexual object, all at the same time. These roles often conflict with one another: adolescent girls' sexuality is usually condemned even as society tells them that's all they have to offer; women are expected to be dazzling in the bedroom but submissive and demure in daily life; women's youthful appearance is considered their most important quality even as society relies on their services as homemakers, cheap laborers, sexual servants and baby incubators.
>
> That's a lot of irony and symbolism for one little word. Which is why it's the perfect title for this project.
>
> (wench.com/about/)

This quote from *Wench* demonstrates mimesis at work in women's and grrrls' e-zines. The writers of *Bitch* adopt a similar tactic, drawing attention to the values that have sedimented into 'bitch', the ways in which the term is often used as a means of silencing women, and the reasons why women should use and expose it:

> When it's being used as an insult, 'bitch' is most often hurled at women who speak their minds, who have opinions and don't shy away from expressing them. If being an outspoken woman means being a bitch, we'll take that as a compliment thanks.
>
> Furthermore, if we take it as a compliment, it loses its power to hurt us. And if we can get people thinking about what they're saying when they use the word, that's even better.

And last but certainly not least, 'bitch' describes all at once who we are when we speak up, what it is we're too worked up over to be quiet about, and the act of making ourselves heard.

(bitchmagazine.com)

Deconstructing the meanings that are ascribed to women is one of the 'tactics' used by the creators of grrrl e-zines, and becomes the first step in articulating a feminist identity on the Web.

THE POLITICS OF PARODY

Grrrl e-zines utilize a range of textual and stylistic tactics to subvert dominant discourses of femininity, and to produce new meanings. Through parodic engagements with the products of mass culture – particularly women's and girl's magazines and female stereotypes – grrrl e-zines challenge representations of women and girls.

Parody might be understood as a textual or semiotic tactic that is utilized by grrrls to advance their own interests by entering alternative signifying codes into discourse by attaching them to existing structures of signification. Thus parody becomes a means by which grrrls can enter the systems of representation through the appropriation and manipulation of textual conventions.

The e-zine *Fluffy Mules* parodies the conventions of women's magazines and the celebrity and fashion industries to critique representations of femininity. The makeover, celebrity icons, shopping tips and the fashion pages are appropriated to subvert the dominant codes of femininity. Adopting an ironic voice *Fluffy Mules* defines itself as

Fashion & Facts, Kitsch & Handbags for the Modern Ms. Thing. By Sam and Jules ... fearlessly confronting your fluffy mules issues. Because you are f*cking [sic] fabulous! (even if some fashion magazines suggest via pictures you should resemble an anorexic 14 year old).

(fluffymules.com)

Content that includes 'How to look like', 'Fashion Rants', 'Le Shopping', 'Style Icons', 'Fairy Tale Heroines', 'Eyebrows of the Rich and Famous' and 'Objects of Desire', aims to challenge dominant cultural values and demonstrates a critical awareness of the ways in which consumer culture is constructed as the primary site for the construction of contemporary feminine identities.

In 'Fashion Rants', the writers Jules and Sam offer a critique of the fashion industry and fashion trends with their reviews of 'neck-beards', 'minge-pants' and 'flamingo legs'. 'How to look like' casts an ironic eye on role models. For example, how to look

7.2 Ironic approaches to femininity at *Fluffy Mules* and *Disgruntled Housewife*

like a character from the film *The Matrix*, requires: 'Black ... lots of black ... post-goth meets helmut lang; Boots – big and butch; shiny trousers to show off your tiny butt; Gel to keep you so-chic hair-do in place even in the midst of hurly-burly; Mobile phone, slimmer the better; super slick laptops and hovering in the air.'

Operating in an ironic mode and with a critical awareness of the ways in which contemporary femininities are represented through discourses of performance and style, *Fluffy Mules* interrogates contemporary representations of femininity.

Irony can be a powerful use of the parodic mode, but other sites adopt alternative forms of parody and different tactics to achieve their goals. *Disgruntled Housewife* appropriates the popular image of the 1950s' housewife as a device to subvert the meanings commonly associated with white, middle-class domestic femininities, and to assert a distance from that identity. Utilizing iconography drawn from pop-ular cultural representations of the housewife in the 1950s, particularly images of the 'domestic goddess' in advertising, magazines, film and popular television, *Disgruntled Housewife* parodies this glamorous figure who loved to cook for her man, and took pleasure in the consumption of a growing range of goods and products for the home and of increased consumer choice.

With its book of recipes for meals that men like ('men like meat'), ideas for 'keep-ing men happy', collections of kitsch objects, pin-up girls and lists of essential household products, *Disgruntled Housewife* playfully parodies, exaggerates and mocks domestic femininities and their representation as primary consumers: 'As every good little wifey knows the fastest way to a man's heart is through his gullet. So tie up those aprons, put Wives and Lovers on the record player, and start cooking up a fine little meal' (disgruntledhousewife.com).

Disgruntled Housewife also interrogates the construction of women as sexual objects and encourages women to identify themselves as sexual subjects. 'Slutty' interrogates the discourses that regulate female sexuality, whilst 'Confessions' encourages women to confess to their sexual desires and fantasies ('tell me yours and I'll tell you mine'). The combination of parody, critique and readers' personal narratives exemplifies the tactics employed by *Disgruntled Housewife*.

Developed primarily as a resource for UK women interested in new media and technology, *Planetgrrl* outlines its place on the Web and in relation to women's magazines in its 'about' section.

> We are Not A Portal! We do not want to be 'the' only place for chicks.;) How dull that would be. We are not a bunch of 'angry teenagers'. We will not talk about cracked nipples, husband bashing, how to make your life great by having thighs taut enough to bounce tennis balls off or menu making.
>
> (planetgrrl.com)

Stating that it is '100% fifties housewife and bridget jones free', *Planetgrrl* asserts a grrrl identity that refuses domesticity and dependence on men. The appropriation of the conventions of the 'who's in' and 'who's out' or 'who's hot' and 'who's not' pages so popular in women's magazines becomes a means of separating out the 'girls' from the 'grrrls'. For *Planetgrrl*, grrrls include Germaine Greer, Pamela Anderson, Xena – Warrior Princess, Kathy Burke, Mo Mowlam and Vivienne Westwood. This eclectic mix of academic feminists, celebrities, politicians and characters from the media suggests that the role models for today's young feminists are not limited to those associated with the radical voices of campaigning feminists, but can also be found in the stars and fictional characters of the mass media.

GUERRILLA WARRIORS

Describing itself as '40% political rally, 60% slumber party', *Marigold* is a Canadian-based e-zine, developed and run by 'boss lady' Audra Estrones; it combines six sites that include personal journals from women across Canada, cultural criticism, political activism, art, poetry and a number of forums. The sites are:

- The Lives of Girls and Women – 'Online journals from far and wide'
- Suffragette City – 'Political news, views, and how tos'
- Whoa Nellies – 'Rabble rousers past, present and future'
- Re:Views – 'Our take on pop culture and real life, too'

- Surfacing – 'Artists in electronic residence'

- What's that Marigold? – 'The forums. Talk to us, and each other.'

Inspired by *Bust* (the American magazine that started out as a zine), *Marigold* made its first appearance on the Web in December 1999.

As its slogan testifies, *Marigold* combines a celebration of women's lives and culture with political activism. The forums constitute an important part of *Marigold* and operate as a means to discuss issues and events, but also to arrange meetings between 'Maripeeps', the name used for members of *Marigold*. As with many grrrl e-zines, the forums provide a means for members and non-members alike to discuss issues, but in *Marigold*, they become a means of sustaining a community of like-minded young men (*Marigold* has many male participants who self-identify as feminists) and women across 'virtual' and 'real' space.

Marigold encourages the use of guerrilla tactics to raise awareness about marginalized feminist heroes who have made significant contributions to the arts, politics, feminism, science, and so on, but who are rarely visible in the written history of Canada. Readers are encouraged to download posters of these 'Whoa Nellies' or 'Maple flavoured women' with the cry, 'If you have a printer, or the use of one and you have a staple-gun, some glue, or chewed gum. Then you too can be a guerilla warrior of unsung Canadian women.'

Marigold's guerrilla tactics extend to other aspects of the site, in particular to use of hypertext links to connect readers with resources and information. In Suffragette City, readers are provided with a diverse range of links to feminist and activist sites, links to information about politics and forms of sexism around the globe. This part of the site also includes the contributors' personal bibliographies of feminist texts and fiction as well as articles and essays on a range of political and feminist issues.

CONCLUSION

> Established feminism has lost touch with what some young women are doing – particularly zines, riotgrrrl and the underground culture. Feminism must reconnect with what is going on in the underground.
>
> (thefword.org.uk)

The third wave of feminism should not be understood as representing a radical break from the voices of the second wave: as we have seen, grrrl e-zines adopt some of the practices associated with the radical feminisms of the second wave, for example, through autobiography and speaking from experience.

Yet there is evidence that Web grrrls are blurring the distinction between the 'feminist' subject and 'feminine' subject, a distinction that was largely formed in the second wave. The voices that are found in young women's and grrrls' e-zines claim both feminism and femininity for themselves, recognizing both the problems and pleasures of being a young woman in the contemporary western world.

The feminine/feminist spaces created by grrrl e-zines clearly illustrate and are informed by an engagement with feminist discourse, but it is the popular 'celebrity' feminisms that appear most often in the pages of grrrl e-zines. Feminists such as Naomi Wolf, Rene Denfeld, Germaine Greer, Susan Faludi and Natasha Walter, are often quoted with their forms of 'power feminism', alongside a rejection of academic feminism and a call to reclaim feminism for the majority.

However problematic (and many feminists take issue with the Wolf and Denfeld brand of 'power feminism'), celebrity feminism has helped to inspire a new generation of young women to reclaim the f-word. But it is important to remember that the third wave cannot be reduced to a feisty rebranding, or those e-zines that are produced by the young, predominantly white, educated and heterosexual grrrls discussed here. Third wave feminism emerged primarily as a critique of the homogenization of the category 'woman' and insists on recognizing the diversity of women's experience and on differences between women. Many grrrls' e-zines encourage contributions from women and girls, recognizing and celebrating that diversity, and there are many more that specifically foreground identity politics, particularly politics of race and sexuality, such as *Slander* (worsethanqueer.com), and *Techno-Dyke* (technodyke.com). This chapter foregrounds some of the tactics adopted by young feminists but confesses to significant gaps and omissions, particularly with regard to questions of diversity and difference.

USEFUL WEBSITES

Barbara J. Duncan's Cyberculture Resources: http://barbara_duncan.tripod.com/tlpnew.html

Includes links to academic journals and articles on cyberculture, feminism, postfeminism and cyberfeminism as well as links to grrrl zines and riot grrrls, zine resources and people who write about cyberculture.

Grrrl zines: www.grrrlzines.net

Elke Zobl's site contains links to grrrl zines and e-zines around the world, an academic bibliography, interviews with producers and resources on third wave feminism and cyberfeminism.

Zinebook: www.zinebook.com

Chip Rowe's site refers primarily to zines, but has some good e-zine resources including links to e-zine directories, articles and essays, interviews and e-zine help.

Chapter 8

MOVIE-MAKING IN THE NEW MEDIA AGE

GRAHAM ROBERTS

Oh brave new world that has such people in it.

(Miranda, *The Tempest*, Act V, Scene 1)

Technology doesn't matter. Nobody pays to see it, nobody cares. Any discussion of where cinema goes must remember this. There is a danger that those promoting technology see it as an attraction in itself, and those ignorant of it are overawed by the enthusiasm.

(Owen Thomas, producer, Elemental Films)

It is worth reminding ourselves that, from the documentary shorts of the Lumière Brothers through the introduction of synchronized sound and the development of the classical narrative mode of Hollywood, cinema was *the* New Media for a period of forty years (1898–1938). Cinema (superseding photography) remains the pre-eminent bringing together of art and technology. Cinema's demise as the mass entertainment medium was facilitated by new technology (television) but was caused by sociological changes (including the demographic shift caused by the post-Second World War 'baby boom'). Contemporary changes in patterns of consumption, both public and domestic (allied to new technologies), might just be bringing cinema back to its rightful pre-eminent place.

Much of this chapter takes a positive (if hesitant) approach to the subject of 'movie-making in the new media age'. For, as Kim Howells puts it in his introduction to the Department for Culture Media and Sport (Creative Industries Division) *Screen Digest Report on the Implications of Digital Technology for the Film Industry* (*Screen Digest*, 2002): 'Digital technology is upon us, but its uses are not yet fully implemented, or maybe not even perceived' (DCMS, 2002: 3).

As the cultural spokesman of Britain's 'New Labour', Howells is bound to take a 'brave new world' attitude to technological change:

> One of the most interesting aspects of digital technology is the possibilities it presents. Films could be seen at the same time all over the world, in different types of venue or in places where there is no easy access to cinema at present.
>
> (ibid.)

In the UK, the Film Council (launched in the spring of 2000 to be 'the strategic organisation set up by the Government to create a coherent structure for the UK film industry and to develop film culture in the UK') is most eager that the British film industry be able to exploit the opportunities afforded by digital developments. These developments will undoubtedly change the nature of cinema production and distribution, whether we like it or not.

NEW MEDIA AND DISTRIBUTION

Digital cinema is the replacement of 35mm analogue film with digital files shown on special high-resolution video projectors. At present these files can be sent to cinemas over satellite or on tapes and discs. The first method demands vast expenditure at start-up, the second method is effectively as logistically challenging as transporting tins of film. However, the whole digital cinema experiment could take off with the utilization of cable or the Web.

The promise of digital cinema has been realized thanks to breakthroughs in electronic image projection and data compression. The digital light processor (DLP) projection system was first used to screen digital versions of *Star Wars: Episode I* in New Jersey and Los Angeles in July 1999. More than 100 DLP prototype projectors have been used in cinemas in the USA, Europe and Asia (with five in the UK). They have screened digitized versions of films primarily from Disney and Warner Bros.

Digital cinema opens up the possibilities that non-cinema venues can be equipped with digital projectors to screen movies. This is particularly attractive for producers who may find it difficult to get a screening at their local multiplex, or for communities that do not have access to traditional cinema venues. In the USA, Emerging Cinemas (www.emergingcinemas.com) is installing alternative venue e-cinemas in museums, and caters for art-house movie audiences, while Network Event Theaters is already showing sponsored previews of Hollywood and independent films on campus at 50 universities.

One form of digital distribution already widely known to the viewing public is the Digital Versatile Disc (DVD). This new medium has penetrated twice as fast in Europe as the now ubiquitous VCR. Of the more than 1700 DVD titles released

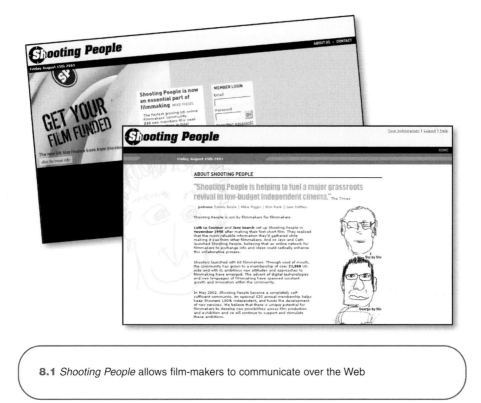

8.1 *Shooting People* allows film-makers to communicate over the Web

in the UK in 2000, 66.3 per cent were feature films (DCMS, 2002: 53). DVD rental now accounts for 60 per cent of business for Blockbuster (the biggest retail rental supplier in the UK). This is from a standing start in 1999. Britain's most popular 'movie' magazine *Empire* carried an editorial in September 2002 stating: 'The catalyst for our own revolution is simply the DVD revolution' (p. 10).

The 'extra features' element of the DVD package may well be the model for future film content. As the DCMS report put it, 'the interactive dimension to DVD has definite potential to enhance a wider appreciation of film culture and extend the possibilities of communication between filmmakers and their audience' (DCMS, 2002: 53). The growth of DVD has itself spurred the flowering of a supporting production sector documenting and celebrating the film-making process with 'making of' documentaries, director profiles, and so on. It has to be said that much of the material packed on to commercial DVDs is largely rehashed from the 'Electronic Press Kit' (EPK) so beloved of lazy journalists, and has very little educational value beyond the study of current press and publicity discourse. Nonetheless the potential is there – not least for portmanteau compilations of films from new directors.

DISTRIBUTION AND THE WEB

The delivery of moving images via the Web is a frustratingly slow and impractical means of movie distribution. As an example, I recently signed up for the (eminently reasonable) legalized 'Napster' site – now named www.ishareit.com. While reasonably quick at supplying audio mp3s, my attempts to download video were less successful: 75 per cent of my attempts to find *Wong Kar Wai* found nothing. When I found the BMW advertising film I was looking for, the eight-minute film took five hours to download. A full download of Martin Scorsese's *Casino* was offered in 43 hours. As easy as a visit to the multiplex – or switching on the TV – it was not.

It is important to bear in mind that the delivery speed depends on how efficiently the film has been digitally compressed. However, the problem of efficient deliverability is almost entirely one of bandwidth and reliability. With a suitably fast broadband connection it should be possible to download a full-length movie in less than its running time. Already 40 per cent of German households have broadband connections. The UK's problem is almost entirely predicated upon the fact that BT's broadband infrastructure can only reach 60 per cent of the country – but the cable companies are moving in to fill the vacuum.

One way in which we can hope that the new and old players in the movie distribution business can operate is 'connected DVD', which links DVD to the Web. The success of this dual technology depends upon producers and publishers seizing an opportunity to build a direct interactive relationship with consumers with the prospect of new revenue opportunities. Some 500 new DVD Web-enabled titles were released in 2001 alone. The PC-bound nature of this activity should soon be lost as DVD player manufacturers plan Web-enabled models. The new game consoles and digital TV set-top boxes that include DVD will also offer internet connectivity.

The current (and indeed immediately foreseeable) time/space problems with downloading moving images are beginning to be addressed via streaming, that is, the real time distribution of audio, video and multimedia by the continuous transmission of the digital media data. With a broadband connection, the image and audio are approaching (or exceeding, with the fastest connections) television quality. Unfortunately, the cost of streaming rises according to the number of simultaneous streams that can be sent out, and the picture and sound quality that is required. This problem may, in the long term, block the widespread use of commercial streaming.

The DCMS document puts 'The Challenge of Internet Distribution to the Industry Establishment' clearly: 'Firstly, there is the emergence of new internet companies employing radically new business models that might overtake the existing industry giants and their traditional modes of business … Secondly, there is the challenge of piracy' (DCMS, 2002: 76). The piracy issue might not trouble us as consumers – but commercial enterprises will simply cease to distribute movies if stealing continues to grow. The end of legitimate distribution would lead – as day follows night – to the end of movie production. We as consumers may not feel too sympathetic to the multinationals who dominate our viewing, but we should remember that piracy affects a small-scale producer with minimal margins much more than it does AOL/Time Warner.

The vast majority of commercially sanctioned 'legitimate' entertainment available on the Web is free, and consists of short movies, film trailers and brief animations. From a total of fewer than 20, the reliable established suppliers are Atom Films (www.atomfilms.shockwave.com) and the more commercially oriented *iFilm* (www.ifilm.com), which are concentrating on delivering short-form content. Recently, more ambitious companies such as *CinemaNow* (www.cinemanow.com) – a subscription service at $9.95 a month – and *Sightsound.com* (where films can be bought outright or 'rented') have been attempting to deliver feature-length movie content over broadband connections. They have yet to secure distribution deals for premium Hollywood movies.

Five of the major studios – Warner, Paramount, MGM, Universal and Sony – are working on a joint venture for a 'video on demand' service. Disney and Fox confirmed a second, similar venture to be offered via Disney's *movies.com* website. These ventures are occupation strategies based on the philosophy 'take the Web before the Web takes you'. They are unlikely to be economically successful for several years to come but, if Hollywood is to avoid being 'Napsterized', it is vital that these moves towards building a compelling and secure commercial alternative begin sooner rather than later.

The revenue models of online entertainment companies have up to now been largely based on a combination of syndication, subscriptions and advertising/sponsorship. These revenue streams have been difficult to come by, not least because audiences have not flocked to e-film sites. Several of the Web companies operating in the short film market are now devoting themselves to generating new sources of revenue by licensing their content 'upstream' to traditional media such as cable television and video, as well as to new platforms such as mobile phones.

The twin uncertainties hanging over the brave new world of movies on the Web are the lack of high-speed access in the home, and resistance to watching films on a PC. These questions are liable to be answered by the next wave of broadband, which will connect broadband to TV. The new digital TV set-top boxes and receivers will increasingly be designed in such a way that internet services are integrated seamlessly into the package. They will also start to include computer-type hard disks and ever-larger measures of processing power. Crucially, these devices should connect to 'always-on' broadband internet pipes. While the PC space has been a notoriously difficult arena in which to make paying services work, viewers of movies on TV are used to paying for movie channels via subscriptions or on a pay-per-view basis. For this reason, it may be easier to make such a model for delivering movies over the internet work as broadband to the TV becomes an economic reality. According to the DCMS,

> each new generation of digital TV technology is becoming more computer-like. In fact, the latest digital TV set-top boxes are really computers in disguise . . . The more important distinction between the different screens in the home will be the manner in which they are used. Some will be used for 'sit-up' activities that are generally associated with the PC (study, information surfing, home banking, shopping, gaming, etc.), while others – probably large hang-on-the-wall flat screens – will be used for more 'sit-back' activities that we currently associate with the TV – and particularly viewing of films.
>
> (2002: 67)

A brave new world for sure – but not one unworried by clouds on the horizon.

The DCMS report also points to the dangers of 'uncertainty and ignorance', a 'widespread lack of understanding about internet developments amongst many British film professionals, coupled with deep uncertainty about how to respond'. This, the DCMS suggests, has led to UK film companies failing to devise any strategies whatsoever regarding either future internet distribution opportunities, or the possible threats to their business posed by internet piracy.

PRODUCTION ON THE WEB

The production process begins with the development of a script. The Web is becoming an essential tool for everybody writing or seeking a story. Scriptwriting programs are available to buy, or are distributed free online. An entire script can be sent around the world within seconds. The internet has spawned discussion groups and global 'communities' that enable scriptwriters to swap ideas and make contacts. Reliable examples of writers' networks are the *Internet Filmmaker's FAQ* (www.filmmaking.net) and *Writers' Exchange* (www.writers-exchange.com).

We have also seen the rise of screenplay submission websites, to which scripts or stories, outlines and pitches can be submitted for peer review or even a prospective sale. These include *ScriptShark.com* and that old warhorse, the BBC (www.bbc.co.uk/writersroom).

Other film professionals have seized the communication potential of the Web rather more tentatively than writers. Nonetheless – beyond the digital production self-help/promotion sites discussed later – there is now a burgeoning sector of film-makers' networks. At the top end of the range, you can explore Francis Coppola's *Zoetrope Virtual Studio* (www.zoetrope.com). Another exceptionally useful site is

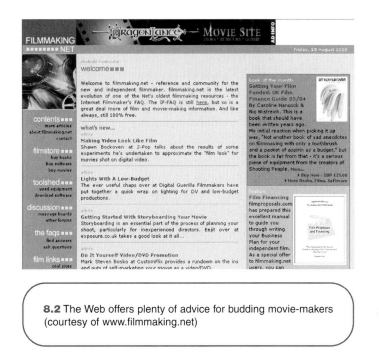

8.2 The Web offers plenty of advice for budding movie-makers (courtesy of www.filmmaking.net)

Shooting People (www.shootingpeople.org), where the 'essential guides' are particularly useful for the inexperienced movie-maker who might feel intimidated when dealing with industry insiders. The facility to discuss and publicize projects with like-minded practitioners is crucial in the fast-changing field of low-budget (almost certainly digital) production.

DIGITAL PRODUCTION

As a medium with a long-standing tradition of innovation and utilization of new technologies, the actual process of capturing images (at least in mainstream cinema) has remained an area of rigid resistance. Recently, while in pre-production for a short feature film to be shot on digital tape, we were told by our cinematographer that 'if you had the money we would be shooting on film'. Sad as it is for those of us old enough to have eroticized Steinbeck editing desks, and yearn for the smell of a chinagraph pencil, *there will soon be no good reason for shooting on 35mm film*. As Wim Wenders put it: 'In the long run, there is no question that DV will replace film. It gives you a more complex and satisfying control over the image than you ever had before' (quoted in an article by Sheila Johnston, *The Daily Telegraph*, 10 November 2000). If you do not believe a darling of the European art-house, then ask George Lucas, who shot the second part of his *Star Wars* saga entirely on CineAlta digital cameras. Citing the savings to be made in production insurance as one reason, Lucas has gone so far as to state that 'I can safely say that

I'll never ever shoot another film on film'. Accordingly, the DCMS states that: 'DV has come to replace 16mm as the preferred low-budget alternative to 35mm film: at the 1999 Los Angeles Film Festival, 10 per cent of submissions were on DV. By 2000 it was 30 per cent; in 2001 it was 60 per cent' (DCMS, 2002: 7).

Two of the key established British directors championing DV are Mike Figgis and Bernard Rose. Figgis made *Time Code* (2000), which narrated several overlapping stories in real-time using four cameras and showing the result in a split-screen format with all four images visible simultaneously. Bernard Rose, who directed *Ivans xtc* (2000), has also set up the provocatively named website *filmisdead.com*, which included self-help materials for putative DV directors and producers. Another notable example of a British DV film is May Miles Thomas' *One Life Stand* (2000), 'shot' for less than £30,000. The crew's experiences of *One Life Stand*, as well as a comprehensive introduction to the world of digital film-making and distribution, are available on the *Project X* website set up by the team behind the film (www.projectx.uk.com).

Director Danny Boyle and producer Andrew MacDonald (who gave us Brit-hits *Shallow Grave* and *Trainspotting*) have since made *28 Days Later* (2002) on DV, but Boyle's attitude is less evangelical than either Rose's or Figgis's. His reasons for using DV are linked to the material more than the allure of the technology: 'You have to have an organic reason to use it. There has to be something in the script that says this story belongs in the digital world' (Floyd, 2002: 19).

If *production* is slowly but surely becoming digital, editing already is. For non-linear editing, film sequences are first converted to video using a telecine film scanner, or DV footage downloaded through a 'fire-wire'. All the material can be stored on a computer hard drive (the rapid fall in the price of disk space and memory has allowed this technology to be utilized by low- or no-budget productions). Every frame can be accessed instantly, and sequences can be assembled in an infinite number of ways with no risk of destroying the original rushes. A vociferous apostle in the use of computer editing – with the Avid system – was legendary film editor Thelma Schoonmaker (*Jaws*, *Raging Bull*). She spoke about the technology after 'cutting' Martin Scorsese's *Casino*: 'It was a revelation, because I had resisted using it for quite a long time … it's just easier to do it faster and without worry; it frees you up' (Boorman and Donahue, 1997: 27). It is worth noting, however, that – as with any powerful tool – there are also hazards: 'The danger of it for an inexperienced director would be to find yourself with sixteen different versions … Marty is a very decisive director … you have to use the system with discipline: you have to think carefully about your options, make sure they are valid' (ibid.).

By the time that Schoonmaker and Scorsese had overcome their resistance to digital editing, Avid was becoming an industrial norm, and the initial whiz-bang overuse had faded. The new 'easy to use' editing technology had had an immediate effect on the aesthetic of Hollywood films. American cinema has historically 'cut' quicker than elsewhere in the world, and the introduction of Avid allowed for films with vastly more rapid cuts, such as Oliver Stone's *Natural Born Killers* (1994). The race for faster and faster editing eventually became a creative dead-end and, in any event, has lost its hegemonic position with the increasing influence of other styles (Hong Kong super slo-mo, for instance) into current Hollywood practice.

HOW THE WEB AFFECTS FILM – HOW FILM AFFECTS THE WEB

The (present) shortcomings of Web delivery have a profound effect on the structure and aesthetics of 'net movies'. Films that work best are short (under five minutes); the camera needs to be close to the action (wide establishing shots and broad vistas look daft on a small viewer); and movement has to be handled with care (frame rate on the Web is not up to the 24–25 frames per second of film and television). The *Shooting People* Essential Guide puts it bluntly: 'Animation films made in Flash are best suited of all for the net – as flash is an internet medium – sharp, clear and fast to download' (*Shooting People*, 2002: 2).

There is no need to despair for the budding *auteur*. The short, simple animation paradigm is a result of only a decade of technical development: art (or commerce) will find a way. The guilty pleasures central to the entertainment value of movies and the Web are very similar. Voyeurism has been at the centre of cinema's pleasures, from the Lumière Brothers and Dziga Vertov, through Hitchcock and Powell, to the latest teen horror self-parody. Voyeurism has given much Web content its point and its selling card. Indeed, one of the few sure-fire ways of being able to 'sell' access to websites is through pornography.

The Web, like gaming, has taken much of its visual language from the movies, and we are now beginning to see film and television borrowing some strategies and aesthetics from the Web. The webcam influence, for example, can be seen in any number of 'reality TV' shows, such as *Big Brother*. The webcam aesthetic is entering into mainstream movie-making with thrillers like *My Little Eye* (2002), while Danny Boyle's motivations for the aesthetic of *28 Days Later* were centred in the *Zeitgeist* of the 'new media' age: 'That's how we see ourselves now – digitally' (Floyd, 2002: 19).

THE WORLD WIDE WEB AND PROMOTION

Since the surprise success of *The Blair Witch Project* (1999), digital marketing (including the ubiquitous website) has become an accepted part of any movie promotion, often beginning in the pre-production phase. Even a small independent company like (my own) Endgame Pictures can use the relatively cheap medium of the home-grown website (www.endgamepictures.co.uk) to promote its product. As a useful spin-off, the site can be used to recruit crew.

A British film-maker like Michael Winterbottom, whose burgeoning reputation had seen him moving into higher-budgeted movie-making, set up a website for his theatrical release *The Claim* (2000) prior to the start of shooting (www.theclaim-movie.com). This site allowed members to view dailies, read production notes and even have a say in aspects of the film via polls, a process that potentially could replace the fraught (and studio-manipulated) process of previews. With films like *The Claim*, the internet is showing its power to build up an online fan base. It is important to remember (returning to one of the quotes that opens this chapter) that the wittiness of your campaign and the audacity of your new media use are irrelevant if the quality of the film is poor – see, for example, the poor critical and commercial reception for *Book of Shadows: Blair Witch 2* (2000).

The Web also provides the movie industry (and those studying the movie industry) with an invaluable source of information on current activity via such sites as *Variety* (www.variety.com), *Screen Digest* (www.screendigest.com) and, most valuable of all (and free), *Screen Daily* (www.screendaily.com).

CONSUMPTION AND THE WEB

The Web offers a uniquely powerful tool to access the collective psyche of the cinema's base. As such, it is a rich resource for investigating the phenomenon of intangible glamour that surrounds all things cinematic – and how that allure is consumed, used and subverted. The most cursory sample of fan-related sites will give just a tiny glimpse of the vast array of material that is cinema related. Thus, we cannot fail to be convinced that the Web is the researcher's tool *par excellence* for what is after all a *popular* art form. Beyond merely academic purposes, judicious use of Web searches can allow a movie-maker valuable primary source material on the needs and gratifications of the very people he or she must sell their product to.

CONCLUSION

The New Media are not just new – they are ubiquitous. To quote the DCMS report: 'Digital technology permeates the production and pre-production phases of filmmaking. Lower-cost digital tools enable almost anyone to create a feature-length film' (2002: 13). What digital will not do, however, is replace the cornerstones of good film-making: talent, inspiration, knowledge, expertise and skills. Nor will digital technology render a script – an orderly plan for the narrative or indeed a rigorous and workable shooting schedule – obsolete. The advice of Thelma Schoonmaker is important here: 'You have to use the system with discipline: you have to think carefully about your options, make sure they are valid' (Boorman and Donahue, 1997: 27).

The Web is already a powerful tool for communications between film-makers, and is becoming a viable conduit between the filmmaking community and its public. As broadband access spreads, the potential for getting movies 'out there' is beginning to be fulfilled. In addition, Web discourse has the potential to change the way stories are told and consumed. But, at the end of the day, whether written on a PC, filmed on DV or streamed on the Web, the future of film is still narratives that are entertaining and engaging. As Alfred Hitchcock once said: 'You need three things to make a good film: a great script, a great script and a great script.'

USEFUL WEBSITES

Atom Films: http://atomfilms.shockwave.com

Devoted to all manner of short films on the Web, this site is highly entertaining and always looking for new material.

Exposure: www.exposure.co.uk

The internet resource for young film-makers, with excellent features on film structure, guerrilla movie-making, and more.

Filmmaker.com: www.filmmaker.com

Includes an online chat page with contacts to film-makers, and a huge links database.

Internet Archive Movie Collection: www.archive.org/movies

A collection of hundreds of short films in MPEG-2 format, which the Prelinger Archives has digitized and donated to the Internet Archive.

Screen Daily: www.screendaily.com

The online version of *Screen International*, the voice of the international film business 'updated around the clock'.

Shooting People: www.shootingpeople.org

The UK film-makers' network: an unpretentious and businesslike community of over 15,000 people working in production.

Chapter 9

'DOING IT' ON THE WEB: EMERGING DISCOURSES ON INTERNET SEX

JODI O'BRIEN and EVE SHAPIRO

> An entire hybrid generation has redefined the concept of 'doing it in the road'.
>
> (McRae, 1996: 243)

Several years ago, just as online communication was becoming more widespread and the subject of scholarly discussion, Shannon McRae offered this variation of the familiar Beatles lyric to characterize what she perceived to be a frontier of sexual expression: virtual sex. McRae began her discussion by acknowledging that the supposed popularity of 'netsex' could indeed be driven by people's fears: fear of AIDS, fear of bodies, fear of strangers, fear of rejection. However, in her estimation, computer-mediated sexual expression also heralded a number of positive sexual shifts including more safety and freedom for women and the opportunity for a more expansive range of sexual practices. Perhaps her boldest introductory remark was the claim that, far from being yet another manifestation of the alienated passivity of an advanced capitalist technology, we can view virtual sex as an occasion in which 'human beings have turned the machinery of power that surrounds them into sources of play and pleasure' (1996: 244). In this regard, her twist on the phrase 'do it in the road' echoes the 1960s' adage that the sexual is also political.

In this chapter, we follow David Silver's notion of 'discoursing cyberspace' (Silver, 2000). Specifically, what are some of the discourses that have emerged regarding computer-mediated sexual practices and expressions? What do these discourses reveal and reflect about more general cultural beliefs and practices regarding sexual expression? How do these beliefs intersect with the debates about internet use and its perceived consequences for social interaction, political organizing and individual expression? We will suggest that the debates and questions that characterize discussions of online sexuality cast into relief age-old questions regarding the character and ethics of sexuality generally. In other words, the discourses, or 'stories' as Silver calls them, that are emerging regarding internet sexuality tell us a lot about long-entrenched beliefs and ideals regarding the meaning, practice and containment of sexuality. What do we perceive to be the implications and consequences of this form of sexual interaction? What do we think we're doing when we 'do it' on the Web, and what do we think these activities may be doing to us?

DEMOGRAPHIC AND DEFINITIONAL OVERVIEW

What sorts of activities constitute internet sex, and what are the range and impact of these activities? According to at least one study, sex is the most frequently searched for topic online (Freeman-Longo and Blanchard, 1998). Several sources concur that online pornography industries are among the most prolific and profitable enterprises on the Web. It has been estimated that over half of all spending that occurs on the internet is related to sexual services and activities (*Guardian*, 27 May 1999). Some scholars have indicated that, just as the pornography industry is usually among the first to exploit new publishing sources, so, to a certain extent, it has driven technological development of the internet (Filippo, 2000). Entrepreneurs of sex-related services are continually seeking new, more efficient and resonant platforms for service delivery. In this regard, sex-related activities can be seen as a major variable in the technological and economic growth and development of the internet.

The venues through which these activities take place include Web-based chat rooms, Bulletin Board Systems (BBSs), Multi User Domains (MUDs), and Internet Relay Chat (IRC). The many studies that have been written on internet sexuality in the past decade may or may not contain a distinction regarding these venues. Empirical case studies of online sexual cultures tend to be located within

Lapdog69 says: Hey there stranger

BeatGirl says: Howdy

Lapdog69 says: What you got on?

BeatGirl says: The radio.

BeatGirl says: whats that in your hand?

Lapdog69 says: Its not my mouse...

BeatGirl says: Can I stroke it anyway?

9.1 Textual intercourse online

specific venues, for example, Correll's ethnography of a lesbian café (1995), Kendall's study of masculinity in a MUD (2002), Shaw's study of gay men's use of IRC (1997), and Berry and Martin's study of BBS use among queer students in Taiwan and Korea (2000). The form or venue through which people engage in online sexual practices is also a significant factor. It is therefore noteworthy that in much of the theoretical and public speculation regarding the implications of computer-mediated sex, the observer fails to make a distinction between venues. Instead, in many of these discussions, the internet is rendered as one vast, undifferentiated 'frontier'.

Responses to this 'sexual frontier' include bored indifference ('it's nothing more than an interactive version of *Penthouse*'), a science fiction-like anticipation of new developments in virtual sexual technology (such as the notion of an internet-connected, full-body 'love suit'), and various entrepreneurial claims regarding the lucrative potential of online sex sites. In this chapter we explore two significant discourses that have emerged in response to the development and proliferation of internet sex: the discourse about a 'brave new frontier' or 'sexual playground', and the discourse regarding a 'perilous vortex of danger and corruption'. These discourses stand in stark opposition and mirror more general and long-standing controversies regarding sexuality – what it is, who can have it, with whom, and how. These discourses also reflect scholarly and public discussions regarding the overall implications and consequences of internet use in our daily lives. To this end, we suggest that studies of internet sex cast into relief questions and debates regarding both sex and the implications of internet use. Thus, an understanding of these discourses can be helpful in understanding these more general debates.

What does 'doing it' on the Web mean?

Before turning to an overview and critical assessment of these two discourses, we wish to point out that there is often a disconnection between what people (including scholars) *think* others are doing with new technologies and forms of communication, and what is actually going on. What *are* people doing when they 'do' internet sex? For the most part, they are doing one or both of the following activities.

- Looking at sexual imagery. This material may be live-feed imagery (real-time images) or posted material. It may or may not be posted on an interactive site. In other words, the images may in fact be an online version of Penthouse or they may be live-feed of an erotic performance (similar to live erotic dancing or peep shows).

- Finding others for sex chats. These activities usually take place in designated chat rooms or IRC. Two or more individuals exchange lines of text describing sexual acts that they are 'doing' to one another. This activity is sometimes referred to as 'one-handed typing'. Much of the activity in chat rooms consists of checking out profiles of others who are logged on, exchanging flirtatious banter and so forth. In this way the sites can be seen as similar to cruising a bar or café. If you're lucky, you may find someone and move to a 'private room'.

Some observers refer to these activities as 'masturbatory enhancement mechanisms'. To this end internet sex sites are providing images and/or forms of interaction that arouse sexual responses in ways presumed to be similar to sexual magazines and/or phone sex. The extent to which internet sex is similar or distinct is the topic of considerable scholarly discussion. This discussion can be interpreted as a debate about what constitutes 'real' sex (Hamman, 1996; O'Brien, 1998; Shaw, 1997; Stone, 1991). For many, 'real' sex requires the physical presence of two or more bodies. For others, sex is as much a matter of imagination and interaction – in any form – as it is an embodied activity. In any case, it is a fact that online real-time *interactive* sexual engagement is primarily text-based (and only occasionally accompanied by live imagery). Text-based communication differs in many ways from spoken exchanges and/or physical contact. Any inquiry into internet sex must take this into account. In the case of some online chat sites, this fact is considered a plus. Note the following quotes that appear on various sites as a reminder that good sex need not be physical.

> All really great lovers are articulate, and verbal seduction is the surest road to actual seduction.
>
> (Marya Mannes, *Naughtychat.com* homepage)

> Language is a skin: I rub my language against the other ... (language experiences orgasm upon touching itself).
>
> (Roland Barthes, *A Lover's Discourse* (1978: 73) (quoted in Shaw, 1997))

In addition to looking at sexual imagery and finding others to 'do it' with online, other sex-related activities on the internet include searching for sex-related information (where to meet others with similar sexual interests; information regarding specific sexual practices, and so on) and hanging out online with others who share a particular sexual interest or culture. To this end, the internet serves as an organizing and information-dispensing mechanism. The discourses which we interrogate here are responses to internet sex both in terms of sexual activities as described above and as an organizing/informational mechanism.

EMERGING DISCOURSES: AN OVERVIEW

The early stories of online sexual activity mirror some of the earliest discourses regarding the directions and implications of internet use more generally. As Filippo (2000) notes in reference to the internet pornography industry, the pendulum swings between those who view the sites as dangerous and damaging, and those who consider the sites to be expanded opportunities for sexual fulfilment and expression. These initial assessments have been based largely on speculation according to particular metaphorical renderings of the internet rather than on empirical studies. Silver notes that the early studies of cyberculture were marked by a 'limited dualism and use of the internet-as-frontier metaphor' (2000: 19). He characterizes a second wave of studies as cybercultural studies wherein the emphases were 'virtual communities' and manifestations of identities in online interactions. These studies were largely uncritical and tended toward a tone of enthusiasm. Most noteworthy for our purposes are Howard Rheingold's (1993) study of virtual communities and Sherry Turkle's (1995) study of identity in the age of the internet. Each author extends the metaphor of a frontier and renders this particular frontier a place where people will be freed from the limitations of space and place and the shackles of ascribed characteristics (gender, ethnicity, race, age, physical ability, and so on) that accompany face-to-face interaction.

Discourses of expansion and liberation: a brave sexual frontier

Regarding sexual expression and practice, scholars and users alike embraced the enthusiastic writings of Rheingold and Turkle and began to talk about the internet as a site for expanding the opportunities to meet people across geographic boundaries. For individuals and activists who identified with marginalized sexual and/or gender positions, the internet was embraced as a 'new space' for forming community. Online bulletin boards provided much greater opportunity for gaining information about alternative sexualities and links to others with similar interests (these links usually leading to chat rooms and IRC activities). Similarly, the internet was also characterized as a 'virtual world' wherein one could try on different gender and sexual identities. Bruckman (1992) enthusiastically dubbed the internet an 'identity workshop'. The internet was also touted as a welcoming space for persons who may feel ostracized in traditional face-to-face dating venues for reasons such as attractiveness, physical ability, and so forth. In these early discussions, the internet was predicted to be a 'brave new frontier' in which more people would be able to 'do it', and do it in less restrictive and exciting new ways.

These speculative discussions of the liberating benefits of the internet as an expanded sexual frontier were followed by a spate of empirical studies which are useful in so far as they attempt to describe what persons are actually doing when they are engaged in internet sexual activities. Several of these studies can be classified together in terms of research on the use and consequences of the internet for sexually marginalized groups and individuals (for example, Correll, 1995; Shaw, 1997; Berry and Martin, 2000). These studies emphasize the significance of the internet in facilitating encounters between people whose marginalized sexualities may limit face-to-face encounters, especially people who are not in large urban areas and who do not have access to public queer spaces. The authors of these studies also point to the role of the internet in facilitating self-expression among persons who feel sexually stigmatized. Shaw, for example, comments that for many people gay male-oriented chat rooms and IRC offer a welcome alternative to the gay bar. For many men who do not feel comfortable in public gay settings, IRC 'presents an opportunity for gay men, who often go through life hiding this most vital aspect of their identity, to try on this real identity' (1997: 144).

Related studies highlight these 'identity-liberating' features of sexually oriented internet sites and also focus on the internet as venue for sexual social support. Adelman (2002), for example, explores what she terms 'the sexual justice benefits of internet sex'. In an interview-based study of internet sex work, she looks at the ways in which persons 'discover' their 'online sexual self' and, subsequently, learn to 'transfer' this 'online sexual self' to a 'real life sexual self' (see Hamman, 1996). To this end, she views internet sex work as a therapeutic activity which is highly beneficial for liberated sexual expression on- and offline.

Shapiro (in press) makes the claim that the internet has been a central factor in the recent history of transgender activism. She interviews several transgender activists, all of whom describe the significance of the internet as a basis for dispensing information, organizing across geographical boundaries, and providing opportunities for persons to explore transgender identities in a safe space. This kind of study is indicative of the emphasis in the literature on the internet as a venue in which identities are liberated and communities are able to emerge.

In sum, these empirical studies take up the same enthusiastic tone as the early theoretical and philosophical discussions. They applaud the potentially anonymous and disinhibiting features of online sexual engagement, as well as the chance to 'play' with various forms of sexual expression and identity. These studies also make claims for the significance of the internet as a basis for providing information, social support and opportunities for organizing and activism among sexually marginalized people. To this end, it can be said that in these studies the internet is rendered a brave new *space* for liberated expressions and practices, and a significant technologically for distributing information and bringing people together.

Discourses of protection and regulation: the 'perilous dangers' of cybersex

The previous empirical studies and related theoretical discussions are focused on groups and individuals who are perceived to have been denied access to traditional embodied sexual arenas (for reasons of physical ability and/or attractiveness, for example), or who identify with marginalized sexualities, which has made it more difficult to find venues for sexual exploration. In contrast, the literature of 'concern' regarding internet sexual practices tends to focus on the vast reach of the

9.2 Sex tips in cyberspace, courtesy of *anneandcathy.com*

pornography industry, its use by men searching for 'masturbatory enhancement material' (such as online pornographic text and imagery), engaging in criminal practices such as paedophiliac 'grooming', or suffering from 'sexual addiction'.

A great deal of this literature has been generated by 'concerned' journalists and politicians, and is rarely grounded in any empirical or theoretical research. In these commentaries, the 'frontier' of internet sexuality is a perilous and danger-ous place. The central discourse that emerges from these texts is that these are dangers from which we should be protected. They usually include a call for regu-lation of some sort or another. Some of the potential evils include sexual stalking (especially of young people) and sexual recruiting (luring young people into com-promising sexual entanglements) (Freeman-Longo, 2000). In the USA, the call for protection and regulation far exceeds the existence of empirical information doc-umenting the veracity of these concerns. Some cautious estimates indicate that the incidence of internet sex crimes may be no greater than related sex crimes that occur in physical public places (although this does not in itself mean we *shouldn't* worry about it, of course). With regard to the risk of sex crimes perpetuated against young people, criminologists repeatedly point out that the most likely per-petrator is still someone known to the child – usually a family friend or relative (see Levine, 2002, for a review). But this information seems to have done little to stem the rising tide of concerned voices who fear the internet may be a 'dark and corrupting force', precisely because it is an uncharted sexual frontier (see Stern and Handel, 2001).

One noteworthy body of literature, primarily written by clinical researchers in psychology and social work, deals with the question of sex addiction. In this recent and prolific line of research, authors acknowledge that internet sexual services may have many benefits, especially in terms of the potential for anonymity and disinhibition (Griffiths, 2000). Still, internet-related sexual addiction is presumed to be a real phenomenon. In a critical evaluation of this literature Griffiths concedes that there is no hard evidence that online sexual addiction does, in fact, exist. He argues, however, that this is due to the lack of a specific and commonly used definition of online sexual addiction. He offers his own definition of the core components of addiction: salience (when the factor becomes the most important aspect of the person's life); mood alteration; problems withdrawing; and conflict with self/others regarding extensive internet sexual activity (Griffiths, 1996).

Our intent is not to dismiss the possibility that excessive online sexual activity may be a source of distress to some individuals and to those around them, nor that the internet holds the potential for criminal sexual activity. However, what we find remarkable about this literature is the language used to describe various activities and expressions. In these discussions there is little enthusiasm for internet sexual activity. Instead, an underlying assumption is that *unless* one is sexually ostracized or physically challenged in some way, there is no good reason for engaging in internet sexual activities. The clinical literature focuses on 'explanations' for why someone would want to engage in 'cybersex' and/or 'cyber relationships'. The accepted explanations seem to be that online sexuality is appealing because it is anonymous and disinhibiting (Cooper, 1998; Joinson, 1998; Young, 1998). This may be a good thing for men who suffer from sexual performance anxieties and women who feel that they are not allowed to explore their full sexuality because it is either considered inappropriate or because they feel physically undesirable (Young, 1998). To this end, a little dabbling is fine. But for the most part, this literature is organized explicitly around the idea that the very features that may make internet sex so attractive – affordability, accessibility and anonymity (Cooper (1998) refers to this as the 'Triple A Engine') – are also the basis for potentially damaging and pathological behaviour.

There is considerable discussion regarding the problems with 'escape'. Schwartz and Southern (2000), for example, conclude that the desire to 'escape' (from the 'real' world?) is a possible indication of 'dissociative reenactment and affect regulation'. Far from being an exciting new space to meet others like oneself, they see 'cybersex as the new tearoom for meeting anonymous partners and engaging in a fantasy world' wherein a person engages in 'secretive illicit sex on the computer and then goes to bed with a spouse without dissonance or discomfort'. This literature repeatedly points to the anonymity of internet sex as a 'consistent factor underlying excessive use' (Griffiths, 1995; Young, 1998). Anonymity is considered additionally problematic in that it leads to the desire to 'lie' about identity and to 'desire' multiple partners. In these discussions, much of what is seen as positive in the 'brave frontier' literature (for instance, the ability to 'experiment' and 'liberate' identities, and have access to multiple partners) is a source of potential pathology.

CRITICAL CONSIDERATIONS

In preparing this chapter, we have been repeatedly struck with the connections between the controversies regarding internet sex and the debates regarding online communication generally. By way of conclusion we offer a brief critical consideration of three of these tensions: alienation, reinforcement of stereotypes, and sexual liberty.

Alienation and disembodiment?

One tension reflected in these discourses is the question of what computer-mediated communication is 'doing' to us. Does online sexual activity really provide an instructive and liberating playground or is it a potentially damaging form of escape? This question anchors many of the scholarly explorations of online communication. It can be summarized in terms of the standard modern question of technology as alienating or expanding for the human experience.

Internet sexual practices in particular are seen as having the potential to alienate us from our embodied selves. This is a complicated debate that reflects limited metaphors based on a mind/body dichotomy. We do not have the space here to review this debate other than to note that it has spurred an intriguing discussion about the connection between the mind, the body and technologies. If nothing else, this particular debate is at least opening the way for expanded metaphors regarding these connections – metaphors that better express the mutual interplay between mental and physical activity and development (see Stone, 1991; O'Brien, 1998). Future inquiries into internet sex, especially those interested in the interpersonal and social implications of this activity, must critically assess some of the assumptions that underlie these concerns regarding alienation and disembodiment. To this end, a pivotal discussion is the debate regarding whether internet sex is 'real' sex; see, for instance, McRae (1996) and Shaw (1997), who both make the case that online sex actually 'magnifies' or 'enhances' the mind/body connection.

Cultural expansion or a reinforcement of stereotypes: 'a crisis of imagination'

A related tension, one that reflects critical scholarship generally, is the question of whether the forms of communication and the types of expression that are emerging in online sexual activities reinforce or challenge socially restrictive stereotypes.

Are internet chat rooms and IRC really an occasion for identity play or just one more venue for reinforcing Barbie and Ken-like images of what is considered desirable?

Initially enthusiastic discourses of the potential of the internet to break down stereotypes relied on the assumptions that, first, online communication transcends the body and physical geography entirely, and, second, that once these physical 'limitations' have been transcended, we really will be free to meet others and present ourselves just as we wish. Cautious critics of this perspective point out that even the most liberated playgrounds have some rules or expectations for interaction. Without an idea of what is expected, interaction grinds to a confused halt. People don't know what to do with one another. Given this, it's likely that people will bring in pre-existing cultural scripts, especially in the form of existing stereotypes for attractiveness, sexual expression and practices. With regard to gender and sexuality, O'Brien (1998) has argued that the initial internet hype ('be anyone you want to be, there are no closets in cyberspace') was situated in a problematic logic which naïvely assumes that people will not drag preconceived notions of attraction and arousal into cyber interactions.

Critical race theories have taken up a similar theme. Chon (2000) and Sharpe (1999) wrote similar critiques regarding the hype surrounding the (de)racialization of online interactions. Countering the prediction that race would lose its salience as a mark of identity, both authors make the case that it is much more likely that the traditionally unmarked race, whiteness, would become the default race yet again. Sharpe suggests that the problem is not the theories of cultural expansion *per se*, but lies with the failure to recognize what she calls a 'crisis of imagination'. She acknowledges that internet engagement *could be* an occasion to 'help reformulate some of the preconceptions about race and the racialized subject' (ibid.: 193). However, she emphasizes that in the absence of alternative racial formulations, there is no reason to assume that we won't 'carry the same borders into virtual space'. O'Brien (1998) develops a similar thesis with an emphasis on the fact that even when people want to engage in radical sexual and gender practices, they're often not sure how to do so. They want to be different but cannot imagine what this might be like. And supposing someone is able to present an unexpected (i.e. alternative) sexual identity, will others know how to respond?

Our observation is that there is considerable expansion taking place in internet sexual forums. Many cultural scripts are being challenged, especially with regard to the traditional braiding together of gender and sexuality. At the same time, there is also a considerable re-entrenchment of existing stereotypes and cultural forms of sexual behaviour (including sexual harassment; see Kendall, 2002). Sharpe's comments regarding a 'crisis of imagination' are especially applicable to sexual expression and activity. For alternative sexual expressions and practices to take hold, there needs to be a coalescing of a critical mass of alternative voices and expressions. Whether this is likely to occur depends both on a stretching of imagination, and on who has access to sites of sexual expression. Clearly this is a subject that deserves careful empirical research.

Libertus quirkus: a question of sexual liberty

A third consideration is the question of sexual liberty. Our central observation throughout this chapter is that all of the emerging discourses on internet sexuality reflect long-standing debates regarding sexual liberation versus containment. These reflect underlying assumptions of what sexuality is and how it should be organized. What is sex? What is acceptable sex? Who can engage in it? With whom? The Latin phrase *libertus quirkus* means, literally, the freedom to be quirky. Many of the controversies surrounding internet sex can be viewed in terms of the question: who has the freedom to be sexually quirky? All cultures have definitions and boundaries regarding acceptable sexual practices. These practices usually grant sexual licence to some classes of people and deny it to others. In the history of modern culture, sexual experimentation is tolerated, perhaps even encouraged, among the upper classes, but tends to be a source of shame and silence in the middle classes, and seen as a sign of moral corruption among the working classes (see D'Emilio and Freedman, 1997; Foucault, 1990; Gay, 1998; Tannahill, 1992). In addition to seeing themselves as beyond the reach of middle-class morality (the case of Bill Clinton notwithstanding), the rich and powerful have the *means* to engage in a wide variety of sexual activities. For instance, it is much easier to carry on an affair without raising the suspicion of your spouse and neighbours if you have access to hotels and the opportunity to travel. Thus, the freedom to engage in sexual play can be seen, at least to some extent, as a matter of access.

In this regard, the internet does indeed have a potentially democratizing and decolonizing effect on the *organization* of sexuality. People who have internet access (which is also a matter of class) have access to considerably expanded opportunities to engage in sexual discourse, view sexual imagery, and find others with similar sexual interests. Those who wish to see more sexual liberty granted to everyone obviously see this expanded access as a positive development. Those who view sexuality as something that should be contained (i.e. within the bonds of a monogamous marriage between two people who share a face-to-face relationship) and/or as a form of expression that is potentially dangerous if not regulated, view the internet as a threatening development. To this end, it can be said that the regulatory discourses are driven by cultural ideals of heteronormativity. Activities that do not conform to these standards are seen to need regulation and policing. This discourse reflects an old cultural story whereby sexuality is a kind of 'beast within' that must be tamed lest it overwhelm individual and collective civilization. Framed more positively but still in terms of containment, sexuality is intended to be an expression of something special and/or sacred. From this perspective, internet sexuality is seen as one more element contributing to the erosion of our romantic ideals.

Regardless of your views on this, another fact is that computer-mediated sex does indeed change the *forms* through which we relate to one another. Concerns about 'loss of romance', 'disembodiment' and 'alienation' are probably moot at this point in time. Sexual imagery and practice have long been removed from the discourses of romance. Despite perceptions of an attitude of sexual liberation in the media generally, most sexual repertoires continue to be organized around exploitation discourses, patriarchal discourses, and discourses of silence and shame. Expanded opportunities ('workshops') for sexual practices and sexual identities, such as those that may exist on internet sites, are quite possibly a cultural improvement – or at least an occasion for rewriting existing sexual stories. In our assessment, the internet is already facilitating a reorganization and a revisioning of the ways we think about sex and the ways we practise sex. We already are 'doing it' differently. There is indeed more freedom for more people to be sexually quirky. And as has always been the case, this expanded freedom, especially across social classes, is shadowed by expressions of sexual panic manifest in calls for regulation. How sexually quirky we might actually become, and with what consequences, will continue to be matters of both politics and imagination.

USEFUL WEBSITES

Anne and Cathy: www.anneandcathy.com

Two women dedicated to educating people about healthy, safe sex, with information dissemination, tips and online sex guides.

BananaGuide: www.bananaguide.com

'The gay man's guide to sex on the Net', providing information on all aspects of the gay adult Web including a directory of free sites, pay site reviews, advice on meeting men online, weekly sex news, and more.

Clean Sheets: www.cleansheets.com

A weekly magazine devoted to encouraging and publishing quality erotic fiction, poetry, and art, providing honest information and thoughtful commentary on sexuality to the public, and fostering an ongoing discussion of sexuality in the lives of individuals and in a global society.

Cyborgasms: An Ethnography of Cybersex in AOL Chat Rooms: www.socio.demon.co.uk/Cyborgasms.html

A Master's dissertation by Robin B. Hamman of the University of Essex, UK. The author focuses on the issue of cybersex as it relates to cyborg theory. The discussion includes the sociological methods used, narrow bandwidth vs wide bandwidth communication, and case studies of three actual cybersex participants. It also offers a bibliography of sources relating to the topic.

Feminists for Free Expression: www.ffeusa.org

A diverse group of feminists working to preserve the individual's right and responsibility to read, listen, view and produce materials of her choice, without the intervention of the state 'for her own good'.

Chapter 10

ART IN CYBERSPACE: THE DIGITAL AESTHETIC

MARK ANDREJEVIC

If art is a creative, expressive way of organizing information of all kinds, from words and images to body movements, the internet provides artists with a vast new palette of possibilities. Consider, for example, a collaborative artwork called 'Listening Post' that transforms the streams of data generated by thousands of people typing away in chat rooms, online forums and search engines into a symphony of sounds that pulse in time with the flow of data. Thanks to sophisticated algorithms, 'computers analyze the chatter and convert that mass of statistical data into dense chords or a resonant drone that represents the underlying patterns in the online communication' (Mirapaul, 2001a). The result is that someone clacking anonymously at a keyboard becomes an unwitting participant in the creation of a data-driven musical composition. Designed by a New York artist and a research statistician, 'Listening Post' encapsulates several (but by no means all) of the characteristic elements of the digital aesthetic: interactivity, the ability of digitization to transform one medium (words) into another (sound), and the open-ended and evolving form of the final work.

From Daedalus to Dada, artists have experimented with the creative possibilities of the technologies of their time, and the recent burst of creative activity online is no different. Digital technologies have made inroads into every type of artistic practice from poetry and sculpture to dance and film, providing new examples of the complex relationship between art, technology and society. In the modern era, artists have often been hailed for anticipating the potential of new technologies by exploring the ways of understanding and responding to the world these technologies make possible. The result is that social and technological changes come to be associated over time with a particular aesthetic, such as that of high modernism (which typically includes artists such as Picasso and the architect Le Corbusier) or the so-called postmodern aesthetic (Andy Warhol and Frank Gehry, for example). The rather broad and open-ended way in which I am using the word 'aesthetic' hearkens back to its roots in the Greek word for sense perception, suggesting a unique way of organizing our experience of the world. Keeping this in mind, one question facing internet scholars regards the relationship between digital artworks composed or performed online and the historical moment in which they emerge. Is there a particular aesthetic associated with cyberspace, and if so, how does it reflect (upon) and expand our understanding of the information society? The emerging world of internet art does indeed exhibit signs of having its own aesthetic – one based on an exploration of the capabilities of new media and their role in an information-saturated world. Indeed, internet art provides a fruitful vantage-point for thinking about new technology precisely because it can reflect upon the social significance of the medium itself. Catalogues of digital artworks repeatedly invoke one or another of the 'themes' of new media: their ability to foster a sense of virtual community, to create virtual worlds, to enable long-distance collaboration, or to discern patterns in incomprehensibly large amounts of data. However, the danger of abstracting the world of art from that of everyday life is that it allows people to make celebratory claims about the creative potential of new media without taking into account how the technology is being used every day in stores, factories and schools. When we celebrate the interactive potential or the community-building capability of new media in the abstract, we lend weight to the claims of those who tell us that the ability to shop online or to design one's own sneakers on a corporate webpage is empowering. When we uncritically champion the claim that new technologies will set us free, we run the risk of blithely surrendering that freedom to Microsoft.

Indeed, perhaps the defining characteristic of the digital aesthetic – one that emerges in various forms in several of the following sections – is the portrayal of cyberspace as a realm of freedom from material constraint. In cyberspace, artists are liberated from the laws of physics: virtual sculptures can be built that defy the laws of gravity, music can be created that would be impossible for the human voice to sing. In cyberspace, or so the story goes, we will eventually construct a second nature whose only limits are those of the human imagination. This is the somewhat psychedelic world Holtzman evokes in his pioneering discussion of digital art: 'I think of unbounded worlds of intense kaledioscopic images ... abstract three-dimensional mandalas existing only in the ethereal realm of cyberspace ... I imagine the possibilities of a world free of physical constraints and made from the infinitely malleable material of the virtual' (1997: 41). Other predictions are somewhat less abstract, portraying a future in which humans can transcend the limits of their bodies by plugging into a virtual reality that allows them to share physical sensations with others and to escape any and all of the constraints of physical embodiment without, paradoxically, losing physical sensation. In such virtual worlds, humans get to play creator (in all senses of the word) by virtue of their power to build 'a future where evolving artificial and intelligent life-forms will populate vibrant digital worlds' (ibid.: 99). In short, cyberspace is portrayed as the externalization of fantasy: what used to be possible only in the mind can be 'realized' in cyberspace. The following sections explore some of the forms these fantasies are taking.

INTERACTIVITY AND THE FATE OF THE AUTHOR

Unlike more traditional forms of art, which relegate audiences to the role of spectator or listener, online art exploits the interactivity of new media to encourage viewers, readers and listeners to do more than just observe. The online project 'Turns' (www.myturningpoint.com), for example, invites viewers to contribute personal narratives about events that changed their lives. The content of the work is provided by viewers willing to divulge (or invent) the details of dramatic events in their lives, and includes personal tales of illegal abortion, love lost and found, and life in wartime London. Viewers can peruse intimate glimpses into the lives of others, whose stories are sorted by categories such as 'accidents/trauma', 'finance' and 'family/growing up'. The result is an intriguing form of anonymous voyeurism: viewers collect tidbits of the emotional lives of strangers, and are encouraged, in turn, to share their own traumas and triumphs. The 'Turns' website describes itself as a 'new type of social collaboration' made possible by the ability of the internet to foster a sense of online community. At the same time, the site raises questions about just how communal it is to share personal stories with strangers in an anonymous forum. It also challenges the modernist conception of creativity as the sole province of the solitary genius creating works to be appreciated – but not touched – by the masses.

If audiences participate in the creative process, how does this alter their relationship to the artist? The use of hypertext links, for example, invites audiences to help construct their aesthetic experience in tangible ways. Murray argues that hypertext works transform the role of the viewer into that of the interactor, who, 'whether as navigator, protagonist, explorer, or builder, makes use of this repertoire of possible steps and rhythms to improvise a particular dance among the many, many possible dances the author has enabled' (1997: 153). The role of the hypertext author is to write 'the rules by which the texts appear as well as writing the texts themselves. It means writing the rules for the interactor's involvement' (ibid.: 152–3). The text is no longer fixed, but the rules whereby it operates are. The *process* becomes the author-supplied content.

If viewers take an active role in helping to create the artwork, as in the case of a work like 'Turns' – whose title invokes both the idea of turning points and of taking turns – the hierarchical relationship between creator and audience is ostensibly undermined. Moreover, thanks to the infinite reproducibility of digital works, audience members are often invited to take a copy home. Some of the artworks discussed in this chapter (including Mary Flanagan's '[collection]' and Ray

Kurzweil's Cybernetic Poet) are programs that can be downloaded by anyone with internet access. The ability to download art makes it seem more accessible, perhaps less mysterious and unattainable. Lovejoy (1989), drawing on the work of German literary critic Walter Benjamin, argues that infinitely reproducible digital artworks help undermine the 'aura' associated with pre-digital works that remain guarded, like the *Mona Lisa*, in museums that inspire the awe and humility associated with churches or temples.

Taken together, the active role of the audience and the de-mystification of the artwork have been used to suggest that the digital aesthetic is democratizing: more people can participate in and experience creative works. They can access art the same way they get their e-mail and the online newspaper. Thus, Lanham argues that the digital aesthetic, with its emphasis on process, participation and flexibility counters the 'oppressive' nature of the Western artistic tradition itself: 'The traditional idea of an artistic canon brings with it, by the very "immortality" it strives for, both a passive beholder and a passive reality waiting out there to be perceived' (1993: 38). Digital art, by contrast, promotes viewing as an active, transformative process: 'All of this yields a body of work active not passive, a canon not frozen in perfection, but volatile with contending human motive. Is this not the aesthetic of the personal computer?' (ibid.: 51). It is not difficult to see how this assessment of the digital aesthetic underwrites the notion that the internet is a medium that empowers users and challenges traditional forms of authority. This notion is a popular one, but it endows the technology with a power all its own, and fails to take into account the important role played by those who decide how it will be implemented. Even potentially empowering capabilities can be undermined by human choices.

As a society, we have criticized top-down, hierarchical organizations as undemocratic for so long we tend to forget participation is not necessarily politically progressive. For an alternative portrayal of the deployment of interactivity, consider Komar and Melamid's 'The Most Wanted Paintings on the Web' (www.diacenter.org/km/), a series of paintings manufactured according to the dictates of market research. The artists polled residents of several countries (including a separate category they listed just as 'the Web') in order to determine what colours, subject matter and style of painting consumers preferred. They then used viewer preferences to paint a customized set of artworks for each country. The works, on the whole, have the drab and random character of art designed by committee, and are unlikely to capture the imagination of the audiences who 'helped' design them. The real achievement of the project is that, by self-consciously enlisting the tools of market research, the artists wittily challenge the idea that 'interactivity' will enable audiences to access the material of their dreams. As their website puts it, the point was to raise the question: 'What kind of culture is produced by a society that lives and governs itself by opinion polls?' The advent of interactive

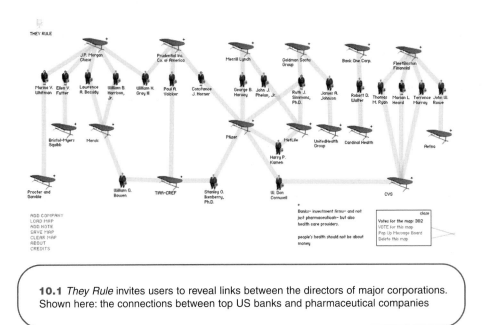

10.1 *They Rule* invites users to reveal links between the directors of major corporations. Shown here: the connections between top US banks and pharmaceutical companies

media forces us to examine more closely the promise of participation and to ask which forms of interactivity pose a challenge to oppressive hierarchies, and which amount to little more than candy-coated market research. Another critical project, Josh On's *They Rule* (www.theyrule.net), uses the information-sharing capacity of the internet to attempt to chart the overlapping board of directors of major US corporations. The site paints a fascinating portrait of the corporate ties between some of the most connected members of the 'power elite', and allows users to contribute by creating annotated maps describing the connections between particular corporations and individuals. The participation is meant to be political and, presumably, empowering: to expose the structure of an ultra-concentrated ruling class.

CYBERSPACE AND THE AUTONOMOUS ARTWORK

The ultimate form of empowerment offered by the digital aesthetic, however, is the paradoxical promise to overcome the limitations associated with humans themselves. Thus, one of the recurring themes of digital art is its freedom not only from the laws of the physical world – but from its creators. Computer programs that can compose their own music and artworks and that can 'evolve' over time are recurring themes in the new media art world. Robertson goes so far as to argue that the perfection of digital audio will render human performers and musicians obsolete:

> many musical forms are already enhanced by digital recording technology to
> the point that they are significantly better than what can be produced by
> human performers ... Eventually audience expectations will outstrip what even
> the finest and most talented performers are capable of achieving.
>
> (1998: 150)

Exhibiting the disdain for the flesh that has become a recurring theme in the world of cyberspace, he portrays this as a step forward, not only in terms of efficiency, but in terms of quality. Robertson points out, for example, that computers tend to be a lot more reliable and a lot less temperamental than humans. He envisions a day in which digital actors will replace the all-too-human ones: 'The next logical step from synthesized dinosaurs is computer-synthesized human actors ... Eventually it will eliminate the problems related to temperamental actors and their attendant high salaries' (ibid.: 152). (It's worth noting that Roberston adopts a particular perspective – that of the producers – when he describes high salaries as 'a problem'.) The first step toward the fully computer-generated movie has already been taken with *Final Fantasy: The Spirits Within*, a science-fiction adventure whose promoters boasted that 'No real locations, people, vehicles or props were used' in the making of the movie (www.finalfantasy.com). Robertson might be gratified, but what about the 'problems' associated with temperamental programmers?

The ultimate fantasy of the creative imagination is not just the ability to generate a separate reality, but to breathe life into it: hence the fascination of the digerati with artificial intelligence and artworks that can compose or create on their own. Holtzman (1997) describes, for example, a computer program that can be used to create new compositions 'in the style of' Mozart or J.S. Bach, drawing on algorithms derived from a close examination of the composers' works. Taken to the limit, procedural authorship refers not only to the creation of the rules for interactions, but to algorithms which can then generate compositions. Ray Kurzweil, who claims that we live at the dawn of 'the age of the cybernetic artist' (1999: 159), has created a program that generates original poetry based on other poems it has analysed. He provides several examples of the Cybernetic Poet's compositions, including this (approximation of a) haiku:

> Scattered sandals
> A call back to myself
> So hollow I would echo
>
> (ibid.: 166)

Although Kurzweil's poet does little to support his assertion that the creative potential of computers will one day surpass that of humans, it does highlight the fascination with artificial intelligence that haunts the digital imaginary: the desire to transcend human creativity itself.

10.2 Mary Flanagan's '[collection]' shows the dreamworld of networked computers – all kinds of files tumble through cyberspace

Can the digital aesthetic be broad enough to incorporate such seemingly mutually exclusive tendencies as autonomy *and* interactivity? In fact, these attributes are not as contradictory as they might seem. Artworks like 'Listening Post' use the interactions of unwitting participants to compose unpredictable musical patterns. Similarly, Mary Flanagan's '[collection]' uses the data stored in the hard drives of the computers on which it is installed to create an eerie 'networked collective unconscious' (www.maryflanagan.com/collection.htm) of words and images that float across the computer screen, dredged up from the computer's memory in random patterns. Like the subconscious processes it is meant to echo, '[collection]' takes the information with which we provide it and imbues it with a 'life' of its own.

The combination of interactivity and autonomy is a recurring theme not only of digital art, but of the online economy envisioned by corporate futurists who imagine a world in which 'smart' programs that monitor our habits may come to know our wants and needs better than we do. Bill Gates (1996), for example, suggests that consumers will not only avail themselves of 'intelligent agents' to seek out low prices for goods and services, but will eventually let their computers monitor their shopping habits in order to provide shopping suggestions. This scenario leads one to start asking for whom the agent is actually working:

> From time to time, your software agent will try to persuade you to fill out a
> questionnaire about your tastes. The questionnaire might include all sorts of
> images in an effort to draw subtle reactions out of you ... The information you
> furnish will go into a profile of your tastes, which will guide the agent
>
> (1996: 191)

As in the case of the artworks described above, the consumer provides the raw
data, but the computer does the 'work'. In gathering a measure of autonomy, the
machines offer to leave the flesh behind – for its own good.

Placed within its social context, the celebration of digital autonomy warrants critical examination. It is not hard to understand the appeal that a virtual 'world'
freed from the constraints of nature might have for a species that has long been
frustrated by the limits of its far-too-frail flesh. But we need to be careful not to
take the claims of autonomy at face value. Indeed, Kurzweil seems engaged in a
bit of sleight of hand when he calls the algorithm he has created a 'poet': he has
downplayed his own creative role in designing the algorithm and shaping its
creations. This same sleight of hand conceals the economic interests behind the
creation of 'intelligent' agents that offer to guide us through the Web and help us
decide what to watch, listen to and buy. The danger of a facile celebration of the
potential of artificial intelligence is that it distracts us from the humans behind
the curtain, pulling the levers.

CONVERGENCE AND DIGITAL DE-DIFFERENTIATION

It might be possible to summarize the aspects of the digital aesthetic introduced
above by observing that digital art challenges conventional distinctions between,
for example, artist and audience, reality and fantasy, and even human and
machine. The digital medium seems appropriate for this kind of challenge, since
it allows for an unprecedented degree of convergence, or de-differentiation,
between media. In cyberspace, the material differences between art forms such as
painting and music, and even between materials such as oil paint and pastel, are
all subsumed to the universal medium of the bit. Thanks to this medium, the
boundary between genres continues to blur, since online artworks often combine
text with graphics, animation, video and music, and may someday be able to
include data for the remaining senses (perhaps the 'feelies' of *Brave New World* are
not far off). In the meantime, works of online fiction like Erik Loyer's *The Lair of
the Marrow Monkey* (www.marrowmonkey.com) use both music and animation to
reinforce narrative effects. In a chapter describing the narrator's inability to sleep
in a sultry hotel room, for example, the viewer's mouse controls a moveable letter
'i', and wherever the 'i' goes, a circle marked 'deafening heat' follows it and surrounds it. Circles marked 'home' and 'rest' move away from the 'i', and the music

evokes the sounds of an insomniac night: droplets of sweat hitting the sheets.

The de-differentiation associated with digital artworks is also spatial: artworks that can be viewed in museums and galleries (like several of the works described in this chapter), can also be viewed in the privacy of the home. As the gallery comes to the home, the home simultaneously comes into the gallery in works like 'Turns' that invite viewers to participate in a shared, public work via modem. Not surprisingly, in an era when we are increasingly watched by the machines that we watch, the reconfigured boundary between public and private is a recurring theme of interactive artworks. Consider the example of a pair of Italian performance artists who have taken their act online with a website (www.0100101110101101.org) that invites the world into their home computer, which they describe as an externalization of their emotional and intellectual lives complete with their writings, e-mail and music files (Mirapaul, 2001b). Similarly, webcam artist Ana Voog (www.anacam.com; see Snyder, 2000), uses digital cameras to turn her home into a stage for her performances, sharing with viewers the details of her private life in her online journals. This transformation of one's home into a stage echoes the de-differentiation enabled by digital media in the economic sphere: the transformation of home, airport, café and any other 'wired' space into a workplace.

Pushing the privacy limit in a different direction, the techno-music artist The Spacewürm, who describes himself as a 'digital voyeur', has composed music based on intercepted mobile phone conversations woven together digitally. The conversations he taps into provide the thrill of voyeurism: we hear the intimate words of a woman comforting a jealous lover overlaid with a conversation between two men casually planning to start a fight. Against the background of such works, the burgeoning trend of reality TV demonstrates its kinship to the world of new media interactivity. In both cases participation often comes in the form of self-disclosure: the sharing of personal data. The fact that this kind of participation is something anyone can do helps call into question one more boundary: that between art and life. If my e-mail messages are contributing to the creation of a symphony, if my phone calls appear in a techno composition, I'm part of the creative process whether I'm working in my office or talking to friends and relatives. Moreover, if computers connect people to the art world as easily as to the shopping mall, the opportunities for participation in the creative process expand exponentially. MIT Media Lab guru Nicholas Negroponte has argued that, thanks to the internet, art will be increasingly integrated into daily life: 'Tomorrow people of all ages will find a more harmonious continuum in their lives, because, increasingly, the tools to work with and the toys to play with will be the same. There will be a more common palette for love and duty, self-expression and group work' (1995: 221). Perhaps, but we should be wary about the notion that all we have to do to foster creativity is to equip ourselves with the appropriate – that is to say, interactive –

technology. Otherwise, instead of a vibrant new world of enhanced creativity, we're in danger of recreating the one we've got and calling it art.

 USEFUL WEBSITES

Artport: The Whitney Museum's Portal to Net Art: www.whitney.org/artport

A museum site that doubles as an online gallery space for commissioned internet art projects. Artport includes gateways to featured artists, an archive of online works and links to other digital art resources.

Critical Art Ensemble: www.critical-art.net/

Online access to projects created by a group devoted to politically motivated projects that mine the connection between art, technology and politics.

Digital Aesthetics Hotlinks: www.ucl.ac.uk/slade/digita/hotlinks.html

The resource page posted by Sean Cubitt in conjunction with his book, *Digital Aesthetics*. Includes links to online artworks, artists and digital art resource sites.

Listening Post: www.earstudio.com/projects/P_subpage/listening_middle.html

Details of an art project that makes music out of the collective 'voices' of data travelling over the internet. The site includes sound samples, project details and statements by the project's creators.

Rhizome: The New Media Art Resource: http://rhizome.org/

An online non-profit organization devoted to discussion and promotion of artworks that incorporate new media technologies. Free online membership allows users to subscribe to e-mail lists, to participate in online discussions, and to submit their own work for inclusion in the site's archives.

Chapter 11

PORNOGRAPHY ONLINE, LESBIAN STYLE

MEREDITH BALDERSTON

With the barriers to entry so low, pornography has found a new life and marketplace online. The high initial costs associated with print publishing and video production have traditionally limited the number of players in the porn industry, and the visibility of differences in production values usually declared who was a major player and who was not (although shoddy production values did not necessarily keep porn start-ups from becoming hugely profitable, as witnessed by Larry Flynt's mega-success with *Hustler*). The revolutionary ease of production and distribution on the World Wide Web has led to an explosion of porn sites run, not just by big corporations like Playboy and Penthouse, but also by housewives, college students and other amateurs. It is often difficult to distinguish between a website run by a large, well-funded company and a site run by one person out of his or her basement or dorm room. With the porn playing field levelled somewhat, there are more women than ever acting as creators and distributors, rather than just models.

While traditional pornography (print and video) has been criticized by some for its allegedly degrading and objectifying depiction of women by and for men, the unique opportunities offered by this new mode of production have affected both the content and consumption of pornography. When women can control production of pornography on a level comparable to their male counterparts, their portrayals can be self-determined, and, thereby, the opportunity arises to articulate a greater diversity of sexualities and sexual practices for women than exists in male-fantasy-as-commodity. Looking at sexually explicit websites provides the opportunity to examine issues of identity, power and control with regards to representation of female sexuality. Such an examination is particularly interesting if those sites are run by women themselves, and if men are largely absent from the sexual depictions. To this end, we shall focus on lesbian porn sites.

So what exactly constitutes 'lesbian' pornography? It can include pornography made *by* self-identified lesbians, pornography made *for* lesbians (by whomever) and pornography *featuring* lesbians (often produced by and for heterosexual men). Since it is the means and manner of production that has been revolutionized by Web technologies, this chapter focuses primarily on sites produced by lesbians, and examines how, if at all, this new medium changes the relationship and importance of women to pornography and vice versa. It is important to note that if a site *claims* to feature or be made by or for lesbians, there is no fail-safe way of ascertaining to any meaningful or consistent degree the 'truth' of such labels and assertions.

WOMEN AND PORN: A BACKGROUND

Pornography has always had a contested place within feminist discourse and has proved to be a divisive issue. Anti-pornography feminists like Andrea Dworkin (1979) and Catharine MacKinnon (1993) argue that pornography demeans and encourages violence against women (creating a rather unexpected alliance between a certain group of feminists and the conservative moral right), but other feminists who identify themselves as anti-censorship or 'pro-sex' feminists (Bright, 1997; Williams, 1999) believe that pornography can allow for positive expression of sexuality. Lesbian porn sites do not fit securely into this dialectic on either side.

There is, in fact, a long history in America of women producing pornography for women. Almost as soon as obscenity laws were established, they were violated by women, partly because sex educational material – explanations of physical changes during adolescence or menopause, and information on birth control – was included in the sphere covered by the laws. In the 1910s, Margaret Sanger was threatened with jail under an early obscenity law (the 1873 Comstock Law) for publishing an educational periodical for women called *The Woman Rebel*, and a 1913 pamphlet on birth control called *What Every Girl Should Know* (Lane, 2000: 17–18; Williams, 1999: 85–6). Though not prurient in nature, Sanger's publications were denounced for their explicitness. Obscenity laws have become more and more lenient, but explicit educational material still runs the risk of being confused with pornography, as happens when Web filters intended to keep porn sites from children's eyes 'catch' and block medical sites with information about breast cancer. Likewise, most filtering software available today restricts access to any kind of gay or lesbian site, regardless of content.

Health education remains an important focus of many feminist groups, and the sexual revolution of the 1970s helped to spark interest in advocating women's explorations of their own sexual desires. This gave rise to Betty Dodson's famous masturbation seminars for women, and Susie Bright's 'sexpert' advice columns in magazines like *Salon* (www.salon.com). The logic of this brand of feminism is that sexual pleasure is an important last frontier where women often still lack the understanding and self-assurance to assert themselves.

In the early 1980s, Bright, along with Nan Kinney and Debi Sundahl, helped found *On Our Backs*, a magazine that promises 'the best of lesbian sex' (originally, it was 'the magazine for the adventurous lesbian') and claims to be the only regularly published lesbian porn magazine in the world. *OOB*, as the magazine is affectionately called by readers, has a website (www.onourbacksmag.com) with the magazine's explicit articles and pictorials, proudly and exclusively featuring 'real' lesbians doing what they really do – make out, play, flirt and have sex. The models' bodies are far from the skinny, white ideal one finds in publications like *Playboy* and *Hustler*. In its spreads, *OOB* features women of colour, women with piercings and tattoos, and women of all shapes, personalities and styles. By portraying a wider variety of women enjoying sensual situations, *OOB* implies that all forms of women's sexuality are natural and worthwhile, and that natural women can be sexy without all the accoutrements of patriarchal capitalism.

REPRESENTATIONS OF FEMININITY

One common criticism of mainstream pornography is that the women featured in it are 'fake' – that is, they have been heavily made-up, surgically 'enhanced' and have had every hair removed from their bodies – and promote an unhealthy and unnatural standard of beauty. In pornographic texts, porn stars are sometimes presented or referred to as ideal women, but a woman – or a man, for that matter – would have to spend copious time, money and energy to achieve this model of ideal womanhood, the net effect of which is to look nothing like a woman looks naturally. Porn stars (and drag queens) can thus be seen as 'hyperreal' women, in that they are 'more real' than reality (Baudrillard, 1994). This 'hyperwomanhood' embodied by traditional porn stars is an exaggerated performance of (socially constructed) femininity (Butler, 1990; Straayer, 1996). The number of female porn stars who currently have breast implants and shaved pubic regions is so overwhelming that a special category of pornography now exists – 'natural' – to denote women with naturally small or large breasts and, sometimes, unshaven genitals. This phenomenon of hyperwomanhood is considerably less prevalent in lesbian porn.

Despite a more visible diversity of women since the sexual revolution, there are still many deeply ingrained expectations, persistent myths and bizarre stereotypes associated with femininity. An example of this is the equation of feminine sexuality with passivity and submission. While the social construction of femininity has been historically limiting, it offers another site of resistance. Since the societal notion of 'what it is to be a woman' is culturally constructed, women who create pornography are in a position to create an alternate concept of femininity and feminine sexuality.

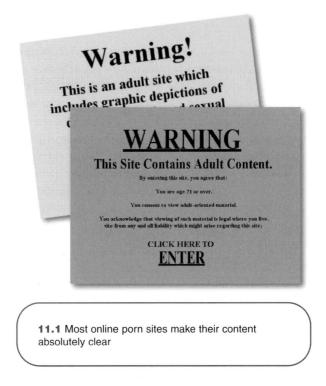

11.1 Most online porn sites make their content absolutely clear

Having the opportunity to construct one's own image, however, does not guarantee a new mode of representation, and some pornography sites made by women are indistinguishable from their man-made counterparts. *Persian Kitty* (www.persiankitty.com), one of the best-known names in Web porn, is in fact owned and operated by a woman. The fact that the site was founded by a Washington State homemaker and mother of two (Lane, 2000: 89) has not kept it from looking 'like pre-Giuliani Times Square' (a common phrase among porn snobs to describe porn sites that are poorly designed and feature lots of ads and pop-up windows), nor made it particularly appealing to women. *Persian Kitty*, however, is primarily a listing service rather than an original content provider, and may not be the best place to look for groundbreaking representations of women.

Other woman-run sites that focus more on original content, like Danni Ashe's *Hard Drive* (www.danni.com) and *Suze Randall's Erotic Photo Gallery* (www.suze.net) look similar to higher-end men's sites. The models they feature tend to be typical examples of porn-star hyperwomanhood – white, tall and slim, with large, often augmented breasts, and long hair on their heads, but little to no hair anywhere else. This could be because both Danni and Suze (and many other successful porn webmistresses) were involved in the pornography industry for years before starting their own websites – Danni as a model and actress, and Suze as a model and then photographer. Their connections to traditional porn may have influenced their style, making their current work still characteristic of traditional porn representation that assumes a male audience.

Meanwhile, *trueLESBIANS* (www.truelesbians.com), an interactive webcam pay site, offers lesbian content ostensibly geared toward a lesbian audience. The couple on the cams is average-looking – neither stereotypically butch nor femme – and plump by mainstream media standards. The site has a 24-hour live feed from five webcams throughout the couple's house, photos from their ventures outside their home, and an online journal by one of the women. By offering themselves and their activities for observation as webcam subjects, these women challenge notions of what kinds of activities are interesting, what activities lesbians engage in, and what can be considered sexy. The fact that the women featured claim to be and identify as true lesbians, not straight women 'acting' for the pleasure of a male audience, is a key component of the site's identity (as the title and domain name suggest).

Lesbian porn sites that loudly and proudly proclaim their status as such tend to stem from the philosophy of pro-sex feminism. Women involved in the production of such sites tend to identify themselves as feminists who actively try to subvert expectations about women and their sexuality. These sites embody a form of activism that promotes sexual health and awareness, and sometimes feature educational sections in addition to sexual entertainment.

HerCurve (www.hercurve.com) is a website that describes itself as 'a community for straight, bi, queer, transgendered women and their partners', although the site began more exclusively as 'an erotic community for queer and transgendered women'. The site offers free content including erotic stories, articles about female sexuality, and interactive forums, as well as pay-personals. The spare design, restrained colour palette and use of relaxed language throughout the site give it a laid-back, but well-organized feel. Though dedicated to sex, *HerCurve* feels more like a webzine than a porn site. This may be partly because 'herSkin' – a section of the site devoted to erotic photography – was eliminated during a redesign.

Strikingly, there is a lot of overlap between sub-genres of lesbian Web porn. It is common in directories of such sites to see the same site listed under several categories. *HerCurve*, for example, might be listed under 'Erotica', 'Webzines' and 'Sexuality Resources', while *OOB* might be classified as 'Pornography', 'Erotica' and 'Webzines'. Many sexually oriented lesbian sites do not fall clearly into a single genre.

WATCHING PORN: THEORIES OF SPECTATORSHIP

Sites like *OOB* and *HerCurve* are an important part of the counter-movement precipitated by the historical (and current) representation of women in all forms of Western (particularly American) popular culture as either desireless, lacking sexual agency, or else dangerous. These characterizations have stigmatized possession and expression of female desire, particularly towards other women. In cinema in particular, several notable film theorists have argued that women are ritually portrayed as objects to be looked at and desired, with the entire industry structured around this fetishistic 'looking'.

Laura Mulvey (1988a, 1988b) uses Sigmund Freud's theories to argue that the spectatorship of women and women's bodies in classical Hollywood cinema is structured by three looks or gazes: (1) that of the camera at the actors; (2) the spectators at the screen; and (3) the actors at each other. The first two are subordinated to the third in an effort to eliminate distance between the spectator and the narrative where all three gazes converge on the body of the female star. The gaze(s) psychologically disempower the woman by fetishizing her image in order to reduce the threat of castration her image represents. Linda Williams (1999) theorizes that porn movies in particular are intended to uncover and display as much as possible the 'mystery' of female sexuality to a male audience.

These theoretical models can be applied to porn in other visual media like photography and the Web. Hardcore porn featuring women – that which shows penetration – can be seen as an attempt to demystify the female body and sexuality for a male spectator by obsessively focusing attention on what is visible. These theories may also account for the existence of some lesbian- and woman-run porn sites that primarily feature the webmistress. A woman may develop exhibitionist tendencies – whereby a person receives pleasure by flagrant display of his or her body – as a psychological mechanism for dealing with the constant gazes of more powerful 'others'. Amateur sites often combine the proprietress's exhibitionist proclivities with an entrepreneurial spirit, though some sites are completely free. One such example is *Glamazon* (www.glamazon.com), a fairly 'vanilla' (uncomplicated) amateur site that's completely free of charge and appears to exist solely for the pleasure of its exhibitionist proprietress.

Though Mulvey's work provides a basis for understanding the tradition of eroticizing and gazing at women and women's bodies, her critics claim that her work, with its reliance on castration anxiety and (male) Oedipal development, does not adequately address the 'problem' of female spectatorship. When these porn sites are intended for other women, straight or gay, Mulvey's model is not very useful for understanding the dynamics of spectatorship.

Judith Mayne (1993) discusses in greater detail ways of thinking about female spectatorship that go beyond the notions of the classical gender division in media, where men produce and consume, and women are merely consumed. While a heterogeneous audience may remain primarily male-identified with regards to the narrative presented, a spectator may be able to inhabit a variety of subject positions within a single narrative. That is to say that an observer/reader/spectator does not always identify with either the intended protagonist, or even a single

11.2 Susie Bright's homepage mixes erotic fiction and sex-positive feminism

character or point of view over the entire course of a text (filmic, literary or otherwise). A heterogeneous theory of spectatorship allows for a 'marginal' spectator – typically understood to be female (Mayne, 1993: 76) – who may read any text against the grain and recode it with subversive meaning (Straayer, 1996). Traditional pornography that is enjoyed or consumed by women can be seen as one such subversive text, where images intended for arousing men are appropriated and used to arouse women. Before the advent of the Web, some lesbians consumed pornography intended for straight men because of the lack of 'appropriate' lesbian texts. In these instances, traditional porn becomes recoded as lesbian porn.

Pornography created by and specifically for women is different, in that its very creation is an act of subversion of an entire textual genre, displacing the moment of resistance from the reception onto the production of the text. Some porn site webmistresses state that they created their own porn sites because they had a hard time finding the kind of porn they wanted to see. The 'editrix' of *HerCurve* writes, 'Why did we create this space? Because, frankly, there just ain't enough sex on the internet already. Not for women, anyway' (www.hercurve.com/stats).

EROTICA VS PORNOGRAPHY

Sometimes even pro-sex feminists share anti-porn feminists' criticism of pornography in view of the abundance of overtly misogynistic portrayals of women as 'semen receptacles' or 'sluts' who want 'to be fucked', rather than as active sexual agents. Mulvey's theory of spectatorship may account for some of this harsh treatment; that is, women are depicted as disempowered (sometimes by pictorial dismemberment, so that a woman is presented as a collection of body parts, not an autonomous whole) in order to negate the threat that they pose to men. It is because of such images and language that some women have difficulty endorsing pornography.

At this point, there are those feminists who, wanting to condemn anything that may perpetuate oppression of or violence against women, yet also wanting to rescue sexual expression for women, introduce alternatives to pornography. Brian McNair proposes that 'pornography is a male creation, and thus a reflection of (misogynistic) male desires and fantasies ... Another category – erotica – can represent sexuality in nonhierarchical, nonsexist, nonsubordinating ways' (1996: 50).

Though objective distinctions between pornography and erotica are elusive, Gloria Steinem differentiates the two thus: 'erotica is about sexuality, but pornography is about power and sex-as-weapon' (McNair, 1996: 50). Both of these categorizations place the onus of exploitation not on the denotative content, but on the connotations of production and reception (including intended market). Hence, a video depicting lesbian sexual activity would be considered pornography if made for men (who cannot seem to get enough lesbian action), yet the same lesbian content would be erotica if made by and for women. Perhaps because of this kind of stigmatization of pornography, erotica has come to be generally associated with women – sexual content for women or by women.

Jane's Net Sex Guide (www.janesguide.com) has a more concrete distinction – 'the difference between erotica and pornography is lighting' – but some people maintain that, in fact, there is no objective difference between the two: one person's erotica is another's pornography, and vice versa. Susie Bright poignantly recalls, 'As I mentioned when it was first published, I masturbated to the Meese Report until I passed out – thank you, taxpayers!' (1997: 77).

McNair hints that the difference may be more semantic than anything else: 'If pornography and obscenity are, as it were, the "evil twins" of the sexuality debate, the word erotica is frequently deployed as a positive counterweight, connoting the healthy, legitimate representation of sex' (1996: 41). This could account for the blurring of categories when it comes to sexually themed lesbian websites.

Along this same line of thought are scholars like Laura Kipnis whose stance is that 'the differences between pornography and other forms of culture are less meaningful than their similarities' (1996: viii). Examining pornography, then, can illuminate key issues of larger culture that have been distilled into a purer form than is elsewhere available. Pornography is made of the same stuff that surrounds all of us everyday – fantasy, power, sex and gender roles, desire and commodification – stripped of the distraction of fluffy filler.

USEFUL WEBSITES

**The Andrea Dworkin Online Library:
www.nostatusquo.com/ACLU/dworkin/**

This is a section of a fan site devoted to one of the most outspoken and prolific anti-pornography feminists. It contains large excerpts from most of Dworkin's published writing, including some pieces co-authored with Catharine MacKinnon.

Concerned Women for America: www.cwfa.org

A public policy women's organization that seeks to promote biblical values, CWFA believes that pornography violates the dignity of human beings created in God's image, and degrades the biblical view of marriage.

CyberDyke Network: www.cyber-dyke.net

A co-operative network of lesbian porn sites, ranging from softcore to hardcore, from written erotica to cartoons to photographs of every style. The sites in the network share an Age Verification System (AVS) that prevents minors from accessing their content and also grants a user access to all sites in the network by joining one of the member sites.

Susie Bright's Home Page: www.susiebright.com

The homepage of one of the original sex-positive feminists, featuring news, a message board, reviews, stories, a photo gallery, tour schedule, book/video/audio store and biography.

Chapter 12

HELP YOURSELF:
THE WORLD WIDE WEB AS
A SELF-HELP AGORA

SHANI ORGAD

> Our modern lives may well be fraught with anxieties and we may well feel in
> the grip of circumstances over which we have little control, yet the internet
> offers individuals many new ways of reimposing new forms of control that are
> more appropriate to our global age.
>
> (Slevin, 2000: 180)

INTRODUCTION

This chapter concerns the question: How do people use the World Wide Web to
help themselves? In popular and academic writings (such as Kraut *et al.*, 1998), the
use of the internet has often been seen as invoking feelings of stress, isolation,
depression and loneliness. For many people, however, the Web is a great source of
self-help – it allows them to engage in different forms of communication and dialogue, enabling them to make social connections and gain emotional, social and
psychological support.

In this chapter, I discuss some of the ways in which people use the Web to help
themselves, for example, to gain support in coping with chronic illness or a
traumatic stage of life. I argue that the use people make of different websites for
self-help plays a significant role in the process of their self-formation and self-
actualization; in particular, their interaction with others online affects their sense
of self in significant ways.

First, I present the theoretical backcloth to the discussion, focusing on the link
between self-help and notions of self-formation (Giddens, 1991) and individualization (Beck and Beck-Gernsheim, 2001). I then provide a brief overview of the
World Wide Web's self-help 'landscape', mapping out the key features of existing
online forms and self-help websites. Next, I discuss three main processes in which

people engage when using the Web for self-help purposes. I then move into look-ing at a particular case study of patients who use the internet to gain support and cope with breast cancer. Based on my research, this case study highlights the sig-nificance of patient-users' online participation in breast cancer websites for the process of their healing. In particular, I show how, by engaging in the online process of narrativization and storytelling (i.e. producing and recounting a narra-tive of the self) patient-users are endowed with powers that enable them to cope with their new life situation.

SELF-HELP, SELF-FORMATION AND INDIVIDUALIZATION

Before getting to grips with people's use of the Web for self-help purposes, it is useful to look at the wider context of individuals' engagement in self-help. People who seek to help themselves are likely to be in a situation of some form of crisis, where their routine is disrupted and the taken-for-granted aspects of their lives are unexpectedly disturbed. In such situations, the process of self-formation and the need for reformulating one's self-identity are fundamentally enhanced.

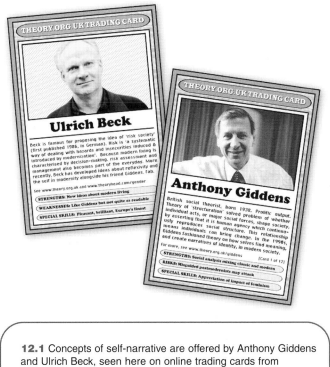

12.1 Concepts of self-narrative are offered by Anthony Giddens and Ulrich Beck, seen here on online trading cards from www.theory.org.uk

Therefore, in cases such as illness, people often attempt to regain normality and a sense of the mundane, and to establish continuity with their 'normal' life before the disturbance imposed by the problem. In other cases, people may decide to change their life course quite radically, having recognized a major emotional dissatisfaction in their lives. These observations are closely connected to Giddens' (1991) concept of the 'reflexive project of the self' and what Beck (Beck and Beck-Gernsheim, 2001) described as the contemporary trend of 'individualization'. Giddens' idea implies that the individual is responsible for what he/she is. In other words, we are what we make of ourselves (1991: 75). 'If they are not to fail,' adds Beck, 'individuals must be able to plan for the long term and adapt to change; they must organize and improvise, set goals, recognize obstacles, accept defeats and attempt new starts' (Beck and Beck-Gernsheim, 2001: 4). Thus, what the individual becomes, especially following a personal crisis, is dependent on their reconstructive endeavours (Giddens, 1991).

People's use of the Web for self-help can be seen as part of their engagement in the 'reconstructive endeavours' of their 'project of the self'. The online space, in its various forms and features, constitutes a key site where such processes of self-formation and self-actualization are facilitated and exercised. This observation is the focus of this chapter. Before moving onto a critical analysis of self-help and the Web, however, it is vital to outline the main features of the online 'landscape' of self-help or, more simply, to address the question: What is happening on self-help websites?

THE SELF-HELP 'LANDSCAPE' ON THE WORLD WIDE WEB

The World Wide Web has become a valued source of self-help for a substantial number of users. The contexts in which people seek self-help on the Web include psychological and identity-related issues (e.g. people who are seeking change in their life), familial matters (e.g. divorce), professional aspects (e.g. job-related advice), financial problems (e.g. handling debt and its consequences), and many other issues that have an emotional aspect. Health-related issues are particularly pertinent in the self-help online landscape. For instance, 73 million adult Americans – 62 per cent of internet users in the USA – have turned to internet sources to seek health information (Pew Internet & American Life, 2002a). According to a recent study, 24 per cent of the internet users who dealt with a major illness said that using the internet was crucial to coping with it (Pew Internet & American Life, 2002b).

Indeed, the heaviest users of the Web for self-help purposes are individuals such as chronic illness patients. Other participants include friends and family, caregivers (other than family), members of medical organizations, medical workers and other related experts. This trend is paralleled by the recent high proliferation of health-related online resources, particularly patient-oriented websites.

Health-related self-help websites commonly consist of *informative textual* features such as downloadable articles, medical research, statistics and glossaries of terms on aspects of a particular problem. There are also some *informative visual* features. For example, using webcam technology, health-related websites broadcast surgical operations to help patients prepare themselves for surgery. Most websites also have *interactive* forums such as peer group e-mails, bulletin boards, discussion lists, newsletters, online personal diaries and text chat rooms. Some websites even use videoconferencing technology as a means of providing health consultations to patients at a distance.

Self-help websites deal with a wide range of social issues: from death through sexual abuse, single motherhood, obsessive-compulsive disorder and chronic illnesses, to mortgage repossession problems (see Burrows *et al.*, 2000; Madara, 2000). Many self-help websites are founded by individuals who are directly involved in a specific project of self-help, for example, patients of a specific illness who run a website to communicate the experience of their disease. Other websites are owned by commercial and non-profit organizations and institutions.

With that rough sketch of self-help on the Web in mind, I now turn to the three main ways in which people use the Web to help themselves. In what follows, I link those processes to Giddens' ideas on the formation of self and self-identity, and to Beck's notion of 'individualization', underscoring the importance of the Web for self-help to the conduct of personal life and the creation of a sense of self.

HOW DO PEOPLE USE THE WEB FOR SELF-HELP?

Appropriation of information on the World Wide Web

When people turn to the Web to help themselves, they are usually seeking information. They start by typing key words related to their problem into a search engine which then links them to a list of websites and sources from which they select those that are relevant and useful to them. The 'stickiness' of specific websites, and the value of their symbolic materials to individual users' personal experience, depends on the users' capacity to relate the website's content to their own circumstances. For instance, in a study on the use of the internet by individuals coping with HIV/AIDS, Reeves (2001) showed that patients valued the information they found on the Web because it was focused and individualized – in other words, it applied to their personal experience.

Although websites' 'stickiness' is partly a function of *similarity* between their content and users' personal contexts, the Web constitutes a significant network of mediated communication that significantly expands individuals' experience and their horizons of understanding beyond their immediate setting. To a large extent, people form a sense of self and develop their autonomy by becoming familiar with objects and events outside their immediate settings (Giddens, 1991).

The symbolic materials that people encounter on the Web provide a glimpse of alternatives, enabling users to reflect critically on the actual circumstances of their lives (Thompson, 1995). Take, for example, the case of a Greek woman who was diagnosed with breast cancer. On a breast cancer bulletin board, she relates how she was first exposed to the option of having reconstructive surgery of the breast through reading about it on the Web. 'In Greece no one told me about the reconstruction,' she says. '[On the contrary] a doctor said: "now you have the cancer, you have to forget the breast".' Using sources such as online medical articles, mailing lists and bulletin boards of breast cancer patients, she became familiar with the implications of such an operation, and decided to go to the USA for a mastectomy. So, the woman's ability to take responsibility for herself and her body was facilitated by symbolic materials (such as messages and online articles) which she encountered on the Web and could relate to her personal experience. Similarly, patients with chronic illness often report that reading on the Web about fellow-sufferers' experiences prompted them to re-evaluate their own situation, and to think differently about themselves. Often, they gained encouragement, hope and optimism.

Exchanging experience on the World Wide Web

Evidently, much of the information individuals encounter on the Web is based on personal experiences. Self-help websites provide various forms of exchange and support such as bulletin boards, discussion groups, e-mail, mailing lists, chat rooms and also more complex communication technologies such as videoconferencing. For example, seeking support and advice, Catalfo, a father of a child diagnosed with leukaemia, started a discussion on The WELL (a computerized conferencing system called the Whole Earth 'Lectronic Link) covering the events, emotions and experiences involved in his son's illness. A lively exchange emerged, resulting in hundreds of postings about the treatment of leukaemia and how to cope with it (McLellan, 1997).

When people exchange experiences with fellow sufferers, they seek self-reassurance, legitimization and validation that their own story has been 'correctly' constructed. In doing so, they work on their self-formation (often unconsciously). As Thompson observes: 'We think of ourselves and our life trajectories primarily in relation to the others whom, and the events which, we encounter (or are likely to encounter) in the practical contexts of our daily lives' (1995: 233). As the Web provides individuals with interactive means of exchanging experience and maintaining reciprocal relationships, it is a key site where processes of self-formation and self-interrogation take place. In fact, patterns of online self-help usage indicate that it is interpersonal exchange, rather than information seeking, that is most salient and valuable to people (King and Moreggi, 1998).

Constructing a 'do-it-yourself biography' on the World Wide Web

As this chapter has shown so far, the mediated symbolic materials that people find on the Web feed into the reflexive process of their self-formation. This involves a continuous construction of one's biography. As Beck argues, today, under conditions of reflexive modernization, individuals must 'produce, stage and cobble together their biographies' (Beck *et al.*, 1994: 13).

The World Wide Web constitutes a central site for the construction and performance of an individual's 'do-it-yourself biography' (Beck and Beck-Gernsheim, 2001), furnishing them with a variety of creative opportunities for working on their self-identity. One of the most explicit ways in which self-help seekers produce their self-biographies on the Web, is through the creation of personal homepages, where they present the story of their personal problem, be it an illness, a traumatic experience or another kind of personal crisis. In his study of homepages of people's illness, Hardey (2002) cites the example of Teresa. Following the onset of Hodgkin's disease, Teresa constructed a personal webpage in which she explains the different aspects of her illness experience. As Hardey observes, Teresa's account of her illness represents an attempt to create continuity with her biography, which was being constructed before the disruption caused by illness.

However, individuals' engagement in the construction of their self-narratives goes beyond the explicit manifestations of personal homepages. In pursuing self-help, people also use more subtle and implicit ways when engaging in the production and telling of their self-narrative on the Web. I argue that, in fact, narrativization and storytelling is a key process which individuals who seek self-help engage in online, particularly when they are patients of chronic illness. As this process has meaningful consequences for the ways in which patients cope with their illness, it is the focus of the remainder of this chapter.

In what follows, I discuss several ways in which the process of narrativization and storytelling is taking place on the World Wide Web, exploring the distinctiveness of the Web for this type of communication and its significance for individuals who seek self-help. The discussion centres on a particular self-help context, namely the experience of patients who cope with breast cancer. My account is based on my study of the online communication of women with breast cancer: an analysis of breast cancer-related websites and patients' accounts of their experience of using the internet in the context of their illness.

CASE STUDY: PATIENTS' USE OF THE WEB IN THE CONTEXT OF BREAST CANCER

In recent years there has been a proliferation of patient-oriented online resources, a substantial number of which relate to breast cancer (Sharf, 1997). On any of the

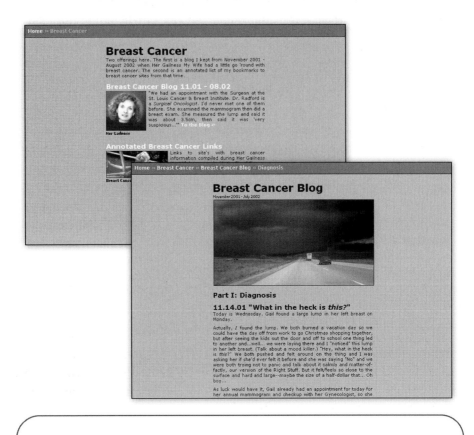

12.2 Blogs such as this one allow people to share personal experiences of breast cancer, as well as information and resources

major search engines, the key words 'breast cancer' retrieve hundreds of related websites. Naturally, the majority of consistently active participants in those websites are women diagnosed with, or worried about, breast cancer. (The disease is overwhelmingly a women's illness; and, in addition, statistics consistently show that women are the main seekers of information on health online.)

Like other self-help-oriented websites, those focused on breast cancer consist of informative features and interactive forms. Breast cancer patients engage in various forms of interactivity including posting messages on bulletin boards, sending e-mails to other sufferers, publishing their 'journey with breast cancer' (as they often call their personal online diaries), discussing aspects of the illness in text chats, sending prayers on 'praying bulletin boards' to women who go through risky stages in their treatment, and reading and responding to breast cancer mailing lists. All these activities are geared towards a wider process of constructing their self-narrative. I argue that the stories patients tell on different health-related online forms help them organize the people, events and information that they have encountered into a coherent framework of meaning, which they can inspect, think about and plan actions around. It is through the practice of storytelling that patients reformulate and redefine their self-identity, following the disturbance created by the cancer.

How does the production of one's personal story and its telling actually take place on the World Wide Web? What consequences does this process have for patients' sense of themselves? I now examine these questions from three perspectives, using examples from different interactions that take place on breast cancer-related websites.

1. Mastering of time

Establishing temporal order is perhaps the most crucial aspect of constructing a coherent narrative. It is particularly important in the context of chronic illness such as breast cancer, where patients are put out of step by uncertainty, being made to wait, and not knowing what is to happen (Frankenberg, 1992). Self-actualization, as Giddens (1991) contends, implies the control of time. Indeed, the publication of patients' personal stories on forums such as bulletin boards, discussion groups and personal homepages appears to be a central means in this process. Consider, for instance, the following account, which was published by a breast cancer patient on a patients' bulletin board:

> When I was diagnosed last November, it was already too late. I found a lump in my left breast last summer. I had benign lumps in my breast for years. Normally they went away after some days. So I thought this time, and forgot them. In September I noticed the lump again. It even was a bit bigger. I went to my doctor who told me not to care. In October the lump was nearly twice as big as the lump I first found in July. My doctor still said I do not have to care, the lump is benign and will disappear from alone. In November I moved to a different town, so I had no time to think about the lump. Late in December, I found the lump was much bigger now. But as Christmas was coming, there was no time, too, and I wanted no illness. Things got worse in January. I awake one morning with my breast red and swollen. I was shocked when I saw little ulceration down the breast. My new doctor was shocked when he saw me. He told me after some test that I have terminal inflammatory breast cancer and only a few months left. It was a shock for me, too, finding out that there is a large cancer killing me. It had already spread to my lung, liver, intestines and bladder.

What is so prominent in this tragic story is the way in which, through writing, the narrator reorganizes the course of her illness as a chain of events, ordered clearly on a timeline. She refuses to let her story so far be that of a 'rollercoaster' over which she has no control. Her narrative is a stubborn attempt to master time, to take control of what is really beyond her control and to relive her experience by organizing her story chronologically, around all the alarming moments she ignored, relating each one to a specific month in the year.

By providing a discursive space that is accessible and immediate, the Web constitutes a central means by which a breast cancer patient can cope with her 'biographical disruption' (Bury, 1991), reformulating her self-narrative along a certain temporal logic. The *written* nature of the medium enhances one's capacity for establishing temporal order and constructing a coherent experience. Crucially, the act of publishing one's story on the World Wide Web bestows status in a very different way from traditional forms of writing, such as a personal journal that one would write just for oneself. The immediacy of using the World Wide Web also plays a central role in encouraging patients to publish their story. While the experience of the illness means the patient is often made to wait, and lacks control over time, the gratification of publishing one's story online is immediate: the narrator gets a sense of control over both the story of her illness and the actual timing of its publication. What is more, through interaction with others (facilitated by features such as bulletin boards and e-mail), she continuously receives feedback on her 'do-it-yourself biography'. In responding to that feedback and exchanging experience with other participants, she has to construct a certain coherent temporal order that makes sense not only to herself but also to her online readers. In a nutshell, the World Wide Web provides a very special space where a breast cancer patient is able to regain control over what she seems to lack the most: time.

2. Construction of a closure

Closely linked to the process of mastering time is the attempt to impose a closure: forming the self as a trajectory of development from the past to an anticipated future (Giddens, 1991). This is particularly true in the case of breast cancer. The reality of the disease does not allow final closure as there is always the risk of recurrence. Interestingly, a close examination of many breast cancer-related websites reveals how they are structured to enable the production of a self-narrative that inevitably entails a closure.

Consider the *Shared Experience* website (www.sharedexperience.org). It is defined as a 'Cancer Support Knowledgebase', designed to enable cancer patients and their caregivers to share their experience of illness online. To search the website's database of patients' stories of their illness, or to add one's personal story, one has to choose a particular cancer type from a dropdown list. The database gives the personal story a coherent structure, using categories such as 'diagnosis', 'chemo drugs', 'treatment', 'quality of life', and so forth, for the entry of particular details. The category list is provided both when users search the existing database (when a user wants to view others' stories) and also when they write their own story. The categories appear onscreen as text boxes. They are static 'grids' of meanings that help the patient, as narrator and reader, to impose meaningful order on the incoherent experience of her illness.

Websites like *Shared Experience*, therefore, offer patients a framework for turning the flux of their experience into a narrative. The sites enable them to impose a closure (both textually and visually) on something over which they have very limited control.

3. Locating the personal within the general

Like the *Shared Experience* website, the design of many breast cancer online forms appears to deliver a clear message to their participants, namely: 'you are not alone'. The idea that publishing one's personal story means inserting it into an existing category (by choosing a particular kind of treatment from a given drop-down menu), clearly locates the individual's story within a wider story, placing it beyond her unique experience. Furthermore, other participants' responses to stories published online inevitably locate the personal in a broader context. Replies to one's story often contain comparisons to other experiences, reassuring the author implicitly (and sometimes explicitly) that she is not alone.

This observation underscores the centrality of interaction with others and their experience in the context of self-help on the Web. As Giddens (1991) argues, negotiating a significant transition in life requires one to grasp the new opportunities opened up by personal crisis. The ability to grasp such opportunities depends on the experience and knowledge gained from encounters with others (significantly, in modern life, *mediated* encounters), and which must be incorporated into the self-narrative one constructs.

In the case of communicating breast cancer on the Web, the encounter with others' experience has a particular expression in the interaction between breast cancer survivors and newly diagnosed women. There is an implicit pattern of 'mentoring' that enables new participants to think of themselves in relation to others, and so help them reflect on their own experience. Survivors of the disease often remain online – even years after being cured – to 'welcome' newly diagnosed women and to mentor them through the course of their illness. This mentoring is often structured in fairly formal kinds of online 'schemes', like 'chemo-angel', an online form by which patients are assigned fellow sufferers as online pals with whom they can correspond and exchange experiences (see www.chemoangels.com).

CONCLUSIONS: TURNING A 'FULL STOP' INTO A 'COMMA'

> Do not place a period where God has placed a comma! I have tried to live my life that way. This [breast cancer] is just my comma in life.
>
> (Message posted on a breast cancer bulletin board)

Individuals' engagement in self-help activities on the World Wide Web is geared towards actively constructing a story out of the symbolic materials available there. It is particularly through the construction and the telling of a story on the World Wide Web (among other processes) that individuals become capable of turning the disruption imposed by their problem into a mere 'comma'.

As discussed in this chapter, in modern life, individuals are confronted with many situations of crisis and unexpected challenges that drive them to seek means of self-help. As Beck (Beck and Beck-Gernsheim, 2001) observes, there is a growing emphasis on the 'individualization of the self'. According to this principle, individuals are encouraged to lead their own independent lives, taking maximum responsibility for their personal choice, self-fulfilment and initiative. As has been shown in the case of breast cancer, this trend is particularly pertinent in contemporary medical environments where the burden of responsibility has shifted onto patients. This chapter has underscored the central role of the World Wide Web in facilitating particular channels for individuals to pursue the 'individualization of the self' and to exercise their 'monitoring of the self' (Giddens, 1991) in relation to self-help matters.

By virtue of their special circumstances, some people are engaged in an intensive process of self-formation and are therefore in need of support. A central implication of the discussion presented in this chapter is thus the need to acknowledge the potential of the World Wide Web as a means for individuals and organizations to provide that support. More particularly, in light of the significance of the process of narrativization, individuals as well as medical organizations should recognize the Web's capacity to provide a platform for people to construct and tell their stories as a means of helping themselves.

USEFUL WEBSITES

Chemo Angels: www.chemoangels.com

A support website for people with cancer, run by cancer survivors themselves, or people whose lives have been affected by cancer.

Faces of Breast Cancer: www.bcforum.org

A site made by Susan Frisius of Massachusetts, USA, who was diagnosed with breast cancer at the age of 46. At this site she invites people to send in photos and information about their own experiences with breast cancer. These are set out in the Faces of Breast Cancer gallery, in tribute to the wide range of people fighting the disease.

GriefNet: www.griefnet.org

An internet community of people dealing with grief, death and major loss, operating 47 e-mail support groups.

National Organization for Single Mothers: www.singlemothers.org

A US-based website dedicated to providing resources, support and information to single mothers, including a bi-monthly newsletter, an online forum, a question-and-answer column and other features based on single mothers' experiences.

Shared Experience: www.sharedexperience.org

A database of cancer patients' stories, searchable by cancer type and designed to enable cancer patients and their caregivers to share their experience of illness online.

Chapter 13

FASCINATION AND HOSPITALITY: ISSUES AND IMPLICATIONS OF INTERNET INTERACTIONS

CHRISTOPHER R. SMIT

The road from early nineteenth-century American freak shows to contemporary internet browsing is not long. Both activities depend(ed) on the consumer's fascination with difference, or the 'other', and both were (or are) driven by commercial gain and commercial persuasion. The rise of freak shows between 1840 and 1940 points to an era of unprecedented fascination with human oddity in the American public sphere. Stifled by guilt and the emergence of political correctness, the American public has stopped viewing freaks in sideshow venues and has instead moved them to film screens, televisions and, most recently, personal computers. Thanks to the internet and the World Wide Web, voyeurs of all types can be fascinated 24 hours a day by practically anything they can imagine. The only difference between the participants of cyber-freak shows and those of the historical sideshow is that ticket buyers no longer wait in lines with other spectators: fascination has been personalized, privatized and made immediately accessible. The world of fascination has been computerized.

What is fascination? The term often carries a sense of shame, perversion or deviance. To place the term 'fascination' in a negative and narrow slot, however, is to deny its possible goodness. Fascination is a moment of enchantment, an allure, an irresistible appeal of something odd, unusual, or at least different – something 'other' than what we are used to. There are reasons to be cautious about fascination, since it can lead us to objectify 'others' as mere things rather than persons. As I will suggest, however, fascination with the 'other' can also open us up to a deeper understanding of the human condition and even to a more fully human understanding of ourselves. To gain from online fascination, however, we must practise the age-old custom of hospitality rather than act merely as voyeurs. Hospitality, as I will discuss at the end of this chapter, challenges the internet browser to realign his or her understanding of 'interactive entertainment' with a sense of responsibility, trust and goodwill.

The historical precedent of contemporary, electronic fascination is important to consider. Recent scholarship on the relationship between mainstream culture and the 'other' (that is, those different from the cultural norm), and the freak, however, has sidestepped the element of fascination; scholars use the term, but fail to conceptualize its significance within the play between spectator and spectacle. As I will argue in this chapter, fascination is an important way that people deal with cultural, physical and mental differences, a process assisted through today's electronic and visual media. These new manifestations resemble the historical models of fascination seen in the American freak show. Finally, these newer media can both foster healthy and destructive forms of fascination depending on whether the parties involved practise what will be referred to later as *hospitable interaction*.

FASCINATION AND CONTEMPORARY TECHNOLOGY

In the late nineteenth century, America was hit with 'cartomania', a compulsion to collect photographs. When scenic landscapes and family portraits grew dull to the privileged collector, an interest in the photography of freaks and circus performers took hold, and effectively initiated the first real surge in American commercialized fascination with the 'other'. Such pictures accompanied the exhibition of particular freaks, and proved to be a lucrative source of capital for performers and proprietors alike. However, it was not until the freak show, which previously had travelled alone, was added to the circus by Barnum and Bailey in 1903, that the financial advancement of freaks and their managers truly began. Among their 47 sideshow attractions, Barnum and Bailey hired Eli Bowen ('The Legless Wonder'), the Hovarth midgets, and Henry Johnson ('What Is It?'), all of whom sold countless freak pictures from the turn of the century until the 1940s (Bogdan, 1990).

The freak show helped transform fascination into a fusion of art and commerce. First, while on stage, the freak often amazed audiences by performing daily tasks using his or her unique physical abilities. Such displays moved the freak from mere object to performer. Second, and most important, the photographs of the freak performers, which were sold by the freaks as extensions of their performances, became artistic representations, strategically constructed to entertain the spectator after the experience of the freak show event. (The freaks themselves often held the rights to their own photographs, and sold them both at shows and when not performing. The best example of this would be seen in the life of Charles Sherwood Stratton, 'General Tom Thumb'.)

Understanding freak show events as part live performance and part photographic product provides insight into the role played by fascination in contemporary media. As Walter Benjamin (1968: 218) points out, when the methods of mechanical reproduction of images are mastered by the modern culture, the 'politics of art' are reshaped. The politics (or power) in new forms of fascination is altered by the staggering availability of images, the responsibility in production of images, and the ethical and moral decisions of the spectator. By looking at each of these aspects of contemporary fascination we can begin to understand and then assess its value in modern life.

First, one must consider the availability of contemporary fascination. Electronic media (via the internet and the World Wide Web) have made multiple images much more accessible to the viewer; digital photography, video, digital sound and webcams all provide images and sounds of the 'other'. In this context, the 'other' stands for any human site of viewer fascination: pornographic players, popular music stars (such as Marilyn Manson), internet fetish photography, and so on, are all to be considered the 'other' in contemporary popular culture. Such availability of images of the 'other' has drastically changed the nature of art, wherein the technology 'enables the original to meet the beholder half way, be it in the form of a photograph or a phonograph record' (Benjamin, 1968: 220). Technology manipulates the space between the art object and the audience, bringing the 'other' 'closer' to the spectator. For instance, the freak show now occurs wherever the spectator gains Web access rather than on the outskirts of a circus tent or seedy trailer.

Second, this change in distance between the original art object and the viewer raises the issue of production responsibility. Inside the 'middle ground' (i.e. the computer monitor), where the art object and audience meet, 'what is really jeopardized … is the authority of the object' (ibid.: 221). Now the spectator controls much of the show: what to see, when and where. When the original

13.1 Visiting an online freak show

authority of an art object is violated in this way, its producer is subtracted from the transaction taking place between spectacle and spectator. While accessing video links and online photography, the viewer is rarely aware of the creator of the images; what matters is the spectacular dynamic of the accessed image. Therefore, the spectator assumes more of the responsibility for how the images are used. Images of pornography, shock photography and sensational advertising techniques, for instance, can be used for good or ill, depending on the intent of the spectator, which would vary from research to critique, adoration, understanding and selfish satisfaction. Left in the abyss of ambiguous production, these spectators become producers, free to manipulate the 'other' for their own fascination.

Third, the individual viewer is left to make his or her own, individual, ethical and moral decisions regarding fascination consumption. Because of technology's expansion of the liminal space of fascination, what Marc Augé (1998) has called the 'non-places of supermodernity', spectators can now access and view the 'other' in a much more privatized fashion. One need only to log on to any of the countless search engines online to understand the outlet for computerized fascination. One could argue that such accessibility to images in a private setting isolates today's viewer from social reality. Rather than attending a public display where other spectators would play a physical, communal part in the fascination event, the online viewer enjoys a guiltless, privatized gaze on the 'other'. The decision to gaze is thus liberated from social pressure, and possibly from social propriety as well.

Mass production of electronic images, through the advent of the World Wide Web, has altered contemporary moments of fascination and holds true to Benjamin's assertion that, 'during long periods of history, the mode of human sense perception changes with humanity's entire mode of existence' (1968: 222). Caught up in the fast pace of modernity, e-mail and 'surfing the Web' have become daily rituals of gazing, urging the viewer to fascinate, or fetishize, his or her desires online. The decision to appear in public with others at a freak show no longer needs to be made. Personal conscience is the only dilemma.

Consider the website *Voyeur Dorm*, which gained a great deal of media attention during the spring of 2000, and still appears to be doing well. *Voyeur Dorm* advertises itself as the hottest thing on the internet, allowing complete and unadulterated, unedited and uncensored video feeds of eight, 'sexy' female college co-eds, captured by 40 secret cameras for the home viewer's pleasure. Thinking about the three elements of mass production discussed above, *Voyeur Dorm* confirms for us the notions of wide availability, shifting responsibility and personal moral decisions. Live video links of eight women are constantly *available* for the consumer willing to pay $34 a month. Because these women, the other, are available as images, they are seen as objects, thus freeing the producers of *Voyeur Dorm* from a sense of *responsibility* to the women being portrayed. And finally, the *decision* of the internet user, to meet the images of these women in the 'middle ground' of their computer screen, is thus freed from social conscience, due to the fact that he or she is alone, without a physical community to guide his or her actions.

Contemporary media images of the 'other' answer 'the desire of contemporary masses to bring things closer' (Benjamin, 1968: 223). Because of this lack of distance between the object and the viewer, spectator satisfaction is only a mouse-click away. The computer keyboard becomes the key which unlocks the autonomy and isolation of electronic interaction. That fascination is at the heart of this technological mass production of images is obvious, yet the definition of the term needs further consideration beyond the cultural isolation and ambiguity attributed to it above. Fascination needs to be separated from purely negative connotations in order for us to understand new ways of reading these planes of interaction. What follows are two possible alternatives to understanding the contemporary sites of fascination.

TOWARDS AN OPEN DEFINITION OF FASCINATION

We have seen in the text above that fascination is a term worthy of more attention. As suggested, the mode in which the term is used in many studies of cultural objectification carries with it a sense of separation, shame and isolation. When other qualities of fascination are ignored, fascination seems purely negative. The alternative variations that follow aim to lighten such preconceptions. Seeing fascination as a means to identity, and as a reflection and identification of the players involved (spectacle and spectator), will expand our use of the term, and give fascination a new vitality within the study of cultural practice. The first section presents an alternative understanding to the American freak show, which uses the concept of fascination as a creator of opportunity and freak identity. We return to the freak show in order to justify the historical need for a re-evaluation of cultural fascination, which precedes our main focus in electronic fascination.

While it is debatable whether or not the financial gains of marketing oneself as a 'freak' outweighed the objectification of these performers, such discussion is not important here. What is relevant, however, is the way in which fascination in the American freak show created an environment for a social, economic and personal definition of the 'other'. First, by establishing the freak as a purchased artefact, as in the pictures discussed above, the 'other' became part of the social action of production and consumption. In this sense, American freaks held an economic as well as cultural place within society. Consequently, freaks were able to be dependent on their own economic fortitude. This was exemplified in the careers of Charles Sherwood Stratton, also known as General Tom Thumb, and his wife Lavinia Warren. Stratton 'sold thousands of ... pictures, and because the markup was good, profits were high' (Bogdan, 1990: 14). Added to Stratton's profit was his wife's enormous capability to sell pictures of her own deformed body. 'She ordered fifty thousand pictures of herself at a time and these were widely available from photography vendors' (ibid.: 15). The couple also found a great deal of success in the circus and private exhibition market, often teaming up with the Ringling Brothers organization as well as Barnum and Bailey. Such a livelihood, made possible through the outcome of fascination, points to the claiming of identity by the 'other'. Whether or not this kind of 'freak entrepreneur' is morally 'good' is a separate but important issue which I will not address in this chapter; certainly self-imposed or market-driven identities are not always good.

The culmination of economic and social opportunities led to the creation of what could be called a freak-identity. Able to function within a society by means of self-objectification, the 'other' was granted a self-consciousness, albeit a twisted one. Using the spectators' fascination to define an independent identity gave the freak show performer a position of cultural power within the emerging freak system. This is not to say that the status of the freak in America was a completely positive label. However, it is important to see the identification of a commodified, empowering 'identity' for freaks as a departure from the predominantly negative critiques of the American freak show (see Drimmer, 1973; Mitchell and Snyder, 1997; Mannix, 2000). Such critiques often cite the phenomenon of isolation and objectification when discussing the freak's social existence. However, by using the term 'fascination' in a more neutral manner, it is possible to see other outcomes of the freak show. This conclusion points to a much-needed alteration and redefinition of the term 'fascination' and its use in analysing cultural interaction.

As we now turn to the modes of contemporary fascination seen in electronic media and in the results of what Benjamin understands as a drastic change in the politics of art, it is important that the same variations be applied. The shift from freak shows under tents to those under the 'big top' of the World Wide Web once again shifts the roles of the 'other' and spectator. Rosemarie Garland Thomson has briefly pointed out that in freak shows, 'the extraordinary body symbolized a potential for individual freedom denied by cultural pressures toward standardization' (1997: 68). While attending the freak show, the spectator may have felt a connection to, or at least an understanding of, the freak performer as an example of the personal freedom to be different and even in some respect 'better'. The 'successful' freak may have symbolized an option, among many, for the pursuit of a productive and self-created lifestyle.

Taking these suggestions further, Garland Thomson also admits that, 'some onlookers probably used the shows to explore the limits of human variation' (1996: 43). While she eventually dismisses the positive possibilities of this speculation in her final analysis, it is relevant here to extend them into the realm of contemporary fascination. I further propose that fascination can be an avenue for exploring difference in order to understand one's own eccentricities and human

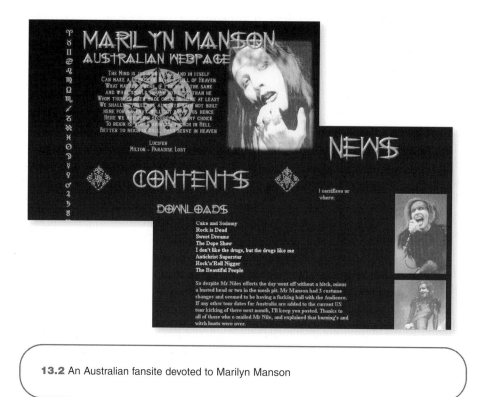

13.2 An Australian fansite devoted to Marilyn Manson

needs. It has already been established that the spectators of online fascination are somewhat freed from the producer of the objects they are viewing. Within that freedom, their gaze is denied the added pressure of personal contact with the images they are encountering. What follows, then, is a moment of exploration that affects both the spectacle and the spectator. The ramifications of such a moment on the 'other' have already been explored. The spectator, following his or her curiosity, delves into his or her own desires – a trait that is subconsciously examined through fascination. The spectator is private, but he or she might still ask the question, 'Who am I that I am so fascinated by these images?' In fact, the spectator might loathe as well as enjoy his or her self-discoveries.

The use of the World Wide Web to access celebrity websites offers a good example of fascination working for the spectator as much as for the spectacle. Obviously, the outcome of capturing a viewer's attention with a particular star image, like Marilyn Manson, is commercially beneficial for Manson due to the publicity involved. However, this resulting publicity, when viewed through the model of fascination suggested above, may also hold positive effects for the viewer. When the spectator finds a commonality with the 'other', and this 'star' quality is added, the justification of 'difference' is established at a completely new level; the viewer, attributing a celebrity's success, both personal and financial, to that performer's oddity, begins to define his or her own peculiarity as a potential for self-betterment. Whatever the consequences, the spectator is better able to self-legitimize a dimension of who he or she is.

A brief discussion of Marilyn Manson leads to a final alternative option for electronic fascination. Manson, whose release of *Antichrist Superstar* launched him into the charts in 1997, has been the target of criticism by several parent organizations and religious groups over the last six years. In addition to playing with norms of identity, spirituality and Christianity – as did Iggy Pop, Alice Cooper, David Bowie, and Kiss before him, and Limp Bizkit, Slipknot and Insane Clown Posse after him – Manson utilizes the grotesque, transgendered aggression of 'shock rock' to lure audiences, listeners and Web surfers. It appears that Manson himself is as fascinated with the religious groups that are against him, as much as they are no doubt fascinated by him. This mode of shared fascination is the dominant model of contemporary cultural activity; when a person is fascinated by the other, they use that moment as a reflection of themselves, in which they can define who they are and who they are not. Thus, fascination moments on the internet can provide the catalyst for self-definition. Moreover, this definition of the spectator is consciously done within the assumed, 'real' presence of another human being, rather than an objectified – thus 'nonhuman' – image of the 'other'. The relationship to the 'other' is thus altered to offer shared humanity as a moment of connection rather than difference. Moments of fascination have allowed people an avenue into understanding the political, ethical and cultural dynamics of the articulation of racial, sexual and physical difference.

However, fascination often carries with it a dark tone, an element of shame, something that historical memory wishes to forget. While this may be partially true, such a one-sided use and critique of fascination ignores the cultural clues which the term holds. Understood through an articulation of electronic media, the internet and the World Wide Web, fascination points towards a multitude of cultural responses. Pushed further, contemporary fascination may enable us to transcend ideas of the relationship between spectacle and spectator, and usher us into a new moment of social realization based on an equality of curiosity and admiration of human difference and sameness.

CONCLUSION: HOSPITABLE INTERACTIONS

In order to facilitate these new moments, however, it is vital to separate harmful Web practices from what might be called *hospitable interactions*, the latter being the necessary step in order to associate a more positive connotation with the practice of fascination. Hospitality, as understood in early Christian writing, entails opening one's home to strangers, or others, allowing them entry into one's life and experience. On a more philosophical level, hospitality calls for an interaction with the 'other' based on trust, openness and goodwill. Furthermore, hospitable interactions allow a space for the perspectives of both the 'other' and us, ensuring that neither participant be consumed completely by each other. Lucien Richard, Professor of Theology at Boston University, suggests that, 'hospitality decenters our perspective; my story counts but so does the story of the other' (2000: 12). Unhealthy instances of online fascination ignore the experiences, or stories, of the other, and as a result frame the 'other' as a mere object to be seen, not heard. Internet pornography is perhaps the best example of this sort of interaction. Chained to his or her desires, the pornography viewer is often guilty of ignoring the humanness, or realness, of the bodies they are viewing. In so doing, he or she favours a private experience of fascination over their communal responsibilities of goodwill for the 'other'. *Voyeur Dorm* subscribers, for example, celebrate the fact that they are unknown, especially by those women being watched.

Hospitality demands that private and public space, represented by the viewer and viewed in online interactions, be merged. As Richard states:

> The stranger is encountered in the public realm; hospitality has to do with the private realm. In the public realm our lives are intertwined with these strangers. The private realm is characterized by mutuality, reciprocity, and intimacy. Hospitality can function as a point of intersection between the private and the public.
>
> (2000: 2)

Hospitable interactions on the World Wide Web, then, would be characterized by a willingness on the part of the viewer to attempt to understand the story of the other, to explore not just the image, but also the self, of the person(s) being viewed. Certainly, this type of interaction is seen above in our discussions of the freak show and Marilyn Manson; both cases prove the necessity of a reciprocal relationship between the spectator and the spectacle, each side being open to each other.

Of course, such openness is theoretical. It is not always possible for the online spectator to literally communicate with the 'other' with whom he or she is interacting (although videocam links and online chatting systems make such interactions more plausible as technologies progress). Nonetheless, I want to argue that the rapidity and pervasiveness of contemporary electronic media compel us to select some guiding principle that will direct our use of them. Hospitality can be that guide. I am suggesting that hospitality can become a lens through which we act and react when participating in online fascination. As has been shown above, hospitable interactions become a way for us to ensure that the recognized humanness we share with the 'other' remains our theoretical and social filter when we see images of them on our computer screens. We can only hope that they use the same principles if, or when, they access images of us.

ACKNOWLEDGEMENT

The author wishes to thank Professor Quentin Schultze of Calvin College for his advice on, and edits to, this chapter.

 USEFUL WEBSITES

Nurple.com: http://nurple.com/sideshow

One of the key arguments made in this chapter is that today's online freak shows are comparative, both psychologically and culturally, to the sideshows of the late nineteenth century in American history. Take a look at Nurple.com and decide for yourself.

'Shock rock' sites:
www.marilynmanson.com
www.insaneclownposse.com

In the macabre style of these artists' websites, we see a present-day example of the 'spectacular' at its most garishly appealing.

'Voyeur' sites:
www.voyeur-dorm.sex-100.com
www.voyeurpic.com
www.1hiddenvoyeurcamera.com

Web directories list hundreds of such 'voyeuristic' porn sites, whose appeals for your credit card details echo the spiel of long-ago sideshow tent 'barkers'.

Part 3:

Web Business, Economics and Capitalism

Chapter 14

STITCHING THE WEB INTO GLOBAL CAPITALISM: TWO STORIES

VINCENT MILLER

In 'Virtual capitalism: monopoly capital, marketing, and the information highway', Michael Dawson and John Bellamy Foster argue that the internet will fail to produce a perfect marketplace. 'One of the great technological myths of our time,' they assert, 'is that the entire system of organised capitalism is being displaced by a new "electronic republic"' (1998: 51). The popular idea that the internet will provide consumers with a wealth of knowledge about products which will lead to 'friction-free capitalism' is, they suggest, quite bogus. Their scepticism lies in the political and economic history of communications, which, as in most areas of economic life, is one increasingly dominated by oligopoly – a state of limited competition between a few powerful companies. They believe the information highway will be no exception to this trend, especially given its recent attractiveness to global capital.

This chapter will examine these theories by looking at two examples of how the internet has been seen as the 'saviour' of capitalism. In particular, it will examine the internet as a focus of capital speculation about 'the future', and investment trends which have involved internet firms. The first example shows how the Web has been viewed as a powerful marketing tool, epitomized in the development, hype and investment boom surrounding 'Web portals'. I will then discuss another example, that of corporate 'convergence' strategies. Here I will show how powerful commercial actors from more established industrial sectors have recently seen the internet as a source of increasing revenues through its potential as a distribution tool, which would increase profits for more established media, IT and telecommunications firms. This involves speculation about a 'new economy' of digital consumption and distribution of media products.

Both cases show the importance of speculation and rhetoric in the commercialization of the Web; that capital investment, while inevitably leading to oligopoly, is enacted in a haphazard pursuit of 'future profits'. My point will be that it is in the development of portals that we can actually see Dawson and Foster's thesis played out. These two examples illustrate how the development of the internet has, in recent years, been tied to commercial interests, specifically how the internet has been the focus of various commodification strategies. The potential of the internet to be, in these cases, a powerful marketing or distribution tool has, to a great extent, controlled its continuing financial saga – and this saga provides evidence of a progressive (although haphazard) trend towards oligopoly on the information highway.

MARKETING, INTERACTIVITY AND THE PORTAL INVESTMENT BOOM

For Dawson and Foster, the attractiveness, and indeed the rhetoric, of the internet as the 'saviour' of economic growth are born out of the stagnation of advanced capitalist economies around the world. Charting the stagnation of (monopolistic) economies of the West with the rise of marketing, they effectively argue that, with decreasing competition, the central problem for a business is not a competitive struggle between firms' products or prices, but a struggle to get consumers to buy more, thereby generating economic growth through an 'artificial stimulation of demand'. In other words, it is a matter of *marketing*. Put simply, products are no longer just produced and then sold to the general public; nowadays, research into consumers creates the basis for a product which can then be sold to a targeted market niche.

The argument is that this ability to target consumers is what makes the internet attractive to business. By its very nature – interactivity – the Web offers the possibility of much more effective 'artificial stimulation of demand':

> There is no doubt that the main reason for corporate interest in the information highway lies in the fact that it is seen as opening up vast new markets, which also means expanding the range and effectiveness of targeting, motivation research, product management, and sales communication – that is, a total marketing strategy.
>
> (Dawson and Foster, 1998: 58)

INTERACTIVITY, MARKETING AND THE ACT OF SEARCHING

Search engines have arguably been the most supported commercial enterprises on the internet thus far. One can argue that this is because search engines (potentially) do two things that make them desirable to those willing and able to invest in the information highway: they help to direct internet traffic, and they increase the potential for consumer profiling.

Search services themselves make the internet practical. By corralling sources of information on any desired topic, search engines greatly increase the chances that a user can find the information they are looking for in the infinite space of the Web. And for those who produce websites, search engines are extremely important as the means by which their pages might actually be found by an audience. This has dramatic consequences, as it paves the way for advertising opportunities, which in turn means that content, funded by advertisers, can be provided free to the consumer.

Thus, search engines provide entry points that users periodically return to when 'surfing'. The idea of wandering around a 'net' is replaced by more of a 'hub and spoke' model, where traffic emerges from one central point and, more often than not, returns to that hub before going out again. What this does is create nodes of traffic, which are predictable – and therefore marketable – to advertisers.

Search services also have the potential to contribute to more effective forms of marketing. The act of searching is itself an act which targets consumers. Most search services are based on hierarchies of categories – such as news, sports, finance, technology – which is one reason that they all look the same. These more general categories are divided into more specific ones (for example, sports into different sports, associations, equipment, and the like). As the user moves on to more specific categories within their search, he or she also becomes an increasingly precise target at which to aim advertising. Because these advertisements are increasingly targeted, they have the potential to be much more effective, and therefore advertisers are willing to pay search companies more for more directed ads:

> We can do a lot more targeting and advertising to people hopefully in a good way and then we can also kind of track how successful things are, and so you can tell instantaneously what people respond to and what they don't respond to … What they like, what their complaints are, all these things.
>
> (David Filo, co-founder of Yahoo!, interviewed 2 December 1997)

Search services have the ability to collect an unprecedented amount of information about their audiences, amassing data on the subjects a user searches for, as well as the types of sites they visit and how long they spend there. (Much of this tracking is carried out using 'cookies'; see Miller, 2000.) The purpose of such information is to obtain more complete profiling about a potential consumer, including their hobbies, interests, and the like. Search services use the information collected to assist them in judging what advertisements a consumer may be interested in, and might therefore be more susceptible to.

These last two points in particular work with one of the major strengths that the internet, and new media in general, have to offer to the commercial world:

interactivity. This has shown itself in search services' ability to 'personalize' the Web environment (such as 'My Yahoo!' or 'My Excite'). Personalization refers to the ability a user has to customize their preferred search service by being able to log on to a search interface which they have constructed, incorporating their specific interests and preferred design. This creates an interesting paradox in Web space, one in which the user is increasingly empowered and yet dominated simultaneously.

On the one hand, the consumer is empowered by being able to customize his or her own space within an interactive environment, but, on the other hand, this is done, in most cases, with the knowledge that this also makes them a clearer target to advertisers. Interactivity, especially in the form of personalization, means giving up more information to advertisers, who can then better understand the user and their motivations. In the case of search engines, controlling your own environment increases the possibility of your environment having a stronger commercial impact on you.

BRANDING, THE RHETORIC OF PORTALS AND THE CONGLOMERATION OF INTERNET TRAFFIC

> I have always thought that a search engine that works well is like a silent author of a book ... you don't really notice the writer. The writer is there but not there, and what has been created is there ... It never calls attention to itself, and it never says 'we are a destination unto ourself' ... we are simply a vehicle for getting from point A to point B.
>
> (Adrian Lurssen, editorial manager of Yahoo!, interviewed 2 December 1997)

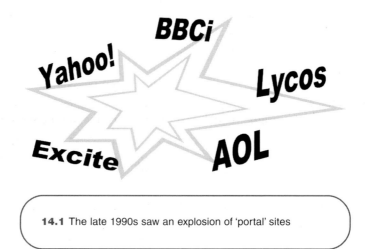

14.1 The late 1990s saw an explosion of 'portal' sites

By the spring of 1998, companies that had formerly been known as 'search engine companies' or 'Web directories' started to call themselves by a new name: 'Web portals' (or simply 'portals'). The philosophy behind these sites is that all of the Web journeys of any particular user should begin in the one place – their own portal to the internet, as it were.

The switch from search engine to portal was based on the adoption of a 'consumer service model' by search services. This was done through the provision of an increasing amount of free services to build upon the search technology already given successfully for free. The first basic steps in this direction were the provision of free e-mail (which Yahoo! began to offer in late 1997, for example), chat services and news. These services expanded over time to include online auctions, shopping, free webpages, and financial information and transactions.

The aim of all this was to increase the amount of 'eyeballs' gazing onto portal sites by attracting and concentrating internet traffic more effectively than through search services alone. In effect, portals want to be all things to all people. They were in a position to achieve this through the fact that they are located at the 'choke points' on the information superhighway, whether as search tools, default browser sites (such as Netscape or Microsoft), or ISP networks (such as America Online).

This conglomeration of internet traffic through service provision was achieved in two ways, either by providing these services 'in house', as was Yahoo!'s strategy, or by purchasing companies that had already established services. Another strategy is to converge traffic by converging companies. Lycos, for example, followed this approach by using its huge market capitalization at the time to buy Tripod, Guestworld, Wired Digital, Quote.com, and WhoWhere, all in 1997/98.

Although portals may have begun with different models (Yahoo!, Infoseek, Lycos, Netscape and Microsoft all started their sites with different intentions, purposes and markets), between 1997 and 1999 they all eventually adopted the basic business model of America Online, the first portal. All portals now look very similar, and provide the same five basic services free of charge: information (news), communication (chat and e-mail), shopping (online retail links and auctions), free Web space and online games. It is this process which O'Leary (1998) argues is demonstrative of the 'law of merging models', whereby, over time, online services come to resemble each other. In organization theory, this process is akin to 'institutional isomorphism'. This phenomenon became known as the 'AOLing of the Web', and is summed up in the following quotation from David Filo:

> Whereas we started out as a directory and search, purely as this kind of navigation thing, we realised ... there are other things we can provide like news feeds and stock quotes and classifieds and whatever ... Early on we looked at AOL and thought that the net, in order to be successful needed

something like AOL ... Once they get the user, they kind of own the user, and they can provide any service they want to the user, and they really control all that the user does.

(Interviewed 2 December 1997)

The presence of the portal created a value that is more than the sum of its parts. The added value created by the portal is the result of branding, and I would argue that the change that transformed search engines into portals heralded the age of internet branding. Whereas, with search engines, content was primary and searching anonymous, with the portal, the reverse was true. This is because portals had moved towards commodity status by becoming the first successful internet brands. As they became gradually similar, the only forum for competition involved 'non-product' elements: marketing and branding (O'Leary, 1998). This process once again echoed Dawson and Foster's central argument, that competition and growth in global capitalism are based on marketing, not on the goods themselves.

PORTALS, INVESTMENT CAPITAL AND OLIGOPOLY

The change in terminology from 'search engine' to 'portal' signalled another change that was to have a notable impact on recent internet history, in the form of the value of stocks. Portals were seen to be the way of the future for capital investment, and many companies who saw the internet as the future for media created or bought a portal. Disney, Microsoft, Netscape, NBC and ABC all developed or invested heavily in portal sites. This, of course, drove up share prices to astronomical levels. With huge market capitalization now in portal shares, these small companies (such as Lycos) were given literally billions of dollars to invest in new services and buy out existing companies. Newly formed portal companies engaged in a competition to attract eyeballs through the development and acquisition of additional consumer services. Such aggressiveness was looked upon favourably by markets and investors, who saw portals as a chance to provide stability and workable business models for the Web. Indeed, during the six months after the use of the word 'portal' became common in early 1998, such companies saw their stocks rise quite dramatically. In that time Infoseek stock rose 223 per cent; Excite 164 per cent; AOL 139 per cent; CNET 125 per cent; and Yahoo! 120 per cent (Bass, 1998). This trend came to a head in June 1998, when 'old media' giant Disney bought a controlling interest in Infoseek, and television conglomerate NBC bought a considerable stake in Snap!, a CNET portal. From then on, portal shares soared to heights that not even seasoned stock market veterans could understand or justify, given the fact that all but Yahoo! were consistently losing money at the time. So what created a situation where a company such as Yahoo! (which, at the time, earned around US$100 million in quarterly revenue, and had roughly 1200 employees worldwide) possessed a market capitalization of over $45 billion in 1999 – more than Xerox or Boeing?

First, the new portal companies were being valued on faith – that the internet 'was the future', and that portals, more than any other type of internet company, had the potential to 'monetize eyeball time' (that is, to capture viewers and hold them long enough to look at advertisements). The conception was that any portals that could be firmly established would be in the enviable position of being global internet brands with access to the loyal eyeballs of hundreds of millions of viewers worldwide. Investors in portal stocks were in part speculating that one or the other portal would eventually build up a presence on the Web.

Second, and perhaps more cynically, investors were speculating that the majority of these portal companies would be bought out (at a favourable share price) by large old media firms increasingly interested in 'hedging their bets' with the internet phenomenon. Investors bet that larger companies (like media giants Disney and NBC, CBS and AT&T) would take over.

Here, one could see a bias in the market. Investors and markets prefer oligopoly, as it is a sign of stability. The internet stock boom (particularly that involving portal sites) showed how companies with the potential to converge and centralize the internet were rewarded with high market capitalization, giving them further resources to buy out smaller firms and aggregate Web traffic. At the same time, investors and markets also like to see traditional oligopolist firms investing, thus providing even further perceived stability and centralization of a potentially decentralized mode of communication.

PORTALS: UNREALIZED POTENTIAL

So far, we have seen how the inflation of portals' and other Web companies' share prices created the conditions for oligopoly on the internet. Such capitalization provided new Web companies with large amounts of capital to buy up smaller firms and consolidate the Web into a more attractive, stable commercial environment (see also Miller, 2000).

Throughout the 1990s, the internet stock boom was fuelled by an ecology where a large amount of start-up capital was available, priming innovation and optimism for the future of the internet. The internet was going to be big, and open up vast new markets, making a lot of money for whichever firms managed to gain a strong foothold. In these conditions, small companies grew quickly, like big fish in a small pond. Anything that showed potential was bought up by larger firms. This was consolidation before the bubble burst.

For the past two years, however, there has been a completely different economic ecology. Commerce on the internet has not grown as much as expected; start-up capital has all but dried up, and, with it, investment in new start-up firms. The remaining firms are worth a fraction of what they once were, with Yahoo!, for example, now worth US$8 billion at the time of writing, down from US$45 billion. (There are, of course, many other reasons for this decline in stock value – economic slowdown in the USA, the aftermath of the attack on the World Trade Center, and recent accounting scandals in several major corporations have all helped in chipping away at the value of stocks overall – but the internet stock bubble had burst before any of these other events had their effect.) The result has been an increasing number of acquisitions from large 'outside' firms. Thus, the trend towards consolidation and oligopoly continues, but has expanded to a cross-industry scale. No longer is it just media and internet companies, but telecommunications firms, book publishers and giant 'old media' companies who are feasting on smaller, low-priced, internet firms (see *Business Week*, 6 April 2001: 118). In other words, the pond got bigger.

There are those who suggest that internet companies like Yahoo! were foolish not to use their outrageously high market capitalization to buy into traditional media giants, and usher in a convergence between these and the new media firms, under the terms of new media. Instead, many internet giants continue to see the internet and the Web as a separate media sphere, apart from 'old media' encumbrances (Katz, 2001). AOL was the one exception, in 2000 effectively buying Time Warner and ushering in a new era of 'convergence'. At the time, everyone thought AOL was making the right decision.

Today, the Web constitutes an established sector of business and media interests, and is being brought into the overall business strategy of the interactive multimedia industry, integrating its digital networking into the telecommunications network and the media machine. This is the convergence strategy.

CONVERGENCE, SYNERGY AND THE INTERNET IN A DIGITAL FUTURE

In July 2000, internet giant America Online merged with 'old media' juggernaut Time Warner, creating the largest media company in the world: AOL/Time Warner. In the same year, what used to be Vivendi Environment, a French water utility company, bought Universal Studios, Polygram records, book publisher Houghton Mifflin, MP3.com, USA Networks, and a stake in Ecostar Satellite Services to become Vivendi Universal, a media and communications giant. A year later, the 167-year-old German publishing company Bertelsmann AG brought RTL, Europe's biggest television company, and Napster, the infamous internet music file sharing service, into the Bertelsmann fold of music publishing and e-commerce websites. At the time, commentators saw these mergers as 'the dawning of the digital century', an era where 'convergence' was seen as the inevitable future of the internet, and modern media in general.

What is 'convergence'?

'Convergence' refers to two things: *digital* convergence and *industry* convergence. Digital convergence has been defined as 'the switch of almost all media and information to electronic format, storage, and transfer' (Herman and McChesney, 1997: 107). Thus, digital convergence is in itself a technological development, simply the ability to reduce communication into digital format – a series of 'ons' and 'offs', or zeroes and ones. Convergence relies on the ability to not only represent all forms of information (voice, text, video, pictures and sound) in this way, but also to transfer it efficiently via increased networking capacity and more sophisticated forms of data compression.

Industry convergence is partially a result of digital convergence, and refers to the coming together of several industrial sectors that deal with communication in one way or another; or, as Herman and McChesney put it, the way that 'media, telecommunications (telephony) and computer industries find their activities are becoming increasingly the same' (1997: 107). Once largely separate industries, with separate agendas, legislative frameworks and modes of delivery, the telecoms industry (consisting of telephone, cable, satellite and broadcasting network companies), information technology sector (computing hardware and software, and internetworking companies), and media content industries (publishing, film, television, radio, AV and information services companies) are said to be in the process of converging. Digitization means that the distinctions between these industries are blurring, as they all now share a common unit of delivery: the digital code. This means that all of these industries and companies are increasingly involved in each other's business, and are therefore potential partners, or competitors.

For example, cable broadcasters, telephone companies and internet sites can technically offer the same services, such as long-distance phone calls. Thus, telephone companies now have a much wider sphere of competition than they did 20 years ago, when all they perhaps had to worry about were other telephone companies. In turn, telephone companies are also able to expand their horizons into, for example, internet service delivery and even the creation of Web portals (competing directly with media content producers and internet firms).

The push towards convergence is based on the idea that, with a shared communications platform, 'synergies' between merged companies in different communications sectors can occur. For example, a cable company that also owns a media company, thus possesses media content that it can distribute on its cable infrastructure, thereby cutting costs and allowing the cross-promotion of both sectors. Thus, one company (or conglomeration of companies) in media, IT and telecommunications can control all aspects of the media production and consumption process: content creation, packaging, marketing, purchase and delivery, all in a digital interactive format that maximizes consumer access.

For a media company, this means that potentially anyone, anywhere can purchase its products without dealing with any kind of middlemen, be they retailers, bankers, or delivery companies. This minimizes overhead costs, making products cheaper, stimulating demand and creating profit. This is profit through oligopoly.

The common assumption is that the result of convergence will be what is variously called the 'interactive multimedia' industry (Østergaard, 1998) or 'info-communications sector' (Herman and McChesney, 1997) – and ultimately a global communications system. At least this is the rhetoric, although no one is quite sure of the form that such a system would take. Visions of this future vary from some sort of interactive 'set-top box' (like Microsoft's WEBTV, or similar efforts by Motorola and BIB), to simply a more efficient World Wide Web, or the ability to watch television on a mobile phone. At this point in time, it is difficult to guess.

This current and uncertain climate has led to larger companies looking for potential allies (or simply fewer 'enemies') in the face of a converged future. Internet, telecoms, computer and broadcasting firms are now looking across these industry sectors for partners and competitors, and, through a series of buy-outs, mergers and partnerships across industries, preparing the way for convergence. As Herman and McChesney note:

> In times of technological upheaval where nobody has a clear idea of exactly where things are heading, the smart course for a firm is to hedge its bets by getting involved in several options so it can be prepared to pounce on any one of them that shows commercial potential.
>
> (1997: 108)

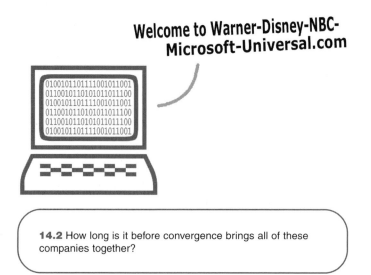

Welcome to Warner-Disney-NBC-Microsoft-Universal.com

14.2 How long is it before convergence brings all of these companies together?

Here, it is the large companies in media, telecoms and IT who are the actors, snapping up smaller internet and other media interests. Aside from the 'old media' acquisitions described above, telecoms and computing firms have been busy investing in 'content' and delivery to prepare for a digital future. Recent activities have included:

- Canadian telecoms giant BCE bought television broadcaster CTV largely for content to put on BCE's series of portal websites

- MCI and British Telecom have teamed up with Microsoft to develop global internet and intranet services

- IBM has partnered with chip manufacturer Intel and cellphone manufacturers Nokia and Ericsson to develop mobile internet technology in Europe.

The big players from three industries are clashing, colluding and colliding. It would seem that the internet, and whatever form digital-based multimedia ultimately takes, is doomed to a legacy of consolidation and oligopoly through convergence investment from outside industries.

THE DEATH OF CONVERGENCE

Despite the best rhetoric of a converged digital future, all would not seem so straightforward. Indeed, the haphazardness from which the internet was born seems to continue, causing problems for firms used to the stability and predictability of oligopolistic economic climates.

First, consumer demand for converged services is hard to determine. Many studies have suggested that consumer demand for interactive multimedia is extremely low (Melody, 1996; European Commission, 1997, cited in Winseck, 1998). Winseck (1998) cites a study undertaken for the European Commission, which concludes that 'convergence is a long way from being a consumer driven phenomenon'. This report goes on to state that 'the rump of users may not change until forced to do so' (KPMG, 1996, cited in Winseck, 1998). It would seem as though consumers themselves will only accept technology that is affordable and useful to them, and, for the moment, prefer the separation of television, internet and telephone. More recent studies, however, suggest that demand is growing as equipment gets cheaper (*Communications Today*, 1998).

Second, the merging of companies has not always gone well. While convergence rhetoric emphasizes the potential 'synergies' and efficiencies of merging across industries, the opposite is often found to be the case, as one observer has noted:

> Inside the merged media companies, employees nursed resentments especially as shareholders beat down their share prices because the promised synergies had not materialised. Stock options, which were once worth more than

salaries, were now worthless. Cultural conflicts deepened between traditional media executives and internet entrepreneurs forced to work together.

(Hiltzik, 2002: A49)

Lack of performance and demand has taken a toll on many companies who followed the convergence strategy. Vivendi shares declined by 75 per cent during 2002, and AOL/Time Warner, which before merging was worth US$290 billion combined, is currently worth only US$51 billion at the time of writing. All of this has spelled doom for the architects of 'convergence' strategies, as the business press has reported: 'The resignation of Bertelsmann AG chief Thomas Meddelhoff was just the latest casualty in the so-called "convergence" craze that has derailed the concerns of the world's leading media executives' (*Agence France Presse English*, 30 July 2002). High-ranking executives in Bertelsmann, AOL/Time Warner (Chief Operations Officer Robert Pittman), and Vivendi (Chairman Jean-Marie Messier) are more visible casualties of boards and shareholders who are increasingly frustrated with convergence policies yet to generate revenues. Unlike four years ago, shareholders currently do not want companies to borrow vast sums of money to wait for a promised future payoff. Indeed, there is pressure on the boards of AOL/Time Warner, Vivendi and Bertelsmann to cut losses by spinning off recently acquired companies, undoing much of the conglomeration that has taken place (Lowry, 2002). Even Disney, whose Web strategy has probably been the most successful of the old media firms, has all but shut down the Disney Internet Group and its 'Go network' portal, losing US$820 million.

THE REVENGE OF THE INTERNET: UNPREDICTABLE EFFECTS OF DIGITIZATION

Convergence has manifested itself perhaps most prominently on the Web in mp3 file sharing, and the resulting trends in audio piracy that have made media headlines, particularly in the notorious Napster case. The mp3 digitization of music files was a by-product of the motion picture industry. Yet, from this, we now have reached a point where 40 million Americans alone use primarily illegal mp3 file sharing services (*Europemedia*, 2002). One can presume that these are mostly used to procure illegally copied digital music files.

Such developments have caused the 'big five' music publishers to completely rethink their business (Shirky, 2001), while vigorously pursuing lawsuits against file-sharing websites at the same time. (Ironically, the chaos of mergers, buyouts and partnerships even led to a situation where one of these, Time Warner, a vehement defender of publishing copyright lawsuits, found itself owning Gnutella, one of the more popular mp3 file-sharing software packages for audio piracy; see Whaley, 2000.) But, in a climate of convergence, there are more players involved than simply music publishers, audio pirates and consumers. All are potential partners or competitors, and it is interesting to note that the *Europemedia* study also found that 53 per cent of those already sharing files (and 24 per cent of all Americans over the age of 12) also have a PC equipped with a CD burner (*Europemedia*, 2002).

In fact, the IT industry has been very vocal in its promotion of the music capabilities of PCs. Sound cards, speakers and software interfaces such as RealJukebox all provide an infrastructure for playing and organizing mp3 files. In addition, Web portals such as Yahoo! list music-sharing sites (as well as host their own), and even AT&T has started the A2B music file-swapping site. At the hardware end, Apple, Philips, Casio and many other equipment manufacturers have all released portable mp3 players to cash in on audio piracy. Clearly there is not much empathy for publishers among the IT, telecoms and consumer electronics industries.

Convergence strategies were originally based on the idea that, with digitization, media companies could bypass distributors and reach consumers directly through the Web. This is consistent with the conception of the internet as a potential global marketplace of perfect competition which ultimately benefits the consumer. However, media oligopolies hoped they could manage this anarchy and advance their market position by using the internet as a more efficient delivery system for media products.

What we have seen in the past two years is the failure of convergence as the instrument of secure markets and established oligopoly that was predicted. Not only have the executives who led convergence strategies lost share value and their jobs, but, at least in the case of music publishers, some are potentially losing revenues, as more and more consumers realize that they can get music (and even films) digitally online for free.

Perhaps there is hope after all. Even though the commercialization of the Web is an issue long settled, the form that commercialization will take is still uncertain. Will it be a new form of marketing and advertising, as were once the Web portal and 'consumer service model'? Or will it change into a distribution-based form of media, as large media companies (following the strategy of convergence) would ultimately prefer? Both cases here illustrate that internet commodification strategies seem logical, straightforward and predictable; ultimately, however, their acceptance is dependent on relationships between consumers, investors and other industries. Whether these actors 'play ball' is a complex issue, but as long as they compete against each other in the current climate of uncertainty, the future of the internet is difficult to determine. For now, it still remains a somewhat separate media sphere, and surprisingly ungovernable.

USEFUL WEBSITES

Center for the Study of Technology and Society: www.tecsoc.org

This weekly updated site devotes a section to issues surrounding media convergence, including interesting articles and recent developments.

Convergence: www.luton.ac.uk/convergence

The *Journal for Research into New Media Technologies* – 'a refereed academic paper journal which addresses the creative, social, political and pedagogical issues raised by the advent of new media technologies'.

The Convergence Center: www.digital-convergence.org

The Convergence Center 'supports research on and experimentation with media convergence'. The site is a bit technical, but interesting nonetheless.

Chapter 15

THE DIGITAL DIVIDE

NICK COULDRY

It's not often that politicians and policy-makers on the world stage talk seriously about whether access to media is evenly and fairly shared; when they do, those interested in studying or researching the media should probably sit up and take notice.

The 'Digital Divide' is the widely used label for a range of policy debates since the mid-1990s about the spread of access to the internet and other forms of 'digital' media. This debate, unusually, straddles political and academic domains, even if politicians' attention since 2001 has started, inevitably, to wane. It is interesting also, because it links the vast, murky currents of global policy discourse to practical, local issues about who is getting something valuable out of the internet, where, and how? It is rare for 'macro' and 'micro' to be connected in this way, and the opportunity for detailed research making a difference on a wider scale cannot be passed over lightly. This is why, for all its confusions and uncertainties, the 'Digital Divide' debate deserves a chapter in a book on the state of Web studies today.

15.1 The 'Digital Divide' strikes again

What exactly is the Digital Divide, you might ask? Who exactly is divided, and how? Good questions, especially when there are almost as many detailed definitions of the term as there are definers. Because this confusion stems from the varied purposes people have in entering into this debate, it makes sense, first, to discuss the broad political context in which something like the 'Digital Divide' came to be debated at all by politicians. At the end of the chapter, we'll discuss where this debate is headed and what its impacts might be on our understanding of how media, economy and democracy interact.

THE EMERGENCE OF A GLOBAL DEBATE

The last time media had featured in the global policy arena was the 1970s' debate within the UN organization, UNESCO, about global inequalities in media production and media flows. At that time, developing nations called strongly for a 'New World Information and Communication Order' (NWICO) where America in particular was less dominant in film, television, news, and so on, and more generally where the balance of the media industries worldwide was less heavily skewed towards the richer nations of 'the West'. These policy debates overlapped with the start of two decades or so of academic debate about the exact nature of the 'imperialism' to which America's media dominance amounted – an important debate that continued long after the policy debate fell silent (following the withdrawal by Reagan's America and Thatcher's UK from UNESCO in the 1980s).

Maybe the Digital Divide debate will be the same: a brief span of political attention, followed by decades of academic discussion falling increasingly on deaf ears. That's something to ponder once we've clarified how this debate emerged. Although the term 'Digital Divide' has a clear political ring to it, the essential precondition, without which the term would never have emerged, was the vision, widespread from the 1980s onwards, of an 'Information Society' in which the possibilities for economic production and social change would be transformed by the new, increased flows of information that computers made possible. The emergence of the internet in the early 1990s from technical obscurity to (potentially) a global network intensified debates about the future of the 'Information Society'. In the USA, the Clinton administration took a lead, with Vice President Al Gore calling in 1994 for a 'Global Information Highway'. Crucially, this new vision was more about the economy than about society or politics: 'it will make possible a global information marketplace, where consumers can buy and sell products' (Al Gore, quoted in Schiller, 1995: 17).

It quickly became clear, however, that this new vision meant little by itself, especially when confronted by continuing global inequalities in informational resources. Long before the internet, telecommunications experts at the United Nations and elsewhere had expressed concern about the impact on world economic development of many countries' staggeringly low access even to the telephone, long since taken for granted in the West. How, they argued, could policy-makers not think seriously about the fact (this was 1995, but it's hardly better now) that 'more than half of the world's population lives more than two hours from a telephone' (UNDP, 1995: 2). The answer was to be not so much a political strategy to reduce world poverty, as an economic one: the opening up of world telecommunications markets encouraged by the (now infamous) World Trade Organization. Already, in 1995, UN experts had made a direct link between the inequalities over who in the world has access to a telephone and the even greater inequalities over who in the world has a modem. They argued convincingly that a poor telecommunications infrastructure was an absolute block to many poor countries' joining the global *online* consumer market for which Microsoft and others hoped (UNDP, 1995: Chapter 5; see also OECD/DSTI, 2001).

Meanwhile, in the USA, there was increasing concern about home-grown inequality in computer access and its impacts on the US domestic market. The Clinton administration commissioned a series of studies by its Department of Commerce (the 'Falling Through the Net' series) which in the late 1990s became crucial reference points in policy discussions about what came to be called 'the Digital Divide'. We'll come back to some limitations of this research later but, for now, it's worth being clear that the main emphasis was, again, on *economic*, not political, consequences. The problem with large numbers of the US population not going online, for whatever reason, was seen above all in terms of restrictions on economic growth. Whatever the wider value of these reports, it's worth remembering that their concern was never political or social inclusion but 'participation in the digital economy' (US Department of Commerce, 2000: 2).

Meanwhile, partly through US influence, the Digital Divide came to the forefront of international political debate. The G8 Summit in Okinawa, Japan (July 2000), issued a Charter for the Global Information Society and even set up a task force to look into what could be done about the Digital Divide. The task force, significantly, was called the 'Digital *Opportunity* Force' (DOTForce), a change of language reflecting growing complaints that talk about the Digital *Divide* was too divisive! A document produced by the Swiss-based World Economic Forum put this point bluntly:

> Instead of fixating on the existence of a divide, it would be far better to focus our attention on the 'global digital opportunity', because that is what really confronts us today – an unprecedented opportunity to move swiftly up the path towards global digital development.
>
> (World Economic Forum, 2000: 10)

In other words, the point of raising something as gloomy as the Digital Divide was to focus more clearly on the possibilities for market growth: short-term political 'pain' for long-term economic gain.

Not all the voices in the debate were so evasive. An interesting *draft* document published by DOTForce (not acted upon but still available on the Web) talked not only about markets but also about fears of 'fragmented globalisation' and 'globalisation backlash' (DOTForce, 2000). We should recall here that around the same time global leaders were getting used to local and very vocal protests at their global meetings, such as the Seattle World Trade Organization meeting in 1999. This political dimension was one reason why talk about the Digital Divide decreased at the highest policy level from 2000 onwards.

Even so, the Digital Divide debate continues to matter in other ways. First, the World Bank in January 2000 set up its own Global Information and Communication Technologies department, which claims explicitly to deal with the 'new opportunities … [to] assist developing countries in bridging the digital divide through economic growth, increased jobs and improved access to basic resources' (GICT, 2002). Second, other countries followed the US lead in investigating the Digital Divide at home. The Blair Government in Britain, when elected in 1997, made social exclusion one of its key concerns, and its Social Exclusion Unit commissioned research on access to and use of information and communications technologies in Britain's poorest areas. The resulting report (UK DTI, 2000) reveals an interesting difference in US and UK rhetoric about the Digital Divide. Whereas US discourse is firmly directed at the economy, the UK report tries to have it both ways, arguing that questions of 'social exclusion' and 'economic development' are 'mutually reinforcing'; in other words, flourishing markets require full social inclusion. A fudge, you might think, since most markets in history have worked perfectly well even though significant groups have been excluded from purchasing power, but an example of the tensions ever present in Digital Divide discourse.

Later in the chapter we'll return to this review of policy debates to see how the Digital Divide has been downplayed by the present US administration. Before that, we need to be clearer about what the Digital Divide is.

WHO IS DIVIDED?

The debate, as you will have noticed, seems to be operating on different scales, where possibly quite different considerations should apply. On the one hand, the international debate would seem to concern the divide in internet access *between* nations; on the other hand, governments have been concerned about the divide *within* nations, or at least within their own nation.

The political scientist, Pippa Norris, despairing of how the 'Digital Divide' has 'entered everyday life as shorthand for any and every disparity within the online community', calls the first division 'the 'global divide' and the second the 'social divide' (2001: 3–4). The first is concerned with the absolute differences between different countries' telecommunications infrastructures, information transmission capacity, numbers of computers, website hosts, and the like; the second is concerned, within one nation, at the gap between those who have access to that society's Web resources and those who don't. Both divides are important.

In fact, these aspects of the Digital Divide are both connected and distinct. They are connected, because, as both global markets and online connections grow, it is likely that not only the divide between rich and poor nations grows, but also that, at least within the poorer nations, the social divide grows between elites (however small), who can afford online access, and the rest (UNDP, 1995: Chapter 5). By contrast, the comparisons in the two cases are very different. Using Norris's terms, the 'global divide' is a macro-comparison of whole countries, operating at the level of *total* numbers of phone lines and modems, *total* numbers of internet users, *total* numbers of Web hosts, and so on. The 'social divide', by contrast, suggests rather different questions about how *individuals* in the same society differ in how they access, and use, the internet.

It is possible, indeed common, to look at the intra-societal 'social' dimension of the Digital Divide without raising any questions about individuals' quality of internet use. Many US reports on the gaps in internet access between different income and educational groups, while demonstrating that a 'social divide' continues to exist in the USA (for example, UCLA, 2001), tell us little about how people differ in the 'quality' of their use, a term that itself, of course, needs some further definition.

In principle, however, thinking about the distribution of online resources within a particular social structure should raise more detailed questions about both the quality and quantity of people's use of the internet. Such questions sometimes arose in debates about different levels of development between nations – for example, when it became clear to many experts that merely increasing the number of phone lines in a poor country such as Tanzania was no solution to its digital 'poverty', given that individual phone line access for most Tanzanians was not a realistic target in the foreseeable future; instead, new thinking emerged which concentrated on providing *social* forms of access to phone links (village phone centres in Bangladesh, 'telecentres' for both phone and internet access in Mexico). Implied here is a move from thinking about the bare fact of access towards thinking about how that fact connects with the real needs and conditions of those to be connected. But it is in relation to the Digital Divide within nations that more elaborate questions about what people are doing with their digital connection arise more obviously.

HOW ARE THEY DIVIDED?

Let us look now, in more detail, at the questions that arise about how individuals access the internet differently, which in turn has implications for the meaning of the 'Digital Divide'. There are many possibilities.

First, we could simply carry over the approach from analysing the 'global divide' and count up who in a society has a computer and who doesn't, who uses the internet (at home or elsewhere) and who doesn't. This is the most basic measure, and fits with the American media sociologist Ronald Rice's seemingly uncontroversial definition of the 'Digital Divide' as 'the differential access to and use of the internet according to gender, income, race, and location' (Rice, 2002: 106). Even if basic, this is the approach of most large-scale studies of internet use, particularly in the USA where, after all, most research funding is concentrated. There are currently under way various country-wide US surveys of internet use: for example, the UCLA Internet Project based in California which returns to the same panel of 2000 or so users and non-users every year (UCLA, 2001) and a series of specific studies of internet use by the Pew Internet & American Life Project based in Washington, DC (Pew Internet & American Life, 2002a). These academic studies have continued, in a sense, where the US Department of Commerce's 'Falling Through the Net' reports left off.

A weakness, which all such studies share, is how little they tell us about the quality of people's internet use, and how *this* might vary. This emerges most clearly when their authors make bigger claims about the significance of their findings. Thus, in the final 'Falling Through the Net' report (published in the last days of the Clinton administration), the Secretary of State for Commerce, Norman Mineta, proclaimed triumphantly in his Preface that 'the data in this report show that, overall, our Nation is moving toward full digital inclusion' (US Department of Commerce, 2000: 2). Full inclusion, if it means anything in a large nation's social and economic life, must surely mean more than that a majority log on regularly for *some* purpose or other. Yet this same report admits that quality of use was not even investigated. As it says at one point (Part II, under 'Location of Internet Use'):

> *Although this survey did not collect data on the intensity or the quality of internet use*, where an individual uses the internet – at home, away from home, or both – *probably* reflects some degree of the quality of his or her internet access.
>
> (My emphasis)

Which tells us precisely nothing, because it has nothing to tell.

An underlying problem here is the way that a research model plausible for, say, telecommunications research is applied to a more complex medium such as the internet – more complex, because it is both interactive and distributive: we use it to contact our friends and receive publicly circulated information. Since (leaving aside specific disabilities) everyone knows how to talk to their friends or order a train ticket by phone, you could argue that knowing the number of phones per square kilometre (the so-called 'teledensity' factor used by telecommunications experts) tells you almost as much as you need to know about telecommunications access in a particular region, although, as we have seen, it may not suggest how to solve extremely low teledensity. The same is not true for computers and internet access. For example, as recent research has shown, there are enormous differences in what 'heavy' internet users and 'light' internet users *do* when they switch on their computers and modems (Katz *et al.*, 2001). Heavy internet users, particularly those with broadband access, are much more likely to spend their time online sending their own documents and information, rather than receiving public information (Pew Internet & American Life, 2002b). Light internet users, by contrast, may do little more than access their Web server, look at the headlines and a few links, and check a train time via a familiar search route. Are these two 'uses' to be given the same weight in measuring the Digital Divide, particularly across a rich and extremely diverse nation such as the United States? Surely not, even though such differences are partly just a matter of individual taste.

To assume, however, that such differences are *only* a question of individual taste ignores the complexity of what is on offer online. The vast online universe of information and services cannot be assumed to be a universal good, having the same value to everyone. The use you or I make of the internet depends not only on the speed and reliability of our modems and our individual predilections, but on our particular needs and capabilities to *do so something with* the resources we believe are available online. Clearly, researching this requires talking to people in detail. One of the rare US internet surveys that went beyond telephone surveys uncovered striking results. A charity, the Children's Partnership, published a study of online use by 'Underserved Americans', a classic euphemism for the poor and disadvantaged (Children's Partnership, 2000). This highlighted what it called 'the Digital Divide's New Frontier': 'content' – that is, the gulf between what people *need* and what they actually *find available* online. This content gap can arise for many reasons: because online information is not what particular people need (they may want job and education information, not weather or sport), because the assumed literacy level is too high for them, because it is not in their first language, and finally because the content is not 'culturally appropriate', a vague phrase to cover the whole range of reasons why people of varying backgrounds might be put off from pursuing information or anything else on the Web. One important dimension here may be the degree of social support – within or beyond the family – available to help when you have technical difficulties with your computer or software (Kling, 1999).

Here we get into deeper waters. I mentioned that some internet users spend much more time sending their own material than do other users. Being an active online producer is related to more than modem speed; it is a question of education and, ultimately, of what type of person you feel yourself to be. 'Low-income people think they're not *legitimate* information producers,' said one community adviser interviewed by the Children's Partnership (quoted in Children's Partnership, 2000: 24). Suppose this were true and widespread; it would surely be a barrier to the expansion of 'full' internet use. Yet none of the factors just mentioned is measured by simple tests of access to a computer and time spent on it.

There's one other confusion we also need to avoid: assuming that the Digital Divide's impacts are, in reality, much to do with the specific properties of digital media as such. What if the same divides in access and use have characterized all or most information and communication technologies? Pippa Norris's analysis of both 'global divide' and 'social divide' concludes precisely this, that there is nothing different about how the Digital Divide tracks underlying social and economic inequality (Norris, 2001: Chapters 3 and 4). In other words, there is nothing *distinctively* 'digital' about the Digital Divide at all. Which means, not that the Digital Divide was trivial, but that there's no reason to think it can be solved by policies directed at computers alone.

SOME LONG-TERM CONSEQUENCES

Once we look more closely at the Digital Divide debate and its omissions, it emerges as one way in which wider social inequalities are worked out through our access to and use of media. As we might expect, the long-term impacts of such a complex debate have been mixed.

First, it has contributed to the development of imaginative projects across the world which confront the real conditions in which people do or do not use online media. A remarkable case is Kothmale FM Radio based in Mawathura in Sri Lanka: an already existing UNESCO-funded community radio station which recently has also become the internet hub for the surrounding rural region, broadcasting information obtained from the Web and encouraging at least the younger and more educated listeners to travel from their villages to the radio station and gain experience of surfing the Web. In this project, the principle of enabling *social* access to the online world, when individual access is largely impossible, has been imaginatively developed: you can follow up details for yourself at www.kothmale.net, especially the section on 'internet'.

Second, by putting inequalities in patterns of media access and use onto the policy agenda, the Digital Divide debate has made it a little easier for players *outside* the magic circle of the World Bank, UN agencies, and the largest and most powerful governments, to call for discussion on the world's media infrastructure: for example, the Association for Progressive Communications which includes in its 'Internet Rights Charter' a call for 'all citizens [to] have affordable access to the means to communicate, via the internet, and community controlled electronic media' (APC, 2002).

Third, and less positively, the Digital Divide debate has now, as it were, paid for its political inconvenience by being rudely moved off centre stage by the current Bush administration. Not only have federal initiatives directed at the Digital

Divide been shut down, but a new Department of Commerce report pointedly avoids Digital Divide language in claiming that 'we are truly a nation online' (US Department of Commerce, 2002: 2). The hollowness of the claim is clear, since, although on some indicators (such as race and gender, once other factors are excluded), the gap in digital access has narrowed, in other respects the new report's own findings show that it is very much alive. Income and education *remain* major determinants of whether people are online and whether, once they get online, they stay online (US Department of Commerce, 2002: 11, 18, 71, 75; see also UCLA, 2001: 13).

All, however, is not lost. One advantage of the Digital Divide debate has been to highlight, for those prepared to look, the range of ways in which significant inequalities are *reproduced* through media access and use. There is a political link here, although one not yet fully developed, between these insights and a separate debate about where, if anywhere, democracy is heading: how much, and what sort of, online access and use are we each going to need in future to have any chance of participating actively as a citizen?

Oscar Gandy (2002) has gone so far as to argue that here lies the 'real digital divide' – the divide between people considered as mere consumers and people considered as participating citizens. If Gandy is suggesting that the differences in access and use discussed in this chapter are of no consequence, then that goes too far. More likely, Gandy means that what is *ultimately* at stake in Digital Divide debates is not, or not only, the health of the national and global economy, but also whether people share the resources to participate in some political space that deserves the name of democracy. If so, then, for all its limitations, the term 'Digital Divide' is worth still keeping in play.

USEFUL WEBSITES

A Nation Online: www.ntia.doc.gov/ntiahome/dn/anationonline2.pdf

2002 report commissioned by the Bush administration's Department of Commerce which tries to consign the Digital Divide debate to history.

Children's Partnership 2000 Report: www.childrenspartnership.org

Controversial US report on the Digital Divide, as suggested by its title: 'Online content for low-income and underserved Americans: the Digital Divide's new frontier'.

Closing the Digital Divide: www.pat15.org.uk

Useful report published by the UK Department of Trade and Industry. An example of the Blair Government's thinking on 'Digital Divide' issues.

Digital Divide Network: www.digitaldividenetwork.org

Useful site run by the US-based think-tanks, the Benton Foundation and the Markle Foundation, that collects information on Digital Divide debates.

Falling Through the Net Reports: www.ntia.doc.gov/ntiahome/fttn

The research report series by the Clinton administration's Department of Commerce, which high-lighted Digital Divide issues within US domestic politics.

OECD Report on Understanding the Digital Divide 2001: www.oecd.org/pdf/M00002000/M0002444.pdf

Thorough background report on the Digital Divide on an international scale.

Chapter 16

COPYRIGHT IN CYBERSPACE: PROTECTING INTELLECTUAL PROPERTY ONLINE

KATHLEEN K. OLSON

INTRODUCTION

Electronic Frontier Foundation co-founder John Perry Barlow (1994) once compared the enforcement of intellectual property rights on the internet to 'selling wine without bottles'. Whereas copyright laws have traditionally been physically based (copyright attaches when the work is 'fixed in a tangible medium'), information flows without physical form on the internet. Some scholars have therefore concluded that the copyright system requires a complete reworking to be relevant online, while others have used the advent of digital technology to revive a long-standing movement to abolish intellectual property rights altogether.

What is so different about copyright on the internet? The short answer is nothing. The copyright laws apply equally to digital works as to works that exist in the physical world, so most material on the internet is protected by copyright. Online news articles and photographs, newsgroup postings, e-mail messages – even symbols, logos and annoying animated graphics – may be copyrighted material. At the same time, digital technology has brought new challenges in protecting intellectual property. In the past, copyright owners could count on physical limitations to control unlawful copying of their work. Photocopying a novel, for example, was laborious and inferior in quality to the original. Digital copies can be easy, cheap and perfect.

Enforcement is another challenge in cyberspace. Tracking down infringers has always been difficult, but identifying pirates in cyberspace is virtually impossible. Instead, many copyright owners have fought back using their own technology, making use of encryption and other security measures to 'lock up' their intellectual property and control its use. They have also lobbied for – and received – new copyright legislation to add legal force to these controls.

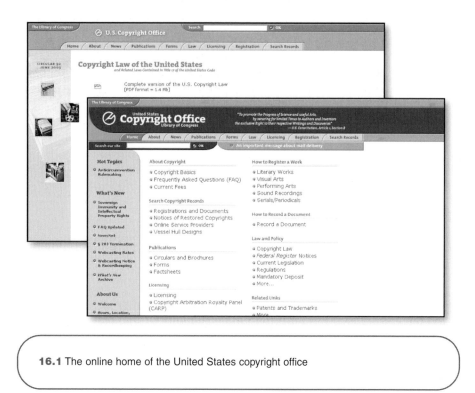

16.1 The online home of the United States copyright office

WHAT IS COPYRIGHT?

Copyright is a property right given to producers of creative expression. Copyright does *not* protect ideas or facts, but it protects works of literature, music, drama, art, sound recordings, photography, movies, software and other original works of authorship. The owner of the copyright in a work owns a set of exclusive rights with regard to that work, including the rights to reproduce, prepare 'derivative' works, distribute copies and perform or display the work. These rights attach to the author of a work as soon as the work is fixed in a 'tangible' medium of expression. Registration is generally not required and the absence of a copyright notice does not mean the work is not copyrighted.

While copyright gives authors important rights, these rights are limited. Once the term of the copyright is over, for example, the work becomes part of the public domain and may be freely used by others. Even before that, exceptions such as the fair use doctrine may allow the use of a work without permission from the copyright holder. Fair use allows works to be used without permission for purposes of scholarship, teaching, news reporting, or comment and criticism, including parody.

While international treaties have standardized the laws regarding copyright to a fair degree, the philosophies underlying copyright protection differ across cultures. American copyright law, for example, is based on an incentive model rooted in the Constitution, which gave Congress the power to grant authors exclusive rights in their works, for a limited time, in order to 'promote the progress of science and useful arts'. Rights transfer with the copyright, so that an author forfeits all control over the work once he or she sells the copyright. In contrast, the continental European model of intellectual property is based on the French concept of 'droit moral', which recognizes an author's moral right to control the fate of his or her creative work.

While the philosophical bases may differ, multinational treaties regarding copyright have brought some uniformity to the rules regarding copyright worldwide. The Berne Convention, adopted in 1866, was the first international effort to ensure that countries provide the same copyright protection to works created in other countries as they would works created in their own countries. The Berne Convention, as revised and amended over the years, remains the primary international treaty and provides minimum standards of copyright protection to which all of its signatories must adhere.

The World Intellectual Property Organization (WIPO), headquartered in Geneva, Switzerland, coordinates and administers multinational efforts to protect intellectual property rights through international treaties, including changes to the Berne Convention. WIPO has 179 member nations, including the United States, Australia, the European Union member states, and China. WIPO has played a central role in attempts to answer the challenges posed by digital technology and the internet to intellectual property rights.

COPYRIGHT PIRACY

That digital technology would challenge the authority of traditional copyright law is not surprising. After all, the printing press is generally credited with creating a need for copyright in the first place, and technological changes throughout the years have spurred changes in intellectual property law to accommodate them. It was not that long ago, after all, that technological advances such as the VCR and the tape recorder were criticized for the assistance they gave to copyright infringers.

The internet, more so than these innovations, is seen by many as a double-edged sword. While it provides an unlimited opportunity to create and distribute one's own creative works, it also provides the opportunity to copy and distribute the works of others without permission. This is the 'digital dilemma', according to the US-based National Research Council (2000), because the internet 'is at once one of the world's largest libraries and surely the world's largest copying machine'.

The need for a new multinational treaty that addressed copyright protections in the context of the internet and digital technology was apparent by 1996, when the Berne Convention was supplemented by two treaties meant to address the issue.

The WIPO Internet Treaties were adopted to crack down on digital piracy by requiring WIPO member states to provide legal remedies against those who circumvent technological protection measures (such as passwords or encryption) or who tamper with copyright management information (such as watermarks) built into digital works.

Before the treaties were ratified by the necessary number of member states to formally take effect, the United States amended its own copyright law to comply with the treaty. The Digital Millennium Copyright Act of 1998 (DMCA) made it a crime to gain unauthorized access to a copyrighted work by circumventing anti-piracy protections built into the work. The DMCA also made it illegal to manufacture, provide, or otherwise traffic in any technology, product, or service that could be used to circumvent copy protection measures. The law provides for both civil and criminal prosecution for violations.

Critics claim that, rather than merely extending existing copyright protection to digital works, the anti-circumvention provisions of the DMCA gave copyright owners too much control over digital works and undermined important principles such as fair use. The Electronic Frontier Foundation and other interest groups claim that the DMCA has been used not just to fight digital piracy but also to chill free expression and suppress legitimate research by journalists, scientists and computer programmers. Others see the Act, in conjunction with recent copyright legislation that extended the length of the copyright term and increased criminal liability for infringement, as another corporate handout for large media corporations such as Disney, Time Warner and the recording studios.

Indeed, Disney and its brothers in the movie industry have not been reluctant to wield the DMCA as a weapon in the fight against what might be called the 'Napsterization' of videos on the internet. 'We're fighting our own terrorist war', Jack Valenti, president of the Motion Picture Association of America, told *The New York Times* in 2002. One of the first battles in that war has been over DeCSS, a decryption software program that allows users to circumvent the anti-piracy encryption code embedded on most DVDs. Circumventing the code allows pirates to make multiple high-quality copies and distribute them over the internet.

Not all those who seek to circumvent the anti-copying devices are pirates, however. Norwegian teenager, Jon Johansen, for example, developed the program in 1999 so that he could make DVDs compatible with his computer's Linux operating system. The software he developed also allowed users to exercise their fair use rights by copying portions of a movie for comment and criticism or for educational or research purposes.

In 2000, Johansen's invention garnered him a prestigious national prize. In 2002, it garnered him an indictment for criminal trespass. Under pressure from American entertainment companies, Norwegian prosecutors in the country's

16.2 The Australian Copyright Council hosts an extensive online information archive

economic crime unit indicted Johansen for violating laws that had previously been applied only to hackers who obtained bank records or other sensitive data. He was acquitted in January 2003. At the urging of the Motion Picture Association of America, Norway's economic crime unit appealed against the decision and a new trial was set for December 2003.

A similar case arose in the United States in 2001, when Dimitri Sklyarov, a Russian PhD student and computer programmer, was arrested in Las Vegas for violating the DMCA. Sklyarov and his employer, software development company ElcomSoft, were indicted for illegally creating and 'trafficking in' a software program that circumvented the anti-copying protection device built into Adobe Systems' eBook Reader. The software allowed legitimate users of the eBook Reader to copy and print digital books and to transfer them from one computer to another.

A federal judge rejected ElcomSoft's argument that the anti-circumvention provision of the DMCA violated the fair use rights of users of the eBook Reader by preventing them from copying portions of the book for legitimate uses. The case went to trial in late 2002, as Sklyarov, who had faced 25 years in prison, agreed to testify against his former employer in exchange for the dropping of charges against him.

Some critics fear that the Act will stifle innovations in software by making it a crime to 'reverse-engineer' encryption technology or to point out flaws in the code of such devices. Indeed, some cases involving the DMCA have gone beyond prosecuting those who manufacture the circumventing technologies to reach those who merely talk about such technologies.

While American principles of free speech would seem to prohibit such prosecutions, federal courts in 2001 rejected First Amendment challenges to the DMCA in two separate cases. In one case, a research team led by Princeton University professor Edward Felten challenged the Act, claiming it prevented the scholars from publishing research they had done regarding security flaws in digital watermarking technology under development for use in digital music. Felten and his team asked a judge to declare that they had a First Amendment right to discuss weaknesses in digital protection measures, but the judge rejected the argument and dismissed the lawsuit.

In the other case, an appeals court in New York upheld a lower court's ruling that the operator of the hacker magazine and website *2600: The Hacker Quarterly* (www.2600.com) violated the DMCA by publishing Jon Johansen's DeCSS code. The trial judge had also ruled that the website could not even provide links to the DeCSS code without violating the DMCA. The court rejected the defendant's First Amendment arguments and concluded that, even if the DMCA made the exercise of legitimate fair use rights more difficult, this result had been taken into consideration by Congress in enacting the DMCA and was beyond the court's authority to rectify.

Thus the early decisions regarding the DMCA have leaned heavily in favour of the copyright owners' rights to protect their works. What is disturbing about the cases so far is that they indicate that the entertainment industry may use the copyright laws not only to control unlawful copying but also to limit legitimate uses of their products and regulate the circumstances in which users read or view or listen to digital works they have legally purchased and rightfully own.

This concern has led several American lawmakers to introduce bills in Congress to amend the DMCA to make it clear that anti-piracy protections should not come at the expense of the public's traditional fair use rights under copyright law. Representative Rick Boucher of Virginia sponsored a Bill in late 2002 that would make it legal to circumvent a technological measure to gain access to a work if the circumvention does not result in an infringement of the copyright in the work. For example, an e-book owner would be able to circumvent the access control in order to read the e-book on a different electronic reader, and researchers would be permitted to produce and use software tools necessary to carry out scientific research into technological protection measures without fear of falling foul of the law. Boucher's Bill, called the Digital Media Consumers' Rights Act of 2002, was strongly endorsed by the Electronic Frontier Foundation and library groups in the United States. Representative Zoe Lofgren of California introduced a similar Bill. (The fate of these Bills is not known at the time of writing.)

OTHER ISSUES IN INTERNET COPYRIGHT

At the same time that courts have been forced to interpret provisions of new legislation regarding copyright, they have also faced the challenge of applying existing copyright law to the unique features of the internet. Many of these cases have involved hyperlinking, a feature unique and integral to the World Wide Web. Web inventor Tim Berners-Lee (1997) sees linking as the *raison d'être* of the medium:

> The Web was designed to be a universal space of information, so when you make a bookmark or a hypertext link, you should be able to make that link to absolutely any piece of information that can be accessed using networks. The universality is essential to the Web: it loses its power if there are certain types of things to which you can't link.

Because hyperlinking is so fundamental to the purpose of the Web, linking without asking permission has been the norm, and an 'implied licence' to link to other sites has generally been recognized. Still, some legal problems have arisen having to do with hyperlinking, and a small but growing body of case law has begun to form.

Deep linking

The first litigation over hyperlinking involved links that took the user directly to an inside page of another website rather than to the homepage for the site. Called 'deep linking', this practice has been the focus of both controversy and litigation. The first case took place in the Shetland Islands, off Scotland, in 1996 in the midst of a small-scale online newspaper war. In that case, the judge temporarily barred *The Shetland News* from linking directly from its website to stories on the website of *The Shetland Times*. These links bypassed the competing newspaper's home page and therefore the advertising on that page. The court found that the potential loss of advertising revenue and the fact that the *News* had copied the *Times'* headlines verbatim to create the hyperlinks, weighed heavily in favour of the *Times*. The parties settled the dispute before an appeal could be heard, with the *News* obtaining permission to link to the *Times* site and agreeing to clearly identify the links as *Times* material.

In a similar case in the United States, the ticket seller TicketMaster sued Microsoft in 1997 for deep linking into TicketMaster's website from Microsoft's 'Seattle Sidewalks' city guide website. Again the issue was the bypassing of lucrative banner advertising on TicketMaster's homepage. TicketMaster claimed Microsoft's deep links diluted the TicketMaster trademark and constituted unfair competition. Unlike the judge in the Shetland case, the judge in this case refused to grant a preliminary injunction to stop the deep linking, but the ruling has little precedential value since the case was settled out of court.

More recent skirmishes over linking have brought mixed results in Europe and the United States. In the summer of 2002, a Danish court ruled that deep linking to 28 newspaper sites by the news search engine Newsbooster.com violated the copyright of those newspapers. In a similar case, a judge in Munich ruled that NewsClub's news search engine violated European Union law, ruling in favour of the publisher of the newspaper *Mainpost* against the German website for linking directly to *Mainpost*'s stories.

During the same period in the United States, on the other hand, several controversies regarding deep linking ended up being settled without resort to the courts. Facing strong public criticism, the National Public Radio network revised its policy that required websites to obtain permission before linking to the NPR site. *Runner's World* magazine publisher Rodale Press sent a cease-and-desist letter to the running website LetsRun.com regarding deep links to its magazine site, but backed down after LetsRun.com pointed out that the *Runner's World* site also used deep links, including some that linked back to LetsRun.com!

While most intellectual property experts do not regard hyperlinking as a violation of copyright law, the case law remains unsettled. According to the website *Don't Link to Us! Stupid Linking Policies* (www.dontlink.com), dozens of corporate websites continue to attempt to prohibit deep linking or otherwise impose restrictions on other sites that link to them.

Framing

A related legal issue involves 'framing', another feature unique to the World Wide Web. 'Framing' refers to websites that appear in the browser in multiple, independently scrollable windows. Each window contains a separate webpage, which may come from a completely different site. Unlike hyperlinks, therefore, the use of frames allows content from one site to be 'imported' into another site. Framing may infringe on a copyright owner's rights to control the distribution of the work and to make derivative works. It may also pose legal problems regarding trademark or unfair competition, especially if website A attempts to 'pass off' website B's content as its own.

In 1997, several large media companies, including The Washington Post Company and CNN, sued TotalNews (www.totalnews.com), a Web-based news service that presented stories from the media companies' websites within frames on the TotalNews site. In their legal complaint, the companies claimed that TotalNews was 'engaged in the internet equivalent of pirating copyrighted material from a variety of famous newspapers, magazines, or television news programs' and packaging the stories as its own. Just as these actions would be considered infringing in the print and broadcasting world, the media companies said, they were equally unlawful in cyberspace. Along with their concern that TotalNews was 'passing off' their content as its own, the media companies disliked that the frame setup on the TotalNews site precluded readers from seeing the banner ads on their own sites.

As part of a settlement in the case, TotalNews was required to obtain from the media companies specific 'link licences' authorizing the hyperlinks, and had to promise to display the media companies' news stories without frames and without deleting accompanying text, graphics or advertising. While no court has definitively ruled on the issue, framing appears to present more obvious legal problems than mere linking, especially if the frames are set up to 'pass off' another site's content as one's own.

CONCLUSION

Copyright is a complex issue and an increasingly important one in the digital age. The tension between protecting intellectual property and promoting creativity and the free flow of ideas is evident in the controversies that surround the DMCA and the cases discussed in this chapter. Striking the right balance between economic interests and freedom of expression is a difficult task for legislatures and the courts, and the stakes are high. The challenge is to prevent the widespread copyright infringement that the internet makes possible without limiting the creativity and access to information that it also provides.

USEFUL WEBSITES

The Copyright Website: www.benedict.com

Published by an American intellectual property lawyer, this site gives a good overview of copyright concepts, and includes case law on visual, audio and digital copyright issues.

Electronic Frontier Foundation: www.eff.org

A non-profit advocacy group dedicated to defending civil liberties on the internet. Topics covered include censorship and intellectual property/fair use.

**Ten Big Myths About Copyright Explained:
www.templetons.com/brad/copymyths.html**

The publisher of an early internet newspaper established this site to clear up some of the confusion about copyright on the Web. It covers e-mail and newsgroup postings.

United States Copyright Office: www.loc.gov/copyright

The definitive guide to US copyright law, includes a 'Hot Topics' section on current issues.

WIPO: www.wipo.org

The official site of the World Intellectual Property Organization includes primers on intellectual property as well as the full text of WIPO treaties and conventions.

Chapter 17

THE MUSIC INDUSTRY VERSUS THE INTERNET: MP3 AND OTHER CYBER MUSIC WARS

IAN DOBIE

This chapter analyses the controversial issues surrounding the distribution and consumption of online music at the turn of the millennium. The consumer-led online music revolution rode on the back of a new technology that enhanced connectivity but disregarded notions of copyright and intellectual property. The increasing popularity of the internet, and the use of the networked computer as a media device, appeared to change the relationship between the major corporations and the public. It enabled artists to create, promote and disseminate their own music, as well as discovering new ways of consuming and interacting with music – but it also meant that the record companies lost control over the copying and distribution of their recordings in the online environment, to the financial detriment of the music industry. I will explore the tensions and conflicts that emerged and came to occupy centre stage as these two opposing pressures battled for supremacy.

On the one hand, the music industry is comprised of the five major record companies (Sony, BMG, EMI, Warners, Universal), all of which are owned and controlled by larger transnational conglomerates. These global corporations invest in the extremely costly business of finding talent, and developing, producing, recording, promoting and distributing musical recordings (Burnett, 1996). The expense involved in this process is generally considered worthwhile because the investment can often be recouped through the sale of vast numbers of CDs that carry copies of those recordings. This is the business model that any cultural industry relies on, and is made possible by an effective and enforceable system of copyright: copyright grants exclusive rights to the creator of a work (in this case the record company as producer of the sound recording), such as the right to authorize the duplication and the dissemination of a work to the public. The major companies are therefore the only parties permitted to reproduce and sell those recordings, thereby guaranteeing (as far as possible) a return on their investment. This is why enforceable copyright is so crucial to the industry – because if the record company invested in the production of a recording, but then everyone was permitted to copy it and sell it, the record company would not be able to cover its costs. The reproduction and dissemination of a work are therefore centralized operations that are restricted to the producer of that work (see Frith, 1993).

On the other hand, a vast number of consumers, who were interconnected by a global electronic communications network, had been experimenting with very different forms of content dissemination throughout the 1990s. This network of networks, now known as the internet, was originally developed so that, for military reasons, attempts to restrict the dissemination of information would be futile. Therefore, the distribution of information by individuals throughout this network had developed in a way that promoted access to, and the sharing of, information or content. In this instance the content in question was produced less by corporations than by individuals or working collectives. The content tended to be more informative, intellectual, technical or scientific in its nature, as opposed to commercial entertainment, and it tended to be disseminated on a non-monetary basis. Rather than a one-to-many model of commercial distribution, this was a decentralized network of individuals who collectively formed an autonomous and self-informing body of thinkers participating in a largely non-monetary exchange of information and ideas (see Rheingold, 1993).

As far as the internet community was concerned, their interests in creating, copying and sharing music throughout the network was the result of a number of different but converging technologies. In contrast with analogue sound, the emergence of digital audio enabled infinite serial duplication of a recording without any degradation. New compression algorithms, such as mp3, enabled the reduction of a large audio file to a relatively minuscule one. The upgrading of public communication networks, and the increased data rate enabled by faster modems, allowed more information to be transferred from one location to another more quickly. Accordingly, the musical uses to which these technologies were put became diverse and varied, but early mp3 use evolved in two distinct directions. The first was rooted in the decentralized model of intellectual exchange, or what Barbrook (1998) called the 'gift economy'; perhaps *MP3.com* epitomized this type of musical activity, where a network of independent producers and consumers shared their own music and information on a non-monetary basis, through the enthusiasm, enjoyment and satisfaction of disseminating their own music in a way that was previously impossible. The excitement surrounding this time was generated by the unprecedented ability to operate independently of the state and the market, and to form inter-personal relationships that were not mediated by capitalism. Engaging in the musical gift economy helped to build a kind of DIY utopia that bypassed the need to engage the interest of a record company, or to target one's music at an identified market category. It was a small act of rebellion against the pressure to 'consume' commercial products, and the internet was hailed by many as a refuge from the continual onslaught of corporate invasion into all areas of everyday life.

Concurrent with the musical gift economy was the emerging practice of 'ripping', or extracting music from copyrighted CDs into mp3 format for personal use, and exchanging them over Internet Relay Chat or posting them up on websites. Where the musical gift economy may have been epitomized by *MP3.com*, perhaps this second strand of activity could be characterized by music-oriented peer-to-peer (P2P) services such as Napster. P2P technology is a recent innovation, and could only have been developed by natives of cyberspace. It embraces the network technology, culture and ethos, is a product of the network architecture, and characterizes the internet's inter-personal structure – a network of relationships on a global scale among millions of people. As far as the music corporations were concerned, the rapid growth of this unauthorized use was the point at which they had to sit up and pay close attention; the rise in popularity of the internet during the mid- to late 1990s meant that a growing majority of users were not rooted in the ethics of intellectual exchange, but borrowed these ideas and extended them to incorporate the free exchange of any content and information. The majority of 'newbies' tended to engage in less interaction and more in standard forms of consumption (Lessig, 1999: 64), and the fact that this occurred within the

17.1 Kazaa is just one of several peer-to-peer (P2P) applications where users exchange a wealth of music, video and software files free of charge

non-monetary framework of networked distribution clearly appeared to violate the corporations' rights to centralize and control the distribution of their own content, thereby conflicting with their interests. Although file exchange was an extension of the now-legal activity of home taping, it was clearly considered illegal by the establishment, and summoned the well-documented wrath of the major record companies.

For the internet community, music use continues to evolve along two strands – the sharing of 'authorized' music files (such as music created by amateurs or semi-professionals, or distributed by Web-savvy independent labels), over sites such as *MP3.com*, and the sharing of 'unauthorized' music files (such as major label copyrighted music) over popular services such as *Kazaa*, which is now more than twice as popular as Napster ever was, with reportedly 120 million users (*Wired Music News*, 25 December 2002). On the authorized front, music can now be produced at home and promoted and disseminated over a global network for minimal cost, and this has allowed a thriving independent online music industry to develop. At one end of the spectrum this is based on the gift economy idea of sharing one's own work on a non-financial basis – a hobby for some, and an act of participating in a mutual community of interest. Even if the user does not identify with the political implications of engaging in the gift economy, such non-commercial exchange is the most efficient means of disseminating one's work when its market has not yet been established.

At the other end of the authorized spectrum, some artists make a substantial amount of money from distributing their music over the net, and perhaps the people most able to benefit from this model of independent distribution are those who have attained stardom through the established music industry, but whose music is now not commercially viable for record company investment. Such artists often have a large and dedicated fan base that can be consolidated and courted, and that can potentially provide a level of support for artists deprived of other sources of funding. Artists such as David Bowie (bowienet.com) and Pete Townshend (pete-townshend.co.uk) can enjoy a successful and direct relationship with their audience that is mediated only by transparent service providers – Bowie provides a successful subscription portal which acts as an outlet for his work as well as a means of cultivating his fan base.

Less renowned artists can also enjoy such a relationship, but they may need either to become part of a community of interest by joining a service that acts as a portal for smaller artists (such as *MP3.com*, which attracts a vast amount of traffic), or procure the services of an intermediary that acts more like a traditional, but perhaps independent, record company. The advantage that the network offers such intermediaries is access to a low-cost global promotion and distribution infrastructure. Through the reduced overheads in bringing a work to the market in this way, a creative online/independent record label, such as Chuck D's *Slamjamz*, may be able to offer artists more equitable contract conditions (such as 50/50 co-ownership of a work) than the major corporations do (Chuck D, 12/2000).

The issues surrounding the notorious activity of unauthorized file exchange focus on consumption rather than production, and represent a radical departure from the traditional means of acquisition and consumption. Although illegal, it has empowered consumers with the ability to find and acquire music instantly (relatively speaking), spontaneously and flexibly, and it encourages a greater degree of experimentation than traditional media. It has finally allowed pop music to be consumed as pop music – track by track, three minutes at a time, rather than on a 74-minute album basis – and the enormous popularity of P2P file-sharing services attests to the overwhelming demand for the ability to exercise such flexibility in the consumption of music (see Fink *et al.*, Fall 2000: 6–13). It also affirms the market appeal of major label-produced music, indicating the majors' continued validity as producers of cultural goods.

And perhaps this is another point of contention between the major labels and the internet users: that the demand for online music is blatantly there, but the supply is nowhere to be seen – the corporations continue to outlaw the illegal activity, yet have provided no legitimate replacement solution until very recently. It remains to be seen whether the corporations' determination to operate strictly within a secure framework has jeopardized their ability to exploit the online market.

The major corporations' desire to pull control of their recordings back in line with the offline environment was born through a necessity to perpetuate the business model that worked for them. Although many users expected the major corporations to lead the development of the online music space by officially releasing their catalogues over the Web, their attitude was to leave the development of online services to others, since the insecure digital market conflicted with their core (offline) business. They recognized that they would eventually be forced to develop their own online services, but that any such ventures would be undertaken using a technology that would restrict the user's ability to copy and distribute their recordings, such as copyright management systems.

For the major record companies it appears that, owing to the vast amount of money involved in the process of music production, copyright is a means to an end. In the past 20 years they have been expanding in size, integrating into other markets, and extending their reach to the point where they are fully global corporations. As throughout the last 100 years, they continue to constitute a tight oligopoly, which in 2002 distributed 80 per cent of the worldwide market for recorded music. They have been instrumental in fine-tuning copyright protection to their own advantage, and they are more than ever reliant upon the offline market structure: the centralized model of production and distribution (Garofalo, 1999).

Therefore, rather than trying to enter the market earlier in an attempt to maintain consumer loyalty, they implemented an anti-piracy campaign that consisted of education, enforcement, litigation and developing new technology, while their longer-term plan consisted of tightening Intellectual Property Rights, litigation, strategic alliances, and again developing new technology. The intention of these strategies was to impede the development of the mp3 market while they developed new technologies to extend their dominance over the converging mediascape, to halt unauthorized activity and to increase their ability to derive revenue through the administration of copyright (see Brindley, 2000).

The corporations' move towards ever-tightening oligopoly was indicative of their attempt to maintain and extend dominance over their markets. In the offline world this manifested itself in horizontal integration: mergers with corporations that could maintain their dominance within the shifting mediascape (such as the AOL/Time Warner merger), and acquisition of companies that would allow them to extend their presence to the further corners of the online music space (such as the buyout of *MP3.com* and *EMusic*). The effect of this was to bring the successful elements of the emergent decentralized music industry under the control of the established centralized industry, as well as to develop their product presentation within cyberspace by, for example, advertising their authorized *PressPlay* service on affiliate sites such as *MP3.com* and *EMusic*.

As well as maintaining a tight oligopoly the majors have also been influential in copyright reform that, in the past 20 years, has increasingly favoured rights holders. The term of copyright has been lengthened, the scope of copyright has been broadened, and any exceptions to the owner's monopoly over copying and distribution have become very specific and narrowly defined (see Marshall, 2001). Since the 1976 US Copyright Act, the objective has increasingly been to expand the owner's protection over his work – partly as a reaction to the increased ease of copying and distribution as technology has progressed, but also because the increasing power of the major corporations since the 1980s has enabled them to set the rules by which the market and society operate. The effect of this has been that copyright reform for the digital environment, such as the 1998 Digital Millennium Copyright Act (DMCA), has effectively granted rights holders the right to use copyright management technologies to determine the terms on which their works are accessed (see Lessig, 1999).

The adverse effect of this tightening of copyrights is that the public's statutory rights have been substantially diminished. Copyright was originally understood to be a bargain that balanced the interests of the author, the publisher and the public; particularly in US copyright, the first consideration was that works should be created in order that the public might benefit through the exchange of ideas upon which future creators might build. The owner's monopoly of copying and distribution was only considered as an incentive for authors to create. It was limited in length and scope, and any public uses that fell outside of the author's rights became known as 'fair use':

> The primary objective of copyright is not to reward the labor of authors, but
> '[t]o promote the Progress of Science and useful Arts.' To this end, copyright
> assures authors the right to their original expression, but encourages others to
> build freely upon the ideas and information conveyed by a work. This result is
> neither unfair nor unfortunate. It is the means by which copyright advances
> the progress of science and art.
>
> (*US Supreme Court, Feist Publications Inc. vs Rural Tel. Service Co. 499
> US 340 (1991),* Findlaw, http://laws.findlaw.com/US/499/340.html;
> accessed 14 January 2000)

As the rights holder's protection over his or her work expanded, fair use and the
public domain diminished, and copyright has become less about promoting the
'progress of Science and the useful Arts' as codified in the US Constitution, than
it is about maintaining the status quo of the market-place (see Théberge, 1993).
The public therefore feel that their rights within copyright are being hijacked, and
that copyright is being used as a tool to outlaw what many consider to be legitimate behaviour. Copyright is the central issue around which the conflicting activities revolve. While the industry has successfully defined (through the triumphant
Napster litigation) that unauthorized file exchange infringes their rights, the public are also concerned that the rights owner's increased protection over his or her
work also infringes their own statutory rights.

Since both industry and internet community are now firmly ensconced in cyberspace, how can the interests of both parties be reconciled? Just as copyright was
originally deemed to serve the interests of the three parties involved in bringing a
work to the market (the author, the publisher and the public), can such a bargain
or balance be struck in the environment that appears to disregard notions of copyright? The corporations want to exploit their recordings, and consumers have
voiced an active demand, so can the conflicting parties be reconciled through
aligned interests, without infringing each other's rights?

For the corporations, perhaps the most effective means of enforcing copyright on
the internet is through the development of technology that restricts the user's
ability to copy and distribute recordings. Recent CD releases that incorporate
restrictive technology have deliberately rendered CDs unplayable on home computers. In the past this strategy has met with little success – BMG found that a
large percentage of CDs were returned by consumers who complained that the
CDs were faulty. However, this is likely to be a tactic that is increasingly attempted
by all of the major labels despite its potential unpopularity with consumers. The
obvious objection will be that since playing CDs on one's computer, and even ripping mp3s for personal use, is still a legitimate activity, corporate moves to block
such activities plainly infringe consumer's rights. This has been the concern voiced
by academics and laypeople alike: that once rights owners are given the freedom

(by new laws such as the DMCA) to control more and more uses through technology, the public's rights diminish accordingly (see Litman, 2001). Perhaps a more popular version of CD-based copy protection technologies would permit legitimate personal use (playing on computers and ripping to mp3) while restricting the ability to redistribute the resulting mp3s over the internet; this was the original plan for the Secure Digital Music Initiative (SDMI) specification.

As far as authorized digital distribution is concerned, any online major-label offering is certain to be released in a format that imposes rules on user behaviour. The SDMI seems almost redundant in 2002, and other rights management systems have been generally slow to emerge and gain acceptance. In terms of luring consumers from illegal services such as *Morpheus* or *Audiogalaxy* onto legitimate subscription music services, the major labels will need to offer added value over the obvious advantage that the illegal services offer: P2P services are free and mp3 usage is well established.

Such added value may emerge when and if legitimate services become available over other networked hardware devices such as mobile phones, cable and satellite TV, and eventually networked hi-fi devices. This would overcome the problem of competing with the established mp3 format, and the services could be tailored to provide value and convenience on different hardware media. The architecture of the devices could enforce user behaviour and even restrict the ability to copy, while the potential for fast data transfer over broadband services could provide an adequate incentive for many users to switch their consumption patterns. If consumers could be encouraged to switch from an overloaded narrowband internet to fully interactive broadband services which included all types of entertainment, then the industry could enforce copyrights within a broadcasting framework that could incorporate the ability to generate copyright royalties and subsequent revenue streams. This could bring a broadband online environment in line with the current market structure while at the same time satisfying demand. It may not actually conflict with the decentralized activities of internet users, but the provision of faster, more comprehensive, and more appealing services may be just what is required to satisfy a demand. This must, therefore, appear to be the major labels' longer-term strategy.

In terms of the future development of the music industry, there are some scenarios that seem likely. The first is that the established model of production, promotion and distribution as practised by the major labels is likely to remain intact for the foreseeable future. It is a model that has evolved slowly over a long period of time, to which the music public is accustomed, and of which it generally approves. The insatiable appetite for charismatic icons and recognizable songs has fuelled the market for mainstream hit records and superstars. The industry structure that has been built to accommodate this market will be increasingly effective as corporations integrate on a global basis and extend their reach into the different corners of the converging multimedia markets. Copyright will remain the central system by which revenue is generated; recent developments within copyright, such as the expansion of owner's rights, indicate that Intellectual Property Rights will grow in stature as they become increasingly significant as a source of revenue, and the economic importance of the cultural industries will expand accordingly.

Alongside this traditional model of music activity is the emergent online music market. This is split into three main strands of activity. The first is the legitimate market for major-label copyrighted recordings. This will work within the logic of the established offline market outlined above. The online market is peripheral to the major labels' core offline market, and development of online services will not be dictated by technological advancement in its own right, but by the ability for technology to function within the logic of the traditional market. As demonstrated by the industry's lawsuits against innovative start-up technology companies, this has been the intention of the corporations all along – that however new or exciting technological development may seem, the majors will not utilize it if it threatens their exclusive ability to derive revenue through the copyright system. Therefore their subscription services *MusicNet* and *PressPlay* are offered within a system that provides some level of copyright protection. As these services were only launched in early 2002 it is too early to say how they will be received by the public, but they are the first stage along the long and winding road to faster and more fully interactive services.

The second strand of activity is the illegal market for major-label music. This looks set to continue unabated, since file sharing seems to be as popular as ever. Although the catalytic *Napster* has folded, other services continue to provide free access to copyrighted music on a P2P basis. Such services are increasingly difficult to target for litigation, as there are no central servers, user anonymity is protected, and these services will increasingly be built with the aim of being litigation-proof.

The third strand of activity is the legitimate market for independent music. At one end this is characterized by *MP3.com*, while at the other end are established artists for whom the major-label system is no longer effective. In either case, independent digital distribution would appear to be a more realistic option than major-label investment, due to the ability of the independent network to accommodate and consolidate a more diverse range of musical styles and niche markets. This is therefore the most likely arena for servicing the markets that are not economically feasible for the major companies to invest in.

The major record companies' attempts to eradicate online piracy are still fraught with difficulties as P2P music services are as popular as ever. Since P2P services will be increasingly elusive targets for litigation, the solution may be to offer attractive services that fulfil consumer demand. Just as *MP3.com* developed innovative services with the new technology, so the majors could follow that lead. Their aim must be to give consumers what they want, within their own framework of copyright, and then the interests of all three parties within the copyright bargain would be fulfilled: the artist, the publisher and the consumer. For although the public's rights have diminished as the owner's rights over their works have expanded, increased competition within the new technology market could render this balance/imbalance irrelevant. The owner's complete protection over the work is pitted against the user's complete disregard for copyright. Therefore the benchmark against which a service is measured will be its practical value to the user. The only amenable solution seems to be an increase in the standard of music service provision by the major labels, to fulfil consumer demand within the commercial framework of copyright. This is no easy task, but at last it may be time for the major record companies to be imaginative and innovative, rather than reactionary and authoritarian.

 **USEFUL WEBSITES**

Bowie Net: www.bowienet.com

A subscription portal from the musical innovator himself. Sites such as these allow established artists to become connected with their fan base.

Insound: www.insound.com

A Web label, zine and forum, contains essays by Jenny Toomey on the plight of the independent artist on the Web.

MP3.com: www.mp3.com

The mother of all independent artist-led music sites. Now owned by Universal it straddles the worlds of the independent Web-musician and mainstream pop acts.

PressPlay: www.pressplay.com

The corporate music service offered by Vivendi-Universal and Sony – also promoted through affiliate sites such as *MP3.com*, the Microsoft Network and Yahoo!.

Quercus Circus: www.quercus-circus.co.uk

Ian Dobie's extensive academic resource on the impact of the internet on the music industry, with a large section of links to related material.

Wired Music News: www.wired.com/news/mp3

Regular and up-to-the-minute news stories on the ever-changing technoscape of digital music: piracy, delivery, independent and corporate artist tales – it's all there.

Part 4:

Global Web
Communities,
Politics and Protest

Chapter 18

THE INTERNET
AND DEMOCRACY

STEPHEN LAX

INTRODUCTION

One of the most prominent among the many and varied claims about the social potential of the internet is that it will enhance the democratic process. At a time when both
interest and participation in politics are perceived to be in decline, commentators
across the world are suggesting that new information and communication technologies (ICTs) can link both government and governed. Others suggest that they could
promote debate and discussion among the electorate. For the British government, this
is part of the 'modernization' of a society in which ideas of class, interventionism and
regulation are seen as old-fashioned. Now, knowledge is the new 'capital' to be accu-
mulated, and information becomes the key commodity for exchange.

ICTs enable novel, 'democratic' practices to take place: people can use the internet
to access government documents or to visit campaigning organizations; groups
of people can engage in discussions through e-mail networks. But to draw the
conclusion that this means society at large will become more democratic is ques-
tionable. Will barriers to access to these technologies mean that participation is
confined to the more privileged? If information provision is central to a better-
informed electorate, should we be concerned about the quality or veracity of that
information? More fundamentally, what are the reasons for supposing that provision of information and access to new (though not necessarily novel) communication channels are any more likely to engage electors and to ensure that more of
the people will be able to exert political influence?

THE CLAIMS

The UK government's White Paper, *Modernising Government*, set out its vision for
electronic government:

We live in an age when most of the old dogmas that haunted governments in the past have been swept away. We know now that better government is about much more than whether public spending should go up or down, or whether organisations should be nationalised or privatised ... Information technology is revolutionising our lives, including the way we work, the way we communicate and the way we learn. The information age offers huge scope for organising government activities in new, innovative and better ways and for making life easier for the public by providing public services in integrated, imaginative and more convenient forms like single gateways, the internet and digital TV.

(*Modernising Government,* 1999)

Behind the rhetoric, for governments the democratic role of ICTs lies in making democracy more efficient, by offering easier public access to government documents, and by allowing more direct communication between representatives and constituents. Further, electronic processing and exchange of some of the functions of government, for example, tax returns and welfare claims, should allow more responsive delivery of services as well as creating cost savings (Taylor *et al.*, 1996). Certainly, examples exist of attempts to deliver services through ICTs, but these remain small in scale or simply experimental, and so there remains little evidence of their effectiveness in either delivering the service or saving money. The more worthy intention expressed above, of a more direct say for the electorate in decision-making by the deployment of new technologies, is still less developed. Coleman (1999: 18) sees the interests of the British government in particular as being economic rather than political, 'efficient government' meaning cheaper government, rather than the involvement of more of the people.

Governments are not alone in arguing the case for the democratic potential of ICTs. Others argue that the new ICTs offer more than the efficient parliamentary democracy described above. Falling numbers of voters taking part in elections, and declining attendances at fewer political meetings, are cited as evidence of a deepening disenchantment with the traditional political processes. If people are to engage with politics and become active citizens, some new means of conducting the political communication process must be developed, and this can be achieved through new technologies. According to *Wired* magazine's Kevin Kelly, 'the internet revives Thomas Jefferson's 200-year-old dream of thinking individuals self-actualising a democracy' (quoted in Ward, 1995). The parallel developments of declining involvement in 'traditional' political processes and the growth of political groups separate from the state, often known as 'social movements' (della Porta and Diani, 1999), have focused debate about ICTs on this 'other politics'. The discussion here will consider two different but overlapping perspectives on ICT use. The first welcomes the new technologies as enabling pressure groups and campaigners more effectively to organize and publicize themselves, to recruit new

18.1 Indymedia sites from around the world, showing online 'democracy' in action. Each has a 'publish' button, where anyone can post news

members, and to co-ordinate activities and campaigns. The second view sees the technology as making possible a political forum where debate can flourish, consensus be achieved and policies put forward. Clearly, there is a continuum between these two possibilities, but the different perspectives suggest particular assumptions about the nature of politics and democracy today.

THE TECHNOLOGY OF DEMOCRACY?

First, what are the technologies we are talking about? One use of technology for democracy is to deliver information, from governments and other organizations. This one-way information flow has traditionally been delivered over a variety of channels – print media (newspapers and mailshots), broadcasting technologies (radio and television), or data communication networks such as teletext or videotex. However, the emergence of the internet has re-energized the debate about technology and democracy.

The internet serves as both a one-way and a two-way network. Much of its use is for people to access documents and other information (text, audio and video) in ways which are, in concept, little more than sophisticated developments of the use of earlier technologies. Certainly, search engines and Web links make navigation easier, and the rapid development of coding techniques enables a variety of media forms and large quantities of data to be delivered. Even so, much of this information is in some way 'official' in nature, for example, from government departments, or commercial or other established organizations, and so it is also obtainable by means other than the internet (albeit often less easily). The 'unofficial', or alternative material on the internet includes personal webpages and small organizations' websites, and this is the sort of information that, for reasons of cost, is unlikely to be found on news stands, or to make its way onto a radio or TV channel, or into newspaper columns. However, the falling costs of computer technology and internet access, and simpler authoring software, mean that it is almost as easy for a solitary individual or tiny group to put their aims and thoughts on the World Wide Web as it is for the corporate or state giants. It is also just as easy *in principle* for someone anywhere in the world to look at those ideas as to seek the views of News Corporation or CNN, for instance.

If the provision of more information from a greater variety of sources were all that were required for an enhanced democracy, then this would indeed represent a democratizing technology (as would satellite and cable television). Certainly, greater availability of information is a prerequisite for improved democracy (though it helps to know where it has come from), and early uses of computer networks, by groups such as Public Data Access, aimed to make public information more freely available (Downing, 1989). However, mere expansion of the quantity or range of information is not enough. The fact that more information is *available* does not mean that access to it is straightforward. More often than not, we find particular ideas or websites either by directly entering the Web address (ironically, often learnt from other, conventional media), or via links from more familiar sites, or by judicious (or accidental) use of search engines. So access to minority views continues to be dependent on forces which mirror the inequalities operating in conventional media – the playing field that is the World Wide Web is far from level.

If the existence of more information does not in itself mean more democracy, where else should we look? The earliest uses of computer networks were for the exchange of e-mail messages. This remains a relatively low-tech application: it is text-based, requiring little bandwidth, and is thus fast and reasonably cheap. The widespread adoption of the standard internet protocol (TCP/IP) in the 1980s meant that rapidly growing numbers of people had access to international e-mail (prior to this common protocol, e-mail traffic was constrained within individual networks which could only interconnect with difficulty). Informal e-mail groups became established, often based on common professional interest (in the universities and research institutes where networking technologies first developed) but organized across nations. They would circulate messages among the whole group rather than to individuals, and 'bulletin boards' allowed the posting of notices, accessible by any group member at any time. Commercial access to these networking technologies and increasing ownership of home computers allowed online information services such as CompuServe, beginning in 1979, to extend this facility into the domestic sphere. Similar groups evolved within these networks, and when in the early 1990s online services began to allow full internet access, e-mail groups expanded rapidly in number – together with a related technology, Usenet, there are now thousands of e-mail groups and newsgroups covering every conceivable subject. It is reasonably straightforward to set up these groups, and internet organizations like Yahoo! provide this service free. Messages are usually archived and so can be reviewed if desired. Since the circulation takes place via e-mail, message downloading does not necessarily require high-speed data links, so is accessible to anyone with quite modest technology linked to the internet. It is claimed that this represents a new 'public sphere' where deliberation can take place between all citizens on an even footing, without intervention from state or corporate interests. 'Chat' technology, which involves a number of people simultaneously connecting to the same server and engaging in real-time dialogue, has been discussed more for its novelty and role playing than for any democratic potential. It certainly offers no more, and probably less, scope for political participation than newsgroups, and so does not merit separate treatment in this discussion.

The use of telephone lines for access to the internet immediately establishes global coverage, and with the development of broadband systems, such as asymmetric digital subscriber line (ADSL), higher data speeds are gradually becoming more accessible at lower costs to both fixed and mobile equipment. Delivery of audio and video material of good quality thus becomes possible, and two-way video-conferencing more user friendly. These are some of the technological developments that are exciting those who argue for the internet's democratic potential.

THE INTERNET AND CAMPAIGNING ORGANIZATIONS

For campaigning organizations, the use of the internet builds upon existing structures. We can see how this works in two different kinds of organization. Some, like Greenpeace and Amnesty International, are well established and have had an international profile far longer than the internet has been around. These organizations have been termed 'professional' in that they operate principally by employing a core of full-time, professional campaigners, and members' and supporters' efforts are aimed at fundraising and other supportive roles. ICTs have been exploited by such groups both for internal organizational purposes and, as internet access became more widespread, for publicity and information delivery. Their websites are full of information about their latest campaigns, with documentation (for example, petitions or letters to MPs) available for download, online membership forms, contact details and often links to other organizations. In this way, the webpages function as a newsletter or magazine that might otherwise be sent only to members. The use of ICTs remains principally directed at more efficient mobilization of resources (such as fundraising and letter writing) and has not fundamentally altered the ways in which these organizations operate.

For other groups, the internet plays a more central role, in galvanizing supporters into activity. For anti-road protests or 'critical mass' cycle rides, for example, the websites serve as detailed information points, perhaps giving the location and time of activities. For international coalitions like the World Social Forum, established at Porto Alegre in 2001, the Web is important in publicizing themselves and announcing events. Lack of funds might prohibit a properly organized mailshot to supporters, so the Web sits alongside otherwise limited publicity in small-circulation magazines and newsletters as a key means of organization. The 'June 18th' protests in cities around the world to coincide with the 1999 G8 summit on world poverty were publicized on the Web with details of activities and contact phone numbers. Dubbed the Carnival Against Capitalism, London's protest achieved significant media coverage after protesters and police clashed in the city's financial district (thereby achieving far greater visibility than it otherwise would have done). Media coverage focused on the use of ICTs, suggesting some sinister, subversive intent in the use of the internet (J18, 1999); the *Guardian* newspaper even reported that the demonstration was entirely dependent on the Web (Dodson, 1999). This is clearly untrue. The full range of other, 'conventional' means of organizing protests were used: posters, leaflets, telephones, word of mouth, and graffiti (ironically, 'www.j18.org' graffiti appeared in many cities prior to the event). No doubt some protesters did turn up through having stumbled across news of the event on the website, but most will have visited that site only after being alerted through one of these other mechanisms.

18.2 Activists have found that 'old' media tactics – such as spraypaint – can bring new media campaigns to life

In these cases, the internet works alongside other technologies as a useful means of organizing and publicizing campaigns: e-mail for contact with and document delivery to activists, webpages for publicity and advertisement. Other technologies play a similar role. Keck and Sikkink (1998) rank cheap and reliable transport (principally air travel) equally significantly as ICT developments in their discussion of transnational campaigns. The group Undercurrents trains activists in the use of compact video cameras to record protests and to document campaigns for distribution by video cassette or by streaming on the Web. To argue that any particular technology uniquely constitutes a force for democracy would be mistaken; the role of new technologies is complex and sometimes contradictory. Three examples illustrate this.

- At the outbreak of NATO bombing of the former Yugoslavia in March 1999, the independent Belgrade radio station B92, which had long been overt in its opposition to the Serbian government, was taken off air by the authorities, who took over its transmission frequency. B92 then began broadcasting instead over the internet. Its programmes (and its plight) reached journalists and human rights organizations through its website, and the closure was widely reported in the traditional media. Other sympathetic radio stations carried its programming. Then, ten days later, state authorities went further and took over the studios, preventing any further internet transmissions.

- In June 1999, the City of London police went to the courts to secure access to all video footage of the Carnival Against Capitalism shot by any journalist in order to identify protesters. It is reassuring that it failed in its quest, but the irony is that a 'democratizing' video technology almost had the opposite effect.

- The capacity of automated digital systems to store and routinely analyse e-mail and mobile phone records has been harnessed in new legislation in many countries following the attack on New York's twin towers on 11 September 2001. Many organizations have condemned the impact on civil liberties that these new laws represent.

So the use of novel technologies does not simply subvert the power of state mechanisms such as the police and judiciary. Certainly, the internet can be an alternative information channel. For example, during the NATO bombing of Serbia, a number of websites carried eyewitness accounts, largely unreported by the Western media (see Philip Taylor's chapter in this volume); 'independent media' organizations have used the Web as an outlet to report anti-capitalist protests around the world (Harding 2001; Moore 2002). But these can only be limited responses to existing imbalances of political power, imbalances which are maintained or even strengthened by the use of new technologies.

Established campaigning groups can use ICTs to great benefit for their internal organizational functions, in the same way that intranets are used by most businesses and public organizations – including political parties (Gibson and Ward, 1999). The promotion of ICTs by groups like GreenNet and trades unionists for campaigning organizations is testimony to the importance of these technologies as a relatively low-cost means of information exchange (Herman and Holly, 2001). There is less evidence, however, to suggest that new ICTs offer unique qualitative advantages for campaigning purposes over other methods and technologies, or that they are spawning mass protest movements. Traditional campaigning techniques such as gaining media coverage (Jordan, 1998), sending mailshots, and political lobbying continue, and 'old' technologies such as telephones and fax machines are equally more important than ever before to the running of an effective campaign.

THE INTERNET AND THE PUBLIC SPHERE

An approach which at first appears rather more radical conceives of electronic networks as forums for deliberation of political ideas and policies – in other words, the creation of an 'electronic public sphere'. (For an account of the concept of the public sphere, see Keane, 2000.) This is not a new idea: 'teledemocracy' experiments include the Ohio *QUBE* experiments of the 1970s, in which cable television subscribers could use a push-button keypad to vote on questions posed on the television screen (Arterton, 1987; Elshtain, 1982). The current conception would exploit the true interactivity of e-mail groups to allow debate, rather than mere electronic voting on questions posed by someone else. The idea is that e-mail discussion groups open up access and draw in all kinds of people: 'the shy, the disabled, and carers … who are socially disadvantaged, obliged to stay at home or otherwise have little voice' (Tsagarousianou *et al.*, 1998: 6). Discussion would lead to opinion formation or to consensus on political issues, thereby involving the electors in decisions which are currently left to elected political representatives. Some proclaim these new forums as replacing 'out-moded' town hall or trades union meetings.

Opinion varies as to the degree to which these forums should determine outcomes: at one extreme, electronic technologies could be provided cheaply enough to allow almost every political decision to be put to the vote; the far more common view, however, envisages retaining a representative democratic structure of some sort, using technology to enable representatives more accurately to gauge the electorate's views.

In a sense, the prototype for this forum already exists in the many newsgroups set up to discuss political issues. Newsgroups or e-mail forums are essentially open to all and can, if desired, be posted to anonymously. However, a number of studies of the use of such forums for debate and opinion formation have raised questions about how successful they are in promoting what Habermas refers to as rational-critical debate, in which views are put forward, considered and reflected upon, and modified in response (e.g., Jankowski and van Selm, 2000). There is also disagreement about the extent of the openness that should exist in these forums – some are moderated while others are not. A moderated forum immediately raises the question of who is doing the moderation; meanwhile, a completely unmoderated list can frequently become a forum dominated by individual dialogues, personal attacks and digressions from the topic under consideration (Wilhelm, 2000). To some extent, these studies expect rather more of the newsgroups than perhaps do the participants themselves. Without the political will, or a model indicating that the deliberations will actually result in having some effect, there may be little incentive for participants to take these forums too seriously.

There are, however, a number of examples of networks that have been established precisely to deliberate policy and develop consensus in order to effect political outcomes. Often, these civic or community networks link up a 'community' which is already in some way established, most commonly on a geographical basis. Among the most familiar are Amsterdam's 'Digital City' and the 'PEN' network in Santa Monica, California (see Tsagarousianou et al., 1998). Others seek to generate debate around specific issues rather than being geographically connected. For example, the UK's Citizens Online Democracy (UKCOD) has hosted a number of e-mail forums on issues such as transport policy or European monetary union. Coleman (1999: 21) described the UKCOD forum on Freedom of Information as 'an unprecedented opportunity for members of the public … to submit comments on the proposed legislation and … receive online responses from the minister with responsibility for the White Paper'. More recently, the Hansard Society has taken over conducting electronic consultations about proposed government policies (www.hansardsociety.org.uk).

Critics of these initiatives point out that forums tend to be dominated by those who already dominate political discourse – inequalities in the 'real world' are replicated in electronic forums (Jankowski and van Selm, 2000; Dahlberg, 2001). Furthermore, there is little evidence that electronic forums have had any significant effect on policy. Brants et al. (1996: 239) report of the Amsterdam initiatives that 'the [pressure groups and citizens] were also dissatisfied with the lack of follow-up in terms of political consequences'. Similarly, the Freedom of Information Bill which emerged from the UKCOD consultation was strongly criticized (for example, Economist, 1999) as falling far short of expectations. This replicates earlier findings of Arterton in his study of numerous US projects. He argued then that participation declined after the novelty factor began to wane and, significantly, the rate of that decline was greater the further that participation was from actual policy influence (Arterton, 1987: 148).

Almost all of these projects have been initiated by a group of 'concerned' individuals rather than as a response to an identified public demand. Arterton (1987: 199) comments on 'elites controlling the agenda' in the 1980s' US projects. In so far as they seek merely to gauge opinion which may (or may not) influence politicians, these projects are actually very conservative in aim. While recognizing that existing democratic practices are flawed, there is no attempt to take power away from politicians and truly place it in the hands of the people; thus, the electorate might simply become still more alienated. Coleman (1999: 21) alerts us to the dangers of mistaking public relations exercises for genuine attempts at public consultation, and without an explicit link to decision-making, participation in electronic consultation is likely to remain low. Budge (1996) argues that new technologies do, for the first time, permit deliberation and genuine decision-making to be made by electors rather than left to politicians. His version of a 'mediated' direct democracy is more sophisticated than crude electronic voting on every issue, retaining a role for political parties and other intermediaries. However, the key question of what mechanism can ensure that those decisions are indeed binding is not answered.

ACCESS TO TECHNOLOGY

That access to ICTs is uneven is self-evident, but it is important to emphasize some of the issues. The demographics of internet access are widely available: a decade after the development of the World Wide Web, the 'average' internet user remains relatively well educated and wealthy; despite falling costs and a large supply of secondhand machines, the growth in ownership of home computers is reaching a plateau in many countries; access via cable networks is hampered by widely varying levels of cable penetration in many countries, with the numbers connected to cable actually in decline in some, such as the UK (for internet demographics, see www.nua.com).

Thus, while cost remains a barrier for some households (just as it does for the telephone, equally an important democratizing technology), a significant limitation to the democratic potential of the internet must be the lack of interest or appeal to electors. Providing networked terminals in public places such as libraries, schools and community centres is not likely to work if there is little perceived need to use them, or, more importantly, a lack of interest in developing the skills required to use them.

Further, the demographic profile of those who do not have access to (or interest in) these technologies, predominantly female, poorly educated, and in lower social classes (C2/D/E), matches those who are already less likely to participate politically, according to Parry et al. (1992). They suggest that women, the working classes (as they put it) and those with few, if any, educational qualifications are more likely to limit their political activity to occasional voting or complete inactivity. Conversely, the groups most likely to participate in political activity are the wealthy, male, well educated, and members of the 'salaried class' (ibid.: 232–4). These are of course the characteristics shared by those most likely to own computers and use new communications technologies like the internet. So any argument that technology might aid democratic participation must acknowledge the likelihood that, first and foremost, it is assisting those who already participate. Consideration of the democratizing potential of ICTs must therefore look beyond the technology and examine access to the democratic process itself.

DEMOCRACY WITHOUT TECHNOLOGY

It is easy to understand why new technologies are held up as solutions to the 'problem' of political apathy or alienation. Voting in elections is declining in Europe and the USA, membership of political parties continues to fall, and political awareness and media coverage are perceived to be in decline (Blumler and Gurevitch, 2001; Tumber, 2001). Proposed remedies include citizens' juries (Delap, 1998; McLaverty, 1998), citizenship lessons in schools (Cassidy, 1999), and of course new technology. The reasoning for the inclusion of technology ranges from the near-deterministic – for example, in Toffler (1980), Rheingold (2000), Poster (1997), Mulgan (1997), in which case the mere existence of ICTs is sufficient remedy (and the only problem then is ensuring equitable access) – to the more realistic, where the market is recognized as an inadequate mechanism for information provision, and so requires regulation by government (Percy-Smith, 1996; Wheeler, 1998). To a greater or lesser degree, however, all these arguments suggest that the principal fault with the democratic process – an imbalance of power between electors and political and corporate institutions – can be rectified by access to better information and argument. Media and communications research has very successfully demonstrated the ways in which political information and debate are manipulated in the interests of the powerful. Yet the problem with democracy is not, and has never been, simply a deficiency in the quality or quantity of information or debate.

The 'knowledge is power' equation is one which fits neatly into a view of a society in which information is king. The UK Chancellor of the Exchequer has written that 'the defining characteristic of economy is less an individual's ability to gain access to capital and far more his or her ability to gain access to knowledge' (Brown, 1996). However, as Hirschkop puts it (1998: 214) 'those who rule do not rule because they know more'. The problem is a lack of political accountability. If electors have little control over decision-making once they have voted their politicians into government, they are unlikely to get very excited about the formal political process. Without some means of ensuring that collective decisions will result in political action, there is no reason to imagine that electors are any more likely to participate in political debate on computer networks than they are currently to vote or write to their representatives. For instance, in their definitive study of political participation, Parry *et al.* found that fewer than one in ten UK electors wrote to their MP (1992: 423), and more recent evidence suggests that, if anything, fewer are likely to do so today (for example, Curtice and Jowell, 1995: 154–6; Margetts, 2000) – even though one could argue that there is far greater access to the 'technology' of letter writing (although it should be remembered that illiteracy remains significant, though under-discussed, in countries like the UK where one in five adults are deemed to have poor levels of literacy (Office of National Statistics, 1997), a factor which itself has a significant impact on political participation (Parsons and Bynner, 2002).

There is little question that corporations have more power and influence over governments than individual electors. That is the reason for the formation and continued existence of trades unions and pressure groups, and suggests that, far from there existing a new form of society with a corresponding need for a new form of democracy, the need for political struggle in all its forms continues. Strikes, demonstrations, lobbies of parliament, and so on, have not disappeared; such methods continue to replace dictatorships with more democratic societies (Indonesia and Serbia being recent examples). In these processes, communications technologies play an important role in organization and information dissemination, but of course the same technologies are used by both sides. How the quest for political power proceeds is dependent on a far greater number of forces than the use of the latest technologies.

The arguments that the internet is an inherently democratic technology, or more cautiously that it can be used in ways which enhance democracy, are therefore flawed, and amount to little more than a technical fix to an old political problem. It is tempting to believe in the rhetoric, and there are none more willing to repeat it than governments seeking legitimacy and hoping to remain in office. Buoyed by the discourse of a new information society, the technodemocracy offers a comfortable route to a more peaceful, more equitable future. But to believe in this means accepting that words and ideas (and wishful thinking) alone are sufficient to bring about fundamental change. If that were the case, then certainly the internet (and a few broadcasting technologies) would be all that were needed. But intellectual activity alone does not redress democratic imbalances. The Carnival Against Capitalism, like so many examples before it, showed that when people take to the streets, the real sources of power (the state, judiciary and big business, in this case) are challenged.

The internet remains a valuable resource in attempts to achieve greater democracy, as are the telephone, fax machine, video camera, photocopier and the printing press, and any organization is likely to benefit from using it. It allows more rapid organization and communication, and it may permit limited deliberation. In so doing it could draw some people into political activity. But while the internet remains in the hands of the relatively privileged minority who are already more inclined to participate, it is doubtful that it will encourage a substantial number of new political participants. To create a more democratic society, political activity must amount to more than the exchange of ideas and information, and, beyond better organizing the already active, the internet's role in nurturing a more democratic, participatory society is likely to remain a minor one.

USEFUL WEBSITES

Alliance for Progressive Communications: www.apc.org

Umbrella organization for the promotion of electronic networking for environmental, human rights, development and peace groups. For example, GreenNet is the UK's APC member organization.

Campaign for Freedom of Information: www.cfoi.org.uk

Campaigns against unnecessary state and corporate secrecy and for a Freedom of Information Act.

Campaign for Press and Broadcasting Freedom: www.cpbf.demon.co.uk

CPBF campaigns for media reform and to promote policies for a diverse, democratic and accountable media. It works principally with media trades unions.

Democracy Forum: www.democracyforum.org.uk

Online forums on parliamentary and other issues, e.g. stem cell research, media legislation. Organized and reviewed by the UK Hansard Society.

Fairness and Accuracy in Reporting (FAIR): www.fair.org

US campaigning group, aiming to democratize the media and challenge bias in reporting.

Indymedia: www.indymedia.org

Independent media organization, with outlets in different countries, offering news, reports and forums on global protest movements. See *NewsREAL*, its monthly video bulletin, at satellite.indymedia.org.

One World: www.oneworld.net

International coalition sharing resources (text, audio and video) on global issues such as environment, debt and poverty.

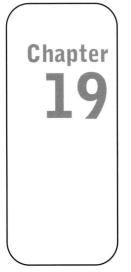

Chapter 19

THE WORLD WIDE WEB GOES TO WAR: FROM KOSOVO TO THE 'WAR' AGAINST TERRORISM

PHILIP M. TAYLOR

Despite their similarities with previous conflicts, every war has its own unique characteristics. Although warfare itself is as old as human history, the ability of people beyond the immediate area of fighting to observe what actually happens there has changed significantly thanks to the communications revolution. As far as media coverage of warfare is concerned, the presence of journalists on the battle-field is a comparatively recent phenomenon, dating back to the mid-nineteenth century with the Crimean War (1854–6) and the American Civil War (1861–5), the latter being the 'first photography war'. Rudimentary silent motion pictures were taken during the Boer War (1899–1902) although cinema newsreels and docu-mentaries were much more characteristic of the First World War (1914–18). Radio came into its own during the Second World War (1939–45), although by then cin-ema had also acquired sound, making it not just a 'war of words' but one of words and images combined. (*The War of Words* was the title chosen by Asa Briggs for his Second World War volume on the history of the BBC.) There were television cam-eras in Korea (1950–3) but it was only towards the end of that conflict, the first true television war, that people in the developed world were beginning to acquire television sets in their own homes. Vietnam (*c.* 1963–73) was thus the first colour television war, while the 'First' Gulf War of 1991 assumes the mantle of the first 'real-time' television war. With the invention of the World Wide Web in 1992, and the subsequent growth of the internet, the Kosovo conflict of 1999 became the 'first internet war' although, by that time, the nature of war itself had become unrecognizable from the days when the 'Glorious 600' rode to their death in the Charge of the Light Brigade.

During the course of the last 150 years, then, the presence of civilian journalists observing fighting forces in action has heightened the level of public scrutiny towards conflicts that were hitherto confined largely to those actually taking part in them. In that period, war first became a mediated event with journalists and photographers acting largely as simple observers of conflict. It is not without significance, however, that the arrival of journalists on the battlefield prompted the creation of modern military censorship. By the time of the First World War, censorship systems served to draw a curtain between what was being observed by the journalists and what they were able to say and show to the public back home. In the process, and what some might see as a paradox, an image–reality gap was opened up, prompted by the fear that if the public could see what actually happened in modern industrialized warfare, they would be so appalled by the brutality and the slaughter that they would be repelled by it, and thus oppose it. However, because military censorship systems proved so effective at controlling the sights and sounds which left the battlefield and reached the public, this hypothesis has never really been tested. Modern communications technologies like the internet are likely to put this assumption truly to the test.

This is because journalists are no longer the only people who are able to communicate, or mediate, events on the battlefield to the people observing those events far beyond it. For the moment, admittedly, they remain the most significant source of information for the vast majority of what is now a global audience. Television, in particular, remains the most trusted source of news and information about contemporary events. But audiences for news and current affairs programmes are in decline and, in the struggle for ratings, television news has adapted by placing more and more emphasis on 'live' coverage, especially following the success of CNN during the Gulf War. The presence of journalists in Baghdad from countries leading the bombing of the 'enemy' capital was unprecedented in modern war coverage. It served to make war a 'media event', although the degree to which the image–reality gap was narrowed remains open to question (Taylor, 1992, 1997).

The problem of censoring live, 'as-it-happens', television coverage is one thing. But when members of the Kuwaiti resistance could use their mobile phones to phone CNN in Atlanta and describe to a global audience in real time what the Iraqi soldiers were doing in Kuwait City, it is not just that the media became actual participants in events, but also that the definition of the war correspondent began to embrace the 'citizen journalist'. As mobile phones became smaller in the years that followed, and as digital camcorders produced high-quality images at high-street prices, it should have come as no surprise to hear ordinary citizens phoning in live traffic reports to their local radio stations or to see dramatic pictures of the Concorde air crash, within hours of the tragedy, that were taken by the wife of a passer-by.

The extent to which these developments have changed the nature of modern war fighting has yet to be fully explored. But there are some preliminary aspects to this phenomenon to be examined here. Since the arrival of modern military censorship, national media coverage of wars has in fact been characterized more by media co-operation than by military–media conflict. A 'deal' is made whereby journalists are given access in return for accepting restrictions of what can be said under the umbrella of what is called 'operational security'. The Vietnam War is often cited – erroneously – as the exception to the norm of media support for 'our boys' in 'our wars' in that the media stand accused of alienating US public support for the war in Southeast Asia by showing, for the first time, the graphic 'realities' of modern warfare. In the transition from Total War to Television War, one consequence of this is that civilian (and, in countries like the USA, military) casualties have become increasingly unacceptable to a watching global television audience, with a corresponding growth of 'smart' weapons technology in an attempt to minimize them. And, as the Gulf War demonstrated, the military were even prepared to place cameras on those weapons to demonstrate to the watching audience that everything was being done to minimize 'collateral damage' in a new era of 'smart warfare'.

At the military–media interface, democratic publics have traditionally relied upon the professional journalist to serve their 'right to know' about the nation's performance on the battlefield and to 'tell them the truth'. This 'spectacle of war' or 'media war' has been likened to mere voyeurism for a global live television audience watching from a safe distance, with all the accompanying problems associated with image–reality gaps, censorship and propaganda. (For a discussion of these issues, see Taylor, 1997.) However, new communications technologies – such as the fax machine, the mobile phone and the video palmcorder – have greatly increased the potential for voyeuristic access to the fighting areas, not least because they are smaller, more affordable and more individualistic – and more difficult to censor. Moreover, these personal media have widened greatly the levels of non-journalistic participation in the process of disseminating news of conflicts from the battlefield that help to shape popular views about them. The internet, as a genuinely interactive medium, is the apogee of this development. 'For the first time anyone on the internet can receive a flow of combatant news, comment and pictures – and, for those with the right equipment, audio-visual programmes and news conferences' (*The Sunday Times*, 1999). But the real point is that anyone with such equipment could also *transmit* their news, comment and pictures to a global audience, bypassing the traditional mass media. And although many still regard internet access as a passive activity, the Serbs in 1999, at least, did not see it as such.

The concept of 'information warfare', or 'information operations' as it is now more commonly being described, is gradually penetrating the military planning process in advanced information societies. Essentially, this is a new concept of war fighting, against new types of adversaries in new forms of battlefields (or battle 'spaces'), that forms part of the so-called Revolution in Military Affairs (RMA). It requires the application of new technologies, especially new communications technologies, to improve military 'command and control' capabilities in defeating an enemy by 'smart' applications, intelligent systems such as computers and satellites, and by applying other advanced technological assets. It is all the more surprising therefore that the main protagonists of such theorizing did not practise in 1999 what they preached.

Much nonsense has been written about information warfare and especially about one of its central 'tools', the internet. Neither the internet itself nor 'information operations' have yet reached the status of accepted concepts in most military establishments, which still tend to regard their business as war fighting. But where the balance of military forces is uneven, these concepts become invaluable tools in asymmetric warfare. In Serbia, it was estimated that a maximum of 50,000 of its ten million population had access to the internet, with fewer than 1000 in Kosovo itself (Mendenhal, 1998). During the 1999 conflict with NATO, television remained the main source of information for 60 per cent of Serbs, followed by newspapers, word of mouth and radio. Four in ten Serbs listened to foreign radio stations (with Radio Free Europe being the most popular) and slightly less foreign television. Less than one in ten Serbs used the internet 'frequently' or 'sometimes' (2 per cent and 7 per cent respectively) for information, but over half of the 'sometimes' users believed that the information they gained was inaccurate. In the first post-conflict survey of Serb media usage, the internet – in terms of usage and credibility – was remarkably placed above NATO television (deployed by flying TV platforms known as the Commando Solo) but actually below the 103 million NATO leaflets that were dropped over the country. (See USIA Opinion Analysis, 1999 – a survey conducted by a market research firm in Serbia (excluding Kosovo) for USIA, and based on face-to-face interviews with 1103 Serbian adults between 26 August and 1 September 1999.)

In due course the internet will undoubtedly gain widespread levels of public acceptance similar to those, for example, in the United States. In 1999, however, most people continued to rely upon traditional mass media as their principal source of information about what was going on in the world around them. Internet users remained an elite, albeit a sizeable and growing one, confined largely to educational and economic circles. Yet this elite was highly influential. It consisted of opinion-makers, people who were in a position to influence much larger numbers of people, and the very type of people who would want to get the story behind the story, for which the internet is an invaluable tool. As such, this was a significant target audience for anyone battling for access to hearts and minds about the rights and wrongs on any given issue. The Serbs realized this, but NATO did not.

It is axiomatic of both the internet and of emerging information warfare thinking that, with comparatively limited resources, a widespread global impact is possible. The Kosovo Liberation Army certainly recognized this by its establishment of a website long before the conflict with NATO began. Nor was it the first to recognize the potential of the internet for political and global communications. Much

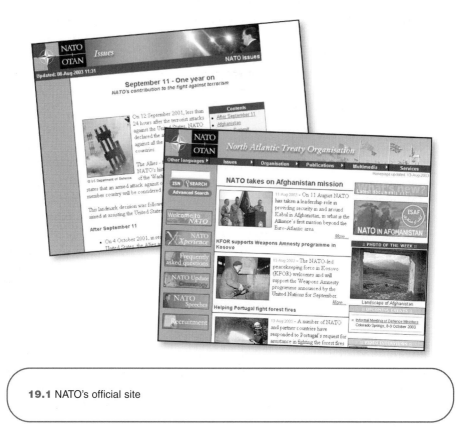

19.1 NATO's official site

has already been written about the Zapatistas' use of the Web from 1995 to promote their cause against the Mexican government over the Chiapas dispute. The
Tamil Internet Black Tigers launched simultaneous e-mail attacks on 18 Sri
Lankan embassies and were even able to disrupt electrical power supplies into
Columbo. We have also seen how electronic information flows increased outside
awareness of what was happening in Bosnia, Zaire and Indonesia. From the
moment the Web was invented in 1992 as the user-friendly 'front end' of the
internet, pressure groups and non-governmental organizations have begun to
seize upon the technology as an ideal instrument of 'electronic democracy' and of
lobbying for a wide variety of causes. Indeed, even in the so-called 'first information war' in the Gulf in 1991, e-mail was added to the arsenal of information
weaponry as a means of communicating with the enemy.

The Serbs were also quick to realize just exactly how far this technology had developed since then, or indeed even since the end of the Bosnian conflict in 1995. As
a result, they were frequently able to place NATO on the defensive as its spokes-
men proclaimed the 1999 conflict to be a 'humanitarian' cause. And because the
Serbs controlled the media in Kosovo itself, where it was too dangerous for most

western correspondents to report from in a consistent way once the bombing had
started, the Kosovo Albanians also seized upon the technology to proclaim their
experience to the outside world. In addition to the KLA's own site, the self-
proclaimed Kosovo government in exile ran its own site from Geneva. When the
Serbs closed down the independent radio station B92, it merely moved to a different location in cyberspace, based in Holland, and continued its protests (the
website can be found at http://helpB92.xs4all.nl).

The Kosovo conflict was unusual in that it created higher levels of uncertainty
amongst the 'chattering classes' about the moral and legal justifications of NATO's
bombing campaign. It will take much more research before any correlation can be
made between these slightly higher than normal levels of ambiguity amongst this
elite audience and their usage of and access to the internet. With only the thinnest
legal backing, and arguably an actual violation of both the UN's and NATO's char-
ters, NATO governments justified the campaign largely in moral terms, as a
humanitarian mission to rescue the Kosovans from genocide. With Britain at the
forefront of the information campaign, the war was framed in terms of the Labour
government's so-called 'ethical foreign policy'. Whereas the majority of people
backed their government's war effort and accepted it as a 'just war', and had the
television images of fleeing refugees to reinforce their support for it, the kind of
people who used the internet for accessing information behind the journalistic
gatekeeping of news stories may not have been quite so sure. It was these very
voices of dissent, which were absent from the traditional patriotic media coverage
of the war, that seized upon the internet as a medium of transmitting their reservations around the world.

The Serbs certainly demonstrated an understanding of all this by devoting considerable resources towards internet communications during the Kosovo conflict.
They saw the Web as a unique instrument for waging their own 'information warfare' against NATO, and for getting their message across to global elite – if not
mass – opinion, while refuting or challenging the arguments of their adversaries.
Indeed, from the moment the NATO bombing commenced on 24 March 1999,
and as it extended into targeting Serbia's military–civil infrastructure, including
Serbian television and radio transmitters and stations, it was perhaps their only
weapon of retaliation.

The problem with trying to analyse traditional war fighting with the internet in
the equation immediately becomes apparent. In cyberspace, it is not really appropriate to talk in traditional terms about battle 'fields', nor can one really distinguish between tactical and strategic battle 'spaces'. Moreover, the internet as an
interactive medium of communications by individuals with access to it – and electricity – redefines not just the way information flows within and beyond an area of
conflict but it also 'demassifies' the traditional monopolistic role of journalists as
observers of other people's miseries. On the internet, the citizen journalist is in his

or her element. When one adds to this that the nature of conflict in the post-Cold War era has increasingly blurred the distinction between soldier and civilian, especially in conflicts that involve 'ethnic cleansing' (such as Bosnia, Rwanda and Kosovo), we also need to rethink our traditional concepts of 'the enemy' and 'enemy soldiers'.

Traditional methods of reaching enemy soldiers and civilians with targeted information and messages – psychological warfare – continued to be used in 1999, as epitomized by the millions of leaflets that were dropped by NATO over Serbia and Kosovo during the conflict (*CNN Interactive*, 1999; Seigle, 1999). Other traditional media such as broadcasting were also employed, not just at the strategic level but through such international radio services as the Voice of America, the BBC World Service and Radio Free Kosovo. The growth of commercial satellite television also meant that Serbs with satellite dishes could watch CNN, Sky News and BBC World. Radio and television signals at the tactical level were supplemented by the Commando Solo, a converted EC 130 airborne television and radio platform operated by the United States out of Hungarian air bases. Commando Solo broadcasts identified themselves as 'Allied Voice Radio and Television', with programming provided by the Serbian service of Radio Free Europe. However, the only true communication innovations in the Kosovo conflict were accessible mobile telephones and internet access. Hence, Serb citizens in Belgrade or Novi Sad could call phone-in shows on networks such as the BBC's Radio Five Live to air their views to a British audience without any censorship, or ordinary Serb citizens could send e-mails to NATO to appeal for the bombing to stop.

A key element of information warfare is information denial to the enemy. When NATO attacked the Serbian state television service (RTS), it may have caused worldwide outrage (mainly, it has to be said, on the part of journalists) but it was militarily logical in the attempt to gain command and control over the information flow both to and inside Serbia. Besides, argued NATO spokesman, Jamie Shea:

> RTS is not media. It's full of government employees who are paid to produce propaganda and lies. To call it media is totally misleading. And therefore we see that as a military target. It is the same thing as a military propaganda machine integrated into the armed forces. We would never target legitimate, free media.
>
> (Global Reporting Network Publications, 1999)

RTS was, however, back on the air within hours. But what about the new media, since the very point of cyberspace is that it exists everywhere there is a computer with which to access it? Certainly, the closely integrated Soviet-style civic–military infrastructure of the Serbian state meant that power installations were also deemed 'legitimate targets' and this frequently meant that electricity supplies and telephone services that used copper-wire technology were badly affected by the bombing. But still the messages and e-mail continued to flow, reiterating the core Serbian official propaganda themes emphasizing the illegitimacy of the NATO = Nazi 'aggression', and the unanimity of the Serbian people united in support of the Milošovic government. We may never know how far the latter was true or, indeed, if it was, how far this was actually caused by the NATO bombing in the first place. Yet within a year of the conflict, Milošovic was ousted by a velvet revolution.

The experience of the Blitz in 1940, or of Hanoi in 1969, would certainly seem to suggest that bombing consolidates rather than shatters morale. Because mass bombing fails to discriminate between ruler and ruled, there is a unifying consequence that cloaks itself in nationalistic slogans. Even though 'smart weaponry' in the form of cruise missiles and laser-guided bombs were used extensively in the bombing of Serbia, whenever a bridge, power station, railway station or TV station is targeted, it invariably affects civilians. Incidents where civilians were 'accidentally' killed added to the sense of outrage. Many Serbs therefore found the internet to be a useful method of letting their anger at NATO's 'fascist aggression' be known. The reasons for that aggression, namely the ethnic cleansing of Kosovo, were largely absent from official Serb media outlets. When foreign satellite stations began showing pictures of fleeing refugees on the Albanian and Macedonian borders, it was explained away by claiming that they were fleeing NATO air raids rather than Serb genocide. As one media analyst observed, 'the ability for each side to create its own reality is almost unlimited' (Kathleen Hall Jamieson, cited in Bruni, 1999). Yet, as another observed, 'the laptop, the modem, the cell phone and the satellite are making it hard for either side to have a complete control over the manufacture of wartime reality' (Wark, 1999).

In the 'fog of war', was the internet able to bring any clarity? The answer is probably not, given the dominance of the polarized propaganda themes disseminated by both sides and reflected in the traditional media that most people still relied upon for their information. Many internet sites merely reflected those themes. However, what the internet user was able to do was to debate the issues (see, for example, Jovanovic, 1999). A number of (mostly American) university campuses hosted sites designed to do precisely this, and to exchange information that was not freely available in the traditional media. Or at least, it was not readily available in one media outlet. The ability to search the internet for information from numerous sources, including online newspaper and television sites, greatly increased the opportunity to accumulate a broad spectrum of news and information – as well as opinions – from one's desktop. But whether this helped anyone to understand better what was actually going on in Kosovo is highly unlikely. After all, despite the proliferation of atrocity stories about Serbian 'ethnic cleansing', it was only when the bombing stopped and NATO troops entered the region that undisputed evidence could be gathered. And the presence of individuals, as distinct from traditional journalists, cybercasting their individual views directly and without mediation to the internet audience may merely have created more confusion than clarity.

Despite the efforts of cyber-Serbia, through such sites as Serbian Ministry of Information, Serb physical control of Kosovo enabled them to limit the damage caused by cyber-Kosovo. For example, before the bombing began, the *Daily Times* (*Koha Ditore*) in Priština was refused access to a recently completed fibre link to Belgrade that would have enabled it to become an internet service provider (Mendenhal, 1998). But how did the Serbs perform against NATO in this cyber-warfare? Preliminary research suggests that they did better than expected. Of course, one reason for this was that most of NATO's 19 member countries enjoyed more sophisticated computerized networks for the Serbs to infiltrate or disrupt. Yugoslavia's own internet infrastructure was pretty limited, but if NATO had decided to target it, it would merely have opened up new routes for cyber count-er-attacks. 'We have lots more to lose than they do if we go down that route,' claimed one expert (Frank Cillufo, director of the information warfare task force at the Center for Strategic and International Studies at Washington, DC, cited in ZDNET, 1999). This did not, of course, prevent Serb attacks on NATO's own homepage, or anti-NATO hackers disrupting the website of the White House (Reuters, 1999). One individual in Belgrade was able to cause considerable damage by e-mailing 2000 messages a day, some containing the Melissa and more pernicious Papa macro viruses, to NATO's website using a 'ping' bombardment strategy to cause line saturation (Associated Press, 1999). The website of the British Ministry of Defence, which translated its website into Serbian to counter Belgrade censorship, at one stage was receiving 150,000 hits per day, 1400 of which were from inside Yugoslavia (Allison, 1999). (We should note that number of 'hits' does not always mean 'number of viewers', since the typical method of counting hits merely describes the number of files – including graphics, logos and bits of frames – served by the host. The actual number of visitors may only be 10 per cent of the number of hits.) It would appear that NATO itself, however, for all its obsession with information warfare/operations, was caught on the hop, and singularly and collectively failed to use the internet as an effective weapon of war. Its own internet site reflected traditional democratic propaganda methods of providing 'straight news and information' as part of a 'strategy of truth'. Of course, it was NATO's truth not Serbia's, and while NATO press conferences (not always successfully) fell into a traditional pattern of attempting to establish the most credible truth about what was happening, they missed an opportunity on the internet where the Serbs attempted to undermine everything NATO claimed by counter-claims, debates and even disinformation.

The Serb infowar nerve centre was based on the thirteenth floor of the Beogradjanka building, where volunteers – mainly students – linked with more than 1000 other computer volunteers at six other centres in Belgrade. Day and night, they debated in chat rooms, translated articles into English, and linked with other anti-NATO groups and individuals worldwide. They were led by 'Captain' Dragan Vasiljkovic, who ran unsuccessfully against President Milošovic in 1992. This 44-year-old former paramilitary veteran of Croatia and Bosnia redirected the funds he had set up for Serbian veterans into the psychological warfare computer centre (Satchell, 1999). 'We are all targets' was the principal slogan deployed to show the outside world that the Serb people were united behind their government under the rain of NATO bombs.

For its 'psychological warfare' against Serbia, NATO appears to have confined itself to traditional 'tactical' methods – leaflets, radio and television – deployed largely on the ground in Kosovo and Serbia. There is no such thing as tactical information on the internet. Yet this is precisely the area that information-age governments need to address. For example, in the United States, US armed forces or government agencies such as the US Information Service are expressly forbidden to conduct 'propaganda' and 'psychological warfare' on US soil. For this reason, defined by the Smith Mundt Act, a US citizen accessing the Voice of America site will find a much more limited service available than his or her European or Asian counterpart. If NATO's US-led campaign against the Serbs were to utilize the internet in its information warfare campaign over Kosovo, it would have violated these traditions quite simply because US citizens would have been able to access the messages contained in that campaign. As a result, no military planner has as yet been able to resolve the geographical problems of the internet's actual or physical location in cyber 'space'.

Moreover, there was another unresolved issue – namely, how reliable is the internet? Further evidence of the breaking of the previous monopoly of the war correspondent to report from the front came in the form of messages from people whose homes had been bombed, or from monks at a Serbian monastery near the Albanian border, all contained in e-mails from addresses ending in '.yu' (Yugoslavia). The difficulty, of course, was in checking authenticity – both of the senders and of the information itself. And whereas it can be argued that one has the same difficulty with reporters and newspapers, the point is that the *profession* of journalism has a tradition of values and responsibilities to such issues as 'the truth' that simply does not, as yet, exist on the Web. Thanks to the internet, therefore, the fog of the war in Kosovo merely got thicker. As subsequent discoveries revealed, the ethnic cleansing was nowhere near on the scale that was portrayed by the mass media at the time. The image–reality gap remained as wide as ever. Nevertheless, the internet was to Kosovo what television was to Korea. NATO's performance was such that it needed to ensure that its next conflict did not become another Vietnam.

The problem was that the next conflict was of such a different character that the media, old and new, are still struggling with ways to report it. The so-called 'war' against terrorism, which began so dramatically, live on television from New York on 11 September 2001, belies the lessons of media coverage of previous conflicts, with the possible exception of the Cold War. 'War' in international law is traditionally defined as armed conflict between two or more states. But the war declared against an international terrorist organization in the form of Al Qaeda does not fit readily into such a definition. At least when the bombing of Afghanistan began on 9 October 2001, the traditional media could begin to 'frame' the conflict against the Taliban in terms similar to that of Kosovo, complete with stories about 'collateral damage'. Even here, however, the media coverage was problematic because it is standard Western military policy not to allow journalistic access to special operations forces, which proved to be the major thrust of the largely Anglo-American military effort. Eight journalists were killed in the process of covering stage one of the war against Al Qaeda, excluding Richard Perle (the *Wall Street Journal* reporter whose execution by extremists in Pakistan

Did Nostradamus Predict 9/11?

BUSH KNEW

UFO Spotted Over WTC

19.2 Conspiracy theories spring up on the Web in the aftermath of September 11

was broadcast on the internet). Even the latest piece of technological wizardry, the videophone, could not help the traditional media coverage to narrow the image–reality gap. And, thanks to the Taliban, Afghanistan was a television-free zone where the internet was barely heard of.

Although there is some evidence to suggest that the 9/11 hijackers may have co-ordinated their attacks using the internet, the use of old-fashioned civilian aviation technology, loaded full of fuel, to carry out the attacks on New York and Washington is a sobering reminder that the internet is not yet the front line of twenty-first-century warfare. For those without traditional instruments of power, it remains an attractive alternative in an asymmetrical conflict, as the Palestinians have been able to demonstrate. In the global information space dominated by Anglo-American multinational media organizations that traditionally can be relied upon to support 'our wars', the internet enables an alternative voice to be heard. That voice can only grow louder as the broadband revolution dawns. It is a voice that is more difficult to censor, especially when it proclaims that '4000 Jews failed to turn up for work on September 11th', or that CNN footage of Palestinians purportedly celebrating the 9/11 attacks was taken during the 'First' Gulf War (Taylor, 2001).

Fear of such nonsense, just like the fear before it of what traditional war correspondents might say, may prove to act as the biggest brake yet on the growth of the internet. Fear of an 'electronic Pearl Harbor' at the hands of international terrorists is already seeing unprecedented legislation designed to restrict and monitor its usage in societies which have valued free speech and freedom of expression. Attempting to control the 'technology without borders' that is the internet, however, will no doubt prove difficult on an international scale. If the 'War' Against Terrorism is, like the Cold War before it, an ideological struggle for hearts and minds between two competing ways of life, between two competing 'realities', the internet provides a unique battle space in which information and disinformation are front-line weapons and where 'citizen journalists' become key participants. As such, it is where the image–reality gap will be both at its widest and at its narrowest. The old axiom that when war breaks out, truth is the first casualty may reflect the historical deal that traditional journalists have negotiated with armed forces to ensure some form of war coverage. But the secret of victory in the new battle space of the twenty-first century will lie not so much in the 'truth' but in which side's 'truth', as told by their info-warriors, is more credible.

USEFUL WEBSITES

BBC News: http://news.bbc.co.uk/hi/english/special_report/1998/kosovo

The *BBC Online* archive about the Kosovo crisis.

CIA: www.cia.gov/terrorism

The US Central Intelligence Agency's page relating to the War Against Terrorism.

FBI: www.fbi.gov/terrorinfo/terrorism.htm

Information, news and alerts regarding the War Against Terrorism at the official site of the US Federal Bureau of Investigation.

Institute for War and Peace Reporting: www.iwpr.net

An invaluable site for monitoring media developments in the Balkans area as a whole.

International Responsibilities Task Force: www.pitt.edu/~ttwiss/irtf/Alternative.html

Alternative news, analysis and commentary on the War Against Terrorism, provided by the American Library Association's Social Responsibilities Round Table.

NATO: www.nato.int

NATO's official site, complete with archives and details on the ongoing situation with KFOR.

Serbian Information Ministry: www.serbia-info.com

The official site of the Serbian Information Ministry – in English, so you need to ask yourself why.

Philip M. Taylor's Links: www.leeds.ac.uk/ics/terrorism.htm

The author's own page of information and links concerning the Propaganda War and the War Against Terrorism.

Chapter 20

WORLD WIDE WOMEN
AND THE WEB

WENDY HARCOURT

WOMEN'S WEAVINGS ON THE WEB

Popular imagery sometimes tends to think of women as reluctant uses of cyber-space, with the typical image of the enthusiastic Web user only recently beginning to include something other than that of a computer-literate man. And, if we were to believe all of the media hype about pornography and consumerism on the internet, it would seem that women are more *caught* in the Web than weaving it themselves. But, from my experience working with women all over the world, this is not so. Women are actively engaged in the cyber-dialogue, creating on the internet strategic information links, lobbying and advocating for change, and building up solidarity among groups that share the same goal even if they never meet face to face. Women's groups are using the internet as a way to break down barriers, exclusions and silences. It is fast becoming a tool for empowerment, changing women's daily lives, their hopes and their future.

In this chapter, I map out briefly some of the ways women are working on the Web and internet. My focus is on the positive side – to counter the images of women as objects rather than subjects of cyberspace. I also focus on women working in the Global South to counter another prevalent image of the Internet as exclusively the tool of the North. Our journey in cyberspace will take up three examples of how women are using the Web in innovative ways. We look at how women are using the Web to help stop violence against women, how the Internet has enabled a vast outreach in women's networking and organizing, and how women are creating new cross-cultural connections on the Web via the group I co-ordinate, 'Women on the Net'. The chapter concludes with a warning note about the limitations of 'women and the cyber-revolution', but I aim to show how women are using the Web to support their political work on women's rights and, in so doing, are creating new cultures across time and space.

THE CYBERFIGHT TO STOP VIOLENCE AGAINST WOMEN

As you surf the hundreds of colourful and professional websites set up by women in every continent – ISIS Manila in the Philippines, Aviva in the UK, FeMiNa in the US, WomensNet in South Africa, Q Web in Sweden, to name just a few – you are struck immediately by the numbers of women using the Web to address the issue of violence against women. Similarly, as anyone hooked into this cyber world knows, e-mail petitions are fast becoming one of the most common and effective lobbying tools by women's groups to protest about violations against women. From all of this activity, one can see how the Web provides a unique tool to empower women by opening up the possibility for international support in the struggle for women's rights locally.

Let us take some examples of women's groups in the Global South using cyber-space for support. In Rajasthan, one of the poorest areas economically in India, Bal Rashmi, an NGO based in Jaipur, is actively involved in the struggle against women's sexual exploitation, including rape, dowry deaths and torture. In 1998, their work drew the negative attention of the (corrupt) State Government domi-nated by a Hindu right-wing party, which filed bogus criminal cases and had the leaders of the NGO arrested. In fighting back, Bal Rashmi members used the Web to immediately contact international human rights and women's networks in India, South Asia, Europe and North America. Their call set off an appeal that, within a few weeks, led to faxes and letters flooding into the National Human Rights Commission, and the Rajasthan State and National Governments. The internet campaign forced an investigation of the cases and, within a few months, five cases were squashed.

Another story comes from Mexico where, in 1997, Claudia Rodriguez spent over a year in prison for the homicide of her would-be rapist, awaiting trial and the possibility of 15 years in prison. Women's organizations and activists in Mexico mobilized support for her case, declaring her innocence and recognizing the precedent a guilty verdict would represent for all women. Their slogan was: 'As long as Claudia is a prisoner, we are all prisoners.'

The women's internet activist network Modemmujer e-mailed Claudia's words and details of her situation to hundreds of women and women's organizations in Mexico, Latin America and North America, with calls of letters to the President, the Secretary of State and the Department of Justice. Mobilization by women's organizations in Mexico City resulted in women coming to the hearing process and making public protests. Letters were sent from all over Mexico, Cuba, Argentina, Colombia, Bolivia, Canada and the United States. Claudia was freed, though the verdict review stated that she used 'excessive force'. The judge refrained from sentencing her to an additional five years in jail.

One more example comes from Shirkat Gah, based in Lahore, one of the very few

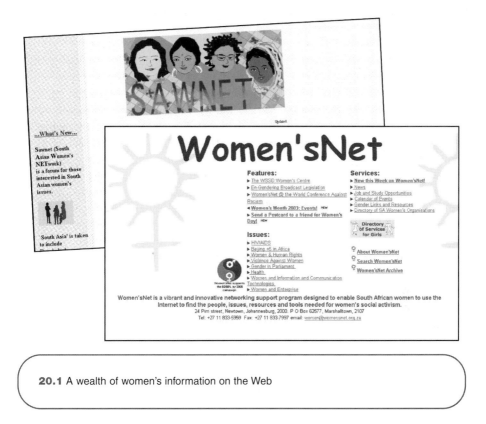

20.1 A wealth of women's information on the Web

human rights and environment women's organizations in Pakistan with the resources and connections to be able to make effective use of e-mail. Using trusted international websites (such as the GREAT network based in East Anglia, with 550 organizations and individuals working on women and gender issues), Shirkat Gah has, since 1999, mobilized around the prosecution of honour killings. As in Rajasthan, because of its work, Shirkat Gah is also fighting for its legitimacy and survival through international cyber-support. Shirkat Gah used its Web contacts to solicit support against threatened closure when the Punjab police and state authorities went to press claiming that Shirkat Gah had illegally received millions of dollars of funds from the World Bank.

What is interesting in these stories (and I could also give examples from Uganda, Senegal, the Philippines, Kenya, Russia and elsewhere) is how women all around the world have been able to use the internet to support their networking, information and communication needs. Through international support, women's groups and individuals under threat locally are able to hold their ground. And, in the process of mobilizing support, they have created a series of networks that quickly and strategically link women's local concerns with the global movement. Another point to note is that, perhaps differently than with other groups using the net for political organizing, women operate by creating safe personalized cyber-spaces. Lelise Regan Shade, in her review of 'globalization from below' and the networking of transnational women's groups, lists hundreds of women's media and cultural activities on the ground using the internet, through e-mail lists, Web conferences and websites (2002: 42–3).

The cyber-network Modemmujer (which engineered the e-mail campaign above that saved Claudia) maintains a relationship with the 400 women's organizations and individuals in Latin America that are part of their list, keeping them up-to-date with information on Mexican women's movements and their counterparts in the Global South. Shirkat Gah works with Women Living Under Muslim Law to keep key strategic information circulating throughout its network. Bal Rashmi is part of the international women human rights movement linked worldwide through the Web. These cyber-networks do not flood women's groups with information frequently too impersonal and distant to local needs to be of interest, but rather focus on creating a safe and intimate space for women. That is why the campaigns can work. The women on the listservs know and trust the message sender and will quickly respond to urgent requests.

CYBER-ORGANIZING FOR WOMEN'S RIGHTS: THE BEIJING EXPERIENCE

The work on violence against women is just one facet of women's work on the Web. E-mail petitions, website links, chat rooms and listservs enable women's groups to empower themselves with up-to-date information flowing in and among countries, regions and internationally, building structures for change and mobilizing struggles for peace, equality and gender justice. Women are using the internet to network, plan and strategize on a level that could never have been imagined just a few years ago. Perhaps the most impressive effort during the 1990s has been in connection with the United Nations Fourth World Conference on Women, held in Beijing in September 1995. The event itself was one of the best-attended UN Conferences ever (thousands of women travelled to Beijing) and the repercussions of the discussions and agreements were felt from far and wide thanks to the internet. As reported by Alice Gittler:

> electronic communication allowed women to bypass mainstream media and still reach thousands . . . Women who met on-line found an immediate network . . . One hundred thousand visits were made to the APC Website on the Conference. . . . When the International Women's Health Tribune Global FaxNet was posted on the Web, over 80,000 hits were recorded in the week before the Beijing Meetings.
>
> (Harcourt, 1999)

One of the key instigators of the link out from Beijing was the International Women's Tribune Center (IWTC), based in New York. The IWTC really launched the information technology process in Beijing. Some 100,000 women worldwide could learn about a problem, instantly making women a very powerful international lobby at the Conference, which still has repercussions for UN policy-making bodies taking up gender and women's interests, feeling that the world's women are watching. For the five-year review of Beijing, the IWTC with other partners have set up a website on the follow-up to Beijing, and have embarked on 'cyber-organizing' with a 16-member coalition launching a global network of websites to share information and track progress. They have also connected to WomenWatch, the website for UN activities related to women. The global website (www.womenaction.org/2000) links regional sites in Asia/Pacific, Africa, North America, Latin America/Caribbean and Europe.

There has also been extensive follow-up through the World Bank/Canadian Global Knowledge process, which has pushed on from the Beijing initiatives to promote gender perspectives in communication plans in order to transcend the gender divide, and the north–south gap (Shade, 2002: 96).

These Web activities involve women who would otherwise never be able to link up – including women who, due to their culture or locality, would not be in a position to voice their opinion otherwise. Arab women, for example, are entering the space created by the net in the face of cultural silencing and questioning of any Western medium. They have to fight the protectionist response of the Arab world to mass media, as well as all manner of gender bias. Nevertheless, the use of the internet allows women to express themselves and their views in ways that would be impossible – even dangerous – in the public sphere. With the impetus and opportunity provided by the Beijing process, religious debate as well as other issues relevant to women's rights and democracy, and subject to government suppression, can be carried on the Web, and Arab women are able to network in order to develop their ideas and activities further. As Lamis Alshejni observes, women NGOs established to promote women's awareness and advocacy for gender, political, social and economic equity are more and more using the internet, and they have realized the importance of this tool for communication, even if it is still largely based on e-mail rather than websites (Harcourt, 1999).

Another marginal female group are the indigenous women living in the 'liquid continent' (their evocative word for the Pacific islands). 'Netwarrior' Kekula Bray Crawford, working with other wired indigenous groups, has been using the Web to connect women's groups based in geographically isolated islands with the aim 'to expand the voice of cultures and peoples' through electronic forums into international arenas. She is creating a cyberculture where she hopes women's indigenous wisdom can achieve a greater recognition through online support. In a cyberencounter in 1998, Kekula wrote: 'including technology in our agendas is imperative in my theory to stand face to face, shoulder to shoulder, back to back with our sisters . . . we can join hands in peace, virtual space can allow us to do it'.

WOMEN ON THE NET: AN EXPERIMENT IN WOMEN'S CYBERCULTURE

Kekula is one of my cybercolleagues in the Women on the Net (WoN) project, set up originally by the Society for International Development with UNESCO funding. WoN was set up to do several things. First, to encourage women particularly in the South and in marginal groups in the Global North (and Central and East Europe) to use the internet more easily as their space, in an effort to 'empower' women to use technology as a political tool. Second, to open up and contribute to a new culture on the internet from a gender perspective that is simultaneously local and global. Third, to bring together individual women and men working from different institutional bases (women NGOs, information technology networks, academe, women activists) to explore a transnational women's movement agenda in response to and shaping evolving telecommunication policies. And, fourth, to create a resource (community and support) base that could be tapped into by different women's groups in terms of analysis, knowledge and internet-navigating skills.

It has been a powerful and unique experience, professionally and personally, hinting at what the Web can do to strengthen women's political and analytical work. The dynamic that has evolved by the WoN online and face-to-face interactions is somewhere between the personal, the political and the professional. The dialogues and meetings have been intense over the crossing of academic and activist knowledge terrain, over language and meanings, over concepts of place and identity. The lively discussion has brought out new ideas and concepts, and stands as another illustration of the type of cyberculture women are creating – in this case, people were communicating with one another as technicians, academics, activists and UN professionals, and women from close to 40 countries.

The WoN discussions on technical and political agendas are intermixed with personal and intimate histories and happenings. The frustrations of being women working in a male environment are shared along with the pleasures: six babies have been born during the group's existence. Health difficulties and managing professional and political life with children and new and old partners are part of the culture being created, creating an intimacy which the solidarity act of typing into a keyboard in front of a screen belies, but which the ethos of WoN embraces (see Harcourt, 1999).

Over the four years of its existence, the group has shaped itself around different needs – from maintaining personal contacts, to planning policy on telecommunications, to supporting advocacy, to reflecting on the gendered aspects of the

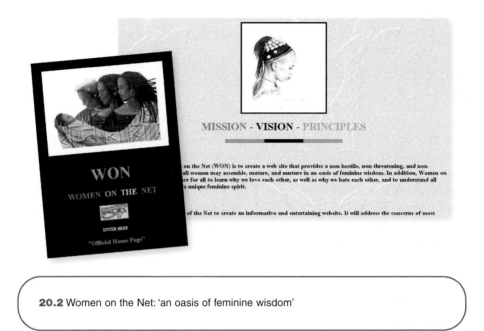

MISSION - **VISION** - PRINCIPLES

on the Net (WON) is to create a web site that provides a non-hostile, non-threatening, and non-
all women may assemble, mature, and nurture in an oasis of feminine wisdom. In addition, Women on
ce for all to learn why we love each other, as well as why we hate each other, and to understand all
a unique feminine spirit.

of the Net to create an informative and entertaining website. It will address the concerns of most

WON

WOMEN ON THE NET

ENTER HERE

"Official Home Page"

20.2 Women on the Net: 'an oasis of feminine wisdom'

north–south digital divide. It is a microcosm of the type of politics that women are creating and shaping on the internet through what the group calls 'meshworking'. Meshworks are non-hierarchical and self-organizing networks that grow in unplanned directions. They are engaging with dominant networks (bureaucracies, government, business groups) and at the same time remain pluralistic and autonomous. The Web lends itself to women's meshworking regionally, nationally and internationally as a cheap and accessible tool to advance their concerns emanating from their own political place. Some of the group are now exploring 'the politics of place' as an exciting new way for women to mobilize transnationally, connecting through the internet in ways that move their concerns to a global level, and yet with a political result that is deeply rooted in the place where they live (Harcourt, 2002).

WOMEN BREAKING DOWN THE BOUNDARIES

What can we learn from this very brief outline of how some women are using the Web? Women are empowering themselves through the Web by breaking down traditional boundaries on many levels. Let us begin with the gender divide. Although it is true that fewer women than men use the internet due to economic, cultural and social reasons – though the gap is lessening daily – once on the net (and overcoming fears of the technology, finding time, and so on, is not a small feat), many women find that virtual encounters can be easier than face-to-face ones. When we encounter people virtually, we do not immediately know what they look like in the flesh, so a vital element of communication – physical attraction – does not come into play. Not knowing the gender or appearance of someone is a virtual robbing of some of the richness of communication, but also offers the possibility for neutral tolerant interchange. Women in particular respond to this possibility, I would argue, and, at least from my experience, the personal and even poetic enters to express who 'I am really' beyond the typing on the screen. Particularly when speaking about issues like violence against women, this neutrality is important, as is the chance to express emotions. The speed of reaction is also vital, as the three examples above from Pakistan, India and Mexico attest. In a less overtly political context, Shade (2002), in her study of how young women are using the internet through cyber magazines, e-mails and chat rooms, shows how whole new worlds are being opened up for creative exploration of self – for example, *Maximag* (www.maximag.com) and *Geek Girl* (www.geekgirl.com.au).

Another boundary continually being crossed is that between intellectual and activist. Labels become fluid as people find the words to understand each other divorced from concrete ways of judging; in cyberspace, there is no actual classroom, no trades union hall, no ancestral ground to defend, no government office to lobby. These remain virtual points of reference that are imagined but not actually embraced and shared. Those who would not meet with professors or high-level policy-makers find themselves in correspondence through e-mail. Papers that would never have reached an African NGO in rural Senegal are translated and sent in a few days of delivery at a scientific or intergovernmental event. Women who will never meet exchange on a daily basis their worries about the men and children in their lives. Women engrossed in their own battles for survival suddenly find that groups living in other countries share the same concerns and are able to exchange valuable strategic knowledge. Academics and activists engage in a vigorous debate that each will use in different contexts enriched by what they have exchanged. A well-known example concerns the women of Chiapas, who have organized and created their own initiatives supported by academics and technicians working on the internet. (See, for example, *Sisters Across Borders*, www.igc.org/ncdm/sisters.html.)

Then there is the crossing of the personal and professional boundaries. For those able to access the Web easily (taking into account cost, equipment, time, and even family needs), it offers a sense of being able to 'share' one's life more easily. People provide the personal in an e-mail communication – something that perhaps would never be placed in a fax or letter. There is something wonderful about this – news of a baby born to a never-met transnational group of cyber-friends, breastfeeding problems discussed among women isolated in rural settings, urgent messages sent by refugee Afghan women throughout the globe.

As is evident from the networking that women are engaged in over the Beijing process, the most obvious and celebrated crossed boundary is the geo-political one – thousands of kilometres fade in chats across the screen. Messages can reach the Pacific, Asia, Europe, North America, Africa, Latin America and the Middle East instantaneously for the cost of a telephone call.

THE DOWNSIDE

Here, however, we need to raise the downside of the cyber-revolution for women. Beyond the fact that many women do not live in places that can afford or have access to the technical infrastructure, the continual crossing of the here and now divide can give an unreality to cyberpolitics. There is a strong need felt by many women to anchor the happenings of their real-life community to the virtual global discourse in order for the online communication space to have meaning. Where do all these cyber-dialogues go? (The time spent? The people fleetingly met?) How are we 'really' relating to others on the Web? Women, with busy lives to attend to in the office and home, can sometimes feel overwhelmed by their e-mails, as they get caught up in responding to reams of messages, and their attention is distracted from other needs.

Another issue concerns those who might be 'masterminding' the Web. It is important to chart how women are more and more using the Web in order to open up new political spaces. Nevertheless, it seems a tiny area that women are inhabiting, controlled and designed usually by others. The nagging questions remain: are women truly connected, or just scratching at the surface of a fast-changing world evolving without their design or needs in mind? If you venture into the world of decision-making and policy agenda-setting on telecommunications and other areas affecting access and use of the internet, where are the women? As Sophia Huyer indicates, there are some brave women charting the ground, but women are yet to venture there as a critical mass (Harcourt, 1999). The world of Microsoft, high finance and telecommunications business are not the spaces in which women or those pushing for an alternative agenda easily find a voice.

A related growing concern since women have started to come online *en masse* from the early 1990s (when women made up only 15 per cent of online traffic) to 2002 (with around 50 per cent female users), is that media and internet behemoths are beginning to target women as consumers, trying to cash in on women's purchasing power (most obviously in the US, European, Japanese and Australian markets) and also, more disturbingly, zeroing in on girls as future consumers (Shade, 2002: 69).

More difficult still is the question of access. There are still many effectively barred from cyberspace. To begin with, a disproportionate 40 per cent of the Web's content is in English, to the inevitable exclusion of non-English-speaking peoples. The illiterate are also obviously excluded, as are the poor in both poor and rich countries, posing a particular problem for many women and old people. Similarly, while access may be increasing among children in poorer areas, it is still a great deal less than that enjoyed by Western 'screenagers'.

It is important to put the stories I have told here in context. The women I have featured are mostly the educated political elite of their countries. Even if the technology gap is closing, the majority of the world's poor and illiterate women still cannot hope to have access to this cyber-world. The infrastructure is not yet in place and, furthermore, the *control* of who has access is a political as well as economic matter.

FUTURE CHALLENGES FOR WORLD WIDE WOMEN ON THE WEB

The challenge for women activists in search of gender justice is to use the Web, not only as an immediate empowering tool for their strategic needs, but also to open up its potential to others. The Web's modality lends itself well to women's traditional support roles and networking. As women begin to train others and learn to create new software, a more interactive, more user-friendly (and female-friendly) type of communication technology could emerge. Greater female-designed Web-weaving could reflect women's sense of community, and move us away from the consumer-focused, alienated, individual interaction that characterizes much communication on the Web today.

Let me end on an upbeat note. Even if many women are excluded from Web-weavings, the potential for shared communication futures has been tapped and needs to be made stronger and more inclusive. In the future, let us hope that the sense of enthusiasm and empowerment that Peggy Antrobus, a respected leader of an interregional southern women's group DAWN (Development Alternatives with Women for a New Era), can be shared by *all* women: 'internet most of all … has empowered us, by giving us the information, the analysis, the sense of solidarity, the experience of shared achievements, the encouragement and moral support that comes from being part of a network, a movement with common goals and visions' (personal cyber-conversation, September 1999).

WoN, in a modest way, has begun that process with small training workshops on the politics of cyberspace with community women's groups. At a meeting held in September 1999 on the beautiful island of Zanzibar off the East Coast of Africa (in both Kiswahili and English), members of WoN discussed with local women the whole nature of the 'virtual world', its possibilities and potential to enable communication across the traditional divides of gender, class, culture and nation. Women who were veiled and had never seen a computer before were given two days to learn how to 'run with' the cyber-revolution. These women are now meeting virtually and face to face to tackle themes such as domestic violence, women and empowerment, social justice and sex education. They draw on the internet to gain knowledge on production processes, health, teaching and cultural industries. They have tapped into a new world, one that they plan to shape and take part in.

USEFUL WEBSITES

Aviva: www.aviva.org

A free monthly webzine run by an international group of feminists based in London, including listings of women's groups and events worldwide.

DAWN: www.dawn.org.fj

Development Alternatives with Women for a New Era is a network of women scholars and activists from the economic South, working for economic justice, gender justice and democracy.

ISIS International Manila: www.isiswomen.org

A feminist NGO dedicated to women's information and communication needs in Asia and the Pacific.

WAVE: www.wave-network.org

Women Against Violence Europe is a network of European women's non-governmental organizations working to combat violence against women and children.

WomenAction: www.womenaction.org

WomenAction's 2000 Network supports women's activities around the world in line with the Beijing Platform of Action.

Women Living Under Muslim Law: www.wluml.org

An international network seeking to both empower Muslim women and harness support to their cause from within and outside the Muslim world.

Chapter 21

CONTINUITY WITHIN CHANGE: THE CHEROKEE INDIANS AND THE INTERNET

ELLEN L. ARNOLD AND DARCY C. PLYMIRE

Current use of the internet by the Cherokee Indians reflects many aspects of the historical situation of the Cherokees since the early 1800s. The Cherokee people, who called themselves *Ani`-Yun`wiya*, or the 'Principal People', at the time of first European contact occupied approximately 135,000 square miles in parts of what are now eight southeastern states. By the early 1800s, their territory had been drastically reduced through treaties and other actions by the US government. One of the so-called Five Civilized Tribes of the Southeast, the Cherokees were quick to adopt many of the ways of the Europeans. In 1821, Sequoyah created the Cherokee Syllabary, which enabled their language to be written, and the Cherokee people quickly gained a greater degree of literacy than their EuroAmerican contemporaries. They drafted their own constitution, published the first Indian newspaper (the *Cherokee Phoenix*, still being published today), and established the town of New Echota in Georgia, which served as both a seat of government and an economic centre for a thriving independent nation.

Under pressure from EuroAmerican settlers seeking gold and land, the US Congress made plans to remove the Cherokee people from their land. Progressive Cherokees, proponents of Americanization, fought in the American courts to force the US government to honour its treaties with the Cherokee Nation, arguing its sovereign status. Many traditionals opposed assimilation into American society; yet the Cherokee Memorials, eloquent documents arguing against removal, demonstrated that even the progressive leaders who drafted them wished to preserve a distinct cultural identity as well as their newly acquired status as 'civilized'. When the Cherokees lost their battle in the courts, 16,000 Cherokees were forced by the US Army to relocate 1000 miles to the west to Indian Territory. On this infamous Trail of Tears, called *Nunadautsun't*, 'the trail where we cried', in the Cherokee language, more than 4000 Cherokees died.

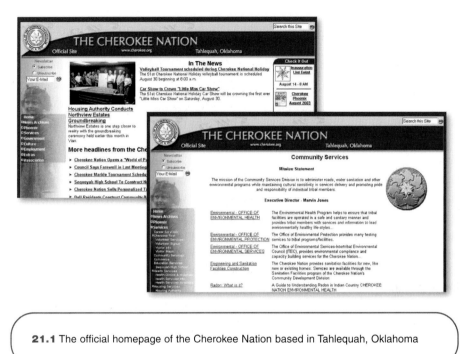

21.1 The official homepage of the Cherokee Nation based in Tahlequah, Oklahoma

Several hundred Cherokee people, mostly traditionals, remained in the East, hiding from settlers and soldiers. Eventually they re-established themselves as a nation and, in 1848, were formally recognized by the US government as the Eastern Band of Cherokee Indians. The Eastern Band now numbers about 12,500 enrolled members, a majority of whom live on the Qualla Boundary in western North Carolina, a 56,000-square-acre portion of their original homeland which has its seat in the town of Cherokee. This land, purchased by Will Thomas, the adopted white son of a Cherokee leader, and transferred to the Cherokees in the late 1800s, is now held in trust for the Cherokee people by the US government and is administered as a reservation. Like other reservations, Qualla Boundary has a complex status as a semi-sovereign nation, exempt from the jurisdiction of state governments in most matters, yet subject to a great deal of control by the federal government. The Western Band of Cherokees, known officially as the Cherokee Nation of Oklahoma, now occupies a jurisdictional service area of 4,480,000 square acres with a capital at Tahlequah, and has approximately 281,000 enrolled members. The United Keetowah Band, a third federally recognized band of Cherokees also located in Oklahoma, numbers more than 7950. The Cherokees, including numerous bands not recognized by the government, form the largest tribal group in the USA.

The question of assimilation remains relevant to contemporary Cherokee Indians.

The construction and use of the official websites of the Eastern Band (www.Cherokee-nc.com) and the Cherokee Nation of Oklahoma (www.Cherokee.org) reflect many elements of the historical relationship of the Cherokee Nation to the nation and government of the USA. (The website of the United Keetowah Band (www.uark.edu/depts/comminfo/UKB) was created in 1997–98 on an academic server, and does not appear to be currently maintained; therefore, we do not include it in our study.) The Oklahoma site primarily serves its community by providing links to human services, political news and organizations, and cultural and historical information. The Eastern Band site provides access to cultural and historical information as well, but because of its proximity to the popular Smoky Mountains National Park and the Blue Ridge Parkway, the Eastern Band has also been able to use its website to help build a thriving tourist economy. Observing the websites as outsiders, we suggest that they are skilfully designed aspects of increasingly successful political and economic efforts to use the dominant paradigm and its technologies to protect and preserve the unique cultural heritage and identity of the Cherokee people and, at the same time, to expand their control over their own affairs and influence on American culture.

THE DEBATES

Cherokee use of the internet must be considered in light of wider debates about whether computer technology and the internet medium help to preserve or tend to destroy indigenous cultures and traditions. Mark Trahant (1996), a member of the Shoshone-Bannock tribe of Idaho, speculates that the internet might be a medium particularly well suited to teaching in Indian communities, because it is more like traditional oral and pictographic forms of communication than are the typical written forms of the dominant culture. The imagery and fluidity of the web, like pictographs, allow the user to enter where he or she will and continue in whatever direction he or she chooses; like the storytelling tradition, in which both teller and audience participate in the exchange of stories and their meaning, the Web undermines both the power of the individual author and the presumed linearity of history. The stories told on the Web, like the stories told in pictographs or oral narration, change according to the teller, listener or user.

According to Trahant, in 1996, the growing numbers of Native Americans using the internet were onto something. He speculated that growing use of the internet by tribal groups would have several beneficial consequences. Since the medium requires less capital outlay than print media, Native groups might get their perspectives on political and social issues into circulation more easily. Second, tribes might use the sites to teach language and history, as do the Navajos and the Cherokees. Third, Trahant states that 'one of the oldest battles in the Native American press is over who controls information' (ibid.: 19). Print media may give tribal governments or federal agencies the power of censorship, while the internet grants individuals a greater voice. Finally, individuals might use the net to communicate with one another, through newsgroups and listservs, to build the bonds of community across time and space.

Trahant's high hopes for the new medium mirrored the utopian tenor of much mainstream scholarship on the internet. Because of the comparative affordability and accessibility of the internet, many came to view the medium as a virtual democratic utopia (Levinson, 1997). If Michel Foucault (1980) is correct that the producers of knowledge have power over those who are the subjects of knowledge, then the established media will typically produce relationships of power that privilege those who already hold positions of social power in capitalist societies. The internet, which opens the publishing field to groups who lack capital and power, can in theory allow marginalized individuals and groups to produce their own knowledge, put it in circulation, and, as a result, gain a greater measure of social power. Kurt Mills (2002) believes the Kurds, oppressed 'inhabitants of a transnational territory' (2002: 81) are living examples of the internet's potential. They use the medium to create a 'cybernation' (ibid.: 81) of Kurdistan to spread political information and to offer a place where Kurds around the world can express their aspirations for self-determination. In an earlier case, the 1994 Zapatista uprising in Chiapas, Mexico, used the internet to generate international support in their struggle against the Mexican government for indigenous self-determination and economic survival.

In addition, scholars such as Sherry Turkle claim that 'on the internet ... people [may] recast their identity in terms of multiple windows and parallel lives' (1997: 72). Theoretically, one may produce an online identity that does not correspond to one's real-life race, class or gender, or one may produce multiple identities, all of which may be in circulation concurrently. This may make the internet a particularly effective medium for negotiating the complex and often conflicting demands of both American and tribal cultural identities. According to the cyber-topian world-view, 'The internet deemphasizes hierarchical political associations, degrading gender roles and ethnic designations, and rigid categories of class relationships found in traditional, visually based and geographically bound communities' (Ebo, 1998: 3). Communities online, therefore, have the potential to create meaningful social groups that do not merely reproduce inequalities among real life social groups. If that is the case, then the medium might be a force for building more egalitarian communities by breaking down race, gender and class barriers.

Many question the cultural implications of virtual community for Native Americans, however. *New York Times* writer Elizabeth Cohen summarized concerns of Native spokespersons she interviewed that 'Web sites may not always represent the people and tribes they say they do, and that certain sacred and guarded cultural knowledge could be misunderstood or misused if it ends up on the Web' (1997: 2); she especially decried '"cyber-shamans" [who] feign tribal affiliation to sell various so-called native goods and services' (ibid.: 3). Lakota scholar Craig Howe argued that, because land and geographic location are fundamental to specific tribal identities, 'the pervasive universalism and individualism of the World Wide Web is antithetical to the particular localities, societies, moralities, and experiences that constitute tribalism' (1999: 7). Or, as Dakota/Salish writer Philip Red Eagle put it in an online discussion of the subject in 1999, 'Community is about responsibility to a specific group of people who practice culture with one another.' Although writing before the invention of the Web, Jerry Mander (1991), a non-Native writer, insisted that the computer destroys ways of thinking and acting fundamental to oral cultures and inculcates values inimical to Indian traditions. Because computers rely on an information exchange model of communication, he argued, they contribute to a world-view that reduces the natural world to resources to be managed and controlled, at the expense of embodied interrelationship with the world that is characteristic of traditional indigenous lifeways. Bowers, Vasquez and Roaf conclude that the problems identified by critics are unavoidable. The computer is not a neutral technology but a teacher of the sort of 'rootless individualism' (2000: 186) endemic to postmodern consumer culture, in which personal tastes and choice take precedence over belongingness and group identity.

The internet also may reproduce rather than challenge social inequalities. Though users cannot see each other, they may not have abandoned all judgements on the basis of race, class, gender and ethnicity. While individuals and minority groups may more easily 'publish' on the internet, readership may be more limited, so knowledge and ideas that challenge the status quo may remain marginalized. Similarly, access to the internet is not equally distributed along lines of race, class, gender and ethnicity. It could be argued that the democratic potential of the internet has not yet been fully realized.

As in many other disciplines, research and critical attention to Indian use of the internet is ghettoized, limited primarily to studies specifically about Native Americans. Such a practice reproduces what many have called 'the vanishing Indian syndrome' by implying that Indians no longer exist as a vital and influential part of the American population. A 1999 report by the National Telecommunications and Information Administration (NTIA) failed to include statistics on Native internet use. The Digital Divide Network (Twist, 2002) reports that the exclusion of Indians from the NTIA study hampers the efforts of individuals and groups lobbying lawmakers for continued funding of federal programmes such as the Technological Opportunity Program (TOP) and Community Technology Centers (CTC) programme, which provide opportunities for Natives to narrow the technology gap. These programmes are important, since Native communities are some of the poorest in the USA, with rates of access to telephone service, computers and the internet currently about two-thirds of the national average (Yawakie, 1997; National Telecommunications and Information Administration, 1999). As a result, Native Americans often rely on community centres for internet access (NTIA, 1999).

Despite this, the *New York Times* reports a 70 per cent increase in Native American use of the internet in the first six months of 1998 alone, and internet sites for and about Indians abound. In 1994, the Oneida Indian Nation was the first Indian nation to 'claim territory in cyberspace' (Polly, 1998: 37). The Indian Circle Web Ring (www.indiancircle.com) now lists 111 active tribal webpages (out of the more than 550 federally recognized Indian tribes of the continental US and Alaska).

THE WEBSITES

The sheer number of sites pertaining to Cherokee Indians makes a general survey impractical; in addition, there are many 'unofficial' sites for and about the Cherokees, many of which are interesting and informative, and some of which are appropriative and/or unreliable. We chose to limit our study to the official home pages of the Eastern and Western Bands. Since our first comparative analysis three years ago, in the first edition of *Web.Studies*, the primary focus of each site remains the same, but there have also been significant changes to the design and content of both sites.

Both homepages are produced by outside organizations under the direction of tribal members, but the two sites still offer striking contrasts. The Oklahoma homepage is designed primarily for Cherokee users. Undergoing revision at the time of writing, it has been retitled from *The Official Site of the Cherokee Nation* to *The Cherokee Nation*, with the words 'Official Site' displayed in smaller font on the line below and an image of the official Seal of the Cherokee Nation displayed to the left. The homepage features changing photographs of community members involved in contemporary activities, and foregrounds news items relevant to local and national Indian politics and services. The site includes links to: the *Cherokee Advocate* and *Cherokee Phoenix*, and their archives; information about tribal government and services; cultural, historical and language instruction sites; employment opportunities; community calendars; and genealogy and enrolment information. A category labelled 'Associations' includes links to Sequoyah High School, Talking Leaves Job Corps, Cherokee Heritage Center, Cherokee Nation Housing Authority, Cherokee Nation Industries, and the Cherokee Gift Shop. Significantly, the only potentially tourist-oriented links on the Western Band homepage, the Gift Shop and the Casinos, are relatively hidden in the 'Associations' category. Furthermore, the gift shop features items that do not seem to be geared toward the tourist trade, such as Cherokee Holiday T-shirts with lettering in the Cherokee syllabary. With the exception of a few of the 'Association' links, the Cherokee Nation now maintains all of the links on the site. Notably, links to Federal Government agencies that appeared on the 1999 page have been removed and replaced with links to services provided by the Cherokee Nation itself, and there are no hints of the internal corruption within the tribal government reported in news releases on the site three years ago. These changes suggest, and have perhaps contributed to, a new sense of self-definition, self-containment and sovereignty on the part of the Western Band of the Cherokee Nation.

Changes in the Western Band page also reflect improved relationships with the Eastern Band. Three years ago, the only link to the Eastern Band homepage was an indirect one via an *Indian Circle Web Ring* link, and the only references to the Eastern Band were historical. The new page offers a direct link to *Cherokee-nc.com* on the Genealogy page, and news stories featured on the site frequently cover recent events in North Carolina. An archived news release reports a historic Joint Council meeting in August 2002, to discuss issues and share ideas of mutual interest, and a September 2002 story covers the opening of a new Cherokee Visitor Center at the Chief Vann House Historic Site in Spring Place, Georgia, attended by both Western Band Chief Chad Smith and Chief Leon Jones of the Eastern Band. Both Chiefs emphasized the need for historical information to combat stereotypes, and 'reiterated the need not to portray the Cherokee as helpless victims of hopeless circumstances' but to remember 'the proud legacy of a strong people who survive and prosper' (www.cherokee.org/NewsArchive/News2002).

In contrast to the Western Band page, the Eastern Band homepage reflects few changes since 1999. The description 'The official homepage of the Cherokee Nation', which appeared at the bottom of the page in 1999, has been incorporated into the body of the text as 'the official home page of the Eastern Band of Cherokee Indians'. The homepage now bears an image of the official Seal of the Eastern Band, similar to that displayed on the Western Band site. The combined effect of changes on the two homepages has been to identify each Band more specifically as a member of a larger Cherokee Nation. Importantly, the link to the Western Band homepage (under 'Related Links'), which was present in 1999 but not working, is now activated. However, many of the links to historical and cultural information have disappeared, and the page of language links which was in an early stage in 1999, has not been developed; as a result, the Eastern Band site at present seems even more directed toward tourism than it did three years ago. Still titled simply *Cherokee*, the homepage features changing images of local attractions, including a potter with her craft, and museum scenes. Links take the user directly to information on tourism and gaming on the Cherokee Reservation and in the Great Smoky Mountains National Park. Attractions on the reservation mirror those in the surrounding park – fishing, hiking and camping – but *Cherokee* also offers visitors cultural attractions, such as Oconoluftee Indian Village, 'Unto These Hills' Outdoor Drama, and Qualla Arts and Crafts Mutual, as well as museums, shopping and an invitation to gamble at Harrah's Cherokee Casino.

In her analysis of 96 official tribal websites comprising the Indian Circle Web ring, Rhonda Fair notes that sites designed for Native American users typically emphasize a 'specific tribal identity' (2000: 204), while those produced for tourists and other outsiders tend to reproduce stereotypical images of the 'White Man's Indian' (Berkhofer, 1978). Fair offers the website of the Eastern Band of Cherokee as an example of the latter trend, but she acknowledges that Cherokee adoption of 'Hollywood' images of Indians reflects a 'dialectical process of identity formation' (2000: 208), in which the Cherokee have the agency to create images for their own purposes. Examination of the current Eastern Band homepage and interviews with its producers reflect that this dialectic process continues. However, at the present time, the Eastern Band Cherokees seem to be recreating their image in ways that will both appeal to non-Native visitors *and* reclaim their specific tribal heritage.

Tribal member Dave Redman (personal communication, 1999), who originated the North Carolina website in 1997, confirmed that the homepage was intended primarily to expand tourism and economic growth on the reservation. 'Gaming' – incorporating casino gambling, video gaming, bingo parlours, stick and bone games, and many other pursuits – is the linchpin of the Cherokees' development strategy, as it has been on other reservations. Like other tribes, many Cherokees view gaming as 'simply a profitable business, upon which economically dormant Indian nations can regain long lost territory, cultural prerogatives, and community

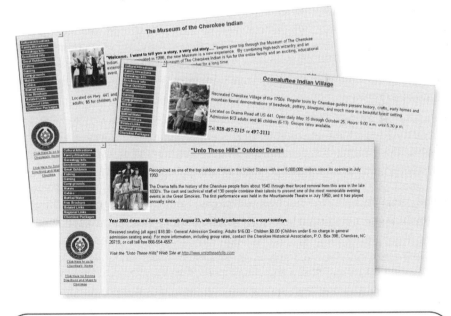

21.2 Cultural attractions on the homepage of the Eastern Band of Cherokee Indians

structures built on respect' (Johnson, 1995: 18). Capital acquisition, however, is not an end in itself for the Cherokee Nation in North Carolina. Gaming proceeds are reinvested in the community. Projects funded by gaming revenues include a new youth centre, which provides access to computers and the internet, and a community computer centre. Other beneficiaries include a new Cultural Resources Division, the newly redesigned museum, a language preservation programme (which records native speakers of Cherokee language on CD-ROM), and the Cherokee school system.

Robert Jumper, who took over management of the website from Redman, reaffirms the Cherokees' interest in building tourism (personal communication, 2002). However, he notes that the nature of tourism has changed. Tourists, especially those from the USA and Japan, have become impatient and lose interest in sites that do not change rapidly and are not technologically exciting. In addition, contemporary tourists want more education and more cultural information. Though there is still a market for the generic Indian items sold by Cherokee Publications (such as beaded belts, medicine wheels and '"Totemscents" Ceremonial Packs'), a growing number of tourists prefer interactive media that teach Cherokee culture, language and history. The site's content already reflects some of the changes Jumper describes. For example, links to the outdoor drama 'Unto These Hills' and the recreated Oconoluftee village contain video clips as well as text and still pictures. To match the 1998 renovation of the Museum of the Cherokee Indian, which combines 'high-tech wizardry and an extensive artifact collection' (www.cherokee-nc.com), the Museum website has been redesigned to feature colour graphics of traditional artefacts, and an online demo of a virtual tour of the Museum available on CD, as well as opportunities to buy historically and culturally specific books, and video and audio tapes.

At the time of writing, Jumper is taking bids for the design of a new website, to be launched early in 2003. Planned to meet both the changing desires of tourists and needs of the Cherokee community, the new website will feature more cultural information and education in the Cherokee language, which Jumper expects to be used by local people engaged in language reacquisition. An exciting element missing from the present webpage is a link to the Cherokee Elementary School and the homepages of Cherokee fifth graders. In 1999, users could access each child's page, with a photograph, his or her name in Cherokee, and an autobiographical statement. The site also invited visitors to click on a 'culture' option to hear a native storyteller recite Cherokee legends in English with Cherokee translations. Unfortunately, while computer use continues among Cherokee students, links to the Elementary School's pages have been discontinued in the interest of the security of the students. Jumper hopes that security issues can be worked out so that the link can be restored, and with it, an additional involvement of the Cherokee community with the website.

CONCLUSION

In our examination of the two websites, we attempted to address the question: does use of this potent Western technology necessarily lead to the degeneration of Native communities, or can Indians use the medium to further the goal of 're-indigenization' – the process of strengthening tribal ties while asserting sovereign rights and fostering self-determination? We conclude from our study of the Cherokees that tribal websites can be powerful agents for community development and cultural continuity within change. The Cherokee Nation of Oklahoma site offers the possibility of developing community by linking people to services, organizations, news, language instruction and free e-mail accounts; both Bands' sites literally enlarge community by providing information about genealogy and enrolment that will assist people with Cherokee ancestry to become members of the tribe, while screening out non-Native 'wannabes' or those merely interested in gaming profits.

The Eastern Band website and its links continue to both reflect and contribute to increasingly successful efforts by Cherokees to recover and retain participation in the capitalist economy of the larger nation. Profits are not only channelled into community services and cultural preservation, but have also expanded the actual land base of the community by funding the purchase of an ancient burial site, and supported business ventures such as the Nation's new bottled water industry and small business loans. Thus the Eastern Band website actively alters the way Qualla interfaces with surrounding cultures, drawing non-Natives from around the world to contribute to cultural preservation and economic recovery (a large percentage of site visitors are German, French, Japanese and other nationalities). At the same time, the internet helps to control access by the dominant culture to Eastern Band Cherokee culture and its representations, and appears to be a significant part of a recovery of their success in the early 1800s as a thriving community in the intersections of EuroAmerican and tribal cultures. While the internet may not yet have become the 'great equalizer' that many had hoped, these two websites suggest that some communities are now beginning to realize the internet's potential for democratic and material equality.

USEFUL WEBSITES

Indian Country Today: www.indiancountry.com

The website of America's largest Indian newspaper, offering news, editorial features, archives and more.

National Congress of American Indians: www.ncai.org

The website of the oldest and largest organization of tribal governments, which serves as a forum for developing consensus-based policy among its membership of 250 tribal governments.

NativeCulture.com: www.nativeculture.com

An award-winning comprehensive portal site for Native American resources on the internet, including educational sites, news and events nationwide, games and products.

NativeWeb: www.nativeweb.org

A non-profit educational organization for the dissemination of information from and about indigenous nations, peoples and organizations around the world.

The Virtual Library of American Indians: www.hanksville.org/NAresources/

A vast index of Native American resources on the internet, ranging from history, museums and language instruction, to legal and health resources, job notices and activist organizations.

Chapter 22

VIRUS WRITERS: SUBCULTURE AND THE ELECTRONIC MEANING OF STYLE

DOUGLAS THOMAS

Within the world of the computer underground there is a subculture devoted to the creation and dissemination of viruses. These programs, which range from code which prints humorous messages across the screen to programs which delete or destroy information, are produced and exist in relation to a clearly marked and defined subculture of virus writers. Unlike the image of virus writers as 'high-tech vandals', many of these programmers are often very talented and see virus writing as a social, cultural and political project. In contrast to the commonly held assumptions about virus writers, the history and motives of this subculture are revealed in the conditions under which that subculture was born and evolved, as well as in the shifting cultural and political contexts to which these programmers have responded. Accordingly, the creation of viruses is not merely a malicious act of vandalism or a senseless act of high-tech destruction, but, instead, functions as a means of subcultural signification and as a strategy for the preservation of a subcultural style in an age of increasing incorporation and commodification of underground computer culture. Like hackers, a distinct subculture that rarely overlaps with the world of virus programmers, virus writers create their own loosely affiliated groups, publish their own underground journals, and engage in

22.1 Your stereotypical computer virus. Mean and deadly ... or misunderstood?

competition and technological one-upmanship, constantly striving to outdo each other in feats of programming. As outlined in 'The Constitution of Worldwide Virus Writers', published in *40Hex*, under the title MOTIVATION: 'In most cases, the motivation for writing a virus should not be the pleasure of seeing someone else's system trashed, but to test one's programming abilities' (*40Hex*, 1992a).

VIRAL STYLE

In their programming, virus writers have adopted a sense of style, which I designate as 'viral style', in an effort to mark themselves as being outside of the computer science community as well as resistant to the computer and anti-virus industry. Virus subculture, like most subcultures, is difficult to define, primarily because as Dick Hebdige has argued, the meaning of subculture is itself always in dispute (Hebdige, 1979: 3). That dispute centres on the primary function of the subculture itself – the use of style to make and remake cultural meaning. Because style is, for subcultures, 'the area in which opposing definitions clash with most dramatic force', what is at stake for virus writers is the meaning of not only the programs they create, but the broader social, cultural and political meanings of technology within contemporary society (ibid.). In much the same way that viruses are related to the history and function of the computer, virus writers are inherently tied to the history of programming.

Virus programmers have a long history of sharing code and ideas, a process which is similar to the early computer programmers of the 1960s and 1970s. What these hackers used to refer to as 'bumming code' is a standard for development in the virus community. In the 1960s and 1970s, it was believed that software should be free, both in terms of its cost and in terms of its ability to be modified. If a programmer could find a way to make software run better, do more, or work more efficiently, then he or she had not only the right, but the responsibility to improve it. It became an ethic among programmers to share code, often referred to as the 'Homebrew ethic' (named for the Homebrew Computer Club, where it was widely practised) or the 'Hacker Ethic' (as documented in Steven Levy's 1983 book, *Hackers*). The idea behind the ethic was that each successive iteration of coding would improve and alter the program for the better, making it do more or run more efficiently. It is a model that virus writers adopted immediately, making their source code available and even distributing it freely in underground journals and through electronic bulletin board systems and the internet. Indeed, most virus writers relate their experience of writing their first virus in a way that mirrors that ethic identically. As one virus programmer (Skism One) explains, after being infected with the Jerusalem virus himself, I 'examined the copy of Jeru for months. Then one day I used a Hex editor to change the suMSDOs string to SKISM-1. Then I went to all the computers I could find and infected them. The next thing you know my friend shows me this list with my name on it' (*40Hex*,

1991). The hex editor was able to change the name of the program, and attribute authorship to Skism One, but it didn't actually modify the code. In order to become a virus writer, he needed to learn how to create virus programs on his own. At that point, Skism One, following in the tradition of computer programmers before him, built his own virus from what he learned from Jerusalem, 'Then I started to learn how to modify the code and all that. The next thing you know I had made my own virus from the scraps of Jeru.' Before long, he had learned enough to begin constructing his own code, 'Then I guess I grew out of the scavenger mode and started writing my own shit, from scratch' (ibid.). While the ethic is similar, the goals and desires of the computer programmers of Homebrew and the virus writers of the 1980s and 1990s are markedly different.

As a subculture, virus writers present themselves as what Dick Hebdige identified as *noise*, 'as an actual mechanism of semantic disorder: a kind of temporary blockage in the system of representation' (1979: 90). Subculture, Hebdige argues, manifests itself in *style* as an intentional form of communication whereby the cultural and social negotiation of signs takes place. Marked as a kind of deviant behaviour, subcultural style is often 'incorporated' through the process of commodification that results in the 'conversion of subcultural signs into mass-produced objects (i.e. the commodity form)' (ibid.: 94). The result is a 'diffusion of the subculture's subversive power' – such as the way in which 'punk innovations fed back directly into high fashion and mainstream fashion' in the 1970s (ibid.: 95).

THE COMMODIFICATION OF HACKER STYLE

The birth and growth of virus culture can be traced directly to the commodification of the computer in the form of the PC and as a response to the incorporation and dilution of computer culture which accompanied the mass marketing of the PC. In terms of technology, the mass appeal of the personal computer, particularly in the mid-1980s, produced a widespread incorporation of computer culture, taking the essentially subversive 'hacker style' which demanded an intimate knowledge of these machines and how they worked, and stripping it of its transgressive character for mass consumption. With the introduction and growth of GUIs (graphical user interfaces), computer users have become increasingly distanced from the machines and software they use. As a result, the technology has been rendered increasingly opaque, even as it has become easier to use and more 'user friendly'.

Virus writers are reacting with a kind of digital violence to these transformations that have taken place in computer culture. The dynamics of the production of a commodified opaque technology have created two motives for virus production. First, viruses force the end user to become aware (or at least more aware) of his or her blind reliance or dependence on technology. In doing so, the threat of viral infection forces him or her to take note of the technology itself. The threat of viral infection forces the end user to understand how his or her computer works, to take precautions, to be aware of how viruses are spread and how to protect one-self. As one writer commented about the threat arising from the Microsoft Word macro viruses: 'Control is in your hands. Don't panic. Take this as an opportunity to learn more about the features of the software you use, to test and verify any security features you plan to utilize and then to configure accordingly' (quoted in Platt, 1996: 149). To the virus writer, the philosophy is simple – there are risks associated with ignorance, especially with ignorance about technology. Typically, virus writers are more hyperbolic in their assessments. But these assessments also betray an underlying metaphor, consonant with earlier theories of viral infection, namely, evolution. As Dark Angel, one of the more vitriolic virus writers, wrote in 1992:

> Virii [sic] are wondrous creations written for the sole purpose of spreading and destroying the systems of unsuspecting fools. This eliminates the systems of simpletons who can't tell that there is a problem when a 100 byte file suddenly blossoms into a 1,000 byte file. Duh. These low-lifes do not deserve to exist, so it is our sacred duty to wipe their hard drives off the face of the Earth. It is a simple matter of speeding along survival of the fittest.

While many, even most, virus writers in the subculture do not harbour such malicious intent, few would disagree with the assessment of the typical computer user as an 'unsuspecting fool' and many see viruses as a natural extension of computer programming and as a logical step in programming and the computer's evolution.

The second motive stems from the fact that virus writers see the broader cultural implications of such dependence on technology as well. They see the commodification of the computer and of computer culture as leading to the possibility of technological domination, and viruses provide a sense of protection. Accordingly, the targets for viral infection are not just individual users. Instead, the inspiration for such coding comes from precisely the kind of blockage that is characteristic of subcultural style. As one virus writer explains, the typical virus writer

> is usually just this angry kid who happens to be very clever, and what's going through his head when he codes this thing is how fuckin' cool it'll be when it starts blowing holes through the infrastructure of some industrial monolith like IBM, where a bunch of drones will start going bugfuck when everything stops working.
>
> (quoted in Platt, 1996: 145)

The idea of being able to 'smash the system' has its roots in narratives about computers as far back as John Brunner's sci-fi classic *The Shockwave Rider*, which tells the story of a computer programmer who liberates society from the tyranny of technology by releasing a virus-like program throughout the government's network. Like Brunner's hero, virus writers see themselves as maintaining the fragility of the system, keeping it in a state of precariousness such that its power over us is always limited by our ability to destroy it.

As the culture of virus writers evolved, journals like *40Hex* underwent transformations as well. *40Hex* started in 1990 as a purely technical journal with the sole mission of disseminating virus code. By 1995, the journal had taken on an entirely different tone: 'We are going to get a little bit more political then we used to be, but we will still keep cranking out the high quality technical information that you all enjoy. I would strongly recommend that you don't skip over the political parts of the magazine, because there are people who want to make laws that will affect every reader of this magazine' (*40Hex*, 1995). The political message of *40Hex* was remarkably similar to that of the early 1960s and 1970s hackers. Predicated on freedom of information, the editors of *40Hex* would argue that efforts to legislate against virus production were misguided. They maintain it is not the production of viral code but its distribution that should be made illegal. The *40Hex* attitude towards viruses also betrays a deeper philosophy about the place of viruses in networks. Viruses have become so deeply embedded in the network environment, they argue, that they are no longer able to be contained:

> Unfortunately, it is too late to start working on anti-virus writing legislation now. The damage has been done. The virus issue is fairly similar to the AIDS issue. You have to use protection, no matter what. There will never be an end to virii. Even if everyone stopped writing virii, the infection rate wouldn't decrease. I don't know of many people that get hit by the newer strains that have been coming out. Most people still get hit by Jerusalem, Stoned, and other 'classics'.
>
> (*40Hex*, 1992b)

NARRATIVES OF INFECTION

The lessons of science fiction are a primary target for the contested meaning of technology between the computer science community and the computer underground. In the late 1980s, the emergence of 'cyberpunk' signalled a shift in the ways that the underground was thinking about technology, and it would be reflection on Robert Morris's internet worm (the first major, internet-based infection) which would lead to that realization. 'More often than we realize, reality conspires to imitate art. In the case of the computer virus reality,' Paul Saffo wrote, 'the art is "cyberpunk," a strangely compelling genre of science fiction that has gained a cult following among hackers operating on both sides of the law' (1989: 664). What Saffo would find interesting was the 'generation gap' between the computer science community (most of whom, including Robert Morris, had read and been fans of Brunner's *The Shockwave Rider*) and the underground world of virus writers, who were more devoted to the work of writers like William Gibson. With respect to Gibson's cyberpunk classic *Neuromancer*, Saffo would report 'I am particularly struck by the "generation gap" in the computer community when it comes to *Neuromancer*: virtually every teenage hacker I spoke with has the book, but almost none of my friends over 30 have picked it up' (ibid.: 665).

Virus writers have learned an important lesson from the past. Watching the process of commodification, whereby computer style has been commodified and stripped of its potentially subversive force, virus writers have adopted a different sense of style that has made them more resistant to cultural incorporation. Accordingly, viral style represents a break from Hebdige's initial notion of subculture in an important respect. The culture surrounding viruses is a subculture which demands constant innovation and which accounts for mainstream culture's (and the industry's) ability to commodify and incorporate aspects of subversive style. Viral style is a response to a response, a *mutation* of style that is negotiating precisely the moment of incorporation of earlier computer style and culture by the mainstream.

With the mass production of the personal computer and the widespread incorporation of computer culture, viral style emerged as a style that negotiates a *previously incorporated style*. Cognizant of the dangers and possibilities of incorporation itself, viral style is *self-replicating* and *polymorphic*, continually changing with each iteration. It is a style that enacts its own defence mechanism against incorporation. It is a style that is constantly evolving, reclaiming the earliest trope that defined the discourse of computer viruses themselves. The antecedents of virus culture, the impact of virus culture on computer culture generally, and the context which situates virus culture are both politically and culturally reactive to the incorporation of hacker style in mainstream, dominant culture.

Virus writers were not the only group to respond to the discourse of infection, public health and hygiene that followed in the wake of Morris's internet worm. The discourse of industry and the mass media also seized on the opportunity to exploit the network-wide infection. In the wake of Morris's worm, public perceptions of viruses and virus writers were formed, and a multi-million-dollar industry was launched.

THE IDEA OF THE COMPUTER VIRUS IN THE POPULAR IMAGINATION

The emergence of computer viruses in popular culture was coincident with an evolving discourse of AIDS and infection that had risen to the level of a public health epidemic. In this sense, the discourses of infection, contamination and hygiene were narratives that had already been mobilized with dramatic effect, and provided an immediate and highly charged context for understanding computer viruses.

Unlike other types of infection, AIDS was constructed in the popular imagination as a kind of smart virus. As Marita Sturken (1997) argues, the discourse of AIDS disrupted the conventional narratives of infection in part because AIDS was endowed with agency and intentionality, learning how to mutate in response to the body's immune system. AIDS, Sturken argues, has transformed the nature of viral infection in the popular imagination:

> A virus is not 'alive,' according to science, yet neither is it dead; it can be killed. It is a 'bundle' of genes, an incohesive tangle. It 'contains instructions' but apparently did not write them itself. It is 'pure information,' yet information that acquires meaning only when in contact with cells.
>
> (1997: 245)

Within this context, the transformation of the virus into the discourse of information, it becomes clear that just as computer science had co-opted the discourse of biology, biological science was now turning to information sciences for its metaphors. The issues which most directly affected the discourse of how AIDS functioned had to do with how it learns, propagates and mutates, properties which were well understood and easily modelled in self-replicating computer code, and computer models and simulations.

While the body was the site of discourse for AIDS, the larger social body and networks are the space in which the discourse of computer viruses is localized. In the wake of the 1988 worm, for example, Peter Denning would write:

> Certainly the vivid imagery of worms and viruses has enabled many outsiders to appreciate the subtlety and danger of attacks on computers attached to open networks. It has increased public appreciation of the dependence of important segments of the economy, aerospace systems, and defense networks on computers and telecommunications. Networks of computers have joined other critical networks that underpin our society – water, gas, electricity, telephones, air traffic control, banking, to name a few.
>
> (1998: 128)

It is a sentiment which would be picked up on by the press, media and in the popular imagination.

CONCLUSION

Until the release of Morris's internet worm, the concept of a computer virus was abstract, limited and contained. Viruses were occasional programs that spawned a few variants each year. For example, prior to Morris's internet worm, there were 11 known viruses for the IBM PC. In the year after the worm, that number nearly doubled (to 21) and in the next few years that followed, the number grew rapidly, doubling roughly every ten months. Even so, the number of virus programs still numbered in the low hundreds until Microsoft released a version of the Word word-processing program which had a built-in macro function. The macro function allowed users to embed commands inside of Microsoft Word documents, giving near complete control over file access, creation and deletion to the Word program. In doing so, Microsoft created a new virus delivery system that made it possible to transmit viruses through text documents (rather than as executable code). It also allowed viruses to be created without any knowledge of assembly language or computer programming. Macros were their own high-level language, easily understood and quickly apprehended by even computer neophytes. It was a language that was designed to be simple to utilize.

The release of Microsoft Word would turn out to be the most significant event in virus production. By 1994, the year of Word's release, the number of viruses was in excess of 5000; nearly all of the new additions took advantage of the Word macro function. The trend continued throughout the 1990s. In 1998, the number of known viruses in the wild was in excess of 18,000. By April of 1999, roughly one year later, McAfee and Associates reported 40,000 known viruses (see www.mcafee.com/anti-virus).

The very idea of a virus connotes illness, sickness and even death. Interestingly, however, the majority of viruses do not cause significant damage. In a 1996 survey, viruses were found to be the 'most common type of security breach', with half of the companies surveyed reporting 'virus incidents', however only 5 per cent of those incidents were described as having a 'serious or significant impact' (quoted in Denning, 1998: 39). What surveys routinely show is that industry spends huge sums of money protecting against virus attacks and attributes large losses to virus infection (usually first on the list of 'sources of financial loss' for organizations reporting virus infections), but that a very small number of actual 'attacks' account for most of the damage. Even recent reports of the top 10 viruses reported on the internet find that only one carries any 'payload' at all.

As a result, viruses, like many aspects of computer culture and high technology, appear to most people as dangerous, mysterious and alien forces. They reflect not only the dissatisfaction of underground culture with the ways in which their style and culture are turned into a product and sold, but they also reflect a broader cultural anxiety about technology itself. Therefore, as viruses become an increasingly common aspect of our everyday experiences with computers, it becomes more and more important to understand the history and motives of the programmers who write them and the culture of programming that has produced them. In doing so, we can better understand not only how viruses and viral code functions, but also we can better reflect on our own relationships with technology and the industries that produce it.

USEFUL WEBSITES

AntiOnline: www.antionline.com

Hosts a collection of more than 600 viruses which may be downloaded for analysis and study. 'AntiOnline is not a place where the community's knowledge is used or passed on to others in order to carry out illegal or immoral acts,' it notes sternly.

CERT Coordination Center: www.cert.org

CERT, the first Computer Emergency Response Team, handles threats to the internet and serves as a major reporting centre for internet security problems.

Symantec's Security Response Center: http://securityresponse.symantec.com

Provides updates on the latest virus releases and security threats.

Vmyths: Truth about Computer Security Hysteria: www.vmyths.com

A site which examines virus myths and hoaxes, as well as providing useful information on viruses and malicious programs.

Chapter 23

DIGITAL MEDIA FUTURES

RICHARD BERGER

Predicting any kind of future is always going to be hard. George Orwell, when he published *Nineteen Eighty-Four* in 1949, had no idea that his core ideas would end up as a reality TV show – *Big Brother* – and a chat show – *Room 101*. But sometimes it worked out, as sci-fi codger Arthur C. Clarke foresaw communications satellites and William Gibson was scarily on the right track when he coined the term 'cyberspace' in his novel *Neuromancer*, published in, er, 1984 – a full 12 years before Tim Berners-Lee's World Wide Web became viewable on Marc Andreessen's Mosaic browser, giving us the internet experience we know today.

In the first edition of *Web.Studies*, David Gauntlett suggested, amongst other things, that a two-tier internet may emerge – a split between broadband and dial-up modem users. And a two-tier structure does indeed seem to be emerging. However, this may not be the most important divide, because we are easily ignoring those who are not online at all – the digital underclass – never mind those who use broadband or narrowband. The internet, as slick and shiny as it seems, depends on a technology invented by Alexander Graham Bell in 1876, and 50 per cent of the world's population don't have access to a telephone. So, what now?

LET'S PLAY ...

It's almost a certainty that a new, emerging generation of users will have a huge impact on the way people use new media. When we talk about the internet, we're really talking about the World Wide Web, and that's only been about since the early-to-mid-90s. However, many primary schools now have their own websites; children as young as five are uploading their schoolwork and projects. E-learning will change the way in which young people develop their skills, and high schools, colleges and universities throughout the world are already beginning to work this way.

This new generation will be one that is ultimately comfortable with new media, and as they grow older, those unsavoury elements that – as the right-wing press would have us believe – seem to flourish online, will be just as marginalized online as they are in the 'offline' world. The web will be increasingly full of educated and responsible users; a generation that has grown up with this technology, and that is comfortable in using it properly. This is nothing new, as *Wired* magazine founder and MIT head-honcho Nicholas Negroponte (1995), said pretty much the same thing some time ago.

THE REGULATIONS 'TRADE-OFF'

Those unsavoury elements have always been a problem: in the 1880s the penny dreadful comics were blamed for their possible effects on society; it was video nasties in the 1980s and hip-hop music in 2002. As James Slevin has suggested, the problem is that governments treat the internet as if it's a broadcast medium, like film, TV and radio – whereas users treat it like the telephone (2001: 219). Robert Burnet and David Marshall also recognize this. They argue that the ways in which governments and institutions treated technology were based largely on metaphors; remember phrases like 'The Information Superhighway'? This limited the scope and vision of government policy (2003: 128). In some respects, these approaches are clumsy, but you could still argue that to a fairly great extent, it seems to be the main strategy used to try and introduce more content regulation. But there's a crucial paradox here that will become increasingly visible.

First of all, new media is very important to the economy. The old manufacturing industries are pretty much in their death throes, and the long awaited e-economy is no longer the fantasy of technophiles and dusty academics. This does cause a problem for regulation: how do you impose more content regulation, but not in a way that damages the new economy? It's a tough problem, but one answer is that more internet watchdogs will emerge – voluntary bodies such as the *Internet Watch Foundation* (www.iwf.org). This is similar to the way in which much of the press in Europe is controlled. There are many who argue that this type of regulation is ineffective, but that's the muddy trade-off that seems to be on the cards. In fact, most European policy seems to be heading that way, and the US government is still smarting from having the Communications Decency Act rejected outright by its Supreme Court in 1997, and having its Child Online Protection Act overturned by the US Appeals Court in 2000, only for it to be reinstated in 2001.

Many established businesses have moved services online, but this was really a cost-cutting measure; we all live near wine bars that used to be banks. Successful companies that just existed online were pretty rare when the first edition of *Web.Studies* was published. Now Amazon.com is turning a healthy profit, and so are others including Lastminute.com – once the laughing stock of the supposed 'dot-com crash'. More will follow and the last thing governments want to do is to hinder that growth with yet more draconian legislation. As in the case of cinema in the UK, already existing laws, such as the Obscene Publications Act and the Protection of Children Act, will be invoked if necessary. And that's fine.

NEW ENVIRONMENTS

The Wi-Fi revolution that David Gauntlett predicted is happening pretty much to plan. But why should we be surprised? The radio was originally called 'the wireless' after all and now many of us have had cordless telephones – and even cordless kettles – for years. Many workplaces take advantage of wireless technology, so that people can wander around with their laptops and not have to worry about plugging them in. This has halved the number of insurance payouts for industrial accidents where people kept tripping over cables all the time.

Now on the horizon are new internet environments. The World Wide Web is something that sits *on top* of the internet, and makes it far easier to use. The next generation of environments will be different in that the information and the computing power will actually exist in cyberspace all the time. At the moment, information sits on other computers, or servers, waiting for people to access it. Now, when you visit a website, you are essentially *downloading* that site to your computer. If the site is slow and clunky, or you can't fully experience all its features, the

23.1 Some people wondering about the availability of wireless internet access, yesterday

chances are that you don't have the required software, and your computer may be too slow. At the moment, there's really no such thing as 'virtual' information, it has to be hosted somewhere.

The new environments, possibly called Internet2 or The Grid, will mean that all the information will be in cyberspace, all the time. It won't be held on other computers or servers. The next stage of the internet will see it move from something that is still centred on old-fashioned telephone networks and big computers, to vast tracts of virtual knowledge. So you won't have to download it. In theory, this will means that even if you have a computer that's so old it has the word 'Sinclair' or 'Commodore' on it, you'll still be able to engage fully with the internet. So, computers will become more like a window, or portal, into a mass of information, and will move ever closer to William Gibson's vision of cyberspace. These new environments will not only make the internet more efficient, but will have huge implications for the technologically disadvantaged. The internet *should* be cheaper to use, and this could change problems we now have with access.

ACCESS ALL AREAS?

The same problems with access that were in existence when the first edition of *Web.Studies* came out are still prevalent. It doesn't matter what you're making or writing, you want, or need, an audience to see it; interactive media needs a user to *initiate* or request it. If you are living in Europe or North America, you are already in a privileged position. The West does seem to have had a 'head start' in terms of access. However, even the most blinkered person can see that the print and visual media are dominated by Western values, and perhaps even more obviously, American values. The phenomenon of conglomeration – which began in the late 1970s – continues today, and will spread further in the near future. For instance, media tycoons such as Rupert Murdoch don't just own newspapers, but TV stations, film studios, record companies, book publishers and computer games manufacturers as well.

However, it's not all bad news. It still is very expensive to set up and run your own newspaper, or TV or radio station. So a lot of people are turning to the internet as a more plural media form. Cyberspace doesn't seem as cluttered and as regulated as conventional media. However, cyberspace is full of companies like Microsoft, and at first glance English is the most common language used. Most browsers and search engines seem to be set up in English as their default option. You could argue convincingly that the English language dominates cyberspace, but even if this was true, it's certainly no longer the reality as large parts of Southeast Asia, Africa and India embrace this new technology. However, the USA has had a huge cultural influence on the world; many leaders of developing nations have been educated in America, and US foreign policy is seemingly at odds with global institutions such as the United Nations, and the World Trade Organization. The USA is also increasingly hostile to notions of further European integration, which will dominate the political landscape for the next few years, at least. American media dominates the world, with Hollywood cinema and CNN giving a US perspective on world affairs. The World Wide Web does suggest a global media community, but it clearly isn't. Yet. Some writers, such as Herbert Schiller (2001) have suggested that America is using new media to gain more control over global markets. At the moment it seems like no one can compete with America, but will this change in future?

When people first stared talking about the internet, it was mainly academics in the West that had access to it. So from the start, the internet has always been a realm of inequality. It is fairly apparent that the most serious divides in cyberspace are those based on what country you live in, how old you are and how much money you have. This is slowly changing, as parts of the developing world are increasing their access, and this will continue. Connection does still depend on a reliable telephone network at the moment, but new environments such as Internet2, Wi-Fi and The Grid may weaken the stranglehold of the telecommunications industry and this will further facilitate access for the technologically disadvantaged. The lower-income countries are home to around 80 per cent of the world's population. Just as in the West, developing nations see the economic value of an e-economy, and are making major inroads into this new sector. The developing world often feels left behind and views these new technologies as a way of keeping up and an entry point into the new e-economy. Many developing countries see the internet as a way of participating in the wider global economy and, therefore, a way to get themselves out of debt and increase their quality of life. Just as in the West, though, they are already experiencing problems of regulation and content control. Daniel Miller and Don Slater's study of Trinidad's emerging e-economy reported claims that over 60 per cent of internet traffic was pornographic in nature. The Trinidad government does not want to create conditions that stop growth, so it is wary of drafting new content legislation (2000: 32).

Western corporations are helping the developing world, but this could be a Faustian pact, as emerging technological countries and markets may find themselves dependent on the West for training, and software upgrades. No developing nation's government is going to turn down free hardware and software, as they are increasingly worried about the increasing gap between the world's rich and poor. Many of these nations are dependent on the West anyway, because of aid and debt, loans and debt relief, and Western co-ownership of communications networks. Only time will tell if the gap between the info-rich and the info-poor increases, or decreases, although there is cause to be optimistic that the outcome will be a good one for all, especially the developing world.

AN OLD CHESTNUT?

Since the early days of new media, people have been predicting some form of convergence, where all media will somehow fuse together. It's often not certain whether people mean a *technological* convergence, an *aesthetic* convergence, or both. So far, it has not really happened, although something is clearly going on. In the UK there has been quite a bit of pressure from the government for people to go out and get digital TV, whether they want to or not. The old analogue TV frequencies have been sold off to telecommunications companies, and the government claims it will switch off the analogue signal sometime in the next decade. So if you haven't 'gone digital', your TV and radio sets will fall eerily silent. The take-up of digital TV has been slower than anticipated, but that will change as cheaper technology becomes available, and more broadcasters and providers get involved. This climate will be further promoted by a whole raft of new legislation and media ownership laws that will facilitate further deregulation across Europe. The BBC's entry into the digital provider market in the UK has led to a significant consumer digital take-up. More and more digital TV and radio channels are appearing all the time. Many of these will vanish, true, but this flurry of new content providers will continue at an increasing rate. There is still some uncertainty and anxiety about the proposed switching-off of the analogue signal. However, there is of course a historical precedent: in 1953 we had the Queen's Coronation in the UK, and thousands of people rushed out to buy TV sets for the occasion. In 1955, ITV started broadcasting for the first time and many of the by now two-year-old TV sets, couldn't pick up the UK's first commercial TV channel. But ITV and broadcast television survived, and it will in the future.

Advertisers may have cause for concern, as technologies such as TiVo (www.tivo.com) will allow you to record hours of your favourite TV, but without the adverts. So marketing gurus will have to adopt similar techniques to those they use online: more tailored and targeted campaigns aimed at individuals. Distinct channel branding may not be as important, as the new generation of digital recorders are generic and only recognize programmes, not channels. These devices also learn what you enjoy watching, and will eventually pre-empt your choices by recording programmes that suit a profile built up of your preferences over time. This is nothing new, as many web-based retail outlets (such as Amazon) have been doing this for some time. So is there going to be a convergence between TV and new media?

TV CHOICE

What about so-called interactive TV (at the moment unhelpfully tagged 'iTV' by some writers)? What about interactivity? This is all still a bit of a fudge, as no one quite seems to know what it is. Or where it is. In the UK, the BBC has reorganized its new media provision, and BBCi is no longer just its web-based services, but now includes interactive TV and broadband provision. Much of this, you could convincingly argue, is just *enhanced* television; it 'looks' like it's interactive and non-linear, but it isn't really. If the first edition of *Web.Studies* predicted a *participatory* era, with people actually authoring content, then TV isn't there yet. However, some pockets do exist, and new digital games channels such as the continuous live bingo channel, AVAGO, and the jokey gambling show, *Banzai*, are getting there. Interactive drama is also something that could be along in a few years, but these will be one-off events, rather than the established programme genres. After all, TV is TV, and most people are happy with that. We watch TV specifically because we like narratives and we still want to be entertained and told a good story with the capacity to surprise. That's what TV is.

If we're talking about participatory experiences, then hasn't TV being doing that for years anyway? Many children's programmes have depended on content from their viewers, and others actively encourage kids to go off and make or create things. Children's TV does always seem to be at the forefront of what's possible with the medium, and much of today's children's programme content (in the UK at least) depends on e-mail and text or picture messages. This will only increase, and will be further proof that the digital divide may well be drawn along *generational* lines as well. Consumer programmes have been around since television began and have always needed audiences to provide content, usually in the form of complaints about household technologies. If Marcel Duchamp (cited in Rush, 1999: 25) claimed in the 1930s that *all* art needs an audience to complete it, then by the same token, isn't *all* media interactive?

INTERACTIVE AND NON-LINEAR MEDIA

When writing about computer games, Steven Poole (2000: 106–9) splits the narrative into the diachronic (the fixed story) and the synchronic (the present 'real-time' plot). Essentially during game-play, you can only influence the synchronic narrative according to the rules of the diachronic narrative. Whatever you do, you won't be able to alter or influence the diachronic narrative one bit. So, in a sense, interactivity just gives you the *illusion* of control. This will surely change, and this illusion of new media as pure spectacle or just a superficial mode of 'the aesthetic of surface-play', as Andrew Darley (2000: 194) suggests, will perhaps over time become increasingly democratic and two-way. More sophisticated interactive and non-linear media will be the purest form of media yet, as it will be one the perfectly maps the cognitive processes of the brain. We don't think in a linear way; we are able to jump about and access information in our brains in a wholly non-linear way. We can all instantaneously recount jokes that were once told to us years ago; so we're constructing narratives all the time from bits and pieces of our own experiences and those narratives are our lives. By the same token, we are all used to using libraries and textbooks, often employing a non-linear system – the alphabet – to help us look for what we want. Cinema, from *Citizen Kane* (Welles, 1941) to *Pulp Fiction* (Tarantino, 1994), *Memento* (Nolan, 2000) and *Irreversible* (Noe, 2003) has often thrilled audiences by telling stories out of conventional sequence. New and interactive media are non-linear and user-initiated, and, after all, this is how we function as human beings, so new media will increasingly reflect the way in which we function, and the way in which we think. Marshall McLuhan was right when he said that 'the user is content', way back in the 1970s (cited in Levinson, 2001: 39).

The definitions of interactive media will still stay in flux for some time yet. But the future will see new types of participatory experiences, with differing levels of participation. These definitions will continue to evolve, but will probably be concerned with *physical* interactivity, and a more sophisticated two-way transaction between content providers/broadcasters and users/audiences.

EMERGING TRENDS: REMEDIATION AND MULTI-PLATFORM SCENARIOS

The way in which different media 'speak' to each other will continue to evolve and become ever more refined. Different media have always borrowed conventions from each other; early cinema was originally just a sideshow, a fairground 'attraction'. The first movie spectators would sit in large tents and were gripped by short films of railway trains coming out of stations. The first narrative films looked like theatre productions, as did early television; and the formative years of cinema were dominated by literary adaptation. It's not so different now, with the 'look' of media constantly borrowing and recycling styles from elsewhere. Lucy Mazon argues that since its earliest days, narrative cinema has always, 'adapted, copied, plagiarised and been inspired by other works' (2000: 2). Now, in a process that Jay David Bolter and Richard Grusin (2000) call 'remediation', new media is having an effect. Some TV programmes look very 'webby' and even films as far back as *Starship Troopers* (Verhoeven, 1997) appropriated a clear internet aesthetic. Bolter and Grusin further suggest that this trend is now two-way, and that older, more established media, have to 'reaffirm their status within our culture as digital media challenge that status' (2000: 5). Television is the most obvious example, as you can now e-mail to the technology itself, and many types of television programming have very obvious stylistic similarities with web-based media, especially television news.

Again, this is nothing new, and it is really a product of further conglomeration, and the influx of new digital acquisition, production and exhibition technologies over almost all media now. It is a strange fact that films are now shot and edited digitally, but a negative is still printed which is copied thousands of times on strips of celluloid, made up of frames – 24 of which equate to one second of screen time. Nearly all films are still exhibited on technology that is over a hundred years old in principle: the projector. This will change.

There will also be an acceleration of ideas and stories deployed over several media at the same time. Increasingly, the summer blockbuster film events also include websites, computer games, tie-in books/magazines, published screenplays, toys, clothing and even tie-in sweets and breakfast cereals. Computer games are being made into films and vice versa; films are being made into TV serials; websites are being turned into TV dramas. These trends will continue and will emerge as the dominant strategy for mainstream media. It's no wonder that some elements of the George Lucas *Star Wars* prequels look like platform computer games – that is exactly what they are. And the same corporation makes them all. It will be interesting to see which media forms become dependent on which, if at all. It seems that cinema is the most dominant form at present, with all other media clustered around it; the logic goes that if the film fails, then so will the tie-in subsidiary texts, such as computer games. In the future, this relationship may leaven out to one of mutual exchange, with no one media having the upper hand.

CONCLUSION

The future may be faster, and there may be more new media, but things won't necessarily get smaller. Telecommunications, both in terms of technological innovation and its place in future media policy and regulation, will still have an important part to play. However, there will be a sudden halt to the increasing miniaturization of mobile phones. With the advent of new visual-based communication – such as picture and video messaging – handsets will have to get bigger again, because trying to watch images on something the size of a baked bean is frankly stupid, and bad for your eyes. These innovations will mean that people will be able to update their websites immediately, wherever they are – great for those backpacking holidays, where friends and family can continuously monitor your progress. Also, television sets are getting bigger, flatter and more rectangular, while IMAX cinemas and 3D experiences are on the increase. On the other hand, your local three-screen cinema probably changed into a 24-screen multiplex some time ago. So cinemas are perhaps the last vanguard of the miniaturization trend.

There is a new generation of children that have been using new media since they were five years old. They will grow up using these technologies without even thinking about it. They will be a generation that is comfortable with this media and who are competent and responsible in its use. They will be a generation that is used to non-linear and interactive forms of media. Therefore there will be a lot more of it about. It should be no surprise that older, more established media starts to appropriate conventions of new media and vice versa. This has always happened. Don't forget, however, that new media used to be called 'multi-media', and that's exactly what it is: a mixture of all that's gone before – in the same way that TV was a mixture of radio, theatre, literature and cinema.

In the early days of cinema, after they'd shown their trains coming out of stations, the Lumière brothers filmed people going to work, in what we can now claim were the first documentaries. It didn't take long for film to develop conventions and a language of its own, and that's where we are now with new media. The next few years will see a move from this period of 'attraction' into an era that firmly establishes the internet as a media form in its own right, with its own codes and conventions. Furthermore, cyberspace is generally a quiet place at present, with hardly any attention paid to sound online. Most websites are strangely silent, and the software that supports sound is a long way behind the level of sophistication of its visual counterparts. So extra layers will be added to the Web to make it even more vibrant and exciting than it is now, as sound does seem to be rather a new media orphan. New media is greater than the sum of all its parts, but not all those parts are in place yet.

So the second edition of *Web.Studies* pretty much ends at the same place the last edition did. It's up to you to move things forward. The internet is still very malleable and there's still vast room for manoeuvre and innovation. The advent of cheap and affordable digital acquisition formats, such as movie cameras, stills cameras, and picture and video messaging, will mean that it is easier than ever before to get involved, and to be creative. It was arguably D.W. Griffith who moved cinema out of its infancy as a sideshow, and away from boring filmed plays, by inventing multiple camera set-ups and editing almost overnight. New media writers and digital theorists are searching for the cyber equivalent – someone who will initiate the next stage. So get involved: we are the new community who can make things better.

GLOSSARY

This glossary of a selection of technical terms – plus a few people, acronyms, programs and companies – was compiled by David Gauntlett and David Silver in 2000, and then revised by David Gauntlett for this 2004 edition. As usual, for further detail on any of these things, or others, you can do a Google search and find much more information.

Accessibility – The principle that websites should be available to as many people as possible, including the blind, and also people with old or slow computers or browsers. Some websites are much more accessible than others. Blind users, for example, may use software that converts webpages to speech, but such programs are often flummoxed by fancy, graphics-heavy sites (especially ones using a lot of **Flash** with no simple **HTML** equivalent).

Acrobat, Adobe – Software which runs on different platforms (computers with divergent operating systems), allowing documents to be viewed exactly as originally intended, complete with layout and graphics. This is often handy, but is also used lazily by people who can't be bothered to convert their documents into webpages. The Acrobat viewer is free; Adobe makes its money by charging for the software which converts documents into Acrobat files.

ADSL – Asymmetrical Digital Subscriber Line, a fast, broadband way of sending data down standard copper phone lines.

Andreessen, Marc (1972–) – While a student at the National Center for Supercomputing Applications (NCSA) at the University of Illinois, Andreessen produced, with staff member Eric Bina, the first Web browser with a graphical point-and-click interface (like Apple and Windows operating systems), called **Mosaic**. This popular early browser, first distributed free over the internet in February 1993, really kick-started interest in the Web. In 1994, Andreessen and

Jim Clark launched Netscape Communications Corporation, and Netscape dominated the browser market for around four years, although Microsoft later succeeded in its late-starting bid to seize power in this area.

AOL – Leading commercial online service that serves as an entry point to the internet for over 34 million users worldwide. (A merger in 2000 saw the company become global media superpower AOL/Time Warner.) As a result of its user-friendly interface and wall-to-wall marketing, AOL attracts countless network newcomers which, in turn, attracts hostility from internet old-timers towards 'AOL newbies'.

ARPANET – An experimental computer network created by the US military during the Cold War. Established in 1969 by the Advanced Research Projects Administration (ARPA) to support military research and nuclear attack-proof communication, ARPANET stands as the original ancestor of the internet.

Attachment – A file (such as a document, spreadsheet, or graphic) sent 'attached' to an e-mail message.

Banner advert – Long, thin advert appearing on a webpage. ('Banner ads' may also refer to online adverts generally, regardless of their shape.) Many sites make some money by selling banner advert space. Banner ads are often animated, and considered annoying by many. Some ads even include little games in a bid to get the user to click through to the advertiser's website.

BBS – Short for bulletin board system, a BBS is an open computer system which members can dial into (via a phone) in order to send e-mail, join discussion groups and download files. Around since the 1970s, BBSs were originally locally based but now often provide access to a broad spectrum of internet applications, including e-mail, telnet and FTP.

Berners-Lee, Tim (1955–) – Invented the World Wide Web during 1990–1, while working at CERN, the European Particle Physics Laboratory in Geneva (see Chapter 1). In 1994 he later established the World Wide Web Consortium (W3C) to oversee the Web's development and recommend universal standards. His book, *Weaving the Web* (1999), gives a valuable account of the development of the Web, and his original ideas and intentions for it.

Blog – Short for 'weblog', a blog is a regularly updated diary of a person's fascinations, thoughts and/or experiences. See Chapter 1 for a discussion of the rise of blogs.

Bluetooth – Named after an ancient Danish king, apparently, Bluetooth is a wireless connectivity technology, enabling a range of devices to speak to each other using radio waves. See also **Wi-Fi**.

Broadband – Generic term for a fast internet connection, via cable or telephone lines (using **ADSL**). Typically at least ten times as fast as the old 56K modem.

Browser – Software for viewing and travelling around the Web, such as Microsoft's Internet Explorer.

Bug – Computerese for a software error or programming glitch which causes the computer to malfunction or crash. Bugs are always around, seldom liked and never entirely eliminated.

Cache – A small, fast area of computer memory used to hold recently accessed data. Most often applied to Web browsers' cache, memory spaces used to hold recently visited websites.

Cascading Style Sheets (CSS) – An extension to **HTML** which allow styles (colour, font style, and font size, for example) to be specified for certain elements of a **hypertext** document. CSS are especially useful when preparing many, slightly different HTML pages.

CD – See **compact disc**.

Chat – A form of online communication which allows users to have conversations in real time. When participating in a chat discussion, users' messages instantaneously appear on another user's computer monitor or, while in a chat room, on the screens of multiple users.

Common Gateway Interface (CGI) – CGI scripts are computer programs which are placed on Web servers, and allow webpages to process data entered by the user.

Compact disc (CD) – A disc used to store large amounts of digital information. CD burners are increasingly commonplace in computers and can be used to save files or, more notoriously, to burn audio CDs. The CD-R can only be written to, and then used or played; the CD-RW is more versatile as files can be erased and rewritten.

Compression – Files can be compressed (in various ways) so that they can be downloaded more quickly. For example, 'red dot, red dot, red dot, red dot, red dot', is the standard long-winded way in which a computer would describe a graphic which, when displayed, looks like a red line. But it could just say '5 red dots'. That's compression.

Cookie – A bit of information, such as a reference number, saved on a Web user's hard disk drive by a website, so that the site can 'remember' information about that particular user. These cookies are saved in one cookies file, which is a simple text file which cannot, in itself, do any harm. Cookies only enable websites to recall information which the user has given to them; they do not send information like your name or e-mail address to a website of their own accord.

Cracker – A hacker who causes damage to systems, or uses stolen data for illegal means. Some hackers like this term to be used, to differentiate 'bad' hackers (crackers) from ordinary hackers, who (in this use of two terms) just enjoy trying to access supposedly secure systems, but don't do any harm.

Cybercafé – A café offering internet access. They range, like all cafés, from the very stylish to the very smelly.

Cyberpunk – A subgenre of science fiction inspired largely by William Gibson's (1984) novel *Neuromancer* and characterized by futuristic computer network-based societies. Recently, the term cyberpunk has been (incorrectly) co-opted to refer to any cultural phenomenon involving digital technology and tight black leather.

Cybersex – Sexual activity or arousal which takes place within online environments such as chat rooms, or even e-mail.

Cyberspace – A more mainstream and literary term for the internet, cyberspace refers to the conceptual space where computer networking hardware, network software and users converge. The term was originally coined by William Gibson in his (1984) novel *Neuromancer*.

Cybersquatting – The practice of buying domain names with the intention of selling them on, subsequently, to companies that are willing to pay lots of money to have them. In the mid-1990s, enterprising people would buy up '.com' domain names which just happened to be those of well-known companies, knowing that soon the companies would be willing to spend a lot of money buying rights to their brand's domain. Others just bought names like 'toothpaste.com' knowing that someone would be bound to want to pay lots of money for them soon. Some legal precedents have now made the purchase of domain names which are the same as existing well-known trademarks illegal (in some countries).

Default – The original arrangement of something – the 'factory setting'.

Digital – A description of data which is stored or transmitted as a sequence of discrete symbols from a finite set, most commonly as binary data (zeroes and ones) represented by electronic or electromagnetic signals. The less precise form of data that preceded digital was analogue. CD-ROMs are to digital as vinyl records are to analogue.

Digital camera – Digital cameras take photographs like normal cameras but save them in digital form (as **JPEG** files, for example), thereby allowing fast and easy transfer to the Web.

Digital versatile disc or **digital video disc (DVD)** – A high-density compact disc used for storing large amounts of data, especially high-resolution audio-visual material. Currently, DVDs provide over seven times the storage capacity of CDs and are often used to store and trade pirated versions of films and television shows. Commercial DVD releases of movies contain a host of bonus features, such as interviews and 'making of' films, except for those designed towards the end of the week, when the makers can't be bothered.

Domain – The location of a website, ending in a suffix such as '.com' (for commercial sites), '.org' (non-profit organizations), '.edu' (education), '.gov' (government), '.net' (internet-related), or regionally specific variants such as '.co.uk' (UK company), '.ac.uk' (UK higher education), '.gouv.fr' (French government). A domain may contain several websites at different addresses within it; it is the very broadest description of where a site resides (GeoCities.com, for example, gives a home to millions of sites). A domain name doesn't *necessarily* lead to a website, as they can be bought and then not used, or used only for e-mail. See also **Cybersquatting**.

Domain Name Server (DNS) – A server on the internet which matches domain names to IP addresses, telling computers where to look for requested pages or files.

Downloading – Simply means taking data from the internet into a computer (or other device). To 'download' a file often, but not necessarily, suggests that you have actively *saved* it as well. But of course data is downloaded every time you view a website, and temporarily stored in the **cache**, though you don't necessarily keep it permanently.

Dreamweaver – Popular and effective webpage-making and website-managing software, produced by Macromedia. Takes a **WYSIWYG** approach but is particularly appreciated by website authors because it doesn't mess up your **HTML**. (Other programs are more arrogant and sometimes rewrite the code – often in a way that the user does not appreciate.)

DVD-R – See **digital versatile disc**.

E-commerce – Electronic commerce: money-making business on the internet.

E-mail – Messages sent via the internet from one user to another. As new internet applications come and go, e-mail remains the most simple and most cherished use of the net.

FAQ – See **Frequently Asked Questions**.

File – A collection of information (a graphic, a software program, an e-mail, for example) recognized and treated as a single unit by a computer.

Flame – An abusive e-mail, usually sent to someone who has made an ignorant, offensive or commercial contribution to an e-mail or newsgroup discussion.

Flash – **Vector-based graphics** and animation format developed by Macromedia, popular on the Web because it can deliver attractive websites – with interactive graphics and sound – with small file sizes.

Freeware – Software distributed free of charge, with no restrictions, over the internet (or by other means).

Frequently Asked Questions (FAQ) – Common form of webpage which provides answers to questions frequently sent to the website.

FTP – Short for file-transfer protocol, FTP refers to (1) a method of transferring one or more files from one computer to another on a network or phone line, and (2) an application program which moves files across the internet using the file-transfer protocol.

Gates, Bill (1955–) – Chief Executive of Microsoft from 1975 to January 2000, when he became Chairman and Chief Software Architect. Extremely rich, obviously. Not always popular with internet people, who often feel that Microsoft has tried to turn the universal internet into Microsoft Internet (TM).

GIF – A graphics file common on the Web, which uses a palette with a limited number of colours to keep its file size down.

Google – Excellent search engine (www.google.com). See Chapter 1 for an explanation of how Google works so well.

Gopher – A menu-driven program developed at the University of Minnesota which helps users explore, locate and retrieve information on the internet. Gopher organizes all information via a series of hierarchical menus. Actually, lots and lots of menus. Happily, the World Wide Web has basically replaced it.

Hacking – Gaining access to supposedly secure computer systems without the consent of the system's owners.

Hard copy – The printout, on paper, of data (such as a website).

Hard disk – Often referred to as a hard drive, a hard disk is a magnetic disk mounted permanently in a computer's central processing unit, or CPU. Hard disks are used to store data, primarily permanent operating applications and temporary files.

Hits – Often taken to mean the number of visitors to a webpage or site: people say 'My site received one million hits last month' and assume this means one million people visited the site. But it doesn't. The number of hits is the number of requests for files made to the web server. An average webpage is made up of one **HTML** file and several graphics files (containing logos, pictures, buttons, bars, and so on). So loading one webpage might notch up ten hits, for example. And then the same visitor might look at other pages, easily generating 50 or 100 hits. So 'one million hits' would never mean one million visitors; it would more likely represent, say, 50,000 visitors, although the percentage of actual visitors (compared to number of hits) will vary from site to site. (Note: to confuse matters further, sometimes people say they had '1000 hits' when they actually know that they had 1000 visitors, but they think that 'hits' is a more trendy word for that, which it isn't.)

HTML – Hypertext Markup Language, simple computer language which most webpages are written in, devised by **Tim Berners-Lee**. An HTML webpage is basically a text document with added HTML tags; these tags, in <angular brackets>, tell the browser how to arrange and format the text, where to add graphics, where links are, and so on.

HTTP – Hypertext Transfer Protocol, devised by **Tim Berners-Lee** as a fast, universal protocol for passing files around the internet, particularly suited to the hypertext system on the Web.

Hyperlink – On a webpage, a hyperlink (or simply 'link') is text or a graphic which the user clicks on in order to proceed or move to a related page.

Hypertext – Text which includes links or short-cuts to other documents, allowing the reader to jump easily from one text to related texts, and consequentially from one idea to another, in a multi-linear, non-sequential manner. Originally coined by Ted Nelson in 1965, hypertext serves as the organizational foundation for the World Wide Web.

Instant Messaging – This is conducted via (usually) free software such as Microsoft Messenger, which allows users to chat in real time in a text window. Graphics and other files, such as video, can also be sent using these tools (leading to: **video messaging**).

Internet – A worldwide network of networks which connects computers around the world. First incarnated as the ARPANET in 1969, the internet has transformed from an internal military network, to an academic research net, to the current communication and commercial internet of today. It supports services such as e-mail, the World Wide Web, file transfer and Internet Relay Chat. The internet is commonly referred to as 'the net', 'cyberspace', and 'the information superhighway'. It's also what all the commotion is about.

Internet Explorer – Web browser, produced by Microsoft from 1996, and given away free (and bundled or 'integrated' with Windows) in order to compete with Netscape Navigator. Despite being shunned by those opposed to Microsoft's dominance of the software market, IE had become the most-used browser by 1998.

Internet Service Provider – Company or organization providing access to the internet. When a home internet user goes online, their computer phones their ISP (via a modem), which provides a gateway to the internet.

Intranet – A network used for internal communications within an organization.

ISDN – Short for Integrated Services Digital Network, ISDN is a set of communications standards offered by telephone carriers which provides users with extremely fast internet connections. ISDN allows a single wire or optical fibre to carry voice, digital network services and video, and is believed by many to be the network which will ultimately replace the telephone system.

ISP – See **Internet Service Provider**.

Java – A programming language created by Sun Microsystems, and featured on many websites. As a platform-independent language, Java programs can be run on any computer, either as a free-standing application or as an applet placed on a webpage. While Java has served to increase Web interactivity and expand multimedia, it is scorned by others for increasing download time and fostering a more commercially focused World Wide Web.

JPEG – A compressed graphics file common on the Web, which can contain up to 16 million colours and thus is used for 'photographic' type images.

Kazaa – Popular tool for **peer-to-peer file sharing**. Statistics show that Kazaa can normally provide you with any music track by anybody, quickly and for no money. That's simple; the moral and legal debates are more complicated.

Killer application – Software (or more broadly, an idea) which is so appealing to users that they will change their computer in order to be able to use it, or buy a new one. The World Wide Web was the 'killer app' which made the internet sufficiently desirable that people would go out of their way to get the equipment to access it.

Linux – A platform-independent operating system created by Linus Torvalds and friends starting about 1990. Unlike other operating systems such as Windows 98, Linux can be downloaded and distributed free of charge. For that reason, many consider Linux to be the most worthy threat to Microsoft's computing hegemony. Assembled collaboratively by literally thousands of users, Linux is often referred to as the world's greatest hacker project in history.

Listservs – Often (technically incorrectly) called mailing lists, listservs refer to (1) the software which makes possible automated mailing list distribution systems, and (2) the online communities which arise from such lists. Listservs can be either moderated or unmoderated, and differ from mailing lists by their automated means of subscribing and unsubscribing.

Microsoft – Founded in 1975 by **Bill Gates** and Paul Allen, Microsoft is the world's largest supplier of operating systems and other software for personal computers. Some of its software products include MS-DOS, Microsoft Windows, Windows NT, and, most recently, Microsoft Internet Explorer. Because of its heavy-handedly aggressive marketing tactics, many internet enthusiasts actively hate Microsoft.

Modem – A device which enables a computer to send and receive information over a telephone line.

MOO – A type of **MUD**, MOO is short for Multi-User Domain, Object-Oriented and differs from MUDs by allowing users to interact with programmable objects. In keeping with MUDs, these objects are usually dungeons, dragons and whips.

Mosaic – Popular early Web browser. See **Andreessen**, who co-wrote it.

Mp3 – Popular format of audio files which provide good-quality digital sound but take up (relatively) few kilobytes. Mp3s are therefore popular on the internet, because you can download good-quality music quite quickly.

MUD – Short for Multi-User Domain or Multi-User Dungeon, MUDs are online role-playing environments. MUDs occur in text mode – similar to a chat room – where players assume a spectrum of identities and explore a range of environments, often based on fantasy fiction or sexual situations.

Multimedia Messaging Service (MMS) – A mobile phone service which allows users to send a combination of text, sounds, images and video to other MMS-capable handsets.

Napster – Now defunct tool for **peer-to-peer file sharing**; still mentioned here because the word 'Napster' is still used by some as a general term for such programs and the phenomenon of online music exchange.

Netscape – See **Andreessen**, who founded this company.

Newbie – Someone new to the internet. Newbies are sometimes sneered at by established internet users, such as long-standing members of e-mail discussion lists (listservs) who tend to be annoyed when a 'newbie' joins and starts posting 'ignorant' questions.

New media – Term which embraces all of the 'new' forms of electronic media – newer than TV and radio, that is – such as multimedia CD-ROMs, the internet and video games. Sometimes it is taken to mean 'the Web' although it is really a broader term.

Newsgroups – A public online space where messages are posted for public consumption and response. The most available distribution of newsgroups is USENET, which contains thousands of newsgroups devoted to all kinds of (diverse and perverse) topics. Often referred to as the original public sphere of cyberspace, newsgroups are currently overrun by spam.

Open source software – A way of developing software in which anybody with programming skills can read, redistribute and modify the source code for a piece of software, so that the program evolves, being fixed and improved by enthusiasts around the world (as opposed to the conventional model where only a few programmers working for a particular company create the code). Enthusiasts argue that the open source approach is a surprisingly rapid way to create more reliable software. The popular operating system **Linux** was developed in this way.

Peer-to-peer file sharing – Programs such as **Kazaa** (www.kazaa.com) allow users to exchange files online. Peer-to-peer (P2P) programs are most often used for disseminating copies of music CDs, DVDs, and other video and software files. The files are not stored on a central server but are exchanged directly from one hard drive to another, with the P2P program merely acting as an agent that brings them together.

Plug-in – An extra bit of software which has to be added to a browser before a certain type of file can be viewed. For example, **Flash** animations cannot be seen unless one has the Flash plug-in. Recent browsers come with a number of the most common plug-ins pre-installed.

Portal – A website which aspires to be your primary point of contact with the Web, usually offering a bundle of news, search facilities, free e-mail, chat areas and other gimmicks. Examples include Yahoo!, BBCi, MSN, and many more.

Program – Used as a noun to describe a series of instructions which tell a computer what to do, or as a verb to describe the act of creating or revising a program.

QuickTime – Refers to both a standard and an application used by Apple computers for integrating full-motion video and digitized sound into programs and websites.

Ripping – The act of copying copyright audio or video files, often for exchange in a **peer-to-peer file sharing** program. Ripping a CD, for example, typically involves converting the data on the CD into the more compressed mp3 format, which makes it easier to share over the internet.

Scanner – Machine which scans an image, such as a photograph or newspaper article, and turns it into a file which can be displayed and manipulated on a computer.

Search engine – Search facility based on a database of as much of the Web's content as possible, compiled by electronic 'spiders' or 'robots' which roam around the internet cataloguing content. (Therefore search engines are different to directories, such as Yahoo!, which are more selective and are compiled by humans.) Examples include AltaVista, Google and Excite.

Server – A computer or set of computers that provides client stations with access to files and printers as shared resources to a computer network. The most common servers are Web servers which send out webpages, mail servers which deliver e-mail, list servers which administer mailing lists, and FTP servers which hold FTP sites and deliver files to users who request them.

Shareware – Software which is usually free initially, but may ask you to register the product and pay its creator after a certain trial period, or to make a voluntary payment if you like the software and use it regularly. Shareware is often distributed over the internet.

Site – See **Website**.

Spam – Junk e-mail, sent to several people at once. Any e-mail that is not written for your personal attention can be seen as spam. E-mail advertising or promoting something is spam; chain letters and virus hoaxes are also regarded as spam by most sane people.

Style sheet – See **Cascading Style Sheets**.

Surfing – Popular term for wandering around the Web, like 'channel surfing' television, and therefore a regrettable term since it positions the Web user as rather passive.

Torvalds, Linus (1970–) – Created the first version of **Linux**, a one-time experimental version of the **UNIX** operating system whilst a student at Helsinki University. A hero among netheads and the antithesis to **Bill Gates**, Torvalds worked with thousands of programmers to alter, tweak and perfect Linux and to keep it free of charge.

UNIX – The operating system upon which the internet was developed. UNIX was developed in the late 1960s/early 1970s as a joint venture between General Electric, AT&T Bell Laboratories, and MIT. Later, UNIX grew with support from the University of California, Berkeley, and other universities. There are several free versions of UNIX, including **Linux** and FreeBSD. Among many, knowledge of UNIX is the bar which separates technical netheads from newbies.

URL – Uniform Resource Locator: the address beginning 'http://' (see **Hypertext Transfer Protocol**, which can point to a file on a Web server anywhere in the world. Some people call this URI, for Universal Resource Indicator (suggesting that the same address will always point to the same file in the same place), as preferred by **Tim Berners-Lee**, but most people ignore that.

Vector-based graphics – A graphics or animation system which can deliver complex or large graphics but small file sizes, by describing the shape and position of elements, rather than describing them pixel by pixel (as conventional graphics formats do). Vector-based graphics can be scaled up or down but always retain a smooth appearance, because instead of explaining the layout of square pixels, the format is saying, for example, 'draw a curve from the centre of the shape to the top-left corner'.

Video Messaging – The addition of video clips to **Instant Messaging**.

Virtual – A commonly used adjective which refers to anything happening in 'cyberspace' or, more concretely, on the internet. Online discussions become known as virtual communities; online environments are called virtual realities; and a bunch of dodgy e-mails are described as virtual sex.

Web – The World Wide Web. According to its inventor, **Tim Berners-Lee**, Web should be written with a capital 'W' when used as abbreviation of World Wide Web.

Webcam – A camera which publishes regularly updated pictures to a website. A webcam does not necessarily have to be online all the time, but some have taken the idea to extremes: Jennifer Kaye Ringley (www.jennicam.com), for example, has webcams all over her house, and has been living her life online since 1996.

Webmaster – Grandiose (and arguably sexist) term meaning the person responsible for creating or maintaining a website.

Webpage – One page of the Web. Usually an '.htm' or '.html' file, which then may call for various graphics or multimedia files to complete its appearance on a user's screen. Normally a webpage is part of a **website**.

Website – A group of related webpages, produced by one person, group or organization, which are closely interlinked. For example www.newmediastudies.com is a **website** containing many **webpages** about new media.

Webzine – Written, edited and designed by individuals, collectives or corporations, webzines are zines which exist on the Web. Some are electronic versions of existing print magazines, but the 'true' webzine exists solely in cyberspace.

Wi-Fi – Wireless Fidelity. Wireless technology, like a mobile phone, enabling computers to be connected to a local network, and/or the internet, without cables. Devices need to be in range of a base station. Wi-Fi connections are fast, and Wi-Fi technology is seen to offer bold new horizons in terms of sending and getting data from 'anywhere'. Tied to voice-recognition software, and a transmitting microphone badge, Wi-Fi can also offer the *Star Trek*-style opportunity to shout 'doctor' and get a doctor, or whatever.

***Wired* (magazine)** – Originally established in 1993 by Louis Rossetto to cover impending digital culture, *Wired* has become a mainstream mouthpiece for the new digital economy, with an occasional libertarian nod towards the more social and political ramifications of the Information Age. Glossy, full of ads and overflowing with self-importance, *Wired* represents all the unfulfilled promises of cyberspace.

World Wide Web (WWW) – A global web of interconnected pages which (ideally) can be read by any computer with a Web browser and internet connection. More technically and specifically, the WWW is the global web of interlinked files which can be located using **HTTP**.

WWW – See **World Wide Web**.

WYSIWYG – An abbreviation for What You See Is What You Get, and pronounced 'wizzywig'. In Web terms, WYSIWYG programs allow website designers to design webpages on screen. The software displays what the page will actually look like when viewed in a browser – as opposed to showing a screenful of **HTML** code.

REFERENCES

Adelman, M. 2002: Notes from an internet sex worker. Paper presented at the annual meeting of the National Communications Association, New Orleans.

Agence France Presse English 2002: Vision of internet convergence sinks media companies. *Agence France Presse English*, 30 January.

Allison, R. 1999: Belgrade hackers bombard NATO website. www.infowar.com, 31 March.

APC 2002: Website of the Association for Progressive Communications. www.apc.org

Arterton, F.C. 1987: *Teledemocracy: Can Technology Protect Democracy?* Newbury Park, CA: Sage.

Associated Press 1999: Serb hackers disrupt NATO e-mail. *Las Vegas Sun* website (www.lasvegassun.com), 31 March.

Augé, M. 1998: *A Sense for the Other: The Timeliness and Relevance of Anthropology.* Stanford, CA: Stanford University Publications.

Banks, M. and Morphy, H. (eds) 1997: *Rethinking Visual Anthropology.* London: Yale University Press.

Barber, L. 2001: Harry, the saucy boy sorceror. *The Australian*. 3 Sept. (accessed online 3 Oct. 2002).

Barbrook, R. 1998: The hi-tech gift economy: organizing collective labour in cyberspace, Hypermedia Research Centre, Westminster University, http://first-monday.dk/issues/issue3_12/barbrook/index.html.

Barlow, J.P. 1994: The economy of ideas: everything you know about intellectual property is wrong. www.wired.com/wired/archive/2.03/economy.ideas.html.

Bass, D. 1998: Portal? What's a portal? The latest, hottest internet stocks. *Fortune*, 26 October, 143–4.

Baudrillard, J. 1994: *Simulacra and Simulation.* Trans. by Glaser, S.F. Ann Arbor, MI: University of Michigan Press.

Baym, N. 2000: *Tune In, Log On: Soaps, Fandom, and Online Community*. Thousand Oaks, CA: Sage.

Baym, N.K. 1995: The emergence of community in computer-mediated communication. In Jones, S.G. (ed.), *CyberSociety: Computer-Mediated Communication and Community*. Thousand Oaks, CA: Sage Publications, 138–63.

Beck, U. and Beck-Gernsheim, E. 2001: *Individualization: Institutionalized Individualism and its Social and Political Consequences*. London: Sage.

Beck, U., Giddens, A. and Lash, S. 1994: *Reflexive Modernization: Politics, Traditions and Aesthetics in the Modern Social Order*. Cambridge: Polity Press.

Becker, H. 1998: Visual sociology, documentary photography, and photojournalism: it's (almost) all a matter of context. In Prosser, J. (ed.), *Image-based Research: A Sourcebook for Qualitative Researchers*. London: Falmer, 84–96.

Benjamin, W. 1968: *Illuminations: Walter Benjamin, Essays and Reflections*. New York: Schocken.

Berkhofer, R. 1978: *The White Man's Indian: Images of the American Indian from Columbus to the Present*. New York: Vintage-Random House.

Berners-Lee, T. 1997: Realising the full potential of the Web. www.w3.org/1998/02/Potential.html.

Berners-Lee, T. 1999: *Weaving the Web: The Past, Present and Future of the World Wide Web by its Inventor*. London: Orion.

Berry, C. and Martin, F. 2000: Queer 'n' Asian on – and off – the net: the role of cyberspace in queer Taiwan and Korea. In Gauntlett, D. (ed.), *Web.Studies: Rewiring Media Studies for the Digital Age*. New York: Oxford University Press, 74–81.

Blumer, H. 1969: *Symbolic Interactionism: Perspective and Method*. Englewood Cliffs, NJ: Prentice-Hall

Blumer, J.G. and Gurevitch, M. 2001: The new media and our political communication discontents: democratizing cyberspace. *Information, Communication and Society* 4(1), 1–13.

Bogdan, R. 1990: *Freak Show: Presenting Human Oddities for Amusement and Profit*. Chicago: University of Chicago.

Bolter, J.D. and Grusin, R. 2000: *Remediation: Understanding New Media*. Cambridge, MA: MIT Press.

Boorman, J. and Donahue, W. (eds) 1997: *Projections* 7. London: Faber & Faber.

Bowers, C.A., Vasquez, M. and Roaf, M. 2000: Native people and the challenge of computers: reservation schools, individualism, and consumerism. *American Indian Quarterly* 24 (2), 182–99.

Braidotti, R. 1994: *Nomadic Subjects*. New York: Columbia University Press.

Braidotti, R. 1996: Cyberfeminism with a difference. http://www.let.uu.nl/womens-studies/rosi/cyberfem.htm.

Brants, K., Huizenga, M. and Van Meerten, R. 1996: The new canals of Amsterdam: an exercise in local electronic democracy. *Media Culture and Society* 18, 233–47.

Bright, S. 1992: *Susie Bright's Sexual Reality: A Virtual Sex World Reader*. Pittsburgh: Cleis Press.

Bright, S. 1997: *Susie Bright's Sexual State of the Union*. New York: Simon & Schuster.

Brindley, P. 2000: *New Musical Entrepreneurs*. London: IPPR.

Brown, G. 1996: In the real world. *Guardian* 2 August, 13.

Bruckman, A. 1992: Identity workshop: emergent social and psychological phenomena in text-based virtual reality. ftp://ftp.cc.gatech.edu/pub/people/asb/papers/identity_workshop.rtf (accessed 23 September 2002).

Bruni, F. 1999: Two duelling views of reality vying on the airwaves. Reproduced from *The New York Times* on the Reagan Information Exchange (www.reagan.com), 19 April.

Budge, I. 1996: *The New Challenge of Direct Democracy*. Cambridge: Polity Press.

Burk, D.L. 2000: Patenting speech. *Texas Literary Review* 99. www.isc.umn.edu/research/papers/Patent2.pdf.

Burnett, R. 1996: *The Global Jukebox: The International Music Industry*. London: Routledge.

Burnett, R. and Marshall, D.P. 2003: *Web Theory: An Introduction*. London: Routledge.

Burrows, R. *et al.* 2000: Virtual community care? Social policy and the emergence of computer mediated social support. *Information, Communication & Society* 3 (1), 95–121.

Bury, M. 1991: The sociology of chronic illness: a review of research and prospects. *Sociology of Health and Illness* 13, 451–68.

Buten, J. 1996: Personal home page survey. www.asc.upenn.edu/USR/sbuten/phpi.htm

Butler, J. 1990: *Gender Trouble: Feminism and the Subversion of Identity*. London: Routledge.

Califia, P. 1994: *Public Sex: The Culture of Radical Sex*. Pittsburgh: Cleis Press.

Cassidy, S. 1999: Civics to be put on timetable. *Times Educational Supplement*, 26 February, 2.

Castells, M. 2001: *The Internet Galaxy: Reflections on the Internet, Business and Society*. New York: Oxford University Press.

Chandler, D. 1997: Writing oneself in cyberspace. www.aber.ac.uk/~dgc/homepgid.html.

Chandler, D. 1998: Personal home pages and the construction of identities on the Web. www.aber.ac.uk/media/Documents/short/webident.html

Chandler, D. and Roberts-Young, D. 1998: The construction of identity in the personal homepages of adolescents. www.aber.ac.uk/~dgc/strasbourg.html.

Cheung, C. 2000: A home on the Web: presentations of self on personal homepages. In Gauntlett, D. (ed.), *Web.Studies: Rewiring Media Studies for the Digital Age*. London: Arnold.

Children's Partnership, the 2000: Online content for low-income and under-served Americans. www.childrenspartnership.org.

Chon, M. 2000: Erasing race?: A critical race feminist view of internet identity-shifting. *Journal of Gender, Race, and Justice* 3, 439–71.

Chuck D 12/2000: Across the water under the underground ... here come the 'inties', Public Enemy Terrordome, www.publicenemy.com/terrordome.php?item=23.

CNN Interactive 1999: NATO leaflets warn Serb troops of 'certain death'. www.cnn.com, 26 April.

Cohen, E. 1997: For Native Americans, the net offers both promise and threat. *The New York Times on the Web*. www.nytimes.com/library/cyber/week/041697natives.html.

Coleman, S. 1999: Can the new media invigorate democracy? *Political Quarterly* 70, 16–22.

Communications Today 1998: Demand grows for bundled service, 21 August.

Connell, R.W. 1995: *Masculinities*. Cambridge: Polity Press.

Cooley, C.H. 1902: *Human Nature and Social Order*. New York: Scribner's.

Cooper, A. 1998: Sexually compulsive behavior. *Contemporary Sexuality* 32 (4), 1–3.

Correll, S. 1995: The ethnography of an electronic bar: the lesbian café. *Journal of Contemporary Ethnography* 24 (3), 270–98.

Cortese, A., Carey, J. and Woodruff, D. 1996: Alt.sex.bondage is closed. Should we be scared? The net is fast becoming a global free-speech battleground. *Business Week* 3458 (39), 1.

Craig, S. 1992: Considering men and the media. In Craig, S. (ed.), *Men, Masculinity and the Media*. London: Sage.

Curtice, J. and Jowell, R. 1995: The sceptical electorate. In Jowell, R., Curtice, J., Park, A., Brook, L., Ahrendt, D. and Thomson, K. (eds), *British Social Attitudes: The 12th Report*. Aldershot: Dartmouth Publishing.

Dahlberg, L. 2001: The internet and democratic discourse: exploring the prospect of online deliberative forums extending the public sphere. *Information, Communication and Society* 4 (4), 615–33.

Darley, A. 2000: *Visual Digital Culture: Surface Play and Spectacle in New Media Genres*. London: Routledge.

Dawson, M. and Bellamy Foster, J. 1998: Virtual capitalism: monopoly capital, marketing, and the information highway. In McChesney, R., Wood, E. and Bellamy Foster, J. (eds), *Capitalism and the Information Age*. New York: Monthly Review Press, 51–67.

DCMS 2002: *Screen Digest Report on the Implications of Digital Technology for the Film Industry*. Screen Digest.

De Certeau, M. 1984: *The Practice of Everyday Life*. Berkeley, CA: University of California Press.

Delap, C. 1998: *Making Better Decisions: Report of an IPPR Symposium on Citizens' Juries and Other Methods of Public Involvement*. London: Institute for Public Policy Research.

Della Porta, D. and Diani, M. 1999: *Social Movements: An Introduction* Oxford: Blackwell.

D'Emilio, J. and Freedman, E.B. 1997: *Intimate Matters: A History of Sexuality in America*. Chicago: University of Chicago Press.

Denning, D. and Denning, P. (eds) 1998: *Internet Besieged: Countering Cyberspace Scofflaws*, New York: ACM Press.

Denzin, N. 1997: *Interpretive Ethnography: Ethnographic Practices for the 21st Century*. London, Sage.

Denzin, N. and Lincoln, E. (eds) 1994: *Handbook of Qualitative Research*. London: Sage.

Digiovanna, J. 1995: Losing your voice on the internet. In Ludlow, P. (ed.), 1996: *High Noon on the Electronic Frontier: Conceptual Issues in Cyberspace*. Cambridge, MA: MIT Press.

Dobson, S. 1999: A riot from cyberspace, *Guardian* 24 June.

Doheny-Farina, S. 1996: *The Wired Neighborhood*. New Haven, CT: Yale University Press.

Dominick, J.R. 1999: Who do you think you are? Personal home pages and self-presentation on the World Wide Web. *Journalism and Mass Communication Quarterly* 76, 646–58.

Donath, J. and Robertson, N. 1994: The sociable web. *Proceedings of the 2nd International World Wide Web Conference*, Chicago. http://judith.www.media.mit.edu/SocialWeb/SociableWeb.html.

Döring, N. 2002: Personal home pages on the web: a review of research. *Journal of Computer Mediated Communication* 7. www.ascusc.org/jcmc/vol7/issue3/doering.html.

DotForce, 2000: *Global Bridges: Digital Opportunities* (draft report). www.dotforce.org/reports.dotforce-draft-report-v1.doc.

Downing, J.D.H. 1989: Computers for political change: PeaceNet and public data access. *Journal of Communication* 39, 154–62.

Drimmer, F. 1973: *Very Special People: The Struggles, Loves, and Triumphs of Human Oddities*. New York: Amjon.

Dworkin, A. 1979: *Pornography: Men Possessing Women*. New York: Perigee Books.

Dyer, R. 1986: *Heavenly Bodies: Film Stars and Society*. New York: St Martin's Press.

Ebo, B. 1998: Internet or outernet? In Ebo, B. (ed.), *Cyberghetto or Cybertopia?: Race, Class, and Gender on the Internet*. Westport, CT: Praeger, 1–12.

Economist, the 1999: Britain: secret society: the government's freedom of information bill makes a mockery of the idea of more open government, 29 May, 32.

Elshtain, J. 1982: Democracy and the QUBE tube. *The Nation*, 7–14 August, 108–10.

European Commission 1997: *Green Paper on the Convergence of the Telecommunications, Media and Information Technology Sectors*, COM 97, 623. Brussels: European Commission.

European Commission 2002: *Flash Eurobarometer 125: Internet and the Public at Large*. Brussels: DG Press and Communication.

Europemedia 2002: 40m Americans use file-swapping sites. *Europemedia*, 13 June.

Fair, R.S. 2000: Becoming the white man's Indian: an examination of Native American tribal web sites. *Plains Anthropologist* 45 (172), 203–13.

Fielding, N.G. and Lee, R.M. 1998: *Computer Analysis and Qualitative Research*. London: Sage.

Filippo, J. 2000: Pornography on the Web. In Gauntlett, D. (ed.), *Web.Studies: Rewiring Media Studies for the Digital Age*. New York: Oxford University Press, 122–9.

Fink R., Garofalo R., Gebhardt, B. and Partovi, C. 2000: Music as object? A Napster roundtable, *Echo*, Vol. 2, Issue 2, Fall, www.humnet.ucla.edu/echo/Volume2-Issue2/napster/Napsterframe.html.

Fisher, W.A. and Barak, A. 2001: Internet pornography: a social psychological perspective on internet sexuality. *The Journal of Sex Research* 38 (4), 312–24.

Fiske, J. 1992: The cultural economy of fandom. In Lewis, L. (ed), *The Adoring Audience: Fan Culture and Popular Media*. London and New York: Routledge, 30–49.

Floyd, N. 2002: Living Dead visit the digital age. *Metro*, 9 October.

40HEX 1991: Interview with Skism One, A.K.A. Lord SSS (triple S), *40Hex* (unnumbered), Volume 1, Issue 2, File 004.

40HEX 1992a: The Constitution of Worldwide Virus Writers, *40Hex*, Number 5, Volume 2, Issue 1, File 005.

40HEX 1992b: Response to a Letter from Paul Melka, *40Hex*, Number 8, Volume 2, Issue 4, File 010.

40HEX 1995: Welcome to 40Hex Issue 12, *40Hex*, Number 12, Volume 3, Issue 3, File 000.

Foster, D. 1997: Community and identity in the electronic village. In Porter, D. (ed.), *Internet Culture*. New York: Routledge, 23–37.

Foucault, M. 1980: *The History of Sexuality*, Vol. I. London: Routledge.

Frankenberg, R. 1992: *Time, Health and Medicine*. London: Sage.

Fraser, N. 1993: Rethinking the public sphere: a contribution to the critique of actually existing democracy. In During, S. (ed.), *The Cultural Studies Reader* (2nd edn). London: Routledge.

Freeman-Longo, R.E. and Blanchard, G.T. 1998: *Sexual Abuse in America: Epidemic of the 21st Century*. Brandon, VT: Safer Society Press.

Freeman-Longo, R.I. 2000: Children, teens and sex on the internet. In Cooper, A. (ed.), *Cybersex: The Darkside of the Force*. Philadelphia, PA: Brunner Routledge, 75–90.

Frith, S. (ed.) 1993: *Music and Copyright*. Edinburgh: Edinburgh University Press.

Gaiser, T. 1998: *Pushing Methodological Boundaries: On-line Focus Groups (an Interview with Ted J. Gaiser)*. www.bc.edu/bc_org/avp/wfnetwork/newsletter/winter99/boundary.html.

Gandy, O. 2002: The real Digital Divide. In L. Lievrouw and S. Livingstone (eds), *The Handbook of New Media*. London: Sage.

Garland Thomson, R. 1996: *Freakery: Cultural Spectacles of the Extraordinary Body*. New York: New York University.

Garland Thomson, R. 1997: *Extraordinary Bodies: Figuring Physical Disability in American Culture and Literature*. New York: Columbia University.

Garofalo, R. 1999: From music publishing to mp3: music and industry in the twentieth century. *American Music*, Autumn, 318–53.

Garrison, E.K. 2000: US feminism-grrrl style! Youth (sub)cultures and the technologics of the third wave. *Feminist Studies* 26 (1), 141–70.

Gates, B. 1996: *The Road Ahead*. New York: Penguin.

Gauntlett, D. (ed.) 2000: *Web.Studies: Rewiring Media Studies for the Digital Age*, London: Arnold.

Gauntlett, D. 2002: *Media, Gender and Identity: An Introduction*. London: Routledge.

Gauntlett, D. 2003: Preface. In Gottlieb, N. and McLelland, M. (eds), *Japanese Cybercultures*. London: Routledge.

Gauntlett, D. and Hill, A. 1999: *TV Living: Television, Culture and Everyday Life*. London: Routledge.

Gay, P. 1998: *The Pleasure Wars: The Bourgeois Experience from Victoria to Freud*. New York: Norton.

Gibson, R. and Ward, S. 1999: Party democracy on-line: UK parties and ICTs. *Information, Communication and Society* 2 (3), 340–67.

GICT 2002: Mission and strategies. http://info.worldbank.org/ict/gictMS.cfm.

Giddens, A. 1991: *Modernity and Self-Identity: Self and Society in the Late Modern Age*. Cambridge: Polity Press.

Gilbert, L. and Kile, C. 1996: *Surfergrrrls: Look Ethel! An Internet Guide for Us!* Seattle: Seal Press.

Global Reporting Network Publications 1999: Off the air: are NATO air strikes against Yugoslav media outlets justified? www.nyu.edu/globalbeat, 4 May.

Goffman, E. 1959 [1990]: *The Presentation of Self in Everyday Life*. London: Penguin. (Page numbers refer to 1990 edition.)

Goguen, J. 1999: *The Ethics of Databases*. Notes from an invited presentation at the 1999 Annual Meeting of the Society for Social Studies of Science, San Diego. www.cse.ucsd.edu/users/goguen/papers/4s/4s.html.

Goldhaber, M.H. 1997: The attention economy and the Net. www.firstmonday.dk/issues/issue2_4/goldhaber.

Greenfield, D.N. 1999: Psychological characteristics of compulsive internet use: a preliminary analysis. *CyberPsychology and Behavior* 8 (2), 403–12.

Griffiths, M.D. 1995: Technological addictions. *Clinical Psychology Forum* 76, 14–19.

Griffiths, M.D. 1996: Behavioural addicitons: an issue for everybody? *Journal of Workplace Learning* 8 (3), 19–25.

Griffiths, M.D. 2000: Excessive internet use: implications for sexual behavior.

CyberPsychology and Behavior 3, 537–52.

Griffiths, M.D. 2001: Sex on the internet: observations and implications for internet sex addiction. *Journal of Sex Research* 38 (4), 333–43.

Grossberg, L. 1992: Is there a fan in the house? The affective sensibility of fandom. In Lewis, L. (ed), *The Adoring Audience: Fan Culture and Popular Media*. London and New York: Routledge, 50–65.

Guardian, 1999: Blue Money. 27 May, 5.

Gurak, L.J. 1997: *Persuasion and Privacy in Cyberspace: The Online Protests Over Lotus Marketplace and the Clipper Chip*. New Haven, CT: Yale University Press.

Gurak, L.J. 2000: *Cyberliteracy: Navigating the Internet with Awareness*. New Haven, CT: Yale University Press.

Gurley, J.W. 1998: Getting in the way on the net. *Fortune*, 6 July, 188–91.

Haas, G. 2001: New tools, new politics? A rhetorical analysis of the Minnesota Fourth Congressional District Campaign websites. MA thesis, University of Minnesota.

Habermas, J. 1989: *The Structural Transformation of the Public Sphere*. Cambridge: Polity Press.

Hamman, R.B. 1996: Cyborgasms: an ethnography of cybersex in AOL chat rooms. *Cybersociology*, 20 September (available online at www.socio.demon.co.uk/Cyborgasms.html).

Harcourt, W. 1999: *Women@internet: Creating New Cultures in Cyberspace*. London: Zed Books.

Harcourt, W. 2002. Body politics: revisiting the population question. In Saunders, K. (ed.) *Feminist Post-Development Thought*. London: Zed Books.

Hardey, M. 2002: 'The story of my illness': personal accounts of illness on the internet. *Health: An Interdisciplinary Journal for the Social Study of Health, Illness and Medicine* 6, 31–46.

Harding, T. 2001: *The Video Activist Handbook* (2nd edn). London: Pluto Press.

Harper, D. 1994: On the authority of the image: visual methods at the cross-roads. In Denzin, N. and Lincoln, E. (eds), *Handbook of Qualitative Research*. London: Sage, 403–12.

Harrison, A. 2001: Where are they now? Online identities on the commercial Web. Unpublished MA thesis. Georgetown University.

Harvard Law Review 1999: The law of cyberspace, 112 (7), 1574–704.

Heath, D., Koch, E., Ley, B. and Montoya, M. 1999: Nodes and queries: linking locations in networked fields of inquiry. *American Behavioral Scientist* 43 (3), 450–63.

Hebdige, D. 1979: *Subculture: The Meaning of Style*. New York: Routledge.

Herman, E. and McChesney, R. 1997: *The Global Media: The New Missionaries of Corporate Capitalism*. London and Washington: Cassel.

Herman, G. and Holly, J. 2001: Trade unions and the internet. In Lax, S. (ed.), *Access Denied in the Information Age*. Basingstoke: Palgrave.

Herring, S. 1993: Gender and democracy in computer-mediated communication. *Electronic Journal of Communication* 3.2. http://hanbat.chungnam.ac.kr/~leejh/txt/Herring.txt.

Hess, M. 2002: A nomad faculty: English professors negotiate self-presentation in unversity Web space. *Computers and Composition* 19, 171–89.

Hevern, V.W. 2000: Alterity and self-presentation via the Web: dialogical and narrative aspects of identity construction. Paper presented at the First International Conference on the Dialogical Self, Katholieke Universiteit Nijmegen, The Netherlands.

Hiltz, S.R. and Turoff, M. 1993: *The Network Nation: Human Communication Via Computer* (2nd edn). Cambridge, MA: MIT Press.

Hiltzik, M., 2002: For companies, synergy leads to turmoil. *Los Angeles Times*, 7 August, A49.

Hine, C. 2001: Web pages, authors and audiences: the meaning of a mouse-click. *Information, Communication and Society* 4 (2), 182–98.

Hirschkop, K. 1998: Democracy and the new technologies. In McChesney, R.W., Meiksins Wood, E. and Foster, J. B. (eds), *Capitalism and the Information Age*. New York: Monthly Review Press.

Holtzman, S. 1997: *Digital Mosaics: The Aesthetics of Cyberspace*. New York: Simon & Schuster.

hooks, b. 1989: *Talking Back: Thinking Feminist, Thinking Black*. Boston, MA: South End Press.

Horrocks, R. 1995: *Male Myths and Icons: Masculinity in Popular Culture*. Basingstoke: Macmillan.

Hossfeld, K.J. 1994: Hiring immigrant women: Silicon Valley's 'simple formula'. In Baca Zinn, M. and Thornton Dill, B. (eds), *Women of Color in US Society*. Philadelphia, PA: Temple University Press, 65–93.

Howe, C. 1999: Cyberspace is no place for tribalism. *Wicazo-Sa Review* 13 (2), archived at www.ualberta.ca/~pimohte/howe.html.

Hudson, R. 2002: When Hamlet met the A-team. *The Sunday Times* (London), 4 August (accessed online 5 October 2002).

J18 1999: June 18 1999. Media reports. http://bak.spc.org/j18/site/net.html (accessed 11 October 2002).

Jackson, P., Stevenson, N. and Brooks, K. 2001: *Making Sense of Men's Magazines*. Cambridge: Polity Press.

Jankowski, N. and Van Selm, M. 2000: The promise and practice of public debate in cyberspace. In Hacker, K. and van Dijk, J. (eds), *Digital Democracy: Issues of Theory and Practice*. London: Sage.

Jeffreys, S. 1990: *Anticlimax: A Feminist Perspective on the Sexual Revolution*. London: Women's Press.

Jenkins, H. 1992: *Textual Poachers: Television Fans and Participatory Culture*. London and New York: Routledge.

Johnson, T. 1995: The dealer's edge: gaming in the path of Native America. *Native Americas* 12, 16–24.

Joinson, A. 1998: Causes and implications of disinhibited behavior on the internet. In Gackenback, J. (ed.), *Psychology and the Internet*. New York: Academic Press, 43–60.

Jones, S.G. (ed.) 1995: *CyberSociety: Computer-Mediated Communication and Community*. Thousand Oaks, CA: Sage Publications.

Jones, S.G. (ed.). 1999: *Doing Internet Research: Critical Issues and Methods for Examining the Net*. Thousand Oaks, CA: Sage.

Jones, S.G. (ed.) 1999: Studying the net: intricacies and issues. In Jones, S.G. (ed.), *Doing Internet Research*. Thousand Oaks, CA: Sage Publications, 1–27.

Jordan, G. 1998: Politics without parties: a growing trend? *Parliamentary Affairs* 51, 314–28.

Jovanovic, T. 1999: America wages propaganda war concerning Kosovo conflict. UCLA website (www.dailybruin.ucla.edu), 12 April.

Katz, F. 2001: AOL finds a feast in Time Warner merger, but Yahoo is starving for good news. *The Atlanta Constitution*, 12 March, A1.

Katz, J., Rice, R. and Aspden, P. 2001: The internet, 1995–2000: access, civic involvement and social interaction. *American Behavioral Scientist* 45 (3): 405–19.

Kaufer, D.S. and Carley, K. 1993: Some concepts and axioms about communication: proximate and at a distance. *Written Communication* 11 (1), 8–42.

Keane, J. 2000: Structural transformations of the public sphere. In Hacker, K. and van Dijk, J. (eds), *Digital Democracy: Issues of Theory and Practice*. London: Sage.

Kearney, M.C. 1998: 'Don't need you': rethinking identity politics and separatism from a grrrl perspective. In Epstein, J.S. (ed.), *Youth Culture: Identity in a Postmodern World*. Oxford: Blackwell.

Keck, M.E. and Sikkink, K. 1998: *Activists Beyond Borders: Advocacy Networks in International Politics*. Ithaca, NY: Cornell University Press.

Kendall, L. 2002: *Hanging Out in the Virtual Pub: Masculinities and Relationships Online*. Berkeley, CA: University of California Press.

Kiesler, S., Siegel, J. and McGuire, T.W. 1984: Social psychological aspects of computer-mediated communication. *American Psychologist* 39 (10), 1123–34.

Killoran, J.B. 1998: Under construction: revision strategies on the web. Paper presented at the conference of College Composition and Communication, Chicago.

Killoran, J.B. 2002: Under constriction: colonization and synthetic institutionalization of Web space. *Computers and Composition* 19, 19–37.

King, S.A. and Moreggi, D. 1998: Internet therapy and self-help groups – the pros and cons. In Gackenbach, J. (ed.), *Psychology and the Internet: Intrapersonal, Interpersonal, and Transpersonal Implications*. San Diego: Academic Press, 77–109.

Kipnis, L. 1996: *Bound and Gagged: Pornography and the Politics of Fantasy in America*. New York: Grove Press.

Kling, R. 1999: Can the 'net-generation internet' effectively support 'ordinary citizens'?, *The Information Society*, 15: 57–63.

Kotamraju, N.P. 1999: The birth of web site design skills: making the present history. *American Behavioral Scientist* 43 (3), 464–74.

KPMG 1996: *Public Policy Issues Arising From Telecommunications and Audiovisual Services – Main Report*. Brussels: European Commission.

Kraut, R.E., Patterson, M., Lundmark, V., Kiesler, S., Mukhopadhyay, T. and Scherlis, W. 1998: Internet paradox: a social technology that reduces social involvement and psychological well-being? *American Psychologist* 53 (9), 1017–32.

Kurzweil, R. 1999: *The Age of Spiritual Machines: When Computers Exceed Human Intelligence*. New York: Viking.

Lane, F.S. 2000: *Obscene Profits: The Entrepreneurs of Pornography in the Cyber Age*. New York: Routledge.

Lanham, R. 1993: *The Electronic Word: Democracy, Technology, and the Arts*. Chicago: University of Chicago Press.

Lather, P. 1993: Fertile obsession: validity after post-structuralism. *Sociological Quarterly* 34, 673–93.

Lea, M., O'Shea, T., Fung, P. and Spears, R. 1992: Flaming in CMC – observations, explanations and implications. In Lea, M. (ed.), *Contexts of Computer-Mediated Communication*. London: Wheatsheaf/Harvester, 89–112.

Lessig, L. 1999: *Code and Other Laws of Cyberspace*. New York: Basic Books.

Levine, J. 2002: *Harmful to Minors: The Perils of Protecting Children from Sex*. Minneapolis: University of Minnesota Press.

Levinson, P. 1997: *The Soft Edge: A Natural History and Future of the Information Revolution*. New York: Routledge.

Levinson, P. 2001: *Digital McLuhan: A Guide to the Information Millennium*. London: Routledge.

Levy, S. 1983: *Hackers: Heroes of the Computer Revolution*, New York: Dell.

Levy, S. 2002: Living in the blog-osphere, *Newsweek*, 26 August, 42–5.

Litman, J. 2001: *Digital Copyright*. New York: Prometheus.

Lovejoy, M. 1989: *Postmodern Currents: Art and Artists in the Age of Electronic Media*. Ann Arbor, MI: University of Michigan Press.

Lowry, T. 2002: Dashed digital dreams. *Business Week*, 15 July, 42.

MacKinnon, C. 1993: Turning rape into pornography. *Ms*, July–August, 24–30.

MacKinnon, R.C. 1997: Punishing the persona: correctional strategies for the virtual offender. In Jones, S.G. (ed.), *Virtual Culture: Identity and Communication in Cybersociety*. Thousand Oaks, CA: Sage Press, 206–35.

MacKintosh, H. 2003: Talk time: William Gibson, *Guardian*, 1 May (www.guardian.co.uk).

Madara, E.J. 2000: From church basements to world wide websites: the growth of self-help support groups. *International Journal of Self-Help and Self-Care* 1 (1), 37–48.

Mander, J. 1991: *In the Absence of the Sacred: The Failure of Technology and the Survival of the Indian Nations*. San Francisco: Sierra Club Books.

Mannix, D.P. 2000: *Freaks: We Who Are Not as Others*. San Francisco: RE/Search Publications.

Marcus, G. 1995: Ethnography in/of the world system: the emergence of multi-sited ethnography. *Annual Review of Anthropology* 24, 95–117.

Margetts, H. 2000: Political participation and protest. In Dunleavy, P., Gamble, A., Holliday, I. and Peele, G. (eds), *Developments in British Politics 6*. Basingstoke: Macmillan.

Markham, A. 1999: *Life Online: Researching Real Experience in Virtual Space*. Walnut Creek, CA: Altamira Press.

Marshall, L. 2001: Losing one's mind: bootlegging and the sociology of copyright, PhD thesis, Warwick: University of Warwick.

Martin, N. 2000: Web site for men too proud to visit doctor. *Daily Telegraph*, 10 November (archived at www.telegraph.co.uk/news/main.jhtml?xml= /news/2000/11/10/nmach10.xml).

Mayne, J. 1993: *Cinema and Spectatorship*. New York: Routledge.

McChesney, R., Wood, E. and Bellamy Foster, J. (eds) 1998: *Capitalism and the Information Age: The Political Economy of the Global Communication Revolution*. New York: Monthly Review Press.

McDonough, J.P. 1999: Designer selves: construction of technologically mediated identity within graphical, multiuser virtual environments. *Journal of the American Society of Information Science* 50 (10), 855–70.

McGuire, J.F. 1999: When speech is heard around the world: Internet content regulation in the United States and Germany. *New York University Law Review* 74 (3), 750–92.

McKenna, K.Y.A. and Bargh, J.A. 1999: Causes and consequences of social interaction on the internet: a conceptual fsramework. *Media Psychology* 1 (3), 249–69.

McKenna, K.Y.A., Green, A.S. and Smith, P.K. 2001: Demarginalizing the sexual self. *The Journal of Sex Research* 38 (4), 302–12.

McLaughlin, M., Goldberg, S.B., Ellison, N. and Lucas, J. 1999: Measuring internet audiences: patrons of an on-line art museum. In Jones, S. (ed.), *Doing Internet Research: Critical Issues and Methods for Examining the Net*. Thousand Oaks, CA: Sage, 163–78.

McLaughlin, T. 1996: *Street Smarts and Critical Theory: Listening to the Vernacular*. London: University of Wisconsin Press.

McLaverty, P. 1998: The public sphere and local democracy. *Democratization* 5, 224–39.

McLellan, F. 1997: A whole other story: the electronic narrative of illness. *Literature and Medicine* 10 (1), 88–107.

McNair, B. 1996: *Mediated Sex: Pornography and Postmodern Culture*. New York: St Martin's Press.

McQuail, D. and Suine, K. (eds) 1997: *Media Policy: Convergence, Concentration, and Commerce*, London: Sage, 94–106.

McRae, S. 1996: Coming apart at the seams: sex, text and the virtual body. In Cherny, L. and Weise, E.R. (eds), *Wired Women*. Seattle: Seal Press, 242–63.

Melody, W. 1996: Towards a framework for designing information society policies. *Telecommunications Policy* 20 (4), 243–59.

Mendenhal, P. 1998: Kosovo: the wired war. *ZDNET* (www.zdnet.com), 7 August 1998.

Miller, D. and Slater, D. 2000: *The Internet: An Ethnographic Approach*. Oxford: Berg.

Miller, H. and Arnold, J. 2001: Breaking away from grounded identity? Women academics on the Web, *CyberPsychology and Behavior* 4, 95–108.

Miller, V. 2000: Search engines, portals and global capitalism. In Gauntlett, D. (ed.), *Web.Studies: Rewiring Media Studies for the Digital Age*. London: Arnold, 113–21.

Mills, K. 2002: Cybernations: identity, self-determination, democracy and the 'internet effect' in the emerging information order. *Global Society* 16 (1), 69–87.

Mirapaul, M. 2001a: Making an opera from cyberspace's Tower of Babble. *New York Times* 10 December, E2.

Mirapaul, M. 2001b: Your life is in your computer for everyone to see. *New York Times* 16 April, E2.

Mitchell, D.T. and Snyder, S.L. (eds) 1997: *The Body and Physical Difference: Discourses on Disability*. Ann Arbor, MI: University of Michigan Press.

Mitra, A. and Cohen, E. 1999: Analyzing the Web: Directions and Challenges. In Jones, S. (ed.), *Doing Internet Research: Critical Issues and Methods for Examining the Net*. Thousand Oaks, California: Sage.

Modernising Government 1999: *Modernising Government*, White Paper Cm 4310. London: The Stationery Office. http://www.archive.official-documents. co.uk/document/cm43/4310/4310.htm.

Moore, F. 2002: Telling it like it is: news websites and online newspapers. *Global Networks* 2 (2), 171–7.

Morbey, M.L. 2000: Academic computing and beyond: new opportunities for women, minority populations, and the new media arts. *Convergence: The Journal of Research into New Media Technologies* 6, 54–77.

Morley, D. 1980: *The 'Nationwide' Audience*. London: British Film Institute.

Mort, F. 1988: Boy's own? Masculinity, style and popular culture. In Chapman, R. and Rutherford, J. (eds), *Male Order: Unwrapping Masculinity*. London: Lawrence & Wishart.

Mosse, G.L. 1996: *The Image of Man: The Creation of Modern Masculinity*. New York: Oxford University Press.

Mulgan, G. 1997: *Connexity: How to Live in a Connected World*. London: Chatto & Windus.

Mulvey, L. 1988a: Afterthoughts on 'Visual pleasure and narrative cinema' inspired by *Duel in the Sun*. In Penley, C. (ed.), *Feminism and Film Theory*. New York: Routledge, 69–79.

Mulvey, L. 1988b: Visual pleasure and narrative cinema. In Penley, C. (ed.), *Feminism and Film Theory*. New York: Routledge, 57–68.

Murray, J. 1997: *Hamlet on the Holodeck: The Future of Narrative in Cyberspace*. New York: Free Press.

National Research Council Committee on Intellectual Property Rights and the Emerging Information Infrastructure, 2000: *The Digital Dilemma: Intellectual Property in the Information Age*. www.nap.edu/html/digital_dilemma/ch1.html.

National Telecommunications and Information 1999: Native Americans lacking information resources (fact sheet). www.ntia.doc.gov/ntiahome/digitaldivide.

Naughton, J. 2003: If you really want to know, ask a blogger, *Observer*, 1 June (www.guardian.co.uk).

Negroponte, N. 1995: *Being Digital*. London: Hodder & Stoughton.

New York Times on the Web 1998: 1998 study says 70 million American adults use the internet. http://membersaol.com/gleposky/70million.html.

Nielsen/Netratings 2002: Women are gaining on the Web (Hong Kong). Press release 11 June. www.nielsen-netratings.com.

Norris, P. 2001: *Digital Divide: Civic Engagement, Information Poverty, and the Internet Worldwide*. Cambridge: Cambridge University Press.

NUA.COM 2002: How many on line? Survey. www.nua.com/surveys/how_many_online/.

O'Brien, J. 1998: Writing in the body: gender (re)production in online interaction. In Smith, M.A. and Kollock, P (eds), *Communities in Cyberspace*. London: Routledge, 76–105.

OECD/DSTI 2001: *Understanding the Digital Divide*. www.oecd.org/pdf/M00002000/M0002444.rdf.

Oelson, V. 1994: Feminisms and models of qualitative research. In Denzin, N. and Lincoln, E. (eds), *Handbook of Qualitative Research*. London: Sage, 158–74.

Office of National Statistics 1997: *Adult Literacy in Britain*. London: The Stationery Office.

O'Leary, M. 1998: Web directories demonstrate an enduring online law. *Online*, July/August, 79–81.

Østergaard, B. 1998: Convergence: legislative dilemmas. In McQuail, D. and Suine, K. (eds), *Media Policy: Convergence, Concentration, and Commerce*. London: Sage. 94–106.

Papacharissi, Z.A. 2000: The personal utility of individual home pages. Unpublished PhD thesis. University of Texas at Austin.

Pariser, E. 2000: Artists' websites: declarations of identity and presentation of self. In Gauntlett, D. (ed.), *Web.Studies: Rewiring Media Studies for the Digital Age*. London: Arnold.

Parry, G., Moyser, G. and Day, N. 1992: *Political Participation and Democracy in Britain*. Cambridge: Cambridge University Press.

Parsons, S. and Bynner, J. 2002: *Basic Skills and Political and Community Participation: Findings from a Study of Adults Born in 1958 and 1970*. London: Basic Skills Agency.

Penley, C. 1991: Brownian motion: women, tactics, and technology. In Penley, C. and Ross, A. (eds), *Technoculture*. Minneapolis: University of Minnesota Press, 135–61.

Penley, C. 1997: *Nasa/Trek: Popular Science and Sex in America*. London: Verso.

Percy-Smith, J. 1996: Downloading democracy? Information and communication technologies in local politics. *Policy and Politics* 24, 43–56.

Pew Internet & American Life Project 2002a: *Getting Serious Online*. www.pew internet.org.

Pew Internet & American Life Project 2002b: *The Broadband Difference*. www.pewinternet.org.

Pew Internet & American Life 2002a: *Vital Decisions: How Internet Users Decide What Information to Trust When They or Their Loved Ones are Sick*. www.pewinternet.org/reports/toc.asp?Report=59 (22 May).

Pew Internet & American Life 2002b: *Use of the Internet at Major Life Moments*. www.pewinternet.org/reports/toc.asp?Report=58 (8 May).

Pink, S. 2001: More visualising, more methodologies: on video, reflexivity and qualitative research. *The Sociological Review* 49 (4), 586–99.

Platt, C. 1996: *Anarchy Online: Net Crime*. New York: HarperCollins.

Polly, J.A. 1998: Standing stones in cyberspace: the Oneida Indian Nations territory on the internet. *Cultural Survival Quarterly* 21 (4), 37–41.

Poole, S., 2000: *Trigger Happy: The Inner Life of Videogames*. London: Fourth Estate.

Poster, M. 1997: Cyberdemocracy: internet and the public sphere. In Porter, D. (ed.), *Internet Culture*. New York: Routledge.

Reeves, P.M. 2001: How individuals coping with HIV/AIDS use the internet. *Health Education Research* 16 (6), 709–19.

Reuters 1999: NATO confirms site hack, e-mail jam. *ZDNET*, 31 March 1999.

Rheingold, H. 1993: *The Virtual Community: Homesteading on the Electronic Frontier*. Reading, MA: Addison-Wesley Publishing Co.

Rheingold, H. 2000: *The Virtual Community: Homesteading on the Electronic Frontier* (revised edn). Cambridge, MA: MIT Press.

Rice, R. 2002: Primary issues in internet use. In L. Lievrouw and S. Livingstone (eds), *The Handbook of New Media*. London: Sage.

Rice, R. and Love, G. 1987: Electronic emotion: socio-emotional content in a computer-mediated communication network. *Communication Research* 14 (1), 85–105.

Richard, L. 2000: *Living the Hospitality of God*. Mahwah, NJ: Paulist Press.

Richardson, L. 1994: Writing: a method of inquiry. In Denzin, N. and Lincoln, E. (eds), *Handbook of Qualitative Research*. London: Sage, 516–29.

Roberts, L.D. and Parks, M.R. 2001: The social geography of gender-switching in virtual environments on the internet. In Green, E. and Adam, A. (eds), *Virtual Gender: Technology, Consumption and Identity*. London: Routledge.

Robertson, D. 1998: *The New Renaissance: Computers and the Next Level of Civilization*. Oxford: Oxford University Press.

Rose, G. 2001: *Visual Methodologies: An Introduction to the Interpretation of Visual Materials*. London: Sage Publications.

Rosenstein, A.W. 2000: Self-presentation and identity on the World Wide Web: an exploration of personal home pages. Unpublished PhD thesis, University of Texas at Austin.

Rothstein, E. 1996: Can Twinkies think, and other ruminations on the Web as a garbage depository. *New York Times* 4 March, D3.

Rush, M., 1999: *New Media in Late 20th-Century Art*. London: Thames & Hudson.

Russell, D. 1993: *Against Pornography: The Evidence of Harm*. Berkeley, CA: Russell.

Saffo, P. 1989: Consensual realities in cyberspace, *Communications of the ACM*, 32 (6).

Satchell, M. 1999: Captain Dragan's Serbian Cybercorps. *World Report*, 10 May 1999 (archived at www.usnews.com).

Scheeres, J. 2002: Dear member: you've been deleted. *Wired.com*, 11 July. www.wired.com/news/business/0,1367,53658,00.html.

Schiller, H. 1995: The global information highway: project for an ungovernable world. In J. Brook and I. Boal (eds), *Resisting the Virtual Life*. San Francisco: City Lights Books.

Schiller, H.I. 2001: The global information highway: project for an ungovernable world. In Trend, D. (ed.), *Reading Digital Culture*. Oxford: Blackwell, 159–71.

Schwartz, M.F. and Southern, S. 2000: Compulsive cybersex: the new tea room. In Cooper, A. (ed.), *Cybersex: The Dark Side of the Force*. Philadelphia, PA: Brunner-Routledge, 127–44.

Seale, J.K. 2001: The same but different: the use of the personal home page by adults with Down's syndrome as a tool for self-presentation. *British Journal of Educational Technology* 32, 343–52.

Seigle, G. 1999: Alliance plays the psychological game into Yugoslav airspace. *Jane's Information Group* (http://jdw.janes.com), 26 April.

Semans, A. and Winks, C. 1999: *The Woman's Guide to Sex on the Web*. San Francisco: HarperCollins.

Shachtman, N. 2002: Blogs make the headlines, *Wired*, 23 December (www.wired.com).

Shade, L.R. 2002: *Gender and Community in the Social Construction of the Internet*. New York: Peter Lang Publishing.

Shapiro, E. (forthcoming). Trans'cending barriers: transgender organizing on the internet. *Journal of Gay and Lesbian Social Services*.

Sharf, B. 1997: Communicating breast cancer on-line: support and empowerment on the internet. *Women and Health* 26 (1), 65–84.

Sharpe, C.E. 1999: Racialized fantasies on the internet. *Signs* 24 (4), 1089–96.

Shaw, D.F. 1997: Gay men and computer communication: a discourse of sex and identity in cyberspace. In Jones, S.G. (ed.) *Virtual Culture: Identity and Communication in Cybersociety*. Thousand Oaks, CA: Sage Press, 133–45.

Shirky, C. 2001: Where Napster is taking the publishing world. *Harvard Business Review*, February, 143–8.

Shooting People 2002: *Essential Guide: Shooting for the Internet*. www.shooting people.org.

Silver, D. 2000: Looking backwards, looking forward: cyberculture studies 1990–2000. In Gauntlett, D. (ed.), *Web.Studies: Rewiring Media Studies for the Digital Age*. London: Arnold.

Silverstone, R. and Hirsch, E. 1992: *Consuming Technologies: Media and Information in Domestic Spaces*. London: Routledge.

Slevin, J. 2000: *The Internet and Society*. Cambridge: Polity Press.

Slevin, J. 2001: *The Internet and Society* (2nd edn). Cambridge: Polity Press.

Snyder, D. 2000: Webcam women: life on your screen. In Gauntlett, D. (ed.), *Web.Studies: Rewiring Media Studies for the Digital Age*. London: Arnold.

Sproull, L. and Kiesler, S. 1986: Reducing social context dues: electronic mail in organizational communication. *Management Science* 32, 1492–512.

Standen, A. 2001: Massacre at Tripod. *Salon.com* 20 March. http://archive.salon.com/tech/log/2001/03/20/tripod/.

Star, S.L. 1994: *Misplaced Concretism and Concrete Situations: Feminism, Method and Information Technology*. Working Paper 11, Series: Gender-Nature-Culture, Feminist Research Network. Odense: Odense University.

Star, S.L. 1999: The ethnography of infrastructure. *American Behavioral Scientist* 43 (3), 377–91.

Stern, S.E. and Handel, A.D. 2001: Sexuality and mass media: the historical context of psychology's reaction to sexuality on the internet. *The Journal of Sex Research* 38 (4), 283–92.

Stone, A.R. 1991: Will the real body please stand up? Boundary stories about virtual cultures. In Benedikt, M. (ed.), *Cyberspace: First Steps*. Cambridge, MA: MIT Press, 81–118.

Straayer, C. 1996: *Deviant Eyes, Deviant Bodies: Sexual Re-orientations in Film and Video*. New York: Columbia University Press.

Stromer-Galley, J. 2000: Online interaction and why candidates avoid it. *Journal of Communication* 50 (4), 111–32.

Sturken, M. 1997: *Tangled Memories: the Vietnam War, the AIDS Epidemic and the Politics of Remembering*. Berkeley: University of California Press.

Suchman, L., Blomberg, J., Orr, J.E. and Trigg, R. 1999: Reconstructing technologies as social practice. *American Behavioral Scientist* 43 (3), 392–408.

Sunday Times, The 1999: Internet surfers join Web war. 28 March.

Tacchi, J. 1998: Radio texture: between self and others. In Miller, D. (ed.), *Material Cultures: Why Some Things Matter*. Chicago: University of Chicago Press, 25–45.

Tannahill, R. 1992: *Sex in History*. London: Scarborough House Press.

Taylor, J., Bellamy, C., Raab, C., Dutton, W.H. and Peltu, M. 1996: Innovation in public service delivery. In Dutton, W.H. (ed.), *Information and Communication Technologies: Visions and Realities*. Oxford: Oxford University Press.

Taylor, P.M. 1992: *War and the Media: Propaganda and Persuasion during the Gulf War*. Manchester: Manchester University Press.

Taylor, P.M. 1997: *Global Communications, International Affairs and the Media since 1945*. London: Routledge.

Taylor, P.M. 2001: Spin laden: propaganda and urban myths. *The World Today* 57 (12, 6–7).

Taylor Nelson Sofres Interactive 2002: *Global eCommerce Report 2002*. www.tnsofres.com/.

Théberge, P. 1993: Technology, ecomomy and copyright reform in Canada. In Frith, S. (ed.), *Music and Copyright*. Edinburgh: Edinburgh University Press, 40–66.

Thompson, J.B. 1995: *The Media and Modernity: A Social Theory of the Media*. Cambridge: Polity Press.

Toffler, A. 1980: *The Third Wave*. London: Collins.

Trahant, M.N. 1996: The power of stories: Native words and images on the internet. *Native Americas* 13 (1), 15–21.

Tsagarousianou, R., Tambini, D. and Bryan, C. 1998: *Cyberdemocracy: Technology, Cities and Civic Networks*. London: Routledge.

Tumber, H. 2001: Democracy in the information age: the role of the fourth estate in cyberspace. In Webster, F. (ed.), *Culture and Politics in the Information Age*. London: Routledge.

Turkle, S. 1988: Computational reticence: why women fear the intimate machines. In Kramarae, C. (ed.), *Technology and Women's Voice*. London: Routledge.

Turkle, S. 1995: *Life on the Screen: Identity in the Age of the Internet*. New York: Touchstone.

Turkle, S. 1997: Multiple subjectivity and virtual community at the end of the Freudian century. *Sociological Inquiry* 67, 72–84.

Twist, K. 2002: A nation online, but where are the Indians? *Digital Divide Network*. www.digitaldividenetwork.org/contents/stories/index.

UCLA 2001: *The UCLA Internet Report 2001: Surveying the Digital Future*. www.ccp.ucla.edu.

UK Department of Trade and Industry 2000: *Closing the Digital Divide*. www.pat15.org.uk.

UNCTAD 2002: *E-Commerce and Development Report 2002*. Geneva: UNCTAD.

UNDP 1995: *UNDP and the Communications Revolution*. www.undp.org/comm.

US Department of Commerce 2000: *Falling through the Net: Towards Digital*

Inclusion. www.ntia.doc.gov/ntiahome.fttn00.

US Department of Commerce 2002: *A Nation Online: How Americans are Expanding their Use of the Internet.* www.ntia.doc.gov/ntiahome/dn/anationonline2.pdf.

USIA Opinion Analysis 1999: State-run stations remain trusted source for Serbs. Washington: US Information Agency. 16 September.

Vološinov, V.N. 1973: *Marxism and the Philosophy of Language.* Trans. by M. Ladislav and I.R. Titunik, Cambridge, MA: Harvard University Press.

Wakeford, N. 1997: Networking women and grrrls with information/communication technology. In Terry, J. and Calvert, M. (eds), *Processed Lives: Gender and Technology in Everyday Life.* London: Routledge.

Wakeford, N. 1999: Gender and the landscapes of computing in an internet café. In Crang, M., Crang, P. and May, J. (eds), *Virtual Geographies: Bodies, Space and Relations (Studies in Communication).* London: Routledge, 178–201.

Walker, K. 2000: 'It's difficult to hide it': the presentation of self on internet home pages. *Qualitative Sociology* 23, 99–120.

Ward, D. 1995: All power to the cybernauts. *Guardian* 22 February, 20.

Wark, M. 1999: Yugoslavia: air war leads us astray. *The Australian*, 31 March.

Washington Post. 2002: Yahoo's China concession. 19 August, A12.

Whaley, C. 2000: Age of acquisition brings cross-purpose alliances. *Computing Canada*, 26 June, 9.

Wheeler, M. 1998: Democracy and the information superhighway. *Democratization* 5, 217–39.

White, R. 2002: Social and political aspects of men's health. *Health* 6 (3), 267–85.

Wilbur, S.P. 1997: An archaeology of cyberspaces: virtuality, community, identity. In Porter, D. (ed.), *Internet Culture.* New York: Routledge, 5–22.

Wilhelm, A.G. 2000: *Democracy in the Digital Age* New York: Routledge.

Williams, D.R. 2003: The health of men: structured inequalities and opportunities. *American Journal of Public Health* 93 (5), 724–31.

Williams, L. 1999: *Hard Core: Power, Pleasure and the 'Frenzy of the Visible'.* Berkeley, CA: University of California Press.

Winseck, D. 1998: Pursuing the Holy Grail: information highways and media reconvergence in Britain and Canada. *European Journal of Communication* 13 (3), 337–74.

Witmer, D.F., Colman, R.W. and Katzman, S.L. 1999: From paper-and-pencil to screen-and-keyboard: toward a methodology for survey research on the internet. In Jones, S. (ed.), *Doing Internet Research: Critical Issues and Methods for Examining the Net.* Thousand Oaks, CA: Sage, 145–61.

Wong, W. 1998: Search engine companies seek partners. *Computer Reseller News*, 14 September, 79–80.

Woolgar, S. (ed.) 1988: *Knowledge and Reflexivity: New Frontiers in the Sociology of Knowledge.* London: Sage.

World Economic Forum 2000: *From the Global Digital Divide to the Global Digital*

Opportunity. www.weforum.org/digitaldivide.nsf/ (accessed 1 April 2001).

Yawakie, M.P. 1997: Building telecommunication capacity in Indian country. *Winds of Change* 12, 44–6.

Young, K.S. 1998: *Caught in the Net: How to Recognize the Signs of Internet Addiction and a Winning Strategy for Recovery*. New York: Wiley.

ZDNET 1999: Infowarfare part of NATO's arsenal? www.zdnet.com, 26 March.

Zeman, T. 2002: *Geocensored*. www.angelfire.com/mo/geocensored/index.html.

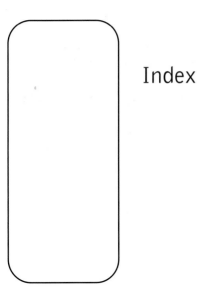

Index